D1443628

Child Therapy Today is a compilation of Volume I, Issues 1-6 of *The Child Therapy News* (October 1993, December 1993, February 1994, April 1994, June 1994, and August 1994).

The Child Therapy News is a bimonthly newsletter for mental health professionals who work with children. Each issue offers up-to-date information on a specific childhood disorder. *The Child Therapy News* is published by The Center for Applied Psychology, Inc., P. O. Box 61587, King of Prussia, PA 19406. An annual subscription is $65.00/year.
For more information or to order, call (800) 962-1141.

The Center for Applied Psychology, Inc. also publishes a collection of psychologically-oriented children's books and textbooks, as well as psychotherapeutic games. For more information, call (800) 962-1141.

CHILD THERAPY TODAY
Publisher: Lawrence E. Shapiro, Ph.D.
Consulting Editor: Charles E. Schaefer, Ph.D.
Senior Editor: Laura Slap-Shelton, Psy.D.
Managing Editor: Hennie M. Shore
Design: Charles Brenna

Published by:
The Center for Applied Psychology, Inc.
P. O. Box 61587
King of Prussia, PA 19406 U.S.A.
Tel. 610/277-4020

The Center for Applied Psychology, Inc. is publisher of Childswork/Childsplay, a catalog of products for mental health professionals, teachers and parents who wish to help children with their developmental, social and emotional growth. For a free catalog of books, games and toys to help children, call 1-800-962-1141.

All rights reserved. No part of this book may be reproduced or transmitted in any form or by any means, electronic or mechanical, including photocopying, recording or by any information storage and retrieval system without written permission from the publisher.

Copyright ©1994 by The Center for Applied Psychology, Inc.
Printed in the United States of America

ISBN 1-882732-12-X

CHILD THERAPY TODAY

Laura Slap-Shelton, Psy.D.
Senior Editor

The Center for Applied Psychology, Inc.
King of Prussia, Pennsylvania

Other Products by The Center for Applied Psychology, Inc.

Play-and-Read Series Books
ALL ABOUT DIVORCE
ALL FEELINGS ARE OK—IT'S WHAT YOU DO WITH THEM THAT COUNTS
FACE YOUR FEELINGS!
TAKE A DEEP BREATH: The Kids' Play-Away Stress Book

Self-Esteem Series Books
EVERYTHING I DO YOU BLAME ON ME!: A Book to Help Children Control
  Their Anger
MY LIFE TURNED UPSIDE DOWN, BUT I TURNED IT RIGHTSIDE UP:
  A Self-Esteem Book About Dealing with Joint Custody
SOMETIMES I DRIVE MY MOM CRAZY, BUT I KNOW SHE'S CRAZY ABOUT
  ME: A Self-Esteem Book for ADHD Children

Workbooks
JUMPIN' JAKE SETTLES DOWN: A Workbook to Help Impulsive Children
  Learn to Think Before They Act
THE BUILDING BLOCKS OF SELF-ESTEEM: A Skill-Oriented Approach to
  Teaching Self-Worth

Reference Books
THE BOOK OF PSYCHOTHERAPEUTIC GAMES

Psychological Games
DR. GARDNER'S PICK-AND-TELL GAMES
KIDS' DAY IN COURT
LET'S SEE...ABOUT ME
LOOK BEFORE YOU LEAP!
MY TWO HOMES
NEVER SAY NEVER
STOP, RELAX & THINK
THE ANGRY MONSTER MACHINE
THE CLASSROOM BEHAVIOR GAME
THE DINOSAUR'S JOURNEY TO HIGH SELF-ESTEEM
THE GOOD BEHAVIOR GAME
THE GREAT FEELINGS CHASE
YOU & ME: A GAME OF SOCIAL SKILLS

Acknowledgements

We gratefully acknowledge the following contributors to *Child Therapy Today*:

Anne Dematatis, M.S.
Michael DeStefano, Ph.D.
Richard A. Gardner, M.D.
Linda Gerstley, Ph.D.
David S. Greenwald, Ph.D.
Beth Jacklin
Toni Cavanagh Johnson, Ph.D.
Dorothy S. Kahler, M.A.
Kevin B. McGovern, Ph.D.
Michele Tortora Pato, M.D.
Steven Rasmussen, M.D.
Barbara L. VanNoppen, M.D.

We wish to thank the following professionals for sharing their expertise:

Flora Colao, M.S.W., The Greenwich House Children's Safety Project,
New York, NY
Kenneth Dodge, Ph.D., Department of Psychology, Vanderbilt University,
Nashville, TN
George DuPaul, Ph.D., Lehigh University Regional Consulting Center for
Adolescents with Attention Deficit Disorder, Bethlehem, PA
Edna B. Foa, Ph.D., Center for the Treatment and Study of Anxiety, Medical
College of Pennsylvania, Philadelphia, PA
Eliana Gil, Ph.D., California Graduate School of Family Psychology, San Rafael, CA
Elizabeth Hembree, Ph.D., Center for the Treatment and Study of Anxiety, Medical
College of Pennsylvania, Philadelphia, PA
Michael Kozak, Ph.D., Center for the Treatment and Study of Anxiety, Medical
College of Pennsylvania, Philadelphia, PA
Peter Lewinsohn, Ph.D., The Oregon Adolescent Depression Project, Eugene, OR
Marion Linblad Goldberg, Divorce and Remarriage Project at Philadelphia Child
Guidance Center, Philadelphia, PA
John March, M.D., Ph.D., Program for Childhood Mental Illness and Anxiety
Disorders, Duke University, Durham, NC
Harvey C. Parker, Ph.D., Children and Adults with Attention Deficit Disorders,
Plantation, FL
Isolina Ricci, Ph.D., California Statewide Office of Family Court Services,
Tiburon, CA
Ronald Slaby, Ph.D., Education Development Center, Newton, MA
Kevin Stark, Ph.D., University of Texas, Austin, TX
Judith Wallerstein, Ph.D., Center for the Family in Transition, Corte Madera, CA
Timothy Wigal, Ph.D., ADD Program at the Child Development Center, University
of California at Irvine, Irvine, CA

Contents

Foreword

Too often in graduate and other training programs the need to learn the basics of practice and theory limits the student's access to current research across a number of clinical areas. As busy clinicians we often have difficulty making time to keep up with the work of our colleagues. *The Child Therapy News* has provided the opportunity to explore in depth the latest developments across a spectrum of psychological disorders and treatments.

Perhaps the most stimulating aspect of working on the newsletter has been the opportunity to speak with dedicated and compassionate psychological researchers and practitioners whose work has made a significant contribution to child psychology. The interviews with Eliana Gil and Flora Calao on child sexual abuse; John Marks, Edna Foa, Elizabeth Hembree and Michael Kozak on Obsessive Compulsive Disorder (OCD); Judith Wallerstein and Isolina Ricci on divorce and child custody, Kevin Stark and Peter Lewinsohn on childhood and adolescent depression; Ronald Slaby and Kenneth Dodge on issues of childhood and adolescent aggression and violence; and Harvey Parker, George DuPaul, and Timothy Wigal on Attention Deficit Disorder (ADD) not only bring us up-to-date on the latest research and treatment developments, but also demonstrate psychology's ability to substantially improve the lives of children and adolescents.

Certain themes seem to appear in every issue of *The Child Therapy News*. One such theme is the impact of a sometimes chaotic, neglectful, and at its worst, violent society on the development of the child. Negative external events impinge on the child's and adolescent's internal integrity, and contribute to depression and aggression. Divorce and sexual abuse are two of the traumatic life experiences whose effects on child development confront many of us regularly in our offices. Even for children with ADD and OCD, whose problems are predominantly determined by genetics, the role and impact of the environment on their recovery and treatment cannot be underestimated. Thus successful treatments for children often include work both with the child and with the systems that support the child.

A second theme involves the need for systems-oriented responses to these childhood problems. While it is fairly common practice to involve parents in treatment or to treat the child by treating the family system, there is an increasing need to involve other systems such as the child's classroom, school system, and local community. Judith Wallerstein and Isolina Ricci speak of the need for society to respond supportively to divorcing families and for adjustments in the legal system that will create equitable and humane custody arrangements. George DuPaul and Edward Shapiro's ADD consulting project works from the school district level down to the individual child, as does James Swanson and Timothy Wigal's special school program for children with ADD.

The American Psychological Association has created a special committee to address the problems of violence and youth, and, as Ronald Slaby reports, efforts must extend from the schoolroom to top governmental levels to mass media programming. Kenneth Dodge describes a program designed to prevent the development of aggressive and violent children which may be implemented on a national level in much the same way as Head Start. Kevin Stark and Peter Lewinsohn describe interventions for depression which involve parents and schools as well as improving the social skills of depressed children. Helping sexually abused children involves interacting with a variety of agencies as well as families in order to create a safe place in which the child may recover and live.

Another theme reflected in the first year of *The Child Therapy News* is the strong relationship between research and treatment, as well as the need for ongoing evaluation of the effectiveness of intervention programs. Related is the expansion of psychological theories to include an understanding of the linkage between children's behavioral and emotional problems and the underlying brain mechanisms and deeper cognitive structures that may contribute to these problems. This trend toward the enlargement of our clinical theories to include neuropsychological data is clearly seen in the theoretical thinking on OCD, depression, ADD, and with Dodge's work on aggression.

In every issue, the importance of accurately identifying and assessing troubled children was highlighted, and the statistics on the number of children needing service in the United States was staggering:

- Three to five percent of children have ADD
- Two percent have OCD
- Suicide is the leading cause of death in 15- to 24-year-olds
- More than 50 percent of children live in a family affected by divorce

And we could continue with statistics on children who have been sexually abused, children affected by youth violence and youth victimization, and so on.

It is not surprising that childhood behavioral and emotional difficulties are making the headlines and front pages of the *New York Times* and *Time* magazine. The challenges to today's therapist are immense. It is our hope that this volume of *Child Therapy Today,* as well as continuing issues of *The Child Therapy News*, will provide a nucleus of information and resources to help you meet these challenges.

—*Laura Slap-Shelton, Psy.D.*
Senior Editor

A Word From the Publisher

In twenty years of working in the mental health field, nothing has troubled me more than our inability to effectively disseminate information about how to help children. Millions of dollars are spent each year in government-funded projects, and millions more are spent in university-sponsored research projects. But in both cases, the findings are ultimately buried amid dozens of journals, or presented to a few hundred participants at a professional convention.

So what about the tens of thousands of front-line practitioners who really need this information, but don't have time to go to the library and keep up with the research? Even if they had the time, the style of most journals is so austere and over-complicated that it would take the average person hours to gather just a few grains of useful information. Eventually some of this information finds its way into expensive textbooks, but by then it is at least several years old and still may be inaccessible to the majority of practitioners who work in schools and clinics with limited funds.

It is my hope that *The Child Therapy News* and this annual compilation, *Child Therapy Today* will be an important step in bridging the gap between the valuable information that is available and the busy people who can most benefit from it. It is my intention that this periodical should above all be practical and accessible. Each issue should cut to the core of a particular childhood problem or disorder. Our writers and editors will continue to do the job that you would want to do if you had the time: to survey and summarize the literature, speak to the experts, focus on practical information that can quickly be used to help children, identify and review the resources that can make your job just a little bit easier, and so on.

When you need the most current information to help a child in trouble, I want there to be sources you can count on for intelligent answers to real-world problems: *The Child Therapy News* and *Child Therapy Today*. Anything less will be unsatisfactory and less than you deserve.

I applaud the courage and tenacity of the people who help our troubled youth, day in and day out, with too few resources and too little appreciation. It is to you that we dedicate this first volume of *Child Therapy Today*.

—*Lawrence E. Shapiro, Ph.D.*
Publisher

CHAPTER 1

Focus on Child Sexual Abuse

An Interview with Eliana Gil, Ph.D.

David Greenwald, Ph.D.: *What advice would you give to a clinician in a situation where there may be some signs of child sexual abuse but s/he is not really sure how to proceed?*

Eliana Gil, Ph.D.: At the outset, one of the most important things to do is to allow a period of time so that some kind of safe environment can be developed for the child, and to become, in the child's mind, a trustworthy person. I think a lot of the children I've worked with who have experiences with abuse have a certain amount of hesitation about trusting others; about opening up, about communicating things that might be bothering them.

This is true especially with kids who are in violent or sexually abusive environments where they've been somewhat threatened, or they experience a lot of generalized fear and anxiety. It's very difficult for these children to really show themselves freely or fully, particularly with someone with whom they're not familiar.

Clinicians need to establish a place where there aren't a lot of demands put upon the child immediately. I think we overemphasize the verbal part of assessment. I think the assessment really has to be of the child's play and the themes in his/her interactions and particular story; how they process, through the use of symbolic play, some of the issues that are underlying their behaviors.

I like the idea of an active observation of the child in different situations. I sometimes, for example, do part of the assessment in the waiting room so that I can see the child interact with other adults and children. Obviously part of the assessment has to be with the parent to see how the child interacts with the people with whom he/she is living and on whom he/she is dependent. Factors such as whether there are similarities or differences in the way he/she responds or interacts with males versus females are important.

DG: *Are there any particular tools that you find most helpful?*

EG: The Children's Apperception Test is sometimes helpful; the Rorschach is useful if the children are a little bit older. But basically I like to give myself the time to really get to know the child. I like using artwork as a therapeutic tool. I use self-portraits and kinetic family drawings. Almost everything a child does and doesn't do is relevant and can be a piece of the puzzle in terms of trying to figure out what's going on.

DG: *And how long does that kind of assessment usually last?*

EG: It varies if you're doing a forensic assessment or you're just doing a regular clinical assessment. If you're doing a clinical assessment, probably something like three months would be a good amount of time to really get into looking at what's going on with the child. If you're doing a forensic evaluation, it can probably be done in a shorter period of time.

DG: *How many of the symptoms of post-traumatic stress disorder do you tend to see with children?*

EG: Let me preface what I'm going to say with the idea that just because a child has been abused doesn't mean that the child has been traumatized by this abuse. I think that we sometimes make assumptions about the impact of the abuse on the child. One of the things we have to look at is the idiosyncratic impact of abuse on this particular child at this particular developmental age and stage, given the personality of that child.

Some children are just more resilient. They have personality structures that allow for them to fend off some of the impact of abuse, and therefore they don't appear to be as traumatized as another child would be. That doesn't mean there can't be some kind of a delayed reaction where at a different developmental age you may get some kind of symptomatology that reveals a relationship to prior abuse.

About 70 percent of the children I see who have chronic histories of abuse also have some post-traumatic stress disorder responses, because I think chronicity is one of the factors that is linked to the potential for trauma. I think you do see this in a lot of children, and these children don't necessarily report in a verbal way, as adults would, those symptoms of PTSD. There's a clear link, as well, between trauma and dissociation; this is an area that children are less likely to tell you about in terms of their feelings.

DG: *In your book* The Healing Power of Play *you quote T. C. Johnson: "The central tasks of post-trauma treatment particularly include re-experience, release, and re-organization." Could you elaborate on how you bring those therapeutic tasks about in treatment?*

EG: The first part is the re-experience. In the field of trauma study, that is, people who have worked with war veterans and holocaust survivors and other groups, there is generally a consensus that the experience has to be brought into some kind of conscious awareness and then processed. The only area where there seems to be more controversy on this involves the trauma of sexual abuse. Sometimes people get concerned that actually helping children remember can be destructive because you're working against their defenses that have helped them to repress this information.

My feeling is that children need an opportunity to remember and face the elements of the trauma that are most disturbing to them. I try to help the child through play re-enactment. Let's say the child's been sexually abused in the bedroom. In the dollhouse, we will set up a bedroom, and if the child is four years old, I'll say a little girl of four is lying down in the bedroom. By doing it that way it distances the child. It's not her necessarily, it's the little girl who's on the bed in front of her, and that gives her a little cushion of distance between herself and the little girl.

A child might say, "Sometimes I think about somebody walking toward me, and I'm in the bed and they're walking towards me." That's an intrusive flashback from PTSD, so I take that, and I start with situational memory, which I think is really helpful. I then say, "Where are you when this is happening? When someone's walking toward you, what are you doing? Where are you?" Then I try to reconstruct the scenario. The idea of helping with this recall is to try to bring in the other dissociated parts of that memory.

I try to bring in all the other elements of a trauma experience as well. For example, I'll ask, "Are there any noises when this is happening? Are there any smells? What's your body doing inside itself, what are you saying to yourself, and how are you feeling?" I help recreate that trauma experience so that the child can begin to actually see what happened to that little girl out there.

I will say to the child, "And how does that little girl feel?" The child might say, "I don't know." And I'll say, "Well, let's look. Her knees are gathered up together and she's shaking, and she's holding her breath. How do you guess she might feel? What do you think?" If there's some kind of affect that's available, the second part of this is to help the child discharge the affect. Most of the time when kids have been hurt they've held it in.

I have this idea that it's almost like an emotional paralysis, like taking a big deep breath and then holding it, and everything's kept inside. We have to help them to release that, because otherwise it never really goes away. It just sits there and sometimes it becomes tapped by another experience and then it becomes bigger. This doesn't mean that the pushing out is always verbal or that it's accompanied by tears. I've actually seen a child who discharged a tremendous amount of feeling just through a sigh.

After the discharge of affect, the next step entails giving the little girl a voice. What does the little girl want to say? What does the little girl want to ask? I encourage the child to take an active role instead of the passive role she had during the traumatization. This process lessens the power of fragmented and vague traumatic memory.

A child needs to process her feelings before she can leave a memory behind. I would say to a child, "Yes, that was a sad feeling, and that was something that happened to you then, but it isn't happening to you now. What should you do with your sad feelings now? If you could have a voice now, what would you say?" It's important to help the child focus her feelings more toward the present. Her present feelings need not merge with the trauma.

DG: *Will you introduce "the little girl in the bedroom" image in the play, or will you wait for the child to do so?*

EG: I think that children have two basic drives. One is to master a situation and resolve it on their own. The other drive is to repress it, to avoid things that are painful. There's a conflict that goes on between these two things. I like to give kids sufficient time to work that conflict out for themselves. I prefer to get out of their way and let them do what they need to do to take care of themselves. I firmly believe that children have their own way of healing, but each child heals differently.

Perhaps half of the children who see a therapist actively approach the material they need to work through on a symbolic level. They will inevitably bring the issue up to you in some way, shape, or form. Maybe they'll draw a picture that is representative of their unconscious feelings or thoughts. Or maybe they'll show you a re-enactment of something that tells you there is something the child needs help with at this time.

But then there's the other half of the children you might see in therapy who resolve this basic conflict through avoidance and repression. I proceed slowly with these children, using non-directive therapy. This protects the child from feeling any kind of intrusion or forcing from the therapist. It also desensitizes them somewhat to the underlying issues, preparing them for the work of eventually dealing with their inner struggles.

I will never force or threaten a child. Giving them space and time and freedom is very important. When children are feeling intruded upon, or they feel that they are not in control of their own situation, they will turn themselves off.

DG: *You're setting a model of a different kind of adult-child relationship.*

EG: Yes. That's why I suggest that the beginning phase of the treatment be non-directive and gathering data. To get a look at the child's inner workings, sandplay and artwork can be helpful, as can any of the expressive therapies that can show more fully how the child might be feeling inside.

This helps them to eventually look at what's happened to them enough so that they can discharge whatever emotions or thoughts they might have had related to that experience.

DG: *How about the reorganizing aspect?*

EG: Reorganizing is basically giving the child an opportunity to have a transformation of the memory in some way. It's difficult to describe exactly which steps you should take. It's a process of separating out the past from the present and the future for the child: "This was something that happened, and under those circumstances you responded in this way, and that made sense given your age and what you could do. And now you are this age, and now you can probably talk and you can probably do other things. And then there's the future and things will be different then."

This reorganizes that whole experience, so if the child has taken on any of the responsibility for what happened or sees himself or herself as unworthy or unlovable or bad because it happened, you can gently give some other possible explanations and meanings for this occurrence. If left alone, the traumatic memory of the experience gets stronger over time.

Abused children are so defenseless in many ways, and if you leave them alone without any kind of intervention, they will make some meaning about what has happened to them. Without intervention, most of the time that meaning is going to be incorrect, and it's going to be self-destructive.

DG: *So the reorganization helps to get a sense of what the meaning of the event was to them.*

EG: Exactly. I've worked with a lot of children who say that they are bad because they didn't say "no," that if they had been able to say "no" they would somehow be relieved of the guilt or shame that they carry. So I will say to the child, "Do you think that there might have been some time when you said "no" without using words?" That makes them stop and think.

I'll never forget this six-year-old who looked up at me and said, "You mean like when I put the safety pin under the zipper so he couldn't pull it down?" And I said, "Exactly, that's what I mean." That's a way to try to say "no" without using words. And once she knew that she had said "no" without words, she felt relieved of this guilt that she had.

I will then go to the next question which is, "Tell me how you said 'yes.'" That really challenges their kind of one-track thinking and they stop and say, "Well, gee, I never really said 'yes' either." And then it's almost like they give themselves permission to be relieved in some way, to not carry around that guilt and that shame anymore. Children don't, unfortunately, have the physical strength to fight anyone off and they can be helped to understand that they were limited in the ways that they could have dealt with the abuse.

I like kids to feel that they are powerful, but, realistically, what are those powers? I tell them that they are powerful because they have their own thoughts and nobody can take those thoughts away. And powerful because they have their own feelings that belong just to them, and because they get to decide who to talk to and who not to talk to, and because they can make choices.

The sad fact is that many of them return to environments that are not the best.

What will happen when someone yells at them and screams at them and calls them names? What can they do for themselves? In this kind of situation I ask, "Is there someone with whom you do feel comfortable and to whom you can talk to when you're feeling really sad or lonely or hurt? It's a matter of trying to teach kids things that are going to be of some use to them outside of the therapy, short of setting them up to fail.

DG: *When is a child going to be able to hear some of your interventions to the play, and when is it time to just let the play unfold?*

EG: I'm constantly asking myself the question, "Why am I using this technique with this child at this time in the therapy?" I really try to watch the child's receptivity and also look for windows of opportunity, anything that has symbolism that might relate back, any metaphor that seems to make sense for the child. I try to enter into metaphors that the child makes available.

Another thing that is very important is to get a sense of when the child is receptive to your comments. I do a lot of wondering out loud. Like I say, "I wonder what a child who has had that happen might feel? I wonder what kids might think about that?"

DG: *How do you involve the family in the treatment?*

EG: I feel that it is really critical to involve the family, although I prefer to have a period of time alone with the child. During that time I'll have the parents give me weekly reports. I have a sheet that I have them fill out that tells me what positive behaviors the child has shown during the week, and if there have been any problem behaviors, and what things they've noticed that have made them feel optimistic or pessimistic. In that way the parents are actively engaged in observing the child and reporting back to me. My frame for that is, "You're helping me help your child."

I always describe what I'm going to do with the children to the family. I explain to them what I call Trauma Resolution and the stages that can be expected. I don't talk about the specifics, just the process and what I'm going to do. Sometimes I'll explain why we're going to pay attention to this particular memory for a period of time. But I also want them to understand that this isn't going to be forever. This helps give the parents a longer perspective.

DG: *You've written a new book on family play therapy in child sexual abuse treatment. Can you talk a bit about that?*

EG: The book's premise is that it's extremely helpful to look at metaphors that can emerge within the family play treatment that might help the family in terms of resolving some of the issues in the long run. I think that those techniques are very, very effective. They really engage the family on a non-intellectual level. They help the child to connect with the family and the family to connect with the child.

DG: *Could you talk a little bit about some of the play techniques you like to use?*

EG: There's a technique called Family Puppet Interview, the idea of which is that you bring a bunch of puppets into a room where the family and the children are together. They have to pick out the puppets that they most like, and tell you a story that has a beginning, a middle, and an end. I usually leave the room, but I have a room that has a one-way mirror so I can observe the family interacting.

I see them address a task together and make decisions about who's going to have what puppet. I get to see how they deal with conflict. It's really very interesting—who starts the story, who develops a theme, who avoids a theme, how people get in role. Then I come back in and ask them to tell me the story, but they can't narrate it. They have to be the puppet.

After they tell the story I relate it back, but not to the people, to the puppets. I will say, "Mr. Turtle, you seem to have a question for the owl. Can you ask the owl your question now?" I do the rest of the therapy session with the family in the roles of their puppets. At the end, I ask everyone what meaning it had for them.

I also use Dr. Richard Gardner's Mutual Story Telling Technique with a family. This technique was developed for use with a single child, but it also works well with whole families. After the family tells a story, then I tell a "therapeutic" story to them.

I think family artwork can also be very interesting. I have people draw a picture together. They draw a picture of their family doing something together, and then talk to each other about what they've drawn. Almost anything that can be done to help the family communicate non-verbally through play can be useful.

DG: *Are there any particular kinds of toys and games that you really find useful with this population?*

EG: I like to have a dollhouse available. I like to have the figures that represent mom, dad, and other adults and children. It's great to use these dolls, but almost any materials can be used therapeutically. I've had children who will use a paper bag and stick a pen through it to represent a penis. They then act out their trauma with these very simple materials.

I keep the anatomical dolls out of reach, and I don't really see them as regular play toys. I see them as being much more a part of a forensic interview where every other method of trying to help the child with some kind of a disclosure has failed, or if the child gets to a certain point and then won't tell me what's happened.

Sunglasses or "Groucho" glasses are wonderful because kids think that somehow they're invisible when they put them on. These help children with issues around privacy or around shame. I like toy telephones for this same purpose. I also like *The Talking, Feeling, and Doing Game* by Dr. Gardner. I ask children sometime during the treatment to write their own questions for other kids who have been hurt and who might play this game.

DG: *Do you ever have to intervene when a child is playing out his or her experience?*

EG: Children who have had traumatic experiences often reenact in their play the exact experiences that they suffered in a traumatic episode in a rigid, literal way. In some circumstances this rigid repetition of the trauma element can actually be counterproductive. Sometimes kids get stuck in the traumatic material, and I think the clinician really needs to be able to intervene and facilitate a more constructive direction.

When I intervene, I will begin to describe, not interpret, what I'm watching the child do in front of me. Most of the time when kids get into this post-traumatic play, they are self-absorbed. I will do verbal descriptions for them of the sequence of the play, but that usually is not very effective.

Another intervention is to actually have the child give the people in the play a voice, because a lot of this is very quiet play. I ask the child, "What is she saying now? What is she saying to him? What's she saying to her?" Sometimes they'll work with that.

I've had most success with videotaping the play. I'll have the child in the session watch her own play, then I'll stop the tape and have her use the controls to fast-forward or stop the play, and I'll say, "Now tell me what's going on right now." It's very interesting because, in a way, when they're in the play they're almost dissociated.

DG: *What do you do to keep children safe after a trauma has occurred?*

EG: That is so hard. I once worked with a child who was raped. We did a lot of work around the notion that his body belonged to him, and that he could say "no," and then he got raped again. He did say "no" this time, but it didn't work. None of our strategies worked.

That really took some wind out of my sails. It became clear to me that sometimes we can do a disservice to these kids by teaching them techniques without really thinking them through. Kids don't have the physical strength to fight adults off— that's an undisputed fact. But I still feel, and will always feel, that we have to teach them that they can say "no," and that they are powerful when they are in charge of their bodies.

Assessing Behaviors Related to Sex and Sexuality in Kindergarten Through Fourth Grade Children

By Toni Cavanagh Johnson, Ph.D.

One of the most difficult tasks for a mental health professional is to determine whether or not inappropriate sexual activity has occurred in a child's life. To make this determination, the therapist must begin with a sound understanding of the "normal" sexual behaviors and interests of the child. Author and lecturer Toni Cavanagh Johnson, Ph.D. has given us some guidelines about what can be viewed as typical and what should be viewed with concern.

The lists on pages 10 through 13 attempt to describe behaviors which relate to sex and sexuality of children of normal intelligence in kindergarten through fourth grade. Available literature and empirical data on child sexuality have been studied and consultation conducted with hundreds of mental health professionals, parents and child care providers to prepare this listing. It is a first step in defining behaviors related to sex and sexuality which are within the normal range, behaviors which raise concern and behaviors which require immediate consultation. This listing is not meant for use by itself in the assessment of child sexual abuse. Comments and suggestions are invited by the author.

The behaviors in the first list are those which are in the normal range. This range is wide and not all children will engage in all of the behaviors, some children may engage in none while some may only engage in one or two. There will be differences due to the amount of exposure the child has had to adult sexuality, nudity, explicit television, videos, pictures and the child's level of interest. The child's parents' attitudes and values will influence the child's behaviors.

The second list describes behaviors which are seen in some children who are overly concerned about sexuality, children who lack adequate supervision and other children who have been or are currently being sexually molested or maltreated. When a child shows several of these behaviors, professional consultation is advised.

The third list describes behaviors which are often indicative of a child who is experiencing deep confusion in the area of sexuality. This child may or may not have been sexually abused or maltreated. It may be that the level of sex and/or aggression in the environment in which the child has lived has overwhelmed the child's ability to integrate it and the child is acting out the confusion. Consultation with a professional who specializes in child sexuality or child sexual abuse should be sought.

Sex Play

Children in kindergarten through fourth grade are trying to understand their bodies, their abilities, how to make friends and what life is all about. The world is a marvelous place full of things to learn and explore; among these are sex and sexuality. Everything related to sex and sexuality, including genitals, breasts, differences between male and female, love, marriage, intercourse, dirty books and pictures, dancing, hugging, touching, etc. is the object of great curiosity.

Young school-age children are often very active in their exploration of these topics. At times children engage in solitary sexual behaviors, at other times similar age children engage in exploratory behavior together or make up games involving sexual themes in which groups of children engage together. Curiosity about sex is natural and is engaged in with liveliness and good humor. Children engaged in sex play mutually agree to participate and are generally giggly and silly. When one child wants to stop, the others stop also. If discovered in sexual behaviors, a child may feel guilty or ashamed, but this passes if the adult treats it as normal.

Areas of Concern

Concern arises when the child focuses on sex and sexuality to a greater extent than 1) other areas of the child's environment or, 2) his or her peers. Sexual interest should be in balance with the curiosity and exploration of all other aspects of the child's life. Most sexual behaviors related to "looking and touching" go underground or stop as children learn that many adults are unaccepting of much of their overt exploration and curiosity.

When a child continues to engage in sexual behaviors in view of adults who say "no," this raises concern. Most sexual behaviors by young school-aged children are engaged in with children of similar age, usually within a year or so, younger or older, of their own age. The wider the age range between children engaged in sexual behaviors, the greater the concern.

Sex play usually occurs between friends and playmates. A child who keeps asking unfamiliar children or children who are uninterested to engage in sexual activity raises concern. Children who appear anxious, tense, confused about sexual issues, or who are continuously involved in sexual activity or do not understand others' admonitions against overt sexual behavior, also raise concern. If a child shows several behaviors which are of concern, professional advice is recommended.

When to Seek Professional Consultation

Generally, there is little concern about peer sexual exploration, yet there can be manipulation and coercion between same-aged peers. When assessing peer sexual behaviors which are considered problematic, the everyday relationship between the children is the best measure of how the children interact. If a child is regularly aggressive and controlling in interactions with other children, this relationship may be the same when sexual behaviors are occurring.

Sexual behaviors between children where one is pressuring the other to engage in the behaviors can be very serious. If other children repeatedly complain about a child's sexual behavior even after the child has been spoken to, assessment by a professional is advisable. When there is anger, anxiety, tension, fear, coercion, manipulation, force or ongoing compulsive interest and activity related to sex and sexuality, professional advice should be sought.

UNDERSTANDING THE SEXUALITY OF CHILDREN (KDG. - GRADE 4)

Normal Range

Asks about the genitals, breasts, intercourse, babies.

Interested in watching/peeking at people doing bathroom functions.

Uses "dirty" words for bathroom functions, genitals, and sex.

Plays doctor, inspecting other's bodies.

Boys and girls are interested in having/birthing a baby.

Shows others his/her genitals.

Interested in urination and defecation.

Touches/rubs own genitals when going to sleep, when tense, excited or afraid.

Plays house, may simulate all roles of mommy and daddy.

Thinks other children are "gross" or have "cooties." Chases them.

Talks about sex with friends. Talks about having a girl/ boyfriend.

Wants privacy when in bathroom or changing clothes.

Likes to hear and tell "dirty" jokes.

Looks at nude pictures.

Plays games with same-aged children related to sex or sexuality.

Draws genitals on human figures.

Explores differences between males and females, boys and girls.

Takes advantage of opportunity to look at nude child or adult.

Pretends to be opposite sex.

Wants to compare genitals with peer-aged friends.

Wants to touch genitals, breasts, buttocks of other same-age child or have child touch him/her.

Kisses familiar adults and children. Allows kissing by familiar adults and children.

Looks at the genitals, buttocks, breasts of adults.

Has erections.

Puts something in own genitals/rectum.

Interested in breeding behavior of animals.

Of Concern
Shows fear or anxiety about sexual topics.

Keeps getting caught watching/peeking at others doing bathroom functions.

Continues to use "dirty" words with adults after parent says "no" and punishes.

Frequently plays doctor and gets caught after being told "no."

Boy keeps making believe he is having baby after month/s.

Wants to be nude in public after the parent says "no" and punishes child.

Plays with feces. Purposely urinates on floor.

Continues to touch/rub genitals in public after being told "no." Masturbates on furniture or with objects.

Humps other children with clothes on. Imitates sexual behavior with dolls/stuffed toy.

Uses "dirty" language when other children really complain.

Sex talk gets child in trouble. Gets upset with public displays of affection.

Becomes very upset when seen changing clothes.

Keeps getting caught telling "dirty" jokes. Makes sexual sounds, e.g. moans.

Continuous fascination with nude pictures.

Wants to play games with much younger children related to sex and sexuality.

Draws genitals on one figure and not another. Genitals in disproportionate size to body.

Confused about male/female differences after all questions have been answered.

Stares/sneaks to stare at nude persons even after having seen many persons nude.

Wants to be opposite sex.

Wants to compare genitals with much older or much younger children or adults.

Continuously wants to touch genitals, breasts, buttocks of other child/ren. Tries to engage in oral, anal, vaginal sex.

French kisses. Talks in sexualized manner with others. Fearful of hugs and kisses by adults. Gets upset with public displays of affection.

Touches/stares at the genitals, breasts, buttocks of adults. Asks adults to touch him/her on genitals.

Continuous erections.

Puts something in own genitals/rectum when it feels uncomfortable. Puts something in the genitals/rectum of other children.

Touches genitals of animals.

Seek Professional Help
Asks endless questions about sex. Sexual knowledge too great for age.

Refuses to leave people alone in bathroom. Continues use of "dirty" words even after exclusion from school and activities.

Forces other children to play doctor, to take off clothes.

Displays fear or anger about babies or intercourse.

Refuses to put on clothes. Exposes self in public after many scoldings.

Repeatedly plays or smears feces. Urinates on furniture on purpose.

Touches/rubs self in public or private to the exclusion of normal childhood activities. Masturbates on people.

Humps naked. Intercourse with another child. Forces sex on other child.

Uses bad language against other child's family. Hurts other gender children.

Talks about sex and sexual acts a lot. Repeatedly in trouble in regard to sexual behavior.

Aggressive or tearful in demand for privacy.

Still tells "dirty" jokes, even after exclusion from school and activities.

Wants to masturbate to nude pictures or display them.

Forces others to play games related to sex and sexuality. Group forces children to play.

Draws genitals as most prominent feature. Draws pictures of intercourse, group sex.

Plays male or female roles in a sad, angry, or aggressive manner. Hates own/other sex.

Asks people to take off their clothes. Tries to forcibly undress people.

Hates being own sex. Hates own genitals.

Demands to see the genitals, breasts, buttocks of children or adults.

Manipulates or forces other child to allow touching of genitals, breasts, buttocks. Forces or mutual oral, anal, or vaginal sex.

Is overly familiar with strangers. Talks in a sexualized manner with unknown adults.

Sneakily or forcibly touches genitals, breasts, buttocks of adults. Tries to manipulate adult into touching him/her.

Painful erections.

Uses any coercion or force in putting something in genitals/rectum of other child. Anal, vaginal, intercourse. Causes harm to own genitals/rectum.

Engages in sexual behaviors with animals.

- Focus on Programs -
The Greenwich House Children's Safety Project

To gain insight into how a successful program for sexually-abused children can be imple-mented, Child Therapy News *editor David Greenwald, Ph.D. visited Flora Colao, M.S.W., Director of the Greenwich House Children's Safety Project.*

The Greenwich House Children's Safety Project, one of New York's oldest and largest settlement houses, was founded in 1987 by Flora Colao to address the problem of child abuse. An internationally-recognized expert in the field of child abuse preven-tion and treatment, Colao's experience has enabled her to create and implement a unique and effective program.

Greenwich House takes a positive approach to treatment of sexually abused, bat-tered and neglected children by placing emphasis on empowerment rather than vic-timization. All of its services are designed to strengthen self-image, provide outlets for pain and anger, and teach children that whatever happened, it was not their fault.

Children are taught that they can and will triumph. According to Colao, "This is the crucial element in healing a hurt child, and essential to strengthening the entire fam-ily, thus enabling them to go on with their lives."

Classes are offered in basic safety, self-defense and crime violence avoidance as an adjunct to individual therapy. Children are taught concrete actions and strategies for dealing with mugging, kidnapping, molestation, accident prevention and other per-sonal safety issues. Specific safety problems being confronted by a particular child are immediately addressed.

The classes provide a release for pent-up anger and give children a sense of empow-erment. "Our program has some rather unique features to allow children to get their stress and anger out. The only two rules are that they're not allowed to hurt them-selves and they're not allowed to hurt anyone else," maintains Colao.

The Center's gymnasium serves as a place children can go to physically work out anger. Colao comments, "Our self-defense program was designed for these children so that we could teach them a way to 're-own' their bodies. A lot of our work deals with venting rage." For example, children are actually taught how to break wooden boards, giving them permission to be aggressive without hurting another person.

Individual art therapy sessions and art expression therapy groups are available to children, providing them with another outlet for their feelings and a means for increasing attention span and ability to focus.

Greenwich House's Counseling Intake Form is a comprehensive attempt to deter-mine concerns of parents and children alike. The form asks such questions as, "Why do you think your child needs counseling?", "Has the child been a victim of or witness to a crime?", "Has the child witnessed domestic violence?", "Are you concerned about a particular person's alcohol or drug abuse affecting your child?", and "Are there any other symptoms or behaviors you are concerned about?"

The Center's Symptom Checklist can be particularly revealing. Colao stresses the importance of having older children fill out their own copy. "This often gives a truer picture of the whole problem," she says. "Some parents will check off one or two items while the child might check almost everything." The checklist asks whether the child has manifested any of the listed symptoms within the last two months, with-in the last year and over one year ago. Listed symptoms are:

Nightmares

Inability to fall asleep

Extremely restless sleep

Waking

Screaming or crying in sleep

Stomachaches

Unexplained nausea
Overeating
Complains of feeling sick
Reversal in toilet training
Easily frustrated
Thumbsucking
Talking in baby talk
Fear of being away from you
Change in school performance
Sexually acts out
Suicidal thoughts or statements
Hitting, biting or kicking
Namecalling
Complains of being teased
Wears clothing that covers body
  when not appropriate
Moves or sits awkwardly
Apathetic

Poor appetite
Headaches
Bedwetting
Uncontrollable rages
Misplaced anger
Withdrawal
Talking little or not at all
Crying spells
Change in peer relationships
Attempts to force or coerce
  others to be sexual
Preoccupation with death
Always victimized
Always frightened
Refuses to change for gym
Complains of soreness
Has sexual knowledge beyond age

David Greenwald, Ph.D.: *What would you tell a clinician who suspects a strong possibility of sexual abuse but is uncertain as to whether or not it should be reported?*

Flora Colao: I don't think it's ever therapeutic *not* to report suspected sexual abuse.

DG: *Then how do you assess the veracity of a child's story?*

FC: Unless a child's health and safety is involved, my first rule is to stress confidentiality. My first question is, "Why are you coming to see me?" Some children will say, "Because of what happened to me." Others will say, "I don't know." I'll say, "Well, what do you think it is? Somebody brought you here. Why did they bring you?" Some say, "My mom says because I'm supposed to say thus and such," or "The policeman said I'm supposed to talk to you." I never ask leading questions like, "Did so and so do this to you?"

I ask them questions about symptomatology. I ask them how they sleep, how they eat, what kind of things bother them. I ask questions like, "Is there anything that you have to think about that you wish you could forget?" When they've told me something, I ask, "What do you think is going to happen now that you've told?" I've been told, "Mom says we'll go to Disney World if I tell you this." This kind of response signals to me that this may be a false report, but it's hard to tell.

I'll often ask, "Why is it so important to Mommy that you tell me this?" I've had kids say, "Because she doesn't want Daddy to ever be around us again," or "She wants to punish Daddy," or "She's angry at Daddy." I've had the same thing with fathers who falsely report against mothers or the mothers' boyfriends.

I also ask, "Is there anything that anybody told you to tell me? Is anybody going to be mad about something you tell me or you don't tell me?" I ask about other details, such as, "Do you remember what else you were doing that day? Do you remember where else you went?" I've interviewed kids who've witnessed murders, and it's these details that sometimes make the case. I once had a kid whose clearest memory is that he was watching TV when the incident occurred. He said, "We were watching Wonderwoman." By finding out about the particular episode, we were able to figure out what day it happened and what happened.

Most children do not readily talk about sexual abuse, so if a child is too forthcoming, that, to me, is a red flag. Kids will walk in and say, "He touched me here, he touched me there, etc." even before they say "Hello." I get very concerned about children who do this, so I look for symptoms when they're talking about what happened.

DG: *What symptoms do you look for?*

FC: I look for any signs or symptoms of anxiety, any change in a child's voice or language, any change in his/her physical demeanor. The expression on his/her face will change when s/he's talking about things that are upsetting. I ask about sensory details: what things feel like, smell like, taste like, look like, because sensory details give me a lot of information. If a four-year-old says, "It was stinging me and it felt like when I skinned my knee but it wasn't my knee that was hurting." That's very different from when a child says, "It doesn't feel like anything."

DG: *What kind of stages do you see in your treatment?*

FC: Often a child will start to deal with what happened and begin to feel stronger and better, and then there's very often a downward swing and depression before they start dealing with it again. In this regressive stage they get frightened when talking about what happened makes it possible for the other things that they haven't dealt with to surface. Many children experience a "rage stage," and a lot of the work we do is simply about venting rage.

DG: *In a situation where the child is really angry, how do you deal with the "rage stage?"*

FC: I have children tumble on mats, hit targets, have sword "fights," and they are taught how to break boards. They have permission to express aggression that's not going to hurt anybody or themselves. I tell them, "It's okay if you want to hit the target and pretend it's your father or your mother or your brother, but it's not okay for you to hit me and or yourself or your little brother. If you want to smash the dolls and the dollhouse, that's fine." I have had kids break toys. That's not an issue; it's all breakable and it's all replaceable.

DG: *How do you work with the symptoms of post-traumatic stress?*

FC: I do a lot of rewriting of nightmares with children. For example, I had a child who had been raped, and what we did in the rewriting of the nightmare was have her parents come into the room and stop the rapist. That helped her for a while, but when she began to feel her fear again, she turned around and said, "Get away from me. The police are coming after you. You're not going to hurt me anymore." I give out notebooks to take home to write in so that they have a place to put the angry or the upset feelings.

DG: *Do you try to get them to shift from acting out to verbalization?*

FC: Only if it seems as though they're going to hurt themselves or someone else. I will tell them it's okay to do it here, but that they've got to keep in mind that this is going to get them in trouble in school. One little girl wrote on the bottom of a painting, "I hate you." For her, that was really contained. Ordinarily she would throw things, kick things, run out of the room, run down the hall, and that kind of thing.

So for her to write "I hate you" was a big step. I told her how proud I was. That picture is still on the wall.

More information on the Greenwich House Children's Safety Project is available by writing 27 Barrow Street, New York, NY 10014 or calling (212) 924-1091 or (212) 242-4140.

Assessing Child Sexual Abuse

By Kevin McGovern, Ph.D.

As of yet, there are no definitive psychological instruments that can infallibly verify claims of child sexual abuse. The inevitable verification occurs through the eventual confession of a perpetrator. It is important to emphasize that the majority of perpetrators will initially deny any claims of sexual misconduct. Who wants to admit that s/he is a sexual offender? However, after a thorough and skillful investigation is completed, the majority of sexual offenders will eventually admit their sexual crimes, especially when they fail a polygraph evaluation.

Although psychological protocols cannot infallibly predict which individuals have been sexually abused or which have committed a sexual offense, certain questionnaires and instruments are especially helpful in assessing the overall psychological damages that have occurred during the sexually abusive incidents. In addition, a number of these psychological instruments have been administered to sexually abused and nonabused children.

Drs. Waterman and Lusk have written an article entitled "Psychological Testing in Evaluation of Child Sexual Abuse." In this article, they discuss a number of protocols that have been used to evaluate these two populations of minors. These authors concluded "that findings have been mixed, with stronger differences between sexually abused and nonabused children generally found on measures completed by parents than on measures administered directly to children...While psychological tests have limited use in validating suspected sexual abuse, they may be extremely useful in the clinical treatment of the child." Reprints can be obtained by writing to Jill Waterman, Ph.D., Department of Psychology, UCLA, Los Angeles, California, 90024-1563.

In addition, the recent construction of the Child Sexual Behavior Inventory and concurrent research by William Friedrich, Ph.D. and his associates have helped identify what types of sexual activities are observed among populations of nonabused and sexually abused children, For example, nonabused children very infrequently engage in oral sexual activities with other children, whereas both sexually and nonsexually abused children will touch their "crotch" or sit with their "crotch" exposed at about the same frequency. These findings are certainly helpful in allowing us to understand what probable sexual behaviors we will normally observe in abused vs. nonabused children. For further information about this instrument and related research, contact Dr. William Freidrich, Section of Psychology, Mayo Clinic, Rochester, MN 55905.

Selected Assessment Tools for Child Sexual Abuse

Child Sexual Behavior Inventory. Friedrich, William. (A 35-item behavior checklist assessing sexual behavior in children 2-12 years old. William Freidrich, Ph.D., Section of Psychology, Mayo Clinic, Rochester, MN 55905.)

Children's Knowledge of Abuse Questionnaire. Tutty, Leslie. (A 40-item questionnaire designed to assess how well children aged 5-12 learn sexual abuse prevention concepts. Leslie Tutty, D.S.W., Faculty of Social Work, University of Calgary, 2500 University Avenue N.W., Calgary, Alberta, Canada T2N 1N4.)

Children's Problems Checklist. Schinka, John A. (Aids in the establishment of rapport and identification of problems. Includes ratings by parents. Publisher: Psychological Assessment Resources, Inc., P.O. Box 998, Odessa, FL 33556-0998.)

Children's State-Trait Anxiety Inventory. Spielberger, C.D., Edwards, C.D., Montouri, J. & Lushene, R. (Assesses state-anxiety, or current level of anxiety, and trait-anxiety, or anxiety-proneness, in children grades 4-8. Publisher: Consulting Psychologists Press, Inc., 577 College Avenue, P.O. Box 60070, Palo Alto, CA 94306. (415) 857-1444.)

Louisville Behavior Checklist. Miller, Lovick C. (1981) (Measures social and emotional behaviors indicative of psychopathological disorders in children ages 4-17. Publisher: Western Psychological Services, 12031 Wilshire Blvd., Los Angeles, CA 90025. (213) 478-2061.)

The Trauma Symptom Checklist (TSC-33): Early data on a new scale. Briere, J. & Runtz, M. (1989) (Journal of Interpersonal Violence, 4, 151-163. Publisher: Sage Publications, Inc., 2455 Teller Rd., Newbury Park, CA 91320.)

Child Sexual Abuse Research Findings

• A study by the National Committee for Prevention of Child Abuse shows that near-ly 3 million U.S. children were reported as suspected victims in 1992. Fewer than half those reports were found to merit further investigation.

• An estimated one of every three girls and one of every seven boys in the U.S. will be sexually abused before age 18. (Lloyd, 1992)

• The National Center of Child Abuse and Neglect reported in 1988 that the rate of female child sexual abuse (3.9 per 1,000) is nearly four times that of males (1.1 per 1,000). (Jackson & Nuttall, 1993)

• It is estimated that 25% of all child sexual abuse occurs before age 7. (Wurtele & Schmitt, 1992)

• One study found that perpetrators in 6% of child sexual abuse cases are cousins and in 4% of cases are siblings. (Lamb & Coakley, 1993)

• Eighty-five percent of female college undergraduates participating in a study of childhood sexual play and games reported that they had engaged in such activities as children. Forty-four percent described sexual play with members of the opposite sex, and many saw their participation as having involved "persuasion, manipulation, or coercion." (Lamb & Coakley, 1993)

• Although teachers are mandated to report suspected child abuse in all 50 states, a 1988 National Incidence Study of the U.S. Department of Health and Human Services found that only 24% of suspected abuse cases are actually reported by school personnel. (Wurtele & Schmitt, 1992)

• The same organization reported no empirical evidence to support higher levels of child sexual abuse among certain races or ethnic groups. But a study of clinical responses to sexual abuse allegations found that clinicians were more likely to view Caucasians as perpetrators than either Afro-Americans or Hispanics. (Jackson & Nuttall, 1993)

• A survey of clinicians revealed that one in five female social workers, psychologists and psychiatrists had personal histories of sexual abuse before age 18. One in five male social workers reported personal abuse, compared with one in 10 male psychologists, psychiatrists and pediatricians. The overall sexual abuse rate for partici-pants in this study was17%. (Jackson & Nuttall, 1993)

• The U.S. Department of Health and Human Services reports a 24-fold increase in the number of sexual abuse allegations between 1977 and 1986. (Jackson & Nuttall, 1993)

• Elevated sexual behavior in sexually-abused children is a consistent research find-ing and one of the most predictable consequences of child sexual abuse. (Friedrich, 1993)

• Manual exploration of an undressed doll's breasts, anus or genitals is a common behavior among non-abused preschoolers, and should not be interpreted as sexualized play. (Kenyon-Jump, Burnette & Robertson, 1991)

• The behavior of sexually-abused and non-abused children does differ with regard to blatantly sexualized actions with anatomical dolls. Most non-abused children under age eight did not spontaneously demonstrate sexual acts with dolls, whereas 90% of children referred for sexual abuse evaluations did. (Kendall-Tackett, 1992)

• Development of a safe, trusting therapeutic relationship is a critical factor in the process of disclosing child sexual abuse. Children are generally fearful about the consequences of "telling." (Heiman, 1992)

• Research shows that young children are able to learn facts about sexual abuse and its prevention, and do not react fearfully to programs designed for this purpose. (Grendel, 1992)

• When the Rorschach test was used to compare effects of early versus late onset of sexual abuse with fathers as perpetrators, the early onset group showed more disturbed thinking, lower self-esteem, poorer body image and higher anxiety level than the late-onset group. (Waterman & Lusk, 1993)

• Parents and teachers of sexually-abused children rate these youngsters as less socially competent and more behaviorally disturbed than the children rate themselves. (Waterman & Lusk, 1993)

• On drawing tests, children alleging ritualistic sexual abuse demonstrate more emotional disturbance than either control group or sexually abused-only participants. (Waterman & Lusk, 1993)

• Studies indicate that sexually-abused children do not have lower full scale or performance IQs than non-abused peers, although their verbal scores may be lower. (Waterman & Lusk, 1993)

Sources: FRIEDRICH, WILLIAM N. (1993) Sexual victimization and sexual behavior in children: A review of recent literature. *Child Abuse and Neglect,* 17, 59-66. GRENDEL, MARILYN A. (1992) Cognitive and emotional effects of brief child sexual abuse prevention program for first-graders. *Dissertation Abstracts International,* 52(11-A), 3826-3827. HEIMAN, MARSHA L. (1992) Putting the puzzle together: Validating allegations of child sexual abuse. *Journal of Child Psychology & Psychiatry & Allied Disciplines,* 33(2), 311-329. JACKSON, HELENE & NUTTALL, RONALD (1993) Clinician responses to sexual abuse allegations. Special issue: Clinical recognition of sexually-abused children. *Child Abuse and Neglect,* 17(1), 127-143. KENDALL-TACKETT, KATHLEEN A. (1992) Professionals' standards of "normal" behavior with anatomical dolls and factors that influence these standards. *Child Abuse and Neglect,* 16(5), 727-733. KENYON-JUMP, RITA, BURNETTE, M. MICHELE & ROBERTSON, MALCOLM (1991) Comparison of behaviors of suspected sexually-abused and nonsexually- abused preschool children using anatomical dolls. *Journal of Psychopathology and Behavioral Assessment,* 13(3), 225-240. LAMB, SHARON & COAKLEY, MARY (1993) "Normal" childhood sexual play and games: Differentiating play from abuse. *Child Abuse and Neglect,* 17, 515-526. LLOYD, ROBIN M. (1992) Negotiating child sexual abuse: The interactional character of investigative practices. *Social Problems,* 39(2), 109-124. WATERMAN, JILL & LUSK, ROBERT (1993) Psychological testing in evaluation of child sexual abuse. Special issue: Clinical recognition of sexually-abused children. *Child Abuse and Neglect,* 17(1), 145-159. WURTELE, SANDY K. & SCHMITT, ANN (1992) Child care workers' knowledge about reporting suspected child sexual abuse. *Child Abuse and Neglect,* 16(3), 385-390.

Recognizing and Responding to Child Sexual Abuse

Every professional who works with children has the responsibility to recognize and report suspected cases of child abuse. Identifying legitimate cases of child abuse involves the professional's ability to interpret behavior, physical signs, as well as the information available from clinical interviews or other legitimate information sources.

Behavioral indicators may run the gamut of psychological symptoms, from acting-out to overly compliant behavior to sleep disturbances, a sudden drop in school performance, clinical depression and suicidal feelings. The clinician must be thorough in ascertaining behavioral patterns both before and after the suspected trauma, and this information should come from a variety of sources, including teachers, relatives, and so on.

Physical evidence of sexual abuse is less common than reported cases, but may involve trauma to the genital or rectal areas, abnormal dilations of the urethra, vaginal or rectal openings, trauma to breasts, buttocks, the lower abdomen or thighs, or the presence of sexually-transmitted diseases.

Information may come as the result of clinical interviews, fact-finding, formal assessments and "credibility assessment." The final evaluation of a child's report must come from the clinical judgment of the professional, but credibility may be influenced by specific factors, including:

1. **The reporting of multiple incidents over a period of time.**
2. **The reporting of a progression of sexual activity from less intimate to more intimate interaction.**
3. **The presence of elements of secrecy in the child's reporting.**
4. **The presence of pressure or coercion by the perpetrator.**
5. **The reporting of explicit details of sexual behavior of the individual child.**

Of course, sexual abuse is only one type of mistreatment from which children must be protected. Physical abuse, neglect, and emotional maltreatment must also be recognized as other forms of trauma to children, and the professional must be sensitive to signs of these types of child abuse as well.

When the sexual traumatization is unknown (or allegedly unknown) to the parents, the professional must proceed with caution. The response of the parents may run the full range of emotional reactions, and their initial response to the report of abuse may have a significant affect on the later treatment of the child. Even as the initial investigation of the incident proceeds, the clinician should assess the child's family and support system.

Professionals must also be aware that certain groups, including children with intellectual, emotional, or learning handicaps, might be particularly susceptible to victimization. Similarly, professionals must consider that abuse can occur from many sources, including family members, strangers, adults known to the child, and other children. The relationship of the alleged perpetrator to the child will have a significant bearing on the child's understanding of the incident or incidents, and the child's willingness and/or ability to reveal the trauma.

Sometimes child abuse will be revealed during the course of therapy and other times it will be uncovered by a teacher or other important adult in the child's life. Schools and other agencies that work with children should have a clear policy of dealing with suspected cases of abuse which conform to local and state regulations. When there is any question of whether abuse has occurred, the advice of an experienced professional should immediately be sought and a representative from child protective services should be contacted as to what kinds of situations or incidents are serious enough to be investigated.

Every reported case of child abuse must be investigated. In every part of the country there are child-protective services that are responsible for receiving reports of alleged abuse and investigating and validating the complaint.

Finally, professionals who work with children and are on the "front-line" in identifying suspected abuse should be forewarned that many cases will not be conclusively resolved. As noted by Burgess, et al (Sexual Assault of Children and Adolescents, 1978): "Despite the most vigorous, knowledgeable, and coordinated efforts, the total facts elicited by investigation frequently will neither prove nor disprove the allegation. Accordingly, every professional who is called upon to assist child victims of sexual assault must learn to live with the irresolution of many cases."

Professionals working with children have the complex obligation to understand the legal and ethical issues involved in identifying sexual abuse and the clinical judgment to act in such a way which will address the immediate needs of the child as well as the long-term issues. Helping and protecting these children is a difficult, but heroic task.

Sources: Burgess, Ann Wolbert, Groth, A. Nicholas, Holmstrom, Lynda Lytle, Sgroi, Suzanne M. (1978) *Sexual Assault of Children and Adolescents.* Lexington, MA: Lexington Books. Everstine, Diana Sullivan & Everstine, Louis (1989) *Sexual Trauma in Children and Adolescents.* New York: Brunner/Mazel. Morrow, Gertrude (1987) *The Compassionate School: A Practical Guide to Educating Abused and Traumatized Children.* Englewood Cliffs, NJ: Prentice-Hall. Sgroi, Suzanne M. (1982) *Handbook of Clinical Intervention in Child Sexual Abuse.* Lexington, MA: Lexington Books. Sgroi, Suzanne M. (1988) *Vulnerable Populations: Evaluation and Treatment of Sexually Abused Children and Adult Survivors, Volume 1.* Lexington, MA: Lexington Books. Sgroi, Suzanne M. (1988) *Vulnerable Populations: Sexual Abuse Treatment for Children, Adult Survivors, Offenders, and Persons with Mental Retardation, Volume 2.* Lexington, MA: Lexington Books.

Recommended Recent Journal Articles
on Child Sexual Abuse

Beitchman, Joseph H., Zucker, Kenneth J., Hood, Jane E., DaCosta, Granville, A., et.al. (1992) **A review of the long-term effects of child sexual abuse.** *Child Abuse and Neglect,* 16(1), 101-118.

Burgess, Ann W. & Hartman, Carol R. (1993) **Children's drawings.** Advocates the use of drawing to help children give voice to their traumatic experiences and reduce trauma associated with disclosing their sexual abuse. *Child Abuse and Neglect,* 17, 161-168.

Conte, Jon R. (Mar., 1992) **Has this child been sexually abused?** Dilemmas for the mental health professional who seeks the answer. Special issue: Sexual child abuse. *Criminal Justice & Behavior,* 19(1), 54-73.

Friedrich, William N. (1993) **Sexual victimization and sexual behavior in children: A review of recent literature.** Reviews empirical research of sexual behavior of sexually abused children. *Child Abuse and Neglect,* 17, 59-66.

Friedrich, William N., Grambsch, Patricia, Damon, Linda, Koverola, Catherine, Wolfe, Vicki, Hewitt, Sandra, Lang, Reuben, Lang, Reuben, Broughton, Daniel (1992) **Child Sexual Behavior Inventory: Normative and Clinical Comparisons.** Normative sample of 880 children was contrasted with a sample of 276 sexually abused children on the Child Sexual Behavior Inventory (CSBI), a 35-item behavior checklist assessing sexual behavior in children 2-12 years old. *Psychological Assessment,* 4(3), 303-311.

Friedrich, William N., Grambsch, Patricia, Broughton, Daniel, Kuiper, James & Beilke, Robert (Sept., 1991) **Normative Sexual Behavior in Children.** Survey to assess the frequency of a wide variety of sexual behaviors in normal preadolescent children and to measure the relationship of these behaviors to age, gender, and socioeconomic and family variables. *Pediatrics,* 88(3), 456-464.

Gonzalez, Lauren Shapiro, Waterman, Jill, Kelly, Robert J., McCord, Jane & Oliveri, Mary Kay (1993) **Children's patterns of disclosures and recantations of sexual and ritualistic abuse allegations in psychotherapy.** Examines patterns of disclosure and recantations during psychotherapy in 63 children who reported sexual and ritualistic abuse in preschool setting. *Child Abuse and Neglect,* 17, 281-289.

Heiman, Marsha L. (1992) **Putting the puzzle together: Validating allegations of child sexual abuse.** Calls for a more systematic assessment protocol when working with suspected victims of child sexual abuse. *Journal of Child Psychology & Psychiatry & Allied Disciplines,* 33(2), 311-329.

Herrera, Michael & Carey, Karen T. (Feb., 1993) **Child sexual abuse: Issues and strategies for school psychologists.** *School Psychology International,* 14(1), 69-81.

Hibbard, Roberta A. & Hartman, Georgia L. (1993) **Components of child and parent interviews in cases of alleged sexual abuse.** Suggests that having a single interview or interviewer may not always be optimal for a thorough evaluation in child sexual abuse cases. *Child Abuse & Neglect,* 17, 495-500.

Jackson, Helene & Nuttall, Ronald (1993) **Clinician responses to sexual abuse**

allegations. Study of a national sampling of clinicians designed to identify factors influencing belief or disbelief of sexual abuse allegations. Special issue: Clinical recognition of sexually abused children. *Child Abuse and Neglect,* 17(1), 127-143.

Kendall-Tackett, Kathleen A. (1992) **Professionals' standards of "normal" behavior with anatomical dolls and factors that influence these standards.** While anatomical dolls are often used in the assessment and diagnosis of child sexual abuse, professionals lack a consistent standard of what constitutes "normal" behavior with dolls. *Child Abuse and Neglect,* 16(5), 727-733.

Kenyon-Jump, Rita, Burnette, M. Michele & Robertson, Malcolm (1991) **Comparison of behaviors of suspected sexually-abused and nonsexually-abused preschool children using anatomical dolls.** Debates usefulness of anatomical dolls in diagnosing sexual abuse of young children. *Journal of Psychopathology and Behavioral Assessment,* 13(3), 225-240.

Lamb, Sharon & Coakley, Mary (1993) **"Normal" childhood sexual play and games: Differentiating play from abuse.** Research has indicated that a significant number of sexually abused children have been molested by other children or adolescents, and that children abused by peers are less likely to disclose abuse to adults than children abused by adults. *Child Abuse and Neglect,* 17, 515-526.

Lloyd, Robin M. (1992) **Negotiating child sexual abuse: The interactional character of investigative practices.** Provides insight into debates about coercion by adults in investigations of child sexual abuse. *Social Problems,* 39(2), 109-124.

Nash, Michael R., Zivney, Olivia A. & Hulsey, Timothy (1993) **Characteristics of sexual abuse associated with greater psychological impairment among children.** Study concluded that characteristics of abuse most often associated with severe psychological disturbance are: the involvment of more than one perpetrator, age of onset before 7, and periods of intense and frequent abuse episodes. *Child Abuse and Neglect,* 17, 401-408.

Rao, Kavitha, DiClemente, Ralph J. & Ponton, Lynn E. (Sep., 1992) **Child sexual abuse of Asians compared with other populations.** *Journal of the American Academy of Child & Adolescent Psychiatry,* 31(5), 880-886.

Wakefield, Hollida & Underwager, Ralph (1991) **Sexual abuse allegations in divorce and custody disputes.** False accusations of child sexual abuse have become a serious concern in vindictive, angry divorce and custody conflicts. Authors call for creation and utilization of more unbiased, empirically-solid tools and techniques for assessment of alleged child sexual abuse. *Behavioral Science and the Law,* 9(4), 451-468.

Waterman, Jill & Lusk, Robert (1993) **Psychological testing in evaluation of child sexual abuse.** Surveys standardized testing results for victims of child sexual abuse. To date, few standardized instruments have been developed specifically for the identification of sexual abuse in children. Tests used routinely have yielded mixed results. Special issue: Clinical recognition of sexually-abused children. *Child Abuse and Neglect,* 17(1), 145-159.

Periodicals Dealing with Child Sexual Abuse

The following periodicals are recommended for use in the treatment and study of child sexual abuse.

Child Abuse and Neglect
(International Society for Prevention of Child Abuse and Neglect)
Pergamon Press, Inc., Journals Division
660 White Plains Road
Tarrytown, NY 10591-5153
(914) 524-9200
Published monthly - Individuals (restricted rate): $108/yr. Institutions: $575/yr.

Family Violence & Sexual Assault Bulletin
(Covers research and treatment issues and offers a clearinghouse networking service, treatment manuals and bibliographies, reference guides to family violence and sexual abuse literature, and conference listings. Services also include membership in the FVSAB Book Club and access to database of professionals in the field.) Family Violence & Sexual Assault Institute
1310 Clinic Drive
Tyler, TX 75701
(903) 595-6600
Published quarterly - Individuals: $25/yr. Institutions: $40/yr.

Journal of Child Sexual Abuse
(Covers research issues, clinical/intervention issues, prevention programs, legal issues, commentary, case studies focusing on child and adolescent victims of sexual abuse or incest, adult survivors of childhood sexual abuse or incest, and sexual abuse or incest offenders.)
Haworth Press, Inc.
10 Alice St.
Binghamton, NY 13904-1580
(800) 342-9678
Published quarterly - Individuals: $30/yr. Institutions: $36/yr.

Journal of Interpersonal Violence
(Devoted to the study and treatment of victims and perpetrators of interpersonal violence. A forum for discussion of the concerns and activities of professionals and researchers working in domestic violence, child sexual abuse, rape and sexual assault, physical child abuse, and violent crime. Focuses on the causes, effects, treatment and prevention of violence.)
Sage Publications, Inc.
2455 Teller Road
Newbury Park, CA 91320
(805) 499-0721
Published quarterly - Individuals: $42/yr. Institutions: $106/yr.

Games for Treating and Preventing Child Sexual Abuse

In the last few years several game developers have found that games have a unique role in both encouraging children to talk about sexual abuse issues and in teaching children the skills that they need to avoid situations that might lead to sexual abuse.

More than just a sensitive game, **Play It Safe...With SASA** is a well-thought-out, structured therapeutic instrument that can be helpful in interview, treatment and prevention of child abuse and child sexual abuse. Designed for 1 to 6 players aged 4 through 14, the game provides an opportunity for comprehensive assessment, discussion of all relevant aspects of the abuse experience and related experiences, and an important training tool for the prevention of child abuse. It features a puppet/doll to comfort children, interview form, body charts, record forms, stickers, and more.

The game also includes Interview cards, which were created with input from law enforcement officials, to be used for the assessment of a child's emotional status as well as to obtain facts surrounding the abuse. Treatment and Prevention cards explore a range of issues, feelings and experiences involved in the abuse. The 720 actual questions from therapists are coded so that the game can be structured for individual needs and situations.

Be Safe...Be Aware! is a colorful board game which teaches young children about healthy and unhealthy touching in a non-threatening way. It stresses the need to identify "safe" and "unsafe" adults, and to always discuss fears and concerns. Be Safe...Be Aware! is designed for 2 to 6 players aged 5 through 10 and is an educational game to be played under the supervision of a mental health professional as a treatment game for children who have experienced some form of sexual abuse. It is appropriate as a prevention tool as well.

Kevin McGovern, Ph.D., the game's developer, notes that some children who have been abused look forward to playing this game, because it provides them an opportunity to talk at their own pace without being "interrogated." The game comes with over 90 question cards, as well as blank cards for personalization.

An effective game for children who act out sexually or who are at risk for molesting other children, **Let's Talk About Touching** focuses on issues related to sexual victimization, sexual abuse, sexual confusion and sexualized and sexually-aggressive behaviors in children. It provides a non-threatening way for 2 to 8 players to deal with thoughts, feelings and behaviors and conversations that relate to sexual abuse. Cards come in pairs of Problems and Solutions, which can be used to play card games life "Go Fish" and "Concentration." Excellent for use with children aged 7 through adolescence as well as family members.

Let's Talk About Touching in the Family uses the same card game format of *Let's Talk About Touching*. It was designed for victims of incest and nonoffending parents to aid in the recovery from adult-child incest and sibling incest, and focuses on the causes, effects, behaviors and feelings involved in incest. An excellent vehicle to foster communication regarding sexual abuse, it is appropriate for 2 to 8 players aged 7 through adolescence.

Organizations and Associations Related to Child Sexual Abuse

These organizations focus on some or all of the following objectives: recovery of child abuse victims, prevention of future child abuse through training programs, publication of instructional materials, research, advocacy of legislation and public policy aimed at protecting children, and resources and referrals to professionals.

Alternatives to Sexual Abuse
P. O. Box 25537
Portland, OR 97229
(503) 644-6600

American Association for Protecting Children
c/o American Humane Association
63 Inverness Drive E.
Englewood, CO 80112-5117
(303) 792-9900

The Center for Child Protection
Children's Hospital
3020 Children's Way
San Diego, CA 92123
(619) 974-8017

The Children's Rights Council
220 "I" Street, N.E.
Suite 230
Washington, DC 20002
(202) 547-6227

Committee for Children
172 20th Avenue
Seattle, WA 98122
(206) 322-5050

Family Violence & Sexual Assault Institute
1310 Clinic Drive
Tyler, TX 75701
(903) 595-6600

The Giarretto Institute
Daughters and Sons United/Parents United
232 E. Gish Road
San Jose, CA 95112
(408) 453-7616

International Society for Prevention of Child Abuse and Neglect
1205 Oneida Street
Denver, CO 80220
(303) 321-3963

National Resource Center on Child Sexual Abuse
107 Lincoln Street
Huntsville, AL 35801
(205) 534-6868 Hotline: (800) 543-7006

National Committee for Prevention of Child Abuse
332 S. Michigan Avenue
Suite 1600
Chicago, IL 60604-4357
(312) 663-3520

Society's League Against Molestation
Women Against Rape/Childwatch
P.O. Box 346
Dollingswood, NJ 08108
(609) 858-7800

The National Resource Center on Child Sexual Abuse provides technical support to all professionals who work with sexually abused children and their families. It is funded by the National Center on Child Abuse and Neglect, U. S. Department of Health and Human Services.

  Among the training opportunities offered by the NRCCSA are comprehensive child sexual abuse intervention training, a national symposium on child sexual abuse, and teleseminars.

  Also offered are referrals for treatment and consultation and a reference library, information papers and a national directory of child sexual abuse treatment programs, monographs, and program and practice briefs. For more information call (800) 543-7006.

The National Directory of Child Sexual Abuse Treatment Programs is a current, annotated listing of approximately 850 child sexual abuse treatment programs operating within the United States and its territories.

  "Programs" are defined as separate and administratively distinct treatment efforts. Information provided for each program includes name and address, contact person, telephone number, host agency, clients served, percent sexual abuse, restrictions, therapeutic services, additional services, professional staff, volunteers, languages, payment accepted, service location(s), area served, and date founded.

  Cost is $25.00 plus $3.50 postage. Send check or money order to National Resource Center on Child Sexual Abuse, 107 Lincoln Street, Huntsville, AL 35801.

About the Contributors

Eliana Gil, Ph.D. is a faculty member and instructor at the California Graduate School of Family Psychology in San Rafael, California, from which she received her doctorate. She is a licensed marriage, family, and child counselor who has worked with adult and child survivors of childhood sexual abuse and their families, as well as sex offenders, since 1973. A past president of the California Professional Society on the Abuse of Children from 1987 to 1989, she currently serves on the Board of the National Resource Center of Child Sexual Abuse.

Dr. Gil has written numerous books on child abuse prevention and treatment, and lectures nationwide. Her books include *Family Play Therapy: The Use of Play in Family Sessions with Young Children* (1994:Guilford Press, NY), *Sexualized Children: Assessment and Treatment of Sexualized Children and Children Who Molest* (with T. C. Johnson, 1993:Launch Press, Rockville, MD), *Foster Parenting Abused Children* (1993:National Committee on Child Abuse Prevention, Chicago, IL), *Outgrowing the Pain Together: A Book for Partners and Spouses of Adult Survivors* (1992:Dell Publications, NY), *The Healing Power of Play: Therapy with Abused Children* (1991:Guilford Press: NY), *United We Stand: A Book for People with Multiple Personalities* (1990:Launch Press, Walnut Creek, CA), *Treatment of Adult Survivors of Childhood Abuse* (1988:Launch Press, Walnut Creek, CA), *Children Who Molest: A Guide for Parents of Young Sex Offenders* (1987:Launch Press, Walnut Creek, CA), *I Told My Secret* (1986:Launch Press, Walnut Creek, CA), and *Outgrowing the Pain: A Book for and About Adults Abused as Children* (1984:Launch Press, Walnut Creek, CA). Dr. Gil is bilingual and bicultural, originally from Guayaquil, Ecuador.

Toni Cavanagh Johnson, Ph.D. is a licensed psychologist in private practice in South Pasadena, California. She has been working in the field of child abuse for 15 years, as a researcher, trainer and clinician. For the past eight years Dr. Johnson has worked in highly specialized treatment programs for children below the age of 13 who molest other children. She is the author of a Curriculum in Human Sexuality for Parents and Children in Troubled Families. Dr. Johnson has developed *Let's Talk About Touching,* a game specifically designed for sexually abused and sexually abusive children, and *Let's Talk About Touching in the Family,* a game for families in which incest has occurred. She has lectured on child abuse throughout the world, and provides consultation to protective service workers, mental health professionals, attorneys, police, probation and courts throughout the United States in the area of sexual victimization and perpetration. Dr. Johnson has authored numerous articles and pamphlets on these subjects and has co-authored a book, *Sexualized Children: Assessment and Treatment of Sexualized Children and Children Who Molest* with Eliana Gil, Ph.D. (Launch Press, 1993).

Dr. Johnson offers a two-day training session on "Children Who Molest," a six- or nine-hour training session on "Fostering the Child with Sexual Behavior Problems," a "Treatment of Child Sexual Abuse Victims" training session, and a 1-1/2- or two-day session on "Caring for Young Children with Sexual Behavior Problems in Residential Care."

Let's Talk About Touching and *Let's Talk About Touching in the Family* are available from Childswork/Childsplay (1-800-962-1141). For more information on Dr. Johnson's publications and training sessions, write 1101 Fremont Ave., Suite 104, S. Pasadena, CA 91030 or call (818) 799-4522.

Kevin B. McGovern, Ph.D. received his Ph.D. from the University of Oregon, is an Associate Clinical Professor of Psychiatry at the Oregon Health Sciences University, and a practicing psychologist in Portland, Oregon. Since 1974, Dr. McGovern has specialized in the treatment of sexual dysfunctions and sexual disorders. He has served as a clinical consultant to the states of Washington and Oregon for the purpose of developing assessment and treatment strategies for sexual offenders.

As a preventive education specialist, Dr. McGovern has designed a children's story book, *Alice Doesn't Babysit Anymore*, and an educational game, *Be Safe...Be Aware*. These educational tools assist parents, professionals, and children in effectively addressing sexual abuse issues. In 1978, Dr. McGovern established an educational resource center called Alternatives to Sexual Abuse, one of the nation's leading sponsors of educational materials and training seminars.

In 1985, he founded the S.A.F.E. Institute (Sexual Abuse Free Environment), a nonprofit organization that publishes Preventing Sexual Abuse. Dr. McGovern also provides both counseling and parental training sessions for victims and families concerned about sexual abuse issues, and viable preventative educational strategies. For more information on Dr. McGovern's programs and products, write Alternative to Sexual Abuse, 1225 NW Murray Rd., Suite 214, Portland, OR 97229 or call 503/644-6600.

CHAPTER 2

Obsessive Compulsive Disorder: The Secret Childhood Epidemic

"Eventually I just dreaded getting up in the morning and facing all the compulsive actions associated with showering and dressing. At one time, I was getting up at 10 A.M. and not getting dressed until 8 P.M." *

"It's hard to put an exact date on when it began. When I was about five, I remember coming downstairs and telling my parents I was bothered about the way I had to put on my pajamas....I was seven, and the school bus would drop me in front of my door. We have a white fence in front of our house. I couldn't get through it. Something made me go back and do it again." *

This chapter is devoted to Obsessive Compulsive Disorder (OCD) among children. Despite the fact that one in every 200 children is estimated to have OCD, very few child therapists are likely to see more than one or two in their practice.

The reason for this under-representation in our clinics and offices is two-fold. First, OCD is a secretive disease by nature, and children with OCD are often very good at hiding it even from their families. Second, we as professionals are often not aware of the signs to look for in diagnosing OCD or of the appropriate questions to ask.

Until recently, childhood OCD was thought to be rare. As a result, no controlled studies of children's treatment were conducted, and therapists of different schools applied psychoanalytically-derived treatments, various cognitive and behavioral treatments and family treatment to children with the illness. Some of these cases are described in the literature. The successful ones generally involved treatments with a behavioral component even if the practitioners did not consider it a mainstay of the treatment.

Only with the recent work of Dr. Edna Foa, Dr. John March, Dr. Judith Rapoport and others, has a successful treatment approach been defined and found to be effective. The treatment of choice for childhood OCD is behavioral therapy combining the two techniques of exposure and response prevention. While this may sound simple, applying these techniques to individual children requires significant clinical skill and a solid understanding of OCD in general and OCD in children.

Children with OCD are often sent to research centers staffed by psychologists and psychiatrists most familiar with OCD treatment. For example, children seen by the staff at the Center for the Study of Anxiety Disorders at the Eastern Pennsylvania Psychiatric Institute in Philadelphia come from all over the country. The staff travels to the children's homes, no matter how far away, for the treatment follow-up (see Focus on Programs).

Fortunately, there are increasing opportunities for child therapists to learn about treating childhood OCD. One of the most exciting advances in this area is the treatment manual *How I Ran OCD Off My Land: A Guide to the Cognitive Behavioral Treatment of Obsessive Compulsive Disorder in Children* by Dr. John March and his colleagues at Duke University. This manual is now available to child therapists who are willing to take time to collect data and return it to Dr. March. It will soon be published in book form (see interview with John March, M.D., Ph.D.).

While OCD remains a chronic disorder, appropriate behavioral therapy and psy-cho-pharmacological treatment can significantly reduce the symptoms in the major-ity of children with OCD. In this chapter, you will learn what OCD is, how to recog-nize it, how it is treated and where to go to learn more about treating it.

We are excited about sharing this information with you and hope that it will con-tribute to the steadily increasing awareness of childhood OCD and its early treat-ment.

—The Editors

From The Boy Who Couldn't Stop Washing: The Experience and Treatment of Obsessive Compulsive Disorder by Judith L. Rapoport, M.D.

Childhood OCD in Brief

Whenever I walk in a London street,
I'm ever so careful to watch my feet;
And I keep in the squares,
And the masses of bears,
Who wait at the corner to eat
The sillies who tread on the lines of the street
Go back to their lairs...

—A. A. Milne, *Lines and Squares*

Childhood obsessive compulsive disorder has many of the same features of adult OCD. There are certain thoughts (obsessions) which the OCD child is unable to stop thinking no matter how stressful or silly they may be and no matter how much the child may wish they would go away. These thoughts typically concern a fear, either of hurting something or someone or of being hurt or contaminated. Swedo and Rapoport reported a study in which they listed obsessions most commonly found in a group of 70 children and adolescents with OCD. Listed in order of decreasing prevalence they were:

- **Fear of dirt or germs**
- **Fear of contamination**
- **A need for symmetry, order and precision**
- **Religious obsessions**
- **Preoccupation with bodily wastes**
- **Lucky and unlucky numbers**
- **Preoccupation with sexual or aggressive thoughts**
- **Fear of harming self or others**
- **Preoccupation with household items**
- **Intrusive sounds, words, etc.**

Compulsions or rituals are the deliberate and repeated behaviors an OCD child uses in order to relieve the anxiety caused by the obsessive thoughts. In some cases, the rituals make sense—for example, children with a fear of germs often have hand-washing rituals, and children with a need for exactness will often redo their letters and numbers until their erasing wears holes in their papers.

In other cases, it is difficult to identify a logical link between the obsession and the ritual. This is especially true when working with very young children who have limited verbal skills. In the Swedo and Rapoport (1989) study mentioned above, the same group of 70 children was found to have the following rituals listed in order of prevalence:

- **Grooming rituals: hand washing, showering, etc.**
- **Repeating rituals involving going in and out of doorways or in general, needing to move through some spaces in a special way, or to check whether the door is locked, the stove is off, etc.**
- **Rituals to undo contact with a "contaminated" person or object**
- **Touching rituals**
- **Rituals to prevent harming self or others**
- **Ordering and arranging objects**
- **Counting rituals**
- **Hoarding and collecting things**

- **Cleaning rituals pertaining to the house or other things**
- **Assorted other rituals such as writing something or moving in a particular way**

It is important to note that rituals play a role in normal child development. It is only when the child's obsessions and rituals become disruptive for the child that they should be considered pathological and receive treatment.

Among different childrens' age groups, toddlers are most well-known for their rituals. For example, toddlers commonly have bedtime rituals which must be repeated exactly each night in order for the child to be able to sleep. Latency-age children often have elaborate and extensive collections of things like bottle caps and baseball cards. Children brought up in religious households may pray regularly before bedtime and important events. The common childhood game of avoiding sidewalk cracks to avoid breaking one's mother's back is another example.

In her discussion of childhood rituals and superstitions, Dr. Leonard compared normal childhood superstitions to childhood OCD rituals and found no particular correspondence between the two. For example, the most common childhood OCD ritual of washing is only rarely seen in normal children. Again the important point is whether or not the child's ritual incapacitates that child.

In some children it is difficult to distinguish whether they have signs of an obsessive personality disorder rather than OCD. Some children with OCD develop obsessive compulsive personality disorder as a means of coping with their rituals. If they always place something in the right place they can maintain diminished levels of anxiety. Others may begin treatment with what looks like obsessive compulsive personality disorder and later develop OCD.

Others still may have OCD and not the personality disorder (Swedo, S. E. et. al. 1992). Dr. Rapoport noted that people with obsessive compulsive personality disorder are not uncomfortable with their personality style and generally find other people at fault. They also tend to have restricted affect and to have trouble enjoying life or making room for non-work activities.

The treatment of choice for OCD is cognitive behavior therapy with exposure and response prevention as the main components of the treatment. While OCD treatments for adults and children are essentially the same, childrens' treatments are a modified version. Additional treatment for the OCD child may be necessary, particularly if s/he has other emotional or developmental difficulties. Support groups for children and the families of children with OCD are very helpful adjunct therapies (see Organizations).

Pharmacotherapy is also used with children to good effect. The serotonin-reuptake inhibitors such as Anafranil (clomipramine) and Prozac (fluoxetine) are the types of medications most often used in the treatment of OCD. A team approach to treatment is important as the treatment of children with OCD may often involve more than one professional, a key person at school, and the family as well as the child.

Sources: Johnston, H. (1992) *Obsessive Compulsive Disorder in Children and Adolescents: A Guide.* Child Psychopharmacology Information Center, University of Wisconsin. Rapoport, J. L. (1989) *Obsessive-Compulsive Disorder in Children and Adolescents.* American Psychiatric Press, Inc. Swedo, S. E., Leonard, H. L., and Rapoport, J. L. (1992) *Childhood-Onset Obsessive Compulsive Disorder.* Psychiatric Clinics of N. A. 15(4). VanNoppen, B. L., Totora Pato, M. and Rasmussen, S. *Living with Obsessive Compulsive Disorder, 2nd Edition.* OC Foundation, CT.

Recognizing Children with OCD

Recognizing obsessive compulsive disorder in children may be difficult, but it is far from impossible. Becoming aware of the behavioral signs of OCD rituals and adding some simple questions to the standard initial clinical interview with the child and/or the child's parents will go a long way towards helping to identify the child with OCD.

Often children will be both surprised and relieved when asked a question relevant to OCD. Because they think no one knows about or understands their problem, they often refrain from volunteering information about it. Once they realize that someone else knows about their secret world, they are often happy to talk. Many children have developed fantasies about the origins of their OCD. It is not uncommon for these fantasies to include ideas about being chosen by creatures from outer space for special purposes or being chosen by God to do some unusual form of work.

Hearing someone else talk about OCD in a rational manner and coming to understand that it is a psychological and even neurological illness helps to relieve these children from feelings of being set apart from others and of having to do special but extremely painful work against unknown forces and for mysterious reasons.

Anyone who works with or cares for children should be aware of the following behavioral signs as possible indicators of OCD. These signs in themselves do not indicate the presence of OCD. But if any of them are present, it would be reasonable to further evaluate the child by asking questions. These behavioral signs are generally the secondary effects of the rituals a child is conducting. The signs include:

- **Raw, chapped hands from constant washing.**
- **Unusually high rate of soap usage.**
- **High, unexplained utility bills.**
- **Unproductive hours spent at homework.**
- **Holes erased through test papers and schoolwork.**
- **Requests for family members to repeat strange phrases or keep answering the same question.**
- **A persistent fear of illness.**
- **A dramatic increase in laundry.**
- **An exceptionally long amount of time spent going to bed.**
- **A continual fear that something terrible will happen to somebody else.**
- **Difficulty leaving the house.**
- **Toilets clogged from too much paper.**
- **Constant lateness.**
- **Chronic irritability.**
- **Chronic fatigue.**
- **Difficulty making simple decisions.**

In screening for OCD in the clinical interview, it is necessary to ask about obsessions and compulsions in a matter-of-fact manner with language the child understands. Dr. March (interviewed in this chapter) recommends the following six questions be asked as part of every standard initial clinical interview:

- **Do you have silly worries or thoughts or images or feelings or urges?**
- **Do you have to check things over and over again?**
- **Do you have to wash either because you're worried about getting contaminated or because you feel sticky?**

- **Do you count?**
- **Do you have problems throwing things away?**
- **Do things have to be "just so?"**

If the child answers "yes" to any of these questions, further questions and observation about the nature of the child's problem are in order. This is necessary because certain behaviors may be age-appropriate. Collecting things, for example, is a common and normal behavior among nine and 10-year-olds. If OCD appears to be a strong possibility, a more formal assessment can be made with commonly-used assessment tools such as the CY-Bocs.

Finally, it is important to ask about the family's history of any OCD, Gilles de Tourette's Syndrome and Tic disorders. OCD has a genetic component, and children with family histories including any of these disorders may be more prone to have OCD. Because of the nature of the illness, however, it may be difficult to elicit a full or accurate family history.

Rather than directly asking about a family's history of OCD occurrences, it is often useful to ask about some of the common behavioral signs or patterns that may indicate OCD. For example, "Did anyone in your family have an exaggerated need to check on things like the door being locked or the stove being turned off?" or "Did anyone in the family hoard unusual objects in the house?"

By becoming aware of the signs of OCD rituals and by taking a few extra minutes to ask about OCD behaviors, child therapists will ensure that OCD is identified and treated at an early stage. Teachers who are familiar with these behavioral signs may also be able to identify children who may have OCD and to bring this the attention of their parents and school counselors.

Sources: *"Could Your Child or Teenager Have Obsessive-Compulsive Disorder (OCD)?"* a pamphlet from Basel Pharmaceuticals, 1991, CIBA-GEIGY Corp. Leonard, H. L., Swedo, S. E., Rappaport, J. L. "Diagnosis and treatment of obsessive-compulsive disorder in children and adolescents" in: Pato, M. T., Zohar, J., Eds. *Current Treatments of Obsessive-Compulsive Disorder.* Washington, DC. American Psychiatric Press, 1991, pp. 87-102. Rapoport, Judith (1989) *The Boy Who Couldn't Stop Washing: The Experience and Treatment of Obsessive Compulsive Disorder.* Penguin Books, NY. Johnston, Hugh (1992) "Obsessive Compulsive Disorder in Children and Adolescents: A Guide." Child Psychopharmacology Information Center, University of Wisconsin.

An Interview with...
John March, M.D., Ph.D.

John March, M.D., Ph.D. is the author of How I Ran OCD Off My Land: A Guide to the Cognitive Behavioral Treatment of Obsessive Compulsive Disorder in Children. *The first of its kind for the treatment of OCD in children, this manual integrates current clinical and scientific knowledge about OCD into a comprehensive treatment program which has proved successful for hundreds of children.*

Dr. March has a master's degree in molecular biology from Berkeley, an M.D.-Ph.D. degree from the University of California in Los Angeles, and is Board Certified in Family Practice and Child Psychiatry. He is the director of Duke University's program for Childhood Mental Illness and Anxiety Disorders where he is in charge of several research projects. He reports that he is a "neuro-psychiatrist by bent."

Since 1986, Dr. March has worked with over 300 children who have OCD. His encyclopedic knowledge about OCD as well as his enthusiasm, clinical wisdom, and creativity were apparent in the recent conversation he had with Senior Editor Laura Slap-Shelton, Psy.D.

Laura Slap-Shelton, Psy.D.: *What signs of OCD would you recommend that a clinician or parent look for in children? At what point should a parent or clinician become concerned about a child possibly having OCD?*

John March, Ph.D.: There are two major groups of children and adolescents with the disorder. The first and perhaps larger group of children with OCD develop it insidiously; that is, there are no antecedent events and there is no family history of OCD or related disorders.

The second group has a very strong family history of OCD and Tourette's Syndrome that goes back through multiple generations. In this group you often have a preponderance of men with Tourette's Syndrome and women with OCD, but many have some combination of Tourette's and OCD or Tics.

LS-S: *Is OCD a genetically-transmitted disease?*

JM: This appears to be the case at least for a significant group of patients. There are fairly decent data now from five family pedigree studies that OCD and Tourette's Syndrome are autosomal dominant with sex specific expressivity and variable penetrance. If the child's family has a history of OCD, Tourette's or Tic disorders and he or she starts having Tics and arranging T-shirts or socks "just so," or tracing and retracing letters, or suddenly begins to do a lot of handwashing or checking rituals due to concern about contamination or some type of catastrophe, it's a good bet that what you're seeing is the emergence of OCD.

LS-S: *For this group, are there specific ages when OCD may be more likely to appear? Does stress increase the chances that a child who is potentially at risk for the illness will have it?*

JM: Yes. There are environmental risk and stress factors that are present in a substantial minority of kids. These include ordinary developmental transitions such as going to kindergarten, moving from third to fourth grade when cognitive demands increase, beginning middle school and high school, leaving home and so on. Significant losses such as when a grandparent dies or the family moves can also constitute environmental risk factors.

LS-S: *We have been discussing children whose families have a history of OCD and related disorders. What about the first group of children you mentioned, the group without family histories? How can we identify this type of child with OCD?*

JM: These children often have affective disorders or things that look like OCD but are not, such as Trichotillomania (compulsive hair-pulling), nail-biting, pore and skin picking or body dysmorphia. It's unusual for a youngster to only have OCD. But even so, many of these kids simply have no identifiable antecedent event and no obvious identifiable family risk other than family history of depression or an anxiety disorder. These children are often more likely to have fearful OCD or OCD where the affect is quite negative like excessive anxiety, disgust or guilt. Their presentation is somewhat different than that of the child with a Tourette's-like OCD. They probably represent a different category with respect to pathogenesis.

LS-S: *Let's say a therapist is treating a child from this category for Attention Deficit Disorder (ADD), but notices that the child needs to have things "just so." Would this indicate that the therapist should be concerned about OCD?*

JM: Yes. This is not an uncommon clinical scenario. The pattern we tend to see is a child who has attention disorganization, daydreaming, and who does better in verbal than nonverbal space on neuropsychological testing, and may have a learning disorder, and in addition to all of this, is showing behaviors that suggest OCD. In this situation the therapist really needs to do a careful evaluation for OCD.

LS-S : *How would a therapist carry out this evaluation?*

JM: There are six questions s/he should ask the child. Actually, I ask every patient I see these same six questions as part of a clinical interview to screen for OCD, and I recommend this practice to all clinicians working with children.
   The questions are basically very simple and are driven by the prevalence of the symptoms. About 80% of children with OCD will have washing or checking rituals, so the first question is, "Do you have silly worries or thoughts or images or feelings or urges?" This question attempts to address the obsession element of OCD in broad terms. The other questions are: "Do you have to check things over and over again?"; "Do you have to wash either because you're worried about getting contaminated or because you feel sticky?"; "Do you count?"; and "Do you have problems throwing things away?" Finally, and very importantly, I ask, "Do you have to do things 'just so?'"

LS-S: *What are you looking for in the responses to these questions?*

JM: We are especially interested in the affective component of the response, the feeling that something hasn't been completed or done enough and that the child will have to continue the behavior until he or she knows it's OK, however long that may take. An example is the child who must trace and retrace letters. I usually give an example for each of these questions when I ask them. I screen out 90 percent of kids just with those six questions.

LS-S: *Let's say that the child answers one of the questions in such a way that OCD cannot be ruled out. What is the next step in making the diagnosis?*

JM: One of the first things to do is try to discriminate age-appropriate behaviors from the behaviors that we see and know a child experiences in OCD. I would want to explore the child's response a little more. There are a fair number of developmentally normal OCD-like behaviors. For example, the childhood game of "Step on a crack, you'll break your mother's back" is a developmentally normal OCD-like behavior in nine-year-olds. Saving things that have sentimental value even when it makes no sense to the parent is not unusual. Arranging and rearranging things in his/her room is a normal activity for a 10-year-old.

You also want to check the context in which the behavior occurs. For example, it's appropriate to arrange the things in your room, but it's not appropriate to be unable to get out of a classroom because you've got to go through the middle of the door exactly in the middle or you haven't been able to arrange your pencils perfectly on your desk.

Another aspect of this is to understand when a behavior is associated with mastery of some developmental event. Mastering organization is an important middle childhood task, but it doesn't make any sense to have to wash your hands for three hours. OCD behaviors not only do not lead to mastery, they're also associated with distress and dysfunction, emotions not experienced in the context of mastery.

So to summarize, it's important to evaluate any affirmative answer to the six screening questions in terms of whether the reported behavior is age-appropriate, whether it is associated with a developmental imperative, and whether it is associated with positive or negative affect. Once you've answered these questions in the direction of OCD you can go on to inventory the symptoms that are characteristic of OCD using one of the standard obsessive compulsive scales or inventories. That's what I do.

LS-S: *How do you collect baseline data in order to evaluate a child's progress in therapy?*

JM: We collect Subjective Units of Discomfort (SUDS) ratings for each of the child's symptoms, and we use this to construct a hierarchy of fears which will determine the shape of the therapy. In doing this we are also creating a within-subject multiple baseline study.

We ask the child to think about each of his/her fears and tell us how uncomfortable it feels using a point system. We use a "fear thermometer" in order to rate discomfort in a way that's understandable for kids. As treatment progresses, the child will rate these situations as being increasingly less stressful. In this way we move up the hierarchy of fears beginning with fairly neutral to mild fears and working toward exposure to the most troubling situations. This means that the behaviors being targeted for exposure and response prevention serve as the baselines in terms of collecting data on the child's improvement.

LS-S: *Are you collecting this data from the clinicians using your manual as well as the general inventory data?*

JM: No. We don't ask clinicians to give that kind of data back to us, partly because they are going to want to publish their papers, and partly because if you really do it you have to collect SUDS on every baseline throughout the whole treatment. This is a time-consuming procedure and some therapists may opt not to be so thorough in their data collection.

LS-S: *Now that we've discussed identification of children with OCD, let's talk about* *treatment. What techniques does the program provide to help the child and the clinician stay focused on the treatment? The title of your manual suggests that you and your colleagues have put significant effort into trying to make your approach appealing and meaningful to children. Is this part of the solution to the compliance issue you mentioned earlier?*

JM: Yes. Let me give you the general framework of the program. First, we establish with the child and the child's family that this a neuro-behavioral illness. It's neural in the sense that it has a clear neurological basis. We stress that it is a medical illness, genetic in some, if not the majority of cases, and that it needs to be approached as a medical disorder. This is important because kids and parents uniformly feel blamed as though they've done something wrong.

We use the terms "hiccups in your head" or "volume control knob turned up too high" and make analogies to medical illness in order to explain OCD to them. We say, "You wouldn't blame yourself for having diabetes; why blame yourself for having OCD? It's no different. It's just that the brain thinks, feels and acts. If you've got hiccups in your head, what we need to do is focus on how to get rid of them." There's no answer to the "who-dun-it" question. The culprit is OCD itself.

LS-S: *This probably provides a lot of relief to the child and the family.*

JM: It does, and it also is an accurate description of OCD. This is not an illness caused by relational distress. I recently saw a youngster with OCD who was concerned with AIDS; he was worried that someone had tampered with his food after having been hospitalized out of state. Because of the concern that someone had tampered with his food and that a few months earlier a teenager had shown him some pictures of nude women while he was eating, the therapist assumed that the child had been sexually abused and that caused all manner of havoc in the family.

In fact, the child had experienced two events that were really not related. The problem causing his distress was AIDS-phobia OCD, a neuro-behavioral disease. The family was enormously relieved to discover this, and they were ready to make the "hiccups in the brain" go away.

LS-S: *What else do you do to encourage full participation in the treatment?*

JM: After removing any blame from the child and the family and explaining the nature of OCD, we continue to help them understand the illness and the treatment with a variety of linguistic or narrative interventions. We borrowed these from Michael White, who is an Australian family therapist. He has a technique he calls "externalization of the problem." Early on, actually at the end of the first session and throughout some of the second session, we have the child give their OCD a nasty nickname. Adolescents sometimes think that's silly and just call it "OCD" as adults do, but younger kids like to give OCD a name which reflects their reproach.

LS-S: *What are some examples of names children have chosen?*

JM: One child I saw had been viciously berated by his teacher, Mrs. T. He had developed tracing and retracing rituals and in a six-month period went from being an "A" to an "F" student. Eventually, he stopped going to school, was hospitalized for school phobia, and was diagnosed with Conduct Disorder. He called his OCD "The Mrs. T Problem."

Children commonly use names like "Silly Worries" and "Terrible Trouble." If they have a particular obsession which is bothersome to them, they'll sometimes name it after the obsession. I had a child who had worries about contamination from plants, particularly at her aunt's house. Unfortunately, she spent a lot of time at her aunt's house so she called her OCD "Plants and Aunts."

LS-S: *How does naming the OCD help the child in therapy?*

JM: The goal is for youngsters to learn how to "boss back" the OCD, to fight back against the nasty nickname they choose because they are at war with the disorder and most of the time the disorder wins. Learning to boss back OCD involves understanding the disorder. To help the child in this we use map metaphors to discuss what the child can control and what the OCD can control. We call this process "mapping OCD." This is where the title of the manual comes from—we teach the child to "run OCD off their land."

To do this we look at the obsessions, the compulsions, the avoidance behaviors, the triggers, the consequences, all of the things that one would do using the traditional cognitive behavioral approach, but we speak about them in terms of territories. There are three territories: the territory in which the child controls everything, the territory in which OCD always wins, and then a middle zone where the child is able to resist the OCD some of the time. We call this third territory the "Transition Zone." Events included in this area turn out to be at the bottom of the child's fear hierarchy.

LS-S: *So now the battle lines are drawn. How does the child engage in bossing back the OCD?*

JM: If you're in a war with the disorder, you need two things. One is allies. Using the nasty nickname and placing OCD in a medical context allows everyone involved with the child's treatment to ally with the child against the disorder. It makes the problem the problem. And we're absolutely intransigent about this with our patients. We refuse to get into blaming. Even when the families are in distress, we absolutely insist that we keep the focus on OCD as the problem. That's an enormous booster for compliance because it's very discouraging when people are attacking each other. Keeping the focus on OCD is a great morale booster.

The second part of what you need is a strategy. No one wants to feel helpless, and the reason that kids do these rituals is they don't feel like they have any alternative. OCD is a powerful negative reinforcer. It's a very aversive stimulus, and once kids get the idea that they can feel better, they're more than happy to do what it takes to get better. We tell them that we're going to give them a tool kit; a doctor's bag and a carpenter's tool kit are the metaphors we often use. We tell them that this tool kit will enable them to write OCD out of their lives.

The tool kit involves two principal elements. One is anxiety management training, which consists of relaxation training, diaphragmatic breathing, and cognitive restructuring. The second tool is exposure and response prevention. We teach kids anxiety management training so that they can use it during the exposure and response prevention tasks to manage the level of their anxiety.

LS-S: *What do you do if the child's anxiety becomes catastrophic?*

JM: We find that by letting children tell us how far up his or her fear hierarchy they are prepared to go, we can avoid creating too much anxiety in them, or flooding. In the first session we tell children that they'll never be asked to do something they absolutely don't want to do.

Once we've gone through these steps, we begin graded exposure in which the child controls the exposure targets and how fast he/she moves up the stimulus hierarchy. The child picks the exposure or response prevention targets for that week. The therapist's role is to control the structure of the treatments. The only thing on which we as therapists insist is the child's willingness to participate in the program. We insist on progress, even if it is in small increments, because we want the child to be successful at every step. We want to build on success.

Building on success is another key to maintaining compliance and participation in the therapy. When a youngster goes home and tries to do something that the therapist thinks is reasonable and then "blows up" in the middle of it, it's unlikely that he/she will want to return. It is also likely that the family will find it difficult to comply if the child's OCD behavior escalates rather than diminishes.

LS-S: *How long does treatment take with most children?*

JM: Our data indicate that the average number of sessions for the children we have treated is 10 weekly sessions. The manual provides for 16 sessions plus a booster session at 22 weeks, but the majority don't even need 16 sessions.

LS-S: *Do you have children keep records of their battles with OCD?*

JM: Yes, we have them keep a symptom diary. This is not a quantitative account of the child's symptoms, but rather a narrative written in terms of the metaphors we have provided as a means of conceptualizing the disorder. The youngsters are authoring OCD out of their story. The diary also provides a written record the therapist can use to see how things went during the week.

Children like the idea of writing away OCD. This method works for very young children as well. The parents or therapist can write down their story if they need help. Of course, some children don't want to do it, and we don't insist on it. But it's a nice option for many children.

LS-S: *How involved are the parents in their child's treatment?*

JM: We involve the parents from the first session on. The manual includes a "Tips for Parents" component which is a book that we give them at the beginning of treatment. The therapist speaks with the parents at the beginning of each session to discuss what happened the preceding week and at the end of each session to explain what the goals are for the coming week. The child has his/her symptom diary and a SUDS checklist, and each session has a set of specific goals and homework assignments which are written out for the child and the parents. Session six and session 12 are specifically devoted to disentangling the parents from OCD. It's an individual-oriented treatment where the parents are involved.

LS-S: *You mentioned earlier that this is an area where the therapist may want to prescribe a treatment goal for the child. How does that work?*

JM: We ask the child to select items from his/her fear or stimulus hierarchy for exposure, response prevention, or extinction which their parents can either help with or work on because they have become part of the stimulus situation. Nine times out of 10 that's all you need to do.

Once in 10 times, the child won't want the parent to stop. This is particularly true with extinction problems. We ask these parents to work on disentangling themselves from a situation they think the child could tolerate. The problem with doing this is that parents aren't given a strategy for managing their youngster's distress. So we anticipate how much distress the child is likely to experience and discuss with the parents what might happen and how they can manage their child's distress in a way that's helpful for the child.

An example would be the child who's concerned about whether s/he's going to be sick because Mom's brought something home from the grocery store and the child's worried that there might be germs on it. The child doesn't want to eat it and will only eat it if the mother reassures him/her that it's not contaminated over and over again.

An extinction procedure would be to stop the reassurance. First we negotiate how that will work with the youngster. So the youngster might say, "Well, I'll ask once and Mom might answer once, 'It's okay,' but if I ask again, Mom won't answer." The case may be that we need to allow Mom to respond five times, because the baseline has been 50 times. Again, it's set up in a way that's negotiated with the parents and the child.

LS-S: *So even though the child doesn't choose the extinction target behavior, he or she does have some control of the way in which therapy will proceed around the behavior.*

JM: Yes. Our goal is to help the child remain in control of his/her battle against OCD and to keep the family allied against the OCD and not each other.

LS-S: *Do you ever involve school personnel in the treatment?*

JM: Yes. When the child has rituals which occur at school, we involve the school personnel. Otherwise, we generally don't, unless the parents want us to talk to the teachers. We are also interested in identifying academic problems the child may be having that are not part of the OCD, but that we have identified as part of our evaluation. We do a fairly careful neuropsychological assessment on all of the children we see and it's amazing how many information processing differences we find that have subtle but important implications for the youngster's academic success.

LS-S: *How does medication fit with your treatment approach?*

JM: There's no question that serotonin reuptake inhibitors such as clomipramine and fluoxetine are the most effective medications for children with OCD, but cognitive behavioral psychotherapy is the treatment of choice for every child with OCD. This is based on research with adults which shows that if you combine medications which are thought to be effective with OCD with anti-exposure instructions, (that is, instructions to avoid the things that make you anxious and if you can't avoid them to do your rituals) the anti-exposure instructions completely attenuate the benefits of medications.

This is a very important clinical result because it means that unless the patient does exposure and response prevention, s/he's not going to get better. Most people who are treated just with medications are doing implicit behavior therapy on their own. Unfortunately, the data are quite clear in children as well as adults that the majority of patients treated only with medications will relapse when the medications are discontinued.

In contrast, our data with children who were treated with a combination of medication and behavior therapy show that we have been successful at getting more than half of our kids off medications and keeping them off with no relapse at follow-up from six to 24 months.

These results will be published next spring. It's quite exciting. The majority of children in our trial either went to a sub-clinical level of symptoms or were symptom-free. Behavior therapy appears to prevent relapse when medications are discontinued.

LS-S: *Does the reduction in anxiety brought about by the medications interfere with the effectiveness of the cognitive behavioral therapy?*

JM: No, much the opposite. The fastest way to get better is the combination of the two therapies. What happens is that the medications enable the behavior therapy to go forward. The therapist has to be very clear that the success is being attributed to the things that the child is doing to resist OCD and not to the medicine, because the attributional issue is one of the things that contributes to relapse. One of the reasons we have high compliance is that we simply tell people that the behavior therapy is the treatment of choice for everybody. It's not an issue. It's the treatment of choice. Medications are an important part of the treatment for the majority of children, so we use a lot of them.

LS-S: *Do you have a preference for any particular medication?*

JM: We use a mixture of medications. I present a "Chinese menu" outlining the plusses and minuses of the different medications and let families pick, because I don't think we have reliable data on which medication is better. There are some things which will rule out a particular medicine; for example, a youngster who has an abnormal EKG isn't a candidate for clomipramine. A child who has had an allergic reaction to one of the serotonin reuptake inhibitors is not a candidate for that drug. We rule out the drugs that are not suitable, suggest which might work the best, and let the parents make their choice.

LS-S: *What do you do if you encounter a family that doesn't want to go through a behavioral treatment regime and just wants the medicine?*

JM: I haven't had that happen. But I don't want to say we work miracles—of the 15 children in the case studies that we have in press, three of them didn't get better. One of them had primary obsessional OCD, for which we don't have a good behavioral or medication treatment. Another was a very sick child with extensive symptomatology who actually is beginning to get a bit better. The third child came from a pathogenic family where there was such a huge amount of yelling and hollering that we could not disentangle the family psychopathology from the OCD, and, unfortunately he dropped out of treatment.

However, in the three-and-a-half years that I've been at Duke, with the exception of patients who come for consultation or live too far away, I haven't had a single family refuse behavioral therapy. I think it's because we present it as the treatment of choice, and most families come ready to trust our recommendations.

How I Ran OCD Off My Land: A Guide to the Cognitive Behavioral Treatment of Obsessive Compulsive Disorder in Children is a manual that integrates current clinical and scientific knowledge about OCD into a comprehensive treatment program which has proved successful for hundreds of children.

The first of its kind for the treatment of OCD in children, it is a research instrument available for replication studies around the country.   Created by Dr. John March, M.D., Ph.D., the manual "will make it possible for any interested child therapist to become competent at providing effective treatment for children with OCD."

Clinicians follow the manual and gather a small amount of global rating scale and baseline data for each patient visit. They then send that information to Dr. March to aid his continuing efforts to validate the efficacy of the treatment manual.

The need for this instrument is clear, Dr. March maintains. "Parents complain that clinicians don't know how to conduct behavior therapy with their OCD children, and clinicians complain that no one will comply with it. Actually, they are both right. Nobody has systematically developed the technique for applying what we know works in adults to kids. That's what we've done," he says.

He maintains that the problem with behavioral psychotherapy and kids with OCD is that the literature is weak. There are approximately 60 published illustrations of treatment of kids with OCD. Six of those are single case designs and the rest are case reports, and they span the range from psychodynamic psychotherapy (where the therapist did use some behavioral techniques but did not identify them as such) to family therapy where the treatment was not conceptualized behaviorally. As an example, Dr. March cites a case that is described in family systems terms where the intervention actually involved extinction procedures.

The manual was written with three goals in mind. The first goal is exportability; that is, to make it accessible to clinicians from all different persuasions. It is written so that someone who has no understanding at all of cognitive behavioral terminology or social learning theory can pick it up and use it immediately. All relevant terms are defined. It is also applicable in any mental health center environment and in any clinician's office; in this respect, it is useful for the hundreds of thousands of children with OCD across the country.

The second goal of the manual is to address compliance issues. "We wanted kids to comply, and we wanted to build in the 'tricks of the trade' that make it work," says Dr. March. "We also wanted the therapists to comply, because often therapists, particularly those trained in other traditions, will get sidetracked by the issues that kids raise, or they'll want to conceptualize OCD problems as having a significant meaning or as a manifestation of some relationship disturbance. They often forget that the treatment is specific for OCD, which is a neuro-behavioral medical illness."

The third goal is that the treatment program have a provision for evaluation. Dr. March explains, "There are two parts to this goal. The first is that we see all of our individual treatments of children as single subject designs. We wanted to stress the idea that the therapist is conducting an experiment, and needs to think about everything in experimental terms as well as in clinical terms so that s/he can evaluate whether or not the therapy is working.

"The second part of this goal is to make sure that treatment results are replicable with different kinds of children with different backgrounds, in different treatment settings, and with clinicians of various theoretical backgrounds. Having the data returned to us by the clinicians using the manual will help us to ensure that the treatment program is exportable, which brings us full circle back to our first goal."

The price for the manual is $14. Send check or money order to Dr. John March, Duke University Medical Center, Suite 2327, Durham, NC 27710 or call Dr. March at (919) 684-4950 for more information.

- Focus on Programs -
The Center for the Treatment and Study of Anxiety

The Center for the Treatment and Study of Anxiety at Medical College of Pennsylvania in Philadelphia is internationally-recognized for its treatment of OCD in adults and children. Its director, Dr. Edna B. Foa, is one of the foremost researchers in the treatment of OCD and other anxiety disorders.

The Center provides cognitive-behavioral treatment for children from all over the country. Treatment is on an outpatient basis whenever possible. The program is divided into three phases: evaluation, treatment and follow-up. The follow-up involves having the therapist travel to the child's home, no matter what the distance, to ensure that the work done at the Center is being carried over within the family.

We visited The Center to discuss its program with Dr. Foa, Dr. Elizabeth Hembree and Dr. Michael Kozak. Dr. Foa emphasized that the Center's cognitive-behavioral work with children provides excellent results, primarily using Dr. John March's manual for treating OCD in children (see interview with Dr. March). Clinicians at the Center often focus on stopping the rituals because children, especially young children, often either do not know why they are acting out their rituals or are unable to put their feelings into words. "We concentrate on stopping the rituals because by definition stopping the rituals brings about exposure," Dr. Foa explained.

In discussing initial evaluations, Dr. Hembree stressed that one of the most important goals during the initial evaluation is "to get a comprehensive idea of all the obsessions and rituals." She added, "We also want to know as much about when and where they occur so that we are able to develop a picture of the context in which they occur." She pointed out that in treating adults, "if we miss one of the obsessions or rituals because the patient hasn't shared the information, the untreated aspect of the OCD often flourishes."

Although there have been no formal studies conducted with children, it is likely that they experience the same phenomenon. This is because although there may be some generalization of the effects from treatment, the ritual or obsession the patient has not shared is likely to be significant. Dr. Hembree explained, "When someone is unable to share an obsession or ritual in the treatment setting, it is generally because it is too frightening and the problem is a large one, not something merely overlooked. One child came back two years after a successful treatment with major problems. She had had inklings of the problem when she was first treated, but was too afraid to bring it up. Over the two years, it had built up and she had a whole new set of rituals."

Dr. Hembree uses a variety of behavioral assessment inventories, such as the Yale-Brown Obsessive-Compulsive Scale, to gain a full picture of the obsessions and rituals, their frequency and the degree to which the child is able to resist them. To screen for depression, she also uses the Beck Depression Inventory. She stressed that the therapist also uses the initial evaluation to collect information to be used in constructing a fear hierarchy with the child. "It is important to question the child carefully about his/her daily routine. This helps to identify when and where the behavior occurs as well as any antecedent behaviors or triggers. It also helps to uncover avoidances the child may have, but does not recognize as being part of his/her problem," she said.

Dr. Hembree stresses the importance of the evaluation phase in terms of setting the stage for therapy. Educating the child and parents about OCD and the reasons behind collecting detailed information and then constructing a stimulus hierarchy are very important in establishing a situation in which the child feels safe. It also helps the child and parents to feel hopeful that the therapy will indeed work. "As uncomfortable as it is to give up rituals, the children really don't like what's been happening to them," Dr.

Hembree explained. "If I've explained the therapy well, they are willing to give it a try."
Dr. Kozak has been working at the Center for more than 10 years and has worked with
a large number of children with anxiety disorders including OCD. He conducts the
treatment phase of the program in which the exposure and response preventions are car-
ried out. Senior Editor Laura Slap-Shelton, Psy.D. spoke with Dr. Kozak regarding
working with children who have OCD.

Laura Slap-Shelton, Psy.D.: *Programs for treating children with OCD are modeled*
on adult programs because the type of treatment, exposure and response prevention is
the same. In what ways should the therapist familiar with the treatment of adults with
OCD modify his/her approach for working with children?

Michael Kozak, Ph.D.: Our treatment program for adults is quite intensive. We've
found it to be very effective and it's been widely validated. It's a rigorous program,
and we've found that it's a good match for most of our adult patients. But children
show a very broad range of capacity to handle such a program because of their varying developmental stages. We see a range of children from ages seven to 17 and
sometimes even younger. A 17-year-old might count officially as a child, but s/he is
capable of pursuing a very different kind of therapy program than a seven-year-old.
We want our work with children to reflect their developmental capacities, so with
children it's important to start off assuming that you're going to have to be more flexible than you might be with an adult.

LS-S: *In the adult program you see the patient every day for three weeks. How does*
this translate to the children's treatment program?

MK: A young child wouldn't be a good match for a program that requires that s/he
come every day for several hours a day and carry out many hours of exercises on
his/her own afterward. Children don't have access to the same levels of concentration and discipline that adults have. Also, we try not to disrupt their school activities
when possible. Taking a child out of school for a month brings problems of its own
which then have to be dealt with. However, we are trying to standardize our children's treatment program to make it more accessible for controlled studies.
Currently, we usually see children once a week for 15 weeks and give them exercises to do at home. Using the operationalized understanding of the child's obsessions
and compulsions and the hierarchy of fears obtained during the evaluation phase, we
plan what we would like to accomplish in each session. These goals are tailored to
what the child can do or tolerate.

LS-S: *In what way might therapists adjust their therapy to meet the developmental age*
of the child?

MK: Let's take a child who is 13 years old and one who is seven or eight. We ask
the 13-year-old to do more on his/her own. Involving his/her parents directly in the
treatment tends to be ineffective as this age group is interested in being more independent. In contrast, when possible we train the parents of the seven-year-olds to
help their children comply with therapy. However, even within these age ranges we
have observed marked differences between children which require adjustments in
therapy.

LS-S: *Please describe a typical treatment.*

MK: The case of a 10-year-old boy typifies the kinds of problems we see in children. The main focus of his obsessions and compulsions was to be perfect. He had to do everything "just so," very often in arbitrary ways which an objective observer would not recognize as superior in any way. In school he was learning how to write letters and would write the same letter over and over again because it didn't quite go to the bottom of the line. The characters he made were perfectly adequate, but they were just not quite perfect. This child erased and erased the letters and made all kinds of holes in his papers. He often was not able to complete his assignments.

LS-S: *What does this feel like for the child?*

MK: For children this is a very, very unhappy experience. Not only are they unable to meet their own standards, but their attempts to be perfect lead to failures in school. Teachers often do not understand the nature of the problem and may misinterpret, thinking that there is a specific academic problem or in some cases a behavior problem.

LS-S: *How did you work with this 10-year-old to stop his compulsion?*

MK: We met once a week, and we practiced doing things "not quite right." For example, we made letters that purposely went underneath the lines and we did homework together. I gave him assignments to do at home.

LS-S: *Did this make the child anxious?*

MK: This child was a bit anxious, but not terrified. Practicing "not doing things perfectly" with somebody and being given permission to make mistakes helped to decrease his anxiety. Creating an exercise where the instruction changed from "You have to do this right" to "You're not allowed to do any of this right" gave him a strong message that is was okay not to be perfect. He worked on this until it became more comfortable for him to just write the letters quickly and not attend to whether they were perfect.

LS-S: *Did you involve his parents in his practice assignments?*

MK: Yes. We let the parents know what tasks he had to do at home and helped them learn some ways of helping the child that would not lead to family conflicts. We also practiced the assignment with the child in the session.

LS-S: *Was this the only symptom the child had?*

MK: No. He also wouldn't touch certain books in the library because they were contaminated. We went and touched things in the library and the cafeteria and so forth. We practiced in the library and cafeteria at this hospital and then assigned homework to be done in his school.

LS-S: *How do you explain OCD and behavioral therapy to the child?*

MK: We try to conceptualize the problem in a way that children can understand. We may identify the OCD as something to work on but not something terrible about the child. We may refer to it simply as habits that can be changed or as a part of the child that's getting in his/her way. We often tell the child that now the OCD is bossing him/her but that in therapy s/he will learn how to boss it instead.

LS-S: *This is a difficult treatment. How do you establish a relationship with the child which will enable him/her to feel safe enough to experience a lot of anxiety and fear?*

MK: We use metaphors and analogies to help them approach therapy as something that is helpful. For example, one approach we often take is to say that the therapist is like a coach. Children are often involved in their school athletics or are aware of sports and can relate to the idea of having a coach. We explain that wanting to make the OCD go away is something like wanting to hit more home runs, get more goals or swim better.

A coach can help them do better than they could alone. The coach looks at what they do and tries to help them by giving suggestions, but they have to follow the suggestions if they're going to get better and they have to practice. Whatever the metaphor, you want the children to feel that you and they are on the same team. This ap-proach also helps to make the assignments feel different from the homework children get in school.

LS-S: *What do you tell them about the treatment?*

MK: We spend some time explaining the way therapy works and what they're going to have to do. We let them know that they are going to have to confront the things that bother them. When the OCD is bossing them around, they are going to have to boss the OCD back and refrain from the ritual.

LS-S: *What techniques do you use to help the child not respond to anxiety-provoking situations? Do you ever use reward systems?*

MK: We have a variety of techniques available and tailor their use to the child's preference. In terms of reward systems, we use them occasionally but not routinely. We have set up formal token systems for some children. For example, and this is an instance in which children of the same age require different approaches, we worked with a 10-year-old girl who really didn't want to have anything to do with therapy. Other children of this age are often eager to learn how to make the OCD stop. For this child we set up a reward system, and it worked very well. She went through the whole list of things she had to do to achieve her rewards and was very happy to attain them. From her point of view, reducing her fears was a secondary gain of the treatment.

We also try to teach kids some techniques that will help them when they have to resist the choice to engage in a ritual. One cognitive technique is simply to have the child tell the OCD, "Go away. I'm the boss here. Get out of here." We teach relaxation techniques, and some of the children take to them while others don't. We always work with the child to find out what is most helpful in carrying out the core of behavioral therapy for OCD, which is exposure and abstinence from rituals.

LS-S: *At what point should a therapist consider referring a child to a psychiatrist for medication?*

MK: We recommend considering that right at the beginning. We try to give our patients and their parents information about what the available treatments are and what the evidence is for their effectiveness. There's no way to predict exactly which treatment will be best for which child so we describe the advantages and disadvantages, the side effects, the cost and the time involved for the different therapies. Drugs have side effects, but they don't involve the kind of time commitment and emotional involvement that therapy does. People tend to stay on medication for a long period of time whereas behavior therapy is a more time limited treatment. We try to detail the pros and cons are and then help them decide.

LS-S: *In what situations should medication be strongly recommended?*

MK: Medication is a good choice if a child has had a good trial with behavior therapy without responding and it's not clear why s/he didn't respond. Medication may be a potentially attractive treatment if the person is too afraid to do behavioral therapy. If s/he says, "There's no way that I'm going to do this" but is willing to do the pharmacological therapy, then you have an attractive alternative.

Parents and clinicians are often conservative with respect to giving medications to children because children are developing and all the possible research you'd like to have about the possible effects on children's growth and development hasn't been done. They often will opt for behavior therapy as a first choice in order to minimize potential drug effects.

LS-S: *How much improvement can be expected in a child who receives treatment for OCD? Is there room for optimism?*

MK: Yes, definitely. The therapies are excellent, and they're much better than they were only a short time ago. But it's also clear that the therapies are not 100 percent effective with all children. Even when they are effective children may need to keep an eye on themselves. Complete elimination of symptoms is unusual even if they have a good treatment that's effective and makes a difference in their ability to function. We don't have a formal data set for children yet, but from our open studies, we see a lot of them getting better, and happily, some get remarkably better.

For more information about The Center for the Treatment and Study of Anxiety, write: 3200 Henry Avenue, Philadelphia, PA 19129, Attn: Dr. Edna B. Foa or call (215) 842-4010.

Guidelines for Living with OCD Children

By Barbara L. VanNoppen, MSW
Michele Tortora Pato, M.D.
Steven Rasmussen, M.D.

Editor's Note: *It is important for the therapist working with children who have OCD to not only involve the child's parents in the treatment when appropriate, but to be aware of the degree of stress the family is experiencing. The better able the family is to align with the child against the OCD, without giving in to the child's demands or becoming divided among themselves, the better the child's ability will be to recover.*

Livingston, VanNoppen, Rasmussen, Eisen et. al. (1991) reported that the interaction patterns of families of OCD children can be classified into three main groups: 1) accommodating with over-involved and permissive behaviors, 2) antagonistic with rigid, detached and hostile interactions, and 3) split with divided reactions in different family members.

Lenane (1989) suggests that it is very helpful to have at least one meeting with the entire family. The goals of this meeting are to: 1) involve the family in treatment, 2) identify all of the relevant OCD behaviors in the child with OCD, 3) gain a full understanding of each family member's style of interacting with the OCD symptoms, and 4) begin to reframe positively the problematic interactions the family brings to the session.

"Guidelines for Living with OCD" was developed by the authors with the help of family members and people with OCD to provide information on the best coping methods when a family member has OCD. It is reprinted here with the permission of Ms. VanNoppen.

Responses of families to the person with OCD vary. There are five typical responses: 1. Families who assist with the rituals to keep peace; 2. Families who do not participate in them but allow the compulsions; 3. Families who refuse to acknowledge or allow the compulsions in their presence; 4. Families who are split in their responses—some family members giving in all the time and some refusing to give in; 5. Families whose members swing from one extreme to the other, trying to find the "right" solution. In any case, extreme and/or inconsistent family responses create more feelings of frustration and helplessness as the OCD symptoms seem to increase.

The natural tendency to put the warning signs of OCD aside seems to prolong seeking professional help. As more is learned about OCD, one can be more optimistic about treatment and recovery. In an effort to help families, the following guidelines have been developed by family members and the people with OCD who have experienced firsthand the difficulty in coping.

1. Recognize Signals

The first family guideline stresses that family members recognize the "warning signals" of OCD. Sometimes OCDers are thinking things you don't know about as part of the OCD, so watch for behavioral changes. Do not dismiss significant changes as "just their personality." Remember that changes can be gradual but overall different from how the person generally has behaved in the past.

Behaviors can be easily mistaken for laziness or manipulation. It is essential that you learn to view these features as signals of OCD, not personality traits. This way, you can join the person with OCD to combat the symptoms, rather than become alienated from the OCD sufferer. OCDers usually report that the more they are criticized or blamed, the worse the symptoms get. (For signals, see Recognizing Children with OCD).

2. Modify Expectations

Consistently, people with OCD report that change of any kind (even positive change) is experienced as stressful. It is during those times that symptoms flare. Along with being able to identify OC symptoms, you can help to moderate stress by modifying your expectations during times of transition. Instead of projecting a frustrating "Snap out of it!" message, a statement such as: "No wonder your symptoms are worse, look at the changes you are going through" is validating, supportive and creates a positive alliance. Further, family conflict only fuels the fire and promotes symptom escalation. It helps to be flexible with an OCDer's behavior program during stressful times.

3. People Get Better at Different Rates

The severity of OC symptoms runs a continuum. Severity is usually rated by the degree of emotional distress and the degree of functional impairment. There is a wide variation in severity of symptoms between individuals. You should measure progress according to the person's own level of functioning not to that of others. You should encourage the sufferer to "push" himself as much as possible, to function at the highest level possible. Yet if the pressure to function "perfectly" is greater than a person's ability, it creates another stress which leads to more symptoms.

For example, you may have observed differences between those with OC symptoms and have said (or thought), "Well, if that person can uphold family responsibilities and work, why can't you?" This may be an unreasonable expectation given an individual's pattern or course of illness. Just as there is a wide variation between individuals regarding the severity of their OC symptoms, there is also wide variation in how rapidly individuals respond to treatment. Be patient. Slow, gradual improvement may be better in the end if relapses are to be prevented.

4. Avoid Day-to-Day Comparisons

Often sufferers feel like they are "back at the start" during symptomatic times. You may have made the mistake of comparing your family member's progress with how he functioned before developing OCD. Due to the "waxing and waning" course of OCD, it is important to look at overall changes since treatment began. Day-to-day comparisons are misleading because they don't accurately reflect improvement. Help the person to develop a realistic "internal yardstick" to measure progress.

On the days that the sufferer "slips," you can remind him that "tomorrow is another day to try," so that the increased rituals won't be interpreted as failure. Feeling as though one is a failure is self-destructive: it leads to feeling guilty, feeling "imperfect." These distortions create stress which can exacerbate symptoms and lead to feeling more "out of control." You can make a difference, if you remind the sufferer of how much progress he has made since the worst episode and since beginning treatment.

5. Recognize "Small" Improvements

OCDers often complain that family members don't understand what it takes to accomplish something such as cutting down a shower by five minutes or resisting asking for reassurance one more time. While this may seem insignificant to family members, it is a very big step for them. Acknowledgment of these seemingly "small" accomplishments is a powerful tool that encourages the person with OCD to keep trying. This lets the sufferer know that his hard work to get better is recognized by you. Verbal praise is a strong positive reinforcer. Use it!

6. Create a Supportive Environment

The more you can avoid personal criticism, the better. It is the OCD that gets on everyone's nerves. Try to learn as much about OCD as you can. Your family member still needs your encouragement and your acceptance of him as a person. Remember that acceptance and support does not mean ignoring the compulsive behavior. Do your best not to participate in the compulsions. Without hostility, explain that the compulsions are symptoms of OCD with which you won't help because you want the sufferer to resist. This projects more of a non-judgmental attitude that reflects acceptance of the person.

7. Keep Communication Clear and Simple

Avoid lengthy explanations. This is often easier said than done, because most people with OCD constantly ask those around them for reassurance: "Are you sure I locked the door?", "Can I be certain I cleaned well enough?" You have probably found that the more you try to prove that the sufferer need not worry, the more he disproves you. Even the most sophisticated explanations won't work. There is always that lingering "what if?"

8. Stick to a Behavioral Contract

In your efforts to help the sufferer reduce his compulsions, you may easily be perceived as being "mean or rejecting," although you are trying to be "supportive." It may seem obvious that family members and sufferers are working toward the common goal of symptom reduction, but the ways in which people do this varies. First, there must be an agreement between family members and sufferers that it is in the sufferer's best interest for family members not to participate in rituals (this includes responding to incessant requests of reassurance). It is ideal for both family members and sufferers to reach this agreement. Often attending a family educational support group for OCD or seeing a family therapist with expertise in OCD facilitates family communication. As a general rule, short, simple responses are best.

9. Set Limits but Be Sensitive to Mood

With the goal of working together to decrease compulsions, family members may find that they have to be firm about: 1) prior agreements regarding assisting with compulsions, 2) how much time is spent discussing OCD, 3) how much reassurance is given, or 4) how much the compulsions infringe upon others' lives. It is commonly reported by sufferers that mood dictates the degree to which the sufferer can divert obsessions and resist compulsions. Likewise, family members have commented that they can tell when the sufferer is "having a bad day." Those are the times when family may need to "back off" unless there is potential for a life-threatening or violent situation. On "good days," sufferers should be encouraged to resist compulsions as much as possible.

10. Keep Your Family Routine "Normal"

Often families ask how to "undo" all of the effects of months or years of going along with obsessive-compulsive symptoms. For example, to "keep the peace" a husband has allowed his wife's contamination fear to prohibit their five children from having any friends in the household. An initial attempt to avoid conflict by giving in just grows. Obsessions and compulsions must be contained. It is important that children have friends in their home or that family members use any sink, sit on any chair, etc. Through negotiations and limit setting, family life and "routines" can be preserved.

Remember, it is in the sufferer's best interest to tolerate the exposure to their fears and to be reminded of others' needs. As they begin to regain function, their wish to be able to do more increases.

11. Use Humor

The ability to distance oneself from irrational fears and to laugh is healthy, especially when done in company. Both family members and sufferers report this to be a relief. Again, sensitivity to the sufferer's mood should be considered before gently poking fun at the OCD. Although humor has been recognized for its healing properties for ages, it may not be best to joke when the OC symptoms are acute.

12. Support the Medication Regime

Always check with the physician about questions, side effects and changes that you notice. Don't undermine the medication instructions the physician and/or clinical professional have given.

All medications have side effects that range in severity. Some are very bothersome (dry mouth, constipation). Discuss these with the treating physician and evaluate the risks and benefits.

For people who cannot pay for medication, it can be obtained at a reduced fee through a special program for OCD medication. The treating psychiatrist can request a copy of the program guide by calling 1-800-PMA-INFO.

13. Separate Time is Important

Often, family members have the natural tendency to feel like they should protect the sufferer by being with him all the time. This can be destructive because family members need their private time, as do sufferers. Give the sufferer the message that he can care for himself.

14. Be Flexible

Above all, these are guidelines! Always consider the severity of the OC symptoms and the sufferer's mood as well as level of stress when making decisions about enforcing limits. Be reasonable, and try to convey caring in your actions.

About the Authors: *Barbara Livingston VanNoppen, MSW is a clinical social worker in the OCD Clinic at Butler Hospital, a private psychiatric facility in Providence, RI. She is a research associate in the Department of Psychiatry and Human Behavior, Division of Biology and Medicine at Brown University. Michele Tortora Pato, MD is a psychiatrist specializing in the treatment of OCD. She is an assistant professor at Brown University's Department of Psychiatry and Behavioral Medicine. Steven Rasmussen, MD is a psychiatrist and the Director of the OCD Clinic at Butler Hospital in Providence, RI.*

Sources: Basel Pharmaceuticals, (1991) *"Family-based Treatment for OCD in Children and Adolescents,"* Summit, New Jersey. Lenane, M. (1991) Family therapy for children with obsessive compulsive disorder. In: Pato, Zohar, (Eds.) *Current Treatments of Obsessive-Compulsive Disorder.* American Psychiatric Press, Washington, DC, pp.103-113. Livingston, VanNoppen, Rasmussen, Eisen et. al. (1991) A multiform group approach as an adjunct to treatment of obsessive compulsive disorder. In: Pato, Zohar, (Eds.) *Current Treatments of Obsessive-Compulsive Disorder.* American Psychiatric Press, Washington, DC, pp.115-134. VanNoppen, B. L., Pato, T. M., Rasmussen, S. (1993). *"Learning to Live with OCD, 2nd Edition."* OC Foundation, P.O. Box 70, Milford, CT, pp.9-14.

Recommended Reading

Books

Husain, S. A. and Kashani, J. H. (1992). *Anxiety Disorders in Children and Adolescents.* American Psychiatric Press, Washington, DC. Provides good summaries of childhood anxiety disorders and their treatment, including OCD.

Jenike, M., Baer, L. and Minichiello, W. *Obsessive Compulsive Disorders: Theory and Management.* 2nd Edition Year Book, Medical Publishers, Inc. To order call: 1-800-325-4177. Provides a comprehensive discussion of OCD and its treatment.

Nezirogulu, F. and Yaryura-Tobias, J. (1991) *Over and Over Again.* Lexington Books. Written for the person with OCD, answers questions and provides support.

Pato, M. and Zohar, J. (Eds.) (1991) *Current Treatments of Obsessive Compulsive Disorder.* American Psychiatric Press. Washington, DC.
Explains current treatment approaches for treatment of OCD in adults and children. Covers behavioral therapy, family therapy, and medication.

Rapoport, J. L. (1989). *The Boy Who Couldn't Stop Washing: The Experience and Treatment of Obsessive-Compulsive Disorder.* Penguin Books, NY. See Book Review.

Rapoport, J. L. (Ed.) (1989) *Obsessive-Compulsive Disorders in Children and Adolescents.* American Psychiatric Press, Washington, DC. An essential text for the clinician working with children with OCD. It provides well-researched reports on every aspect of OCD in childhood.

Zohar, J., Insel, T., Rasmussen, S. (Eds.)(1991). *The Psychobiology of Obsessive-Compulsive Disorder.* Springer Books, New York, NY. Presents current understanding of the biology of OCD.

Steketee, G. and White, K. (1990). *When Once is Not Enough.* New Harbinger Publications, Inc. Oakdale, CA. Provides information on strategies to stop compulsions, self-help, and integrating medication into behavioral treatment.

Pamphlets

Johnston, H. F. (1992) *"Obsessive Compulsive Disorder in Children and Adolescents: A Guide."* Child Psychopharmacology Information Center, University of Wisconsin, Department of Psychiatry. 600 Highland Avenue, Madison, WI 53792.

VanNoppen, B. L., Pato, M. T. and Rasmussen, S. (1993) *"Learning to Live with Obsessive Compulsive Disorder."* OC Foundation, P.O. Box 70, Milford, CT 06460.

"Family-Based Treatment for OCD in Children and Adolescents." Basel Pharmaceuticals. Summit, NJ 07901.

Involving the School in Childhood OCD

It is usually unnecessary to inform school personnel about a child's obsessive compulsive disorder because it often does not interfere with the child's school life. Many times children are able to avoid giving into their fears and doing rituals at school. The urge to do rituals builds up and they can wait until they get to the safer home environment to carry them out.

However, there are certain situations which merit the involvement of school personnel. The following list is not meant to be exhaustive but suggests the kinds of situations that are seen most frequently. Situations that merit informing the school or involving the child's teacher include:

1) The child is on medication and the school nurse and teacher need to be informed.
2) The child repeatedly asks permission to go to the bathroom (to perform cleaning rituals) and thus misses large periods of class time, and in having to leave the classroom disturbs the class.
3) The child asks inappropriate questions repeatedly, again disturbing the class.
4) The child's erasing and rewriting interferes with his/her ability to complete assignments either at school or at home.
5) The child is preoccupied with obsessions to the point that he or she cannot pay attention in class.
6) There is change in the child's behavior, such as being agitated or sedated, which might be a result of medication.
7) The child uses OCD symptoms as a means of getting out of normal expectations for school participation.
8) The child's symptoms lead to teasing and social isolation by classmates.

The best way to approach the child's teacher is for the parents to request a time to meet with and to come prepared to educate the teacher about OCD and how it is affecting their child. This might involve bringing a pamphlet that summarizes essential information about childhood OCD. Sharing the educational video, *"The Touching Tree,"* is an excellent way to raise awareness of OCD in the school setting (see Video Review).

When the child has rituals which are disrupting his/her ability to benefit from school and/or disrupting the class, the teacher may be able to work with the child's therapist to help reduce the disturbing behavior. For example, the teacher and student may collect information about how many times the student requests going to the bathroom. An agreement may be reached, with the help of the therapist, to reduce the number of times by a certain amount, with the goal of stopping the ritualizing completely. In other situations, the therapist may help the child outside of school and the child would practice new behaviors, such as not making letters perfectly on his/her own.

Another important role for the teacher is in modeling tolerance for the OCD child's behavior and stopping teasing and negative responses to the behavior from other children. In the past, ignorance of the disorder has led to some unfortunate and damaging interactions between children with OCD and their teachers. Education goes a long way to putting an end to this unnecessary problem.

Source: Johnston, H. (1992) *"Obsessive Compulsive Disorder in Children and Adolescents: A Guide."* Child Psychopharmacology Information Center, University of Wisconsin, Madison, WI.

Selected Assessment Tools for Childhood Onset OCD

Clinical assessment of children with OCD is done through a combination of clinical interviews with the child and a parent or parents, behavioral assessment inventories and rating scales, and behavioral measures. Structured clinical interviews are used in research settings to obtain complete and standardized information about the child's mental status. For the clinician, the goal is to obtain as thorough a knowledge of the child's obsessions and compulsions as possible so as to address all of the fears and rituals during treatment.

Behavioral Assessment Inventories and Rating Scales

Behavioral assessment inventories and rating scales ask the child to identify their repetitive thoughts and rituals and also evaluate the frequency of their appearance, the degree to which the child tries to resist them, and the degree to which the obsessions and compulsions interfere with the child's life. The scales are derived from adult OCD scales. Teacher rating scales can also be extremely useful in helping to gain a full and complete picture of the child's range of symptoms. Listed herein are some of the inventories and scales in use at present.

Leyton Obsessional Inventory-Child Version (LOI-CV)

(Berg, C. J., Rapoport, J. L., Flament, M. in the *Journal of the American Academy of Child Psychiatry,* 25:84-91, 1986) The LOI-CV is a 44- item questionnaire requiring a yes/no answer and was derived from the adult Leyton Obsessional Inventory. The items are divided into 12 categories including: thoughts, checking, school work, repetition, over-conscientiousness, etc. Each item is presented on a card which the child is asked to place in either the "yes" or "no" box. Items endorsed by the child are further rated according to frequency, resistance and interference. This test has been able to differentiate OCD patients from normal controls, has good test-retest validity, and is sensitive to improvements related to drug treatment.

20-Item Leyton Obsessional Inventory for Adolescents

(Berg, C. J., Whitaker, A., Davies, M. et. al. in Rapoport, J. ed. *Obsessive Compulsive Disorder in Children and Adolescents,* American Psychiatric Press, Washington, DC, 1989, pp. 43-44, 55-56) This inventory was developed from the 44-item inventory for use in an epidemiological study. It is given in a pencil and paper format and asks only about the degree of interference of the symptoms. This inventory is especially useful in identifying those at high risk for having OCD.

NIMH Teacher Rating of OCD

(Printed in: Rapoport, J. ed. *Obsessive Compulsive Disorder in Children and Adolescents,* American Psychiatric Press, Washington, DC, 1989, pp. 44 and 56) This is an eight-item Likert scale which allows teachers to rapidly note behavioral observations of the child/adolescent. The items include questions about excessive checking, repetition, meticulous work, and trouble completing school-work.

Children's Yale-Brown Obsessive Compulsive Scale (CY-BOCS)

(Goodman et. al. printed in: Rapoport, J. ed. *Obsessive Compulsive Disorder in Children and Adolescents*, American Psychiatric Press, Washington, DC, 1989, pp. 45-46 and 61-69) The CY-BOC was developed from the Yale-Brown Obsessive Compulsive Scale (Y-BOC). It consists of 19 items which assess the main OCD symptoms as well as overall severity, improvement, insight, and reliability. The questions are worded for children.

Behavioral Measures
Subjective Units of Discomfort (SUDS)
(Published in Wolpe, J. Psychotherapy by Reciprocal Inhibition. Stanford University Press, Stanford, CA, 1958) After the initial evaluation is completed it is useful to use the SUDS to establish the child's degree of anxiety for each behavior which leads to rituals. A hierarchy of difficult behaviors is then established for use in behavioral treatment.

Sources: Rapoport, J. L., M.D. *Obsessive-Compulsive Disorder in Children and Adolescents,* American Psychiatric Press (1989) pp.41-70. Wolff, R. P., and Wolff, L. S., (1991) Assessment and treatment of obsessive-compulsive disorder in children. *Behavior Modification.* 15(3): 372-393.

Childhood OCD Research Findings

• Ten to 30 percent of patients with ADHD may be etiologically related to the same gene that is believed to be linked to Tourette's syndrome, which is believed to be genetically linked to some forms of OCD. (Comings and Comings,1987b)

• Onset of OCD in males peaks around puberty and in females between the ages of 20 to 24. Thus in the child population the ratio of boys to girls with OCD is 2:1, reflecting the different times of onset, but not the overall prevalence of OCD in men and women, which is about the same. (Rasmussen and Eisen,1990)

• One third to one half of adults with OCD report onset in childhood or adolescence. (Elkins,1980)

• In a study of 100 families of OCD children, 20 percent of the fathers had OCD themselves. Fifty percent of the parents had a psychiatric diagnosis with affective disorders, OCD, alcoholism, and generalized anxiety disorders being the most frequent. Twenty percent of the siblings had a psychiatric diagnosis. (Lenane,1989)

• There is increased incidence of OCD in the families of children with early-onset OCD vs. the families of children with late-childhood and adolescent-onset. (Lenane, Swedo, and Leonard,1988)

• Adult female OCD patients retrospectively report a high incidence of anorexia nervosa and adolescents with anorexia nervosa often have obsessional features. (Wolff and Wolff,1988)

• In a study of the first 69 OCD children seen at the National Institute of Mental Health, depression was secondary to the development of OCD (approximately one half of sample), and anxiety disorders (one third of sample) were the most frequently-occurring associated psychiatric disorders. In this study, ten percent of the sample had Attention Deficit Disorder, and ten percent had Oppositional Disorder. Motor tics were found in about 20 percent of the patients, and occurred more often in acute cases among males and younger patients. (Swedo and Rapoport,1989)

• Treatment of children and adolescents with OCD is more likely to be successful when the therapist involves the family in treatment. Family stress and over-involvement with the child's rituals can be detrimental to treatment. (Lenane,1991)

• Multifamily support groups appear to help families cope better with having a family member with OCD. Common themes in OCD family support groups include: the stigma of mental illness, impact of OCD on other family members, medication, and treatment options. The group process helps to bolster parents' confidence in their ability to make decisions, decrease guilt, reduce isolation of the families, and to provide support and comfort to families. (Fine,1973; Lenane,1989; Livingston, VanNoppen, and Rasmussen,1991)

• Clomipramine has been shown to be effective in creating a 25 to 45 percent decrease in symptomatology in groups of children and adolescents with OCD. (Apter et. al.,1984; Flament et. al.,1985a, 1985b)

• Fluoxetine (Prozac) has been found to be as effective as clomipramine (Anafranil) in treating children and adolescents. Fluoxetine may be better tolerated by some children and adolescents, and may be associated with less relapse when it is discontinued. (Piacentini, Jaffer, et. al.,1992)

• Long term clomipramine treatment may be necessary for children and adolescents with severe primary obsessive-compulsive disorder. However
even long term treatment will not ensure freedom from OCD symptoms whose severity varied in time. Behavior therapy may help patients to
remain off medication (this needs further study). (Leonard, Swedo, Lenane, et. al.,1991).

• OCD patients who are severely depressed, who are on drugs which depress the central nervous system, and who practice covert mental rituals to decrease their discomfort during treatment are the most likely to respond poorly to behavioral therapy. Research is underway to develop more ways to minimize the discomfort of behavioral treatment sessions. (Griest,1992; Jensen, Hutchings and Poulsen,1989)

• Studies show that for most adult OCD patients a combination of treatment with a serotonin reuptake inhibitor and behavior therapy is the treatment of choice. (Greist,1992)

• Neurological imaging studies of adults with OCD have suggested that dysfunction in the basal ganglia and the frontal cortex is associated with OCD. Both increases and decreases in the level of glucose metabolism in these areas relative to normal controls have been shown in patients with OCD. Treatment of OCD has been shown to shift the rate glucose metabolism in the basal ganglia and frontal cortex toward the norm. (Garber, Anath, and Chiu,1989; Luxemberg, Swedo, and Flament, 1988; Benkelfat, Nordahl, and Semple,1990)

• In a study of neuropsychological function in 42 OCD adolescents with 35 matched normal controls the adolescents with OCD scored well within the average range of intellectual ability, but as a group were significantly below the group means I.Q. of the controls. Spatial perceptual dysfunction was the most notable neuropsychological deficit, and there was a tendency toward frontal lobe dysfunction. No correlation between severity of symptoms at the time of testing and level of deficit in neuropsychological functioning was found. At follow-up two to seven years later the OCD adolescents were found to have improved relative to their own performance but to still demonstrate significant impairment relative to the control subjects, suggesting that the initial findings do not reflect a developmental delay in this group. (Cox, Fedio, and Rapoport,1989).

• Many children and adults with OCD have religious preoccupations which would meet the religious phenomena of scrupulosity. Scrupulosity was defined by Saint Alphonus Liguori in 1773 as "a groundless fear of sinning that arises from erroneous ideas." Talmudic legislation has provisions for releasing people from vows, and one of the major Jewish Holy Days, Yom Kippur, is devoted in part to atoning for and being released from vows which could not be upheld during the year. There is a strong similarity between the modern approach to the treatment of OCD and early Judeo-Christian prescriptions for scrupulosity. (Suess, Halpren,1989; Rapoport,1989).

Sources: Apter, A., Bernhout, E. and Tyano, S. (1984) Severe obsessive compulsive disorder in adolescence. *Journal of Adolescence*. 7, pp.349-358.

Benkelfat, C., Nordhal, T. E,., and Semple, W. E. et. al. (1990) Local cerebral glucose metabolic rates in obsessive-compulsive disorder: Patients treated with clomipramine. *Archives of General Psychiatry*. 47, pp. 840-848.

Comings, D. E. and Comings, B. G. (1987b) A controlled study of Tourette's Syndrome. I. Attention deficit disorder, learning disorders and school problems. *American Journal of Human Genetics*. 41. pp.701-741

Cox, C. S., Fedio, P., and Rappaport, J. L. (1989) Neuropsychological testing of obsessive-compulsive adolescents. *Obsessive-Compulsive Disorder in Children and Adolescents*. Ed. Rappaport, J. L. American Psychiatric Press, Washington, DC. pp. 73-85.

Fine, S. (1973) Family therapy and a behavioral approach to childhood obsessive-compulsive disorder. *Archives of General Psychiatry*. 28(5), pp.695-697.

Flament, M., Rappaport, J. L., et. al. (1985a) Clomipramine treatment of childhood obsessive-compulsive disorder. *Archives of General Psychiatry*. 42, pp.977-983.

Garber, H. J., Anath, J. V., Chiu, L. C. et. al. (1989) Nuclear magnetic resonance study of obsessive-compulsive disorder. *American Journal of Psychiatry*. 146, pp. 1001-1005.

Griest, J. H. (1992) An integrated approach to treatment of obsessive compulsive disorder. *Journal of Clinical Psychiatry*. 53(4), Supplement. pp. 38-41.

Jensen, H. H., Hutchings, B., Poulsen, J. C. (1989) Conditioned emotional responding under diazepam: a psychophysiological study of state-dependent learning. *Psychopharmacology*. 98, pp.392-397.

Lenane, M. (1989). Families and obsessive compulsive disorder. in *Obsessive-Compulsive Disorder in Children and Adolescents*. Ed. Rappaport, J. L. American Psychiatric Press, Washington, DC. pp. 237-249.

Lenane, M. (1991) Family therapy for children with obsessive-compulsive behavior. in Pato, M. T. and Zohar, J. Eds. *Current Treatments of Obsessive-Compulsive Disorder*. American Psychiatric Press, Washington, DC. pp. 103-113.

Lenane, M., Swedo, S. and Leonard, H., et. al. (1988) "Obsessive compulsive disorder in first degree relatives of obsessive compulsive disorder children." Paper presented to the American Psychiatric Association, Montreal, May 7-12.

Leonard, H. L., Swedo, S. E., and Lenane, M. et .al. (1991) A double-blind desipramine substitution during long-term clomipramine treatment in children and adolescents with obsessive-compulsive disorder. *Archives of General Psychiatry*. 48, pp.922-927.

Livingston, VanNoppen, B., et. al. (1991) A multifamily group approach as an adjunct to treatment of obsessive-compulsive disorder. In: Pato, M. T., Zohar, J. Eds. *Current Treatments of Obsessive-Compulsive Disorder*. American Psychiatric Press, Washington, DC., pp.115-134.

Luxemberg, J. S., Swedo, S. E., Flament, M. F. et. al. (1988) Neuroanatomic abnormalities in obsessive-compulsive disorder detected with quantitative x-ray computed tomography. *American Journal of Psychiatry*. 145, pp.1089-1094.

Piacentini, J., Jaffer, M. et. al. (1992). Psychopharmacologic treatment of child and adolescent obsessive compulsive disorder. *Pediatric Psychopharmacology*, Psychiatric Clinics of North America. 15(1). pp.87-107.

Rapoport, J. L. (1989) *The Boy Who Couldn't Stop Washing: The Experience and Treatment of Obsessive-Compulsive Disorder*. American Psychiatric Press, Washington DC. pp.259-269.

Rasmussen, S. A. and Eisen, J. L. (1990) Epidemiology of obsessive compulsive disorder. *Journal of Clinical Psychiatry*. 51:2, supplement, pp. 10-13.

Rasmussen, S. A. and Tsuang, M. T. (1986) Clinical characteristics and family history in DSM-III obsessive compulsive disorder. *American Journal of Psychiatry*. 143, pp.317-382.

Suess, L., and Halpren, M. (1989) Obsessive-compulsive disorder: the religious perspective. in *Obsessive-Compulsive Disorder in Children and Adolescents*. Ed. Rapoport, J.L. American Psychiatric Press, Washington, D.C., pp. 311-325.

Swedo, S. E. and Rapoport, J. L. (1989) Phenomenology and differential diagnosis of obsessive-compulsive disorder in children and adolescents. in *Obsessive-Compulsive Disorder in Children and Adolescents*. American Psychiatric Press, Washington,DC., pp.13-32.

Wolff, R. and Rapoport, J. L. (1988). Behavioral treatment of childhood obsessive-compulsive disorder. *Behavior Modification*. 12(2), pp.252-266.

Recent Journal Articles on Childhood OCD

Treatment and Reviews

Apter, A., Bernhout, E., and Tyano, S. (1984) Severe obsessive compulsive disorder in adolescence: a report of eight cases. Provides case studies. *Journal of Adolescence.* 7:349-358.

Capstick, N. and Seldrup, U. (1977) Obsessional states: a study in the relationship between abnormalities occurring at birth and subsequent development of obsessional symptoms. Provides some evidence for link between perinatal events and later development of OCD. *Acta Psychiatrica Scandanavia.* 56:427-439.

Clarizio, H.F. (1991) Obsessive-compulsive disorder. The secretive syndrome. Provides a discussion of OCD in school children. *Psychology in the Schools.* 28(2):106-115.

Dalton, P. (1983) Family treatment of an obsessive-compulsive child: a case report. Presents case study of family treatment of a child with OCD. *Family Process.* 22:99-108.

Fine, S. MB, DPM, CRCP(C) (1973) Family therapy and a behavioral approach to childhood obsessive-compulsive neurosis. Describes two case histories in which childhood OCD was treated with a combination of behavioral and family therapy. *Archives of General Psychiatry.* 28(5): 695-697.

Foa, E. B., Grayson, J. B., and Steketee, G. S. et. al. (1983) Deliberate exposure and blocking of obsessive-compulsive rituals: immediate and long term effects. Important paper discussing the behavioral treatment of OCD. *Journal of Consulting and Clinical Psychology.* 51:287-297.

Francis, G. Childhood obsessive-compulsive disorder: extinction of compulsive reassurance-seeking. Describes extinction procedure in treating common OCD symptoms. *Journal of Anxiety Disorders.* 2(4):361-366.

King, N. J. and Tonge, B. J. (1991) Obsessive-compulsive disorder in children and adolescents: clinical syndrome and treatment. Provides a description of OCD in children and its treatment. *Scandinavian Journal of Behaviour Therapy.* 20(3-4):91-99.

Ishisaka, Y. and Segawa, Y. (1989) The clinical picture and prognosis of obsessive-compulsive neurosis in childhood. Discusses the clinical presentation and prognosis of childhood OCD. *Japanese Journal of Child and Adolescent Psychiatry.* 30(5):367-368.

Swedo, Susan E., Leonard, Henrietta L., M.D., Rappaport, Judith L., M.D. (1992) Childhood-onset obsessive compulsive disorder. Review of OCD in children including treatment and outcome. *Psychiatric Clinics of North America.* 15(4):767-775.

Wolff, Richard P., Wolff, Lisa S. (1991) Assessment and treatment of obsessive-compulsive disorder in children. Review of methods of treatment and assessment of OCD, concluding that multiple measures for assessment are the most effective and that better-designed treatment studies are needed to provide scientific evidence for the best treatment method for children with OCD. *Behavior Modification.* 15(3):372-393.

Medication

Bussing, Regina, M.D., Levin, Gary M., Pharm.D. (1993) Methamphetamine and fluoxetine treatment of a child with attention-deficit hyperactivity disorder and obsessive-compulsive disorder. Presents case study of 11-year-old child with OCD, major depression, and Attention-Deficit Disorder who was successfully and safely treated with a combination of methamphetamine and fluoxetine. *Journal of Child and Adolescent Psycho-pharmacology.* 3(1):53-58.

DeVeaugh-Geiss, M.D, Moroz, Georges, M.D., Biederman, Joseph, M.D. et. al. (1992) Clomipramine hydrochloride in childhood and adolescent obsessive-compulsive disorder. A multicenter trial. Special section: New developments in pediatric psychopharmacology. Presents a study indicating that treatment of child and adolescent OCD patients with clomipramine (CMI) is effective with results similar to those seen in adults. The study also suggests that CMI has a specific anti-OCD function independent of its antidepressant properties. *Journal of the American Academy of Child and Adolescent Psychiatry.* 31(1):45-49.

Leonard, Henrietta L., M.D., Swedo, Susan E., M.D., Lenane, Marge C., MSW et. al. (1991) A double-blind desipramine substitution during long-term clomipramine treatment in children and adolescents with obsessive-compulsive disorder. Presents study indicating that long term clomipramine therapy is necessary for children and adolescents with severe OCD, but that they may still suffer with symptoms of varying intensity over time. *Archives of General Psychiatry.* 48:922-927.

March, J.S., M.D., Johnston, H., M.D., Jefferson, J.W., M.D. et. al. (1990) Does subtle neurological impairment predict treatment resistance to clomipramine in children and adolescents? Presents study which indicates that subtle neurological impairments may be useful in determining which children and adolescents will respond well to clomipramine treatment. *Journal of Child and Adolescent Psychopharmacology.* 1(2):133-140.

Piacentini, J., PhD., Jaffer, M., RN et. al.(1992) Psychopharmacologic treatment of child and adolescent obsessive compulsive disorder. Provides good overview of childhood OCD and discusses efficacy of different drug treatments based on a meta-analysis of several previous studies. *Pediatric Psychopharmacology.* 15(1):87-107.

Riddle, M.A., M.D., Scahill, L., M.S.N. et.al. (1992) Double-blind crossover trial of fluoxetine and placebo in children and adolescents with obsessive-compulsive disorder. Reports a study indicating that fluoxetine (Prozac) can provide a safe and effective treatment in children. *Journal of the American Academy of Child and Adolescent Psychiatry.* 31:(6),1062-1069.

OCD Organizations and Programs

The following organizations and programs devote their efforts to the study and treatment of OCD, improving the welfare of OCD children and their families, and more. This list is not exhaustive and is not intended as an endorsement of any particular program.

Anxiety Disorders Association of America
6000 Executive Blvd.
Suite 200
Rockville, MD 20852
(301) 231-9350; (900) 737-3400 for information on professional treatment, local self-help groups, publications, and membership ($2/minute).

The Anxiety Disorders Center
Department of Psychiatry
University of Wisconsin
Center for Health Sciences
600 Highland Ave.
Madison, WI 53792
(608) 263-6056
Purpose: Nonprofit organization which provides evaluation and treatment of anxiety disorders, training and education for clinicians, and conducts research on the treatment of anxiety disorders.

Center for the Treatment and Study of Anxiety
EPPI Conference Center
Medical College of Pennsylvania
3200 Henry Ave.
Philadelphia, PA 19129
(215) 842-4010
Purpose: Treatment and research of anxiety disorders including childhood OCD.

Childrens Outpatient Psychiatry
Children's Hospital
135 West Mission Ave.
Suite 107
Escondido, CA 92025
(619) 741-8558
Purpose: Group and individual treatment of OCD in children.

Obsessive Compulsive Information Center
Dean Foundation for Health, Research, and Education
Department of Psychiatry
University of Wisconsin
Center for Health Sciences
600 Highland Ave.
Madison, WI 53792
(608) 263-6171
Purpose: To provide information and aid in research on OCD related illness, and their treatments. Staffed by medical librarians.
Publications: *Obsessive Compulsive Disorder: A Guide* by J. H. Greist, M.D., 1992.

Obsessive Compulsive Disorder in Children and Adolescents: A Guide
by H. F. Johnston, M.D., 1992.
The OC Foundation, Inc.
P.O. Box 70
Milford, CT 06460
(203) 878-5669
Info Line: (203) 874-3843; Purpose: The OC Foundation is a volunteer nonprofit organization dedicated to improving the welfare of people with OCD through education, research, and services provided to sufferers, their families, and concerned professionals.
Membership Fee: Basic membership fee is $25/yr. Entitles members to discounts on literature.
Publications: *OCD Newsletter* (bimonthly); *Kidscope* (newsletter for children); *Learning to Live with Obsessive Compulsive Disorder* (2nd Edition) by B. VanNoppen, MSW, M. Tortora Pato, M.D., and S. Rasmussen, M.D.

OCD Clinic
Lucille Salter Packard Childrens Hospital
Stanford University
101 Quarry Rd.
Stanford, CA 94304
(415) 725-0956
Purpose: Treatment of OCD children to age 18.

- Video Review -
"The Touching Tree"

"1,2,3—I'm free!" opens and closes "The Touching Tree," a dramatic videotape featuring Terry, a young student with OCD, and his teacher as they discover the nature of Terry's illness, obtain treatment, and share in his improvement.

Created by the OC Foundation in 1993, this award-winning video helps educators to detect OCD in their students and to understand the nature of the illness and its treatment. The story is set in a school, and provides a compelling case that educators may play in making a significant contribution to the identification and treatment of OCD in their students.

Terry's OCD is first detected while he is playing hide-and-seek on the school playground. When he touches the tree which serves as home base he gets stuck in a counting ritual and cannot stop despite the concern and teasing of his friends, the encouragement of his teacher, and the storm which is threatening in the background.

His teacher observes other problems that Terry is having. Terry cannot play with clay and demonstrates a handwashing ritual, he draws a picture of himself in a box cut off from other children, he cannot complete school work, and he has trouble paying attention in class. His teacher consults the school counselor and eventually a psychologist, who identifies Terry's problem as OCD. He provides behavior therapy and Terry also is given medication.

The film highlights how some areas of behavior may be immune from the rituals, and it describes them as areas in which the child feels most at home, and in control. For Terry this proves to be acting. He gets the lead role in his school play but misses opening night because of a washing ritual.

The following year, after he has been in therapy, he again has the lead in the school play. He is on time, and shares the moments before the opening of the play with his teacher, thanks his teacher, and then takes a moment to run to the tree which he has been avoiding ever since he got stuck there at the beginning of the story. This time he is able to successfully touch the tree three times and leave it, saying "1,2,3—I'm free!"

This is a very touching and moving film which highlights the significant distress children with OCD experience while in school, the courage it takes to go through behavior therapy and the rewards of coming to understand and help a child who has OCD. Patricia Perkins, president of the OC Foundation sums it up when she says, "Since our beginning, one of the Foundation's top priorities has been to raise the awareness of and advocate that professionals check for the existence of childhood OCD. It is a hidden epidemic—one in every 200 children has OCD—and it is being under-diagnosed. This video is an invaluable aid in educating children, parents, educators, and mental health professionals about OCD, its behavioral manifestations, and its effective treatment."

"The Touching Tree" is available from the OC Foundation and is priced at $49.95. For further information write: The OC Foundation, P.O. Box 70, Milford, CT 06460 or call (203) 877-5669.

- Book Review -
The Boy Who Couldn't Stop Washing

In her compelling book *The Boy Who Couldn't Stop Washing: The Experience and Treatment of Obsessive Compulsive Disorder,* Dr. Judith Rapoport tells the story of her experience in treating obsessive compulsive disorders in children, presenting detailed clinical descriptions of the disorder, and a state-of-the-art understanding of its many facets. Dr. Rapoport is Chief of Child Psychiatry at the National Institute of Mental Health, and has devoted most of her professional career to the study of obsessive compulsive disorder.

Once thought to be a rare disease and even rarer in children, OCD was discovered by Dr. Rapoport and her colleagues to have a higher than expected prevalence rate, but to be under-detected, as OCD sufferers tend to be able to hide their symptoms. In speaking with many patients she realized that she needed to rethink her conceptualization of the illness which was based on the state of psychiatric knowledge that existed when she began her work.

Through careful observation and her efforts to find appropriate treatment for her patients, she pioneered the way to a more scientific understanding of the nature of the illness and the most successful treatments. Her dedication to working with people with this illness also led her to try to understand it in terms of normal psychological functioning and from ethological and religious perspectives, as well as to look into her own psyche. In *The Boy Who Couldn't Stop Washing* she shares this wealth of thought about OCD in a non-technical and highly-stimulating manner.

The book is divided into several sections. The first two include personal descriptions of the illness as written by parents of children with OCD who also suffer with the disease, and by the children themselves. These chapters draw the reader directly into the strange and painful world of the patients and into the mysterious world of OCD.

The third section is entitled "A Doctor's Perspective" and makes up the body of the book. In this section the reader is taken on "rounds" and is privileged to be the recipient of Dr. Rapoport's knowledge and her own musings on the meanings of the disease.

Not understanding their problem themselves and not wanting others to think them crazy, children are often ingenious at hiding their compulsions. Dr. Rapoport describes one patient who said, "I put myself into the retarded school." This young girl's counting rituals slowed her down so much that her teachers believed her to be mentally retarded.

A teenager reported a similar strategy of putting on a dumb act to cover her absences and lateness while she performed rituals. She said, "I'm always late for dates and running to the bathroom. My friends think I am such an 'airhead,' and I let them think that. But I'm very organized and serious. Nobody knows me at all. Nobody knows about my counting and checking." A law student is described who slept on park benches rather than return to his apartment where he would be caught up in endless, time-consuming cleaning rituals.

Dr. Rapoport also writes about the effects of OCD on family members, noting the tendency for one parent to become over-involved and the other to withdraw. "I saw how OCD can distort family life, splitting it into warring factions and eliminating ordinary routine. This is familiar now, but at that time, watching a family act out the rituals without understanding was weird. As Charles' mother told me, 'He had never been unreasonable before; he really was no different from most boys. So when he cared so much about something, even though I didn't understand it, I felt I had to go along. And he got so upset when I didn't.'"

Work with adult OCD sufferers led to the conclusion that behavioral treatments rather than verbally-based psychotherapies were more effective for relieving OCD sufferers. The development of the then-new drug Anafranil was also providing new hope for efficacious treatment of the illness. Dr. Rapoport pioneered the study of this drug and found herself at times in the position of helping patients obtain it despite its not having been approved by the FDA. She realistically describes its benefits and reports that it appears to help about two thirds of OCD patients.

Dr. Rapoport writes, "My thesis simply is...that there may be complex behavior patterns programmed into human brains of which modern man is ordinarily unaware. With our fur long gone, is washing a primitive ritual that still remains with us? Compulsions such as washing, arranging, and pulling hair may give us a window into this zoological heritage; in my patients a heritage deranged, gone berserk." On a more hopeful note she suggests that OCD may offer a glimpse into the "biology of knowing."

She ends her book with a section designed to help the reader identify OCD in him/herself or in a family member or close friend. Brief descriptions of treatment options and places to call for further information are presented.

The Boy Who Couldn't Stop Washing represents perhaps the most hopeful sign that OCD, an ancient, and often undetected disease of the brain and psyche may be brought into the light of human understanding so that the great suffering it brings may be identified and stopped at an early age.

The Boy Who Couldn't Stop Washing: The Experience and Treatment of Obsessive Compulsive Disorder. Judith L. Rapoport, M.D., Penguin Books, New York, NY 1991. 269 pp.

CHAPTER 3

Focus on Child Custody:
Who Will Parent the Children?

A small girl, Ramona, sits alone on her bed, which is in the front yard of her now board-ed-up house. Her sister appears behind her. Suddenly, their parents push their separate ways through the broken doors of the house each carrying a suitcase. The mother swings a spatula at the father's head. He ducks. A piece of the house crumbles. They approach Ramona and the father takes her blankets off the bed— after all they belong to him. Ramona grabs her stuffed animal and huddles down. The parents pace and fight, and then walk away, leaving the girls, the house, everything that Ramona knows, behind. Her sister looks up toward a stormy sky and vanishes.
(A scene from Beverly Cleary's "Ramona's Worst Day, Ramona's Perfect Day," Lorimar Home Video, 1988.)

As the story depicted in this children's video unfolds, Ramona wakes up from her nightmare and goes to sleep in her sister's bed. Her sister assures her that her parents won't get divorced. The next morning all is well between the couple who had a fight the evening before. The girls, however, are shaken. Ramona demands and receives an apology. Life returns to normal.

For many children, however, this nightmare becomes reality. The parents do fight, do take everything they can from the family, do leave the house, and in the most extreme instances, do leave the children, either physically or emotionally. This is not news. What is news is the increasing number of more and better studies of families and children experiencing divorce, and the presence of more and better alternatives for settling custody disputes, which provide children with access to both parents and ultimately the right to being parented by both parents.

In this chapter, we focus on child custody as a means of addressing our interest in promoting helpful solutions for children of divorce. The decisions about where and with whom the children will live have a significant impact on children's current and future lives. Divorce is a time of great fear and emotional upheaval for children, and it creates long-lasting effects, some of which may not surface until years after the actual divorce.

Now there is evidence that, when appropriate, children do best when they maintain contact with both parents. Mediation can be used to help reassure the children and re-orient the parents toward maintaining parenting functions despite their own emotional pain and turmoil. It also allows for the possibility of tailor-made parenting arrangements that can benefit the entire family. While more research needs to be done, it seems clear that mediation offers families the best opportunity to reduce to some degree the trauma of divorce.

In this chapter we speak with Dr. Judith Wallerstein about the findings of her ten-year follow-up study of children of divorce and her latest book, *Second Chances*. We also speak with Isolina Ricci, Ph.D., a pioneer of divorce mediation and shared parenting arrangements and the author of the now-classic, *Mom's House, Dad's House*. Dr. Ricci introduces new models of parenting styles which seek to clarify assumptions made about different custody arrangements, particularly joint custody.

While still few, there are several centers whose work focuses on divorced families.

Like Dr. Wallerstein's Center for the Family, these programs are often involved in providing both clinical services and conducting research. Dr. Marion Linblad Goldberg's Divorce and Remarriage Project at the Philadelphia Child Guidance Center (see Focus on Programs) takes the additional step of studying and helping remarried families.

Evaluating children and their parents is a complex clinical process whether it be for mediation or litigation. Herein we have reviewed some of the major areas of assessment for parents and children and reprinted an article by Richard A. Gardner, M.D. on the Parental Alienation Syndrome, a phenomenon he feels is becoming more common and requires special consideration in a child custody evaluation.

Anne Dematatis, M.S. provides guidelines for helping children through the process of custody determination. There are many potential ethical dilemmas involved in conducting of a child custody evaluation. We have summarized the Nebraska Psychological Association's Ethical Guidelines for mental health professionals engaged in custody evaluations. Mediation as a means of resolving child custody disputes is gaining favor throughout the country and is being mandated in some states. In the article "Mediation vs. Litigation in Child Custody" we look at what mediation is and how it differs from litigation in organizing the experience of divorce and resolving parenting issues.

We hope you will find encouragement and challenge as we discuss an issue relevant not only to mental health professionals, but to the welfare of society at large as well.

—The Editors

Evaluating Children in Custody Assessments:
A Brief Review

On the subject of evaluating children in child custody assessments, Dr. Richard A. Gardner (1989) writes, "Evaluating the child in a custody dispute presents examiners with one of their greatest challenges. The primary difficulty relates to children's credibility (or lack of it) and the criteria children may utilize to support their positions."

In order for evaluators to understand all of the dimensions of the child's experience in the family, observation of the child both alone and with the family is essential. A complete child evaluation for a custody assessment includes interviews with each child alone, together with the siblings and with the parents and children (Berry, 1989; Gardner, 1989; Hodges, 1991; Nebraska Psychological Association, 1986). Additional observations of the children at home and at school may be advisable.

According to the Group for the Advancement for Psychiatry report (1981) the following information needs to be gathered and assessed: mental status, developmental history, coping strengths and fantasies for and about the divorce, level of attachment to each parent, degree of psychological impairment and treatment needs if applicable and the ability to make use of other adults to replace a possible missing parent (in Hodges, 1991, pp. 134).

Dr. Gardner (1989) warns of the need to be aware of the presence of Parental Alienation Syndrome, which could lead to a child's expressing a strong desire to remain with one parent despite the fact that this may not be in the child's own best interests (see Dr. Gardner's discussion of Parental Alienation Syndrome in this chapter).

Keilin and Bloom (1986), in their survey of 82 mental health professionals, found that as for adults, the clinical interview was most frequently used to assess children. They found that the most commonly-used formal assessment techniques for evaluating children included the Thematic Apperception Test (TAT), the Rorschach Inkblot Test and the Wechsler Intelligence Scale for Children-Revised. In their study, 69 percent of the professionals used observations of the child interacting with various family members.

Other techniques have been developed but are not as well standardized as the measures listed above. Miller and Veltkamp (1986, in Hodges, 1991) reported using 11 fables, each with its own theme, along with doll play to elicit information about the child's experience. Examples of the themes include Anger, Worry, Incest, and Discipline. Schaefer (1965, in Hodges, 1991) developed the Children's Reports of Parental Behavior in order to assess family relations. This measure is reported to be useful and, unlike other measures, to be psychometrically sound (Hodges, 1991; Weithorn and Grisso, 1987).

Skafte (1985, in Hodges, 1991, pp. 135-136) provides developmental guidelines for the assessment of children. For children under the age of three she recommends observation alone. For children ages three to five, she creates a semi-structured play interview in which she creates several scenarios and involves the child in acting them out or talking about them. For example, one scenario is called "Mommy's house, Daddy's house" and involves playing with dolls or stuffed animals whose "parents" live in two separate places. Another game has the child choose which animal he/she would like to be, explain why, and then identify each family member as an animal and explain why. For children in the five- to eight- year range, she recommends asking them to make three wishes, and to name the best and worst aspects of living with each parent, and then initiates a game in which the child is given a moral dilemma and asked how to solve the problem and to whom to turn for help. Children five and older are often given incomplete sentence tests.

Dr. Gardner (1989) uses *The Talking, Feeling, and Doing Game* to elicit children's perspectives. Hodges (1991) recommends asking older children questions similar to those asked of the parents. There continues to be significant disagreement by professionals as to whether to ask the children directly about their preference for living with one or the other parent. Hodges (1991) recommends against direct questioning in this area. On the other hand, the Nebraska Psychological Association's (1986) guidelines for child custody evaluation insist that the child's preference be taken into account (included in this chapter).

Concerns include not wanting to put the child in a position of having to betray one parent, not knowing how the child has reached his/her decision, the inconsistency of children's decisions around this area, and the possibility that the child is not emotionally free to express or even recognize the choice that would be most beneficial to him/her (Gardner, 1989; Hodges, 1991; Repucci, 1984). Hodges (1991, p. 138) suggests the following questions to assess the child's preference:

1. **When you have a problem, to whom do you go?**
2. **When you are sick, whom do you ask for help?**
3. **When you wake up with a nightmare, whom do you ask for help? Why?**
4. **Which parent do you play games with? Which games?**
5. **Do you have any hobbies? Does either parent help you?**
6. **How is anger expressed in the house?**
7. **How are you punished? Who does the punishing? How do you feel about it? What are you punished for?**
8. **If you are happy (had fun at school, got a good grade), which parent do you tell?**
9. **What do you imagine it would be like if you spent weekdays with mother and weekends with father?**
10. **In which home would you like to spend school nights and why?**
11. **In which home would you like to spend weekends and why?**

Family interviews and parent-child interviews provide extremely valuable information about the child's relationships with his/her parents. The evaluator needs to make careful written observations about the types and quality of the interactions between children and parents. Some professionals recommend having the parents and children engage in a task such as building blocks or planning an event. Videotaping of the sessions provides the opportunity for a more careful study of the interactions. Dimensions of behavior of interest include separation anxiety, the ability of the parents to listen to the child, the parent's ability to nurture and support the child, the degree of comfort the child displays with each parent, discipline and the spontaneity of the child's behavior. (Chasin and Grunebaum, 1981; Gardner, 1989; Hodges, 1991; McDermott, Tseng, Char, and Fukunaga, 1978; Group for the Advancement of Psychiatry, 1981).

Sources: Chasin, R. and Grunebaum, H. (1981). A model for evaluation in child custody disputes. *American Journal of Family Therapy.* 9(1):43-49. Gardner, R. (1989) *Family Evaluation in Child Custody, Mediation, Arbitration, and Litigation.* Creative Therapeutics. Cresskill, NJ. pp. 253-305. Group for the Advancement of Psychiatry (1981). *Divorce, Child Custody and the Family.* Jossey-Bass, San Francisco, CA. Hodges, W. (1991). *Interventions for Children of Divorce: Custody Access, and Psychotherapy.* John Wiley and Sons, Inc. NY. pp. 134-140. McDermott, J., Tseng, W., Char, W., and Fukunaga, C. (1978). Child custody decision making. *Journal of the American Academy of Child Psychiatry.* 17:104-116. Nebraska Psychological

Association. (1986). Special focus: Child custody guidelines. NPA Forum. Summer: 10-14.
Repucci, N. (1984). The wisdom of Solomon: Issues in child custody determination. In Repucci,
N., Weithorn, E., et. al. (Eds.) *Children, Mental Health and the Law.* Sage, Beverly Hills, CA.
pp. 59-78.

ETHICAL GUIDELINES FOR CHILD CUSTODY EVALUATIONS

In 1986 the Nebraska Psychological Association adopted ethical guidelines for the
conduct of child custody evaluations. The main tenets of the guidelines as presented by Berry (1989) are presented here.

• **The child should be considered the major client.** This means that the evaluator should attempt to evaluate every family member involved, and may need to contact the spouse's attorney. If only one parent cooperates the incomplete nature of the
evaluation needs to be communicated. The child's wishes should be taken into consideration. The psychologist in the role of the expert must remain neutral regardless of who is paying for the evaluation. The evaluator must acknowledge the child's
continuing relationship with each parent regardless of custody decisions and take
this into account when making recommendations.

• **Mediation should be considered the preferred prior intervention.**

• **The mental health professional should function as a professional expert.**
The professional should attempt to assist the court in making a decision and should
not assume the role of advocate or sleuth. Descriptive and predictive statements
regarding the post-divorce living arrangements are the appropriate level of information the professional should share with the court. Attempts should be made to base
findings on empirical findings and data.

• **Dual relationships should be avoided.** For example, one of the parents' or children's therapists should not attempt to serve as an impartial expert.

• **Multiple avenues of data gathering are preferred.** Interviews and observations, and, when appropriate, formal testing of all relevant parties are necessary for
an adequate evaluation. Consultation with colleagues from allied professions may be
warranted in order to improve the quality of the evaluation (Berry, 1989; Duquette,
1978; Jackson et. al. 1980).

• **Many factors must be considered.** All possible custody arrangements need to
be considered, and a variety of factors concerning the parents and children need to
be evaluated, not merely mental status. The absence of empirical criteria to determine who is a good parent should be acknowledged.

• **Quality of service should not be dictated by fees.** The evaluator must provide
a full assessment regardless of the fees agreed upon with the client. The evaluator
cannot misrepresent the nature of the work with the client in order to collect from an
insurance company. Fee setting and collection should be established before beginning the evaluation.

Sources: Berry, K.K. (1989) The mental health specialist as a child advocate in court. in *The
Divorce and Divorce Therapy Handbook.* Ed. Textor, M. Jason-Aronson, Inc. Northville, NJ. pp.
143-145. Duquette, D. (1978) Child custody decision making: The lawyer-behavioral scientist

interface. *Journal of Clinical Child Psychology.* 7:192-195. Jackson, A., Warner, N., Hornbein, R. et. al. (1980). Beyond the best interests of the child revisited: An approach to custody evaluations. Journal of Divorce. 3:207-222. Nebraska Psychological Association. (1986). Special focus: Child custody guidelines. NPA Forum, Summer:10-14.

Assessing Parents in Custody Assignments:
A Brief Review

The assessment of parents and children for custody recommendations is a complex clinical process. Therapists evaluating the family for custody decisions must remain neutral and not position themselves as advocates for either of the parents. The parents must be informed that the information they share is not confidential and may be shared with the other parent.

Keilin and Bloom (1986) found, in a survey of 82 mental health practitioners predominantly composed of psychologists, that the most prevalent assessment technique used in evaluating parents and their children is the clinical interview. The same study found that the formal assessment tools most used for the evaluation of parents are the Minnesota Multiphasic Personality Inventory (MMPI), the Rorshach Inkblot Test, the Thematic Apperception Test (TAT), and the Wechsler Adult Intelligence Scale-Revised (WAIS-R). The clinician presenting test findings in a court of law needs to be careful not to attribute more meaning to the test results than they merit and to avoid answering questions from lawyers which cannot be answered from the test results (Hodges, 1991).

The clinical interview for custody decisions is a complex process which involves several meetings with the parents alone, the parents together, the children alone, and observation of the children in the home. Parents need to be evaluated along many dimensions in order to arrive at a reasonable conclusion as to their parenting ability.

Dr. Richard Gardner recommends presenting each parent with an extensive "Parent Questionnaire" which asks many detailed questions about their children's development and current life. The sections in the questionnaire include: Pregnancy, Delivery, Post-Delivery Period, Infancy-Toddler Period, Developmental Milestones, Coordination, School, Peer Relations, Home Behavior, Interests and Accomplishments, and Medical Histories of the children and each parent.

The parent who has scanty or vague knowledge of his/her child's development and current functioning is considered to be less involved with the child. In making this assessment, D'Andrea (1983) recommends asking the parents who has been responsible for the following aspects of the child's life: routine daily care and safety of the child, intellectual growth, discipline, recreational activities, emotional growth, religious and moral development, helping the child to feel part of a family, and making financial decisions.

In assessing each parent individually, it is important to gain a sense of his/her past history. Relevant in this part of the assessment are questions concerning the parent's relationships with his/her parents, whether s/he experienced his/her parent's divorce and if so the nature of that experience, the use of drugs, psychiatric history, games played in childhood, childhood experiences of babysitting, previous marriages, and plans for having children at the time of the marriage (Gardner [1989], The Group for the Advancement of Psychiatry [1981]).

In assessing the recent and current functioning of the parents, one of the most important issues is that of discipline. Dr. Gardner (1989) suggests posing questions about discipline in such a way that the parent feels free to describe his/her behavior honestly without fear of giving the "wrong" answer. He suggests as a way of introducing the subject asking, "Most parents have some problems in the upbringing of their children. What problems have you had with yours?"

In the same vein, in order to assess how appropriately the parent uses punishment he suggests the following opening question: "What things do you find you have to punish the children for?" He notes that it is important to get a sense of the frequency of both the behaviors the child is being punished for and the delivery of the punishment. To gain a sense of the parent's ability to understand and handle different situations calling for some parental intervention he developed the "Typical Child Behavior Problems" questionnaire. It consists of 16 situations and asks for the parent's first, second, and third response. A sample question reads: "You're busy cooking in the kitchen and you tell ____ to stay out for a while. Instead s/he climbs up on a table and knocks over a bowl, spilling all of the food on the floor. First: What would you do? Second: What if s/he came back into the kitchen and climbed on the table again? Third: What if s/he did it once again?" (Gardner, 1989)

Other important aspects of the parents' current relationships with their children include gaining a sense of the parents' hopes and aspirations for the children, what the parents enjoy about their children, what irritates them, how much they support their childrens' interests, whether they promote relationships with the grandparents and peers, and their understanding of each of their children's needs and how the divorce will affect these needs. It is important to find out what the parents feel are their strengths and weaknesses as parents, and also to ask if the strengths and weaknesses are problematic to the spouse (Chasin and Grunebaum [1981], Hodges [1991], Gardner [1989]).

Skafte ([1985], in Hodges [1991]) suggests asking the parents how often they would allow visitation of the noncustodial parent in order to assess their recognition that children benefit from continued relationships with each parent. Chasin and Grunebaum ([1981], in Hodges [1991]) suggest asking the parents questions about different custody arrangements, their preferences and how they might react to them.

Interviewing the parents together provides an opportunity to hear the other side of statements and accusations made during the initial interview. The joint interview can potentially help the evaluator to gain a better sense of the truth of some statements and often brings out statements by the parents which can be used in the report as a direct indication of their performance as parents (Gardner, 1989). The joint interviews can have a therapeutic purpose also, especially if significant acrimony has built up over the course of divorce litigation. Skafte ([1985], in Hodges [1991]) recommends the joint interview and points out that it gives the evaluator an opportunity to gain a better sense of how well a joint custody assignment would work.

Sources: Chasin, R. and Grunebaum, H. (1981) A model for evaluation in child custody disputes. *American Journal of Family Therapy.* 9(1):43-49. Gardner, R. A. (1989) *Family Evaluation in Child Custody, Mediation, Arbitration, and Litigation.* Creative Therapeutics, Cresskill, NJ. pp.148-216, pp. 635-650. Group for the Advancement of Psychiatry. (1981). *Divorce, Child Custody, and the Family.* Jossey-Bass, San Francisco, CA. Hodges, W. F. (1991) *Intervention for Children of Divorce: Custody, Access and Psychotherapy.* John Wiley and Sons, Inc., New York. pp. 125-134. Keilin, W. and Bloom, L. (1986). Child custody evaluation practices: A survey of experienced professionals. *Professional Psychology: Research and Practice.* 17:338-346. Skafte, D. (1985). *Child Custody Evaluations.* Sage Press, Beverly Hills, CA.

Preparing Children for Custody Evaluation

By Anne Dematatis, M.S.

When communication and mediation fail, families are often left in the painful position of using the judicial system to decide how to resolve custody disputes. A court-appointed or mutually-agreed-upon qualified mental health professional is given the responsibility to recommend which is the most capable and available parent. The judge relies heavily on this expert testimony, as the best interests of the child are paramount.

The process can be less anxiety-provoking when children are prepared. Here are some guidelines that a therapist or parent may find helpful to prepare a child for this process.

1) A child from a separated household usually knows the reason for the evaluation, but repeating the reason often allows him/her to be more comfortable. A child should be told that both parents want him/her to live with them, and the judge will decide where s/he will be best cared for. The difference between joint legal custody to decide about issues like education, religion, and activities vs. primary physical custody or residency should be explained. Sometimes, when distance and schools are not a problem, it is possible to have equal time with both parents. Parental availability and capability are primary concerns of the evaluator. It is important to reassure a child that both parents will continue to see him/her regardless of who has primary physical custody.

2) A child's understanding of "truth" will be determined, so it is wise to previously discuss honesty and openness. It is essential to tell the truth and be honest with the judge and mental health professional when they ask questions. Most children are coached to some degree by one or both parents. Rehearsal is usually apparent, and the issues will be probed and explored so different sides are brought out. The custom that a child be seen over a series of sessions, usually three, to observe and hear changes in responses assists the mental health professional in formulating an opinion.

3) Familiarizing a child with the courtroom and proceedings will also assist him/her in coping with the process. Judges sometimes ask children to join them in chambers to state their preference of whom they would like to live with. Showing the youngster a picture of a courtroom and explaining the office or chambers in the back will allow him/her to express opinions and feelings more freely in this new environment.

4) The child's development in social, emotional, intellectual and other developmental areas will be evaluated. Psychological testing may be administered if the mental health professional needs to clarify clinical impressions. School data will also be collected.

5) In a therapy session, guessing at some of the questions a child will be asked may allow him/her to think ahead. Since many children have conflicting loyalties and strong feelings about changes in the family, exploring their answers in the therapy setting may aid in clarifying and articulating their thoughts. Many children worry about taking sides, hurting one parent, or the effects of honestly expressing feelings. A therapist may assist in alleviating guilt and anxiety.

6) The older the child, the more will be given to his/her preference. The reasons for their decision also become more abstract with age. An older child may say, "My father treats me better," whereas the younger child may say, "My daddy gets me more things." It also may benefit a child to have him/her imagine how a parent will react to his/her preference. Exploring whether a child has already discussed the issues and how that parent reacted may be useful in enabling a child to be appropriately assertive. Role playing these discussions is one technique which may be useful.

In one case from my clinical experience, a boy initially preferred to live with his mother. His reasons were actually altruistic and not in his best interests. His mother was erratic, drug-addicted, neglectful and at times, abusive. At the age of 13, he wanted to live with her in order to protect his younger half-sister from abuse and neglect and to continue to enable his mother to receive the income from child support. This case illustrates how a therapist can be helpful in supporting a child to be constructively selfish. The custody evaluator must discriminate between healthy and unhealthy parent-child bonds.

7) Let children know that they will be interviewed with their siblings. They should be told to simply "be themselves." Their communication, affection and alliance to each other will be evaluated. It is not customary to separate siblings unless it can enhance growth, because usually children have enough to adjust to without adding changes in the sibling subsystem. A therapist may assist children in thinking about how they would feel if they lived in a different home than their siblings, if they would feel deserted, and to what extent t hey would feel loss.

Children are often very anxious about a custody evaluation. They can benefit from preparation as well as reassurance that they are not the decision-makers. Their parents' past behavior,and stability will be among the important criteria the judge will use to make a decision.

Sources: Gardner, R. A. (1991) *The Parents Book About Divorce* (revised edition), Bantam Books, New York. Peters, D. and Strom, R. L. (1992) *Divorce and Child Custody: Your Options and Legal Rights,* Makai Publishing Group, Phoenix. Saposnek, D. T. (1991) *Mediating Child Custody Disputes,* Jossey-Bass Publishers, San Francisco. Wallerstein, J. S. and Kelly, J. B. (1980) *Surviving the Breakup: How Children and Parents Cope with Divorce,* Basic Books, U.S.A.

Developmental Table of Children's Experience of Divorce

AGE	REACTIONS	COMMON PROBLEMS	PREVENTION	RECOMMENDED CUSTODY/VISITATION
0-2	Aware of loss of parent	Regression; developmental delays; withdrawal; heightened stranger anxiety	Maintain routines; support caregiver; supplement caregiver	Frequent, short visits with noncustodial parent
2-3	Fears abandonment; misses absent parent	Regression; developmental delays; withdrawal; heightened stranger anxiety; toileting and sleeping problems; sex role confusion	Simple explanation to child; maintain routines/discipline	Overnight visits with noncustodial parent
3-5	Fears abandonment; misses parent; feels unloved	Regression; developmental delays; withdrawal; heightened stranger anxiety; toileting/sleeping problems; sex role confusion; clinging, whining or "perfect" behavior; sadness	Simple explanation to child; maintain routines/discipline; assure that child did not cause divorce; separate bed from parents	Overnight or longer visits no more than ten days apart
6-8	Fears abandonment; misses parent; feels unloved; fears for future; feels guilty; feels betrayed	Anger, behavior/academic problems; withdrawal; depression; dependency	Simple explanation to child; maintain routines/discipline; assure that child did not cause divorce; separate bed from parents; help child to stay out of parents' conflicts; keep as consistent an environment as possible	Longer visits; contact during week; some flexibility around child's school/social activities; involvement of noncustodial parent in school activities
9-12	Fears abandonment; misses parent; feels unloved; fears for future; feels guilty; feels betrayed; may feel rejected; needs someone to blame for divorce	Worries about custody; hostile toward one or both parents; academic/behavior problems; may be parentified	Maintain adult supports for parents; maintain/improve parenting skills; help child process anger	May need to decrease frequency if had high frequency before; regular, flexible visits; involvement in school activities
12-18	Feels grief for loss of family life; fears about own future; feels responsible for family members; feels angry	Withdrawn from family or clinging; decreased self-esteem; academic/behavioral problems; concern about relationships with opposite sex; difficulty with career plans	Maintain discipline; keep low-profile of parental sexual activity; help child cope with ambivalent feelings; support career goals, higher education	Flexible visitation schedule; possible trial living with noncustodial parent
Young adults whose parents divorced earlier		Sleeper effect for girls—in general, difficulty in establishing relationships with opposite sex; confusion about career plans; difficulty with higher education	Therapy; re-involve parents	

Sources: Bray, James H. (1991) *Psychosocial factors affecting custodial and visitation arrangements. Behavioral Sciences and the Law,* 9: 419-437. Hodges, William F. (1991) *Interventions for Children of Divorce: Custody, Access, and Psychotherapy.* John Wiley and Sons, Inc. New York. Wallerstein, Judith and Blakeslee, Sandra (1990) *Second Chances: Men, Women, and Children a Decade after Divorce.* Ticknor and Fields, New York. Wallerstein, Judith and Kelly, Joan Berlin (1980) *Surviving the Breakup: How Parents and Children Cope with Divorce.* Basic Books, New York.

An Interview with...
Isolina Ricci, Ph.D.

Isolina Ricci, Ph.D. is a pioneer in developing educational parenting programs and family mediation. She has worked to improve the plight of divorcing families and especially children of divorce for over 20 years.

In 1984 she was named a Master for the inaugural American Association of Marriage and Family Therapists Master Series. She was the director of the New Family Center in California until 1986, when she became the first and current head of the California Statewide Office of Family Court Services, a part of the Judicial Council of California. In this capacity she is responsible for a five-point program for family courts which includes training for all mediators and non-judicial court staff and evaluates mandatory mediating programs. She recently has provided staff support to the California Commission on the Future of the Courts, and is on the Editorial Review Boards of The Family and Conciliation Courts Review *and* The Journal of Divorce.

In her discussion with Senior Editor Laura Slap-Shelton, Psy.D. she presents a model she has developed through her experience in working with families, called "The Dimensions of Parenting." This model provides guidelines for recognizing the different levels of parenting divorced families achieve. It was partly developed out of Dr. Ricci's concern about the misperceptions and misuses of joint custody, and helps to distinguish between the actual kinds of parenting which exist in joint custody arrangements.

As she describes, with the joint custody framework, some parenting styles are positive for the children and some quite negative. Her strong belief in the ability of couples to put aside their own relationship issues in order to carry on with the important work of raising their children continues to challenge families and the therapists and mediators who work with them to achieve the "best interests of the child."

Laura Slap-Shelton, Psy.D.: *Your book,* Mom's House, Dad's House, *continues to be used today even though it was written over ten years ago. How did you come to be interested in helping families to make shared custody arrangements work?*

Isolina Ricci, Ph.D.: I developed the framework for most of the conceptual and educational models in *Mom's House, Dad's House* between 1971 and 1976. I began as an educational researcher and then became a marriage and family therapist in 1971. My work then included developing parenting programs for family services, community agencies and the University of California Extension which were then used statewide.

My work as a mediator actually began as one of my client's ideas. She had taken my educational courses and had been divorced for several years. She came back to me when her husband was accusing her of being a "bad" parent and threatening to sue for sole custody of their children. She insisted that they could not resolve their differences without help, so I met with the whole family and they were able to develop a parenting agreement. That experience made me realize the potential of appropriate educational interventions coupled with counseling.

By 1974 I had developed a way of mediating custody disputes and began teaching parents, professionals, courts and agencies about mediation. I also continued to work as a couples, family and child therapist.

LS-S: It seems that your focus in mediation has been primarily in helping the parents continue to take care of the children.

IR: In my work with couples with custody disputes I thought of myself as "developing parenting agreements" rather than as a mediator. I found that if the parents had attended my educational workshops about parenting before getting counseling about the custody decision they were far better suited to negotiating with their attorney and their spouse. That led to developing the framework of the business-like relationship between parents which is an important part of *Mom's House, Dad's House.*

LS-S: *What did you want to help a family achieve through the process of custody mediation?*

IR: My goals were to first aid parents in developing a mutually-acceptable plan for reorganizing their roles as parents and fulfilling their responsibilities. Often, this included aiding either the individual or the family to attain a sound sense of personal judgment. People who are going through divorce often lose their ability to make sound judgments, so one of my goals was to help people collect good information so they could make reasonable decisions for themselves and their families. This is especially important for those who have never had to do this sort of planning before, as is the case for some women in traditional marriages. I wanted to help parents resume their day-to-day parenting functioning as soon as possible. Simple educational interventions reduced anxiety and increased self-confidence and self-esteem, while at the same time promoting better decision-making.

LS-S: *What goals for mediation are incorporated in your work for the State of California?*

IR: I currently work for the Judicial Branch of California where I direct a state-wide office of family mediation, family court services, and reconciliation courts. This program is responsible for training family mediators throughout the state and has certain goals set forth in the state statute. These goals include: first, the reduction of acrimony between the parents; second, the arrival at an agreement which serves the best interest of the children involved; and third, that if it is in the children's best interest to remain in close and continuing contact with both parents, that arrangements are made for this. The idea is that the child owns the right to a relationship with each parent.

LS-S: *How many family members should be involved in mediation?*

IR: In the private sector mediators can work with the extended family if it seems important. Every mediator has a style and a manner in which they prefer to work. My preference was to work educationally with the parents for some proportion of the time with the hope that this would lead to a reorganization of and the development of a plan for how they would continue to parent the children. I found that the reorganization process moved more smoothly when parents were able to set some goals with regard to how they would help their children retain a sense of basic trust.

LS-S: *Is it hard for the parents to put aside their involvement and anger with each other to understand that working out the parenting issues is one of the major pieces of work they need to accomplish?*

IR: I think that some parents put it very well when they say, "How can I think about my child when I can't even think?" When one or both of the parents is highly agitated or upset it helps to have them develop a temporary agreement with the understanding that this agreement is temporary and should not influence future legal decisions.

For example, having the parents agree to a common calendar for visitation and agree on how to discuss their separation with the children without bad-mouthing each other can be very helpful for children. I believe it is the psychotherapist's or mediator's obligation to caution the parents that even though their emotions and feelings may be deeply hurt during this time, involving the children is a no-win situation. Even when parents are unable to accomplish a business-like working relationship right away, knowing that this is something they should strive toward can be constructive. If a therapist or mediator does not make parents aware that involving the children in their personal conflicts can be damaging, their destructive behavior is given tacit approval.

LS-S: *As the person in the "expert" role, the parents must look to you for all sorts of help and approval.*

IR: In the crisis stage these parents often need "parents." I found that being supportive also meant modeling positive parenting roles for the parents. It's very difficult to be your own good parent when you feel betrayed, when someone says s/he is going to take your children away, etc. You just couldn't imagine a worse situation. Of all the times you need good judgment, this is it, and often you just don't have it.

LS-S: *How does one become a mediator? Is there a certification process?*

IR: There is no national certification for being a mediator. Interested parties should check with their states to see if there are certain training requirements. Currently there are two major national organizations, The Academy of Family Mediators and The Association of Family and Conciliation Courts. One offers certification in mediation.

In California, mediators who practice in the court system must have a master's degree and two years of experience. Most courts look for five years of experience and a license as a marriage-family counselor, psychologist or social worker. In some courts there is also a requirement that the mediator must have had some experience working in shelters for battered women, but there is no Board of Examiners and no official certificate. It's a topic of great interest at present.

LS-S: *How can one locate a good, well-trained mediator?*

IR: Contacting the Academy of Family Mediators is one way to find mediators who have received good training. It is also important to find out how many mediations the mediator has done over a period of time, and their supervised experience. There are some people who present themselves as mediators after only 40 hours of training.

LS-S: *An important part of your work and contribution to the field is your insistence on using positive language in discussing divorce related issues. I'm wondering how you came to this and why it works so well.*

IR: *Mom's House, Dad's House* is in its 20th printing partly because the section on language is so popular. Cleaning up the language used in divorce is a very simple, effective intervention that a clinician can easily help a parent to use.

I came upon the idea after reading an article by Margaret Mead in which she said something that struck me. I'm paraphrasing, but it was something like, "We have got to find other ways to describe a relationship that has produced four children in the past five years other than the vulgar 'my Ex-'." I thought about that and when I started working with parents, my ideas slowly developed until it all came together. I began to think, "How can he call this woman his Ex- when she is the mother of his children?"

I also found that a good deal of alienation came about as a result of terms like, "broken home," "failure of the marriage" and "intact" to describe non-divorced families. In the 1970s there was a significant stigma attached to divorce. Society tended to view divorced people as being socially irresponsible.

LS-S: *The two sets of language sound so different when you read them side by side. Using positive non-judgmental language must help to boost the morale of the family.*

IR: It makes a big difference for the children. I feel that there is still an accusatory tone that surrounds divorce. I believe that there is such a thing as a "good divorce." We say that a good marriage takes "work" and I believe that a good divorce takes work too. The work of divorce is, among other things, a reorganization of relationships and roles. Like marriage, divorce can have its own set of expectations for success and the rearing of children.

LS-S: *The tendency, certainly, is to think of divorce as the negative, the absence of marriage, rather than as an event in and of itself.*

IR: Divorce is now a part of the fabric of our lives. It's an inevitable social phenomenon. Part of the problem I see is people want the marriage to be over; they want the divorce to be over. They never want to see or hear from the other parent again, not recognizing the process. One of the tasks before them is developing a new type of working relationship centered around parenting their child.

Now that I've been around for a long time—(my children are raised and I'm a grandmother)— I'm even more convinced that we need to take a more deliberate look at what makes a successful divorce and successful parenting after divorce. From another perspective, we now have the economic necessity of having both parents work, so children in non-divorced families often do not have enough time with their parents as it is. When the parents separate the children stand to lose even more contact. The lack of time all parents and their children have together as a family is of profound concern to me.

LS-S: *Are you saying that you are concerned about the quality of parenting in general in this country?*

IR: Yes. I see parents who are making a concerted effort to be solid parents and to raise their children to be contributing members of the community, but then I also see parents who don't even consider that as part of the parents' role. They just go from one day to the next.

LS-S: *A kind of survival mentality?*

IR: Yes. In my work I've spoken with many people who are increasingly concerned over what they see as parenting deficits, parents who were not well-parented themselves.

LS-S: *How can this problem be addressed?*

IR: A major effort to educate parents is called for. Sometimes parents do not seek a parenting education class, but when a good opportunity comes along, they get a sense of, "I can do this! This is making my life as a parent more meaningful" or "This is making life better for my children." I am heartened by the fact that parents who are required by some courts to attend parenting education classes before they can move ahead with the divorce develop a real interest in improving their parenting. At first some may be resistant, but gradually most of them become quite involved.

LS-S: *In* Mom's House, Dad's House *you say that joint custody means maintaining each parent's individual parenting style, yet sharing the parenting. How do children adjust to switching between two households which may be very different from each other?*

IR: It may depend on the level of conflict between the parents. In my work at Stanford University I saw how children behaved differently in different settings. They acted one way with the father, one way with the mother, and another way at school. The sample was too small to generalize to a larger population, but what I saw suggested that the more conflict there was between the parents, the more the children differentiated their behavior. This led me to further develop my ideas and to create a new framework which I call "Dimensions of Parenting."

I also developed "Dimensions of Parenting" in response to seeing people interpret joint custody arrangements as a means of evading the child's need for a good parent-child relationship. I was very concerned about what I felt was an oversimplification of joint custody as a matter of equal time and authority, and about people who believed that joint custody automatically ensures cooperative parenting and good child adjustment.

One of the first messages I wanted to share is that joint custody isn't always equal time or equal responsibilities; that parents don't always cooperate, and that sharing isn't always good. Surprisingly, a lot of people needed to hear that. In my "Dimensions of Parenting" framework I identify five types of parenting relationships for use with parents, as well as for training mediators and clinicians. I believe that clinicians and mediators involved with families have an obligation to point out the problems that they observe in their client's parenting style. I believe this helps parents.

LS-S: *What are the five types of parenting you identify in your model?*

IR: The first is called "Substandard" and includes neglect and/or abuse. The second is "Exclusive," the third is "Parallel," the fourth is "Shared," and the fifth is "Cooperative."

LS-S: *What does the "Substandard" parenting style look like?*

IR: The Substandard style is where one or both parents has/have a serious deficit in parenting skills. The extreme case is where there is abuse or neglect. If the parenting is neglectful or incompetent, any type of relationship between the parents after separation is doomed without substantial intervention.

LS-S: *An "Exclusive" parenting style would be the arrangement of choice in this situation, assuming that one parent was competent.*

IR: Yes. The Exclusive parenting style is typified by the sole custody arrangement. That's when one parent, usually the mother, but not always, makes all the decisions and has all the responsibility and authority. The other parent can pay child support and have visitation rights. This doesn't have to be a poor parenting arrangement. The non-custodial parent can be involved in major decision-making, but may not have functional authority. If the parents are cooperative and the child has consistent access to the other parent, I believe this form of parenting can be very successful.

LS-S: *"Parallel" parenting brings with it images of parallel play when children play side by side with little meaningful sharing of experience.*

IR: Yes. These are the types of parents who will only contact each other in emergencies or in cases of illness. While both parents are actively involved in the children's life, they are unwilling or unable to discuss the children's needs. Children aren't free to talk about what happened to them in the other home, where they went, who they saw, etc. They even have to pretend they don't have another parent. They must choose their words carefully.

Sometimes if a child talks about something that happened in the other home the parent will say, "I don't want to hear it." It's so difficult for the parents to be in the same room together that they will often alternate attendance at school events or activities like soccer rather than risk a scene or bad feelings. The scripts are, "It's too painful or difficult to talk to him or her," "I don't like her," "I have nothing to say to him," or "Every time we talk we have an argument." At least one parent will say the other puts their child in the middle.

So the child may have two parents and two homes, but they're not secure in either. One child said to me in such a situation, "My safe home is the car." My view of this is that the parents didn't share the parenting. These are parents who just divided the time and went their own ways. They divided it and essentially divided the child. It's a form of neglect, and paradoxically creates a negative Exclusive parenting situation. When asked if changing things would help, children in these situations often reply, "No. Keep it the way it is. At least I have them both." They are afraid that if the division is unequal, the losing parent will disappear.

LS-S: *The children lack faith in their parent's ability to communicate on their behalf.*

IR: That's right. And they feel powerless in this situation. The absence of power in these children is of great concern. To me this is the worst kind of parenting style. It became more common after shared custody began to gain favor.

LS-S: *It is very different from the last two styles you mentioned, "Shared" and "Cooperative" parenting.*

IR: Yes. Both of these styles will benefit children. Shared parenting is a more business-like relationship, and I believe most parents can achieve this. Cooperative parenting occurs when there is an ease of give-and-take between the parents that allows for more fluid sharing of responsibilities without either parent keeping a big scoreboard. It builds on the business-like relationship of Shared parenting but goes one step further in ease of communication which benefits the children.

In both arrangements the parents work together and support each other. They respect the child's right to have a relationship with each of them, and they've developed a business-like relationship where they can attend conferences and school events together. The teachers and coaches are free to call either parent without risk of being caught in competitiveness or territorial disputes. The children can share their lives with both parents and there is open phone access. Both are the most desired forms of parenting after a divorce. It's also best for the parents and the community.

LS-S: *How does it benefit the community?*

IR: The community has to allow the separated or divorced family to move through their stages of hurt and recovery and to reorganize so that they can become contributing members of the community again. Unfortunately, some grandparents, aunts, uncles and new spouses do not understand shared or cooperative arrangements. They make statements like, "If you can get along now, you should never have divorced."

LS-S: *These arrangements leave a lot of room for jealousies to arise, and blame to be leveled at the divorced parents.*

IR: Yes. Many parents seem to interpret these statements as encouraging ongoing war with the former spouse in order to justify their decision to divorce. This is just as prevalent now as it was 20 years ago. We may have made rapid strides with regard to mediation and with the legal custody aspects of divorce, but we haven't done much in terms of creating an understanding of divorced families in society. We still target one or the other parent as the one to "blame."
    A general climate of support and understanding for divorced families is still lacking. The five Parenting Patterns can be used with parents to map out the territory and help them move toward the most optimal arrangement they can create for their children.

LS-S: *What are the most important issues children going through custody disputes need to address?*

IR: Children often need help in distancing themselves from the parents' divorce and not taking on responsibility for their parents' pain and the parents' decisions. They can often feel quite guilty for actions over which they had no control. One teenager said to me, "Can you do anything about parents who want us to be their parents?" Switching of roles or the use of children for emotional ballast by the parents is common and has a deleterious effect on children. The child's therapist or family therapist can promote the resumption of the parental protective role by the parent.

LS-S: *Would your preference be to work with children alone or with the parents?*

IR: That's such a hard question because families are so different. If a child comes into therapy because the school says the child is under great stress, and it's affecting his schoolwork or behavior, yet the family is unaware of any problems, I would want to work with the family system. Children have a lot of fantasies at the time of divorce and these fantasies can take on a life of their own if the children are not able to share their worries and confusion with someone.
    One common source of difficulty for the child is when one or both parents attempt to get the child on "their side." That's exceptionally hard for children. While they need to know the basic facts about the divorce, they need to have it explained in a way that is not full of blame for the other parent. When I worked with families in mediation I always saw the children at least once. I would show them the office,

where their parents sat, and explain what we were talking about. I also explained confidentiality issues to the children in a simple way that they could easily understand and to which they could easily relate.

LS-S: *How did you do that?*

IR: I explained that I didn't keep secrets between their parents and that the goal was to help them talk better with each other. I assured the children that if they said something to me about either of their parents I would not repeat it without their express permission. Those were the ground rules, and I found that the parents reported that their children were happier after they came in.

LS-S: *Why do you think this helped the children?*

IR: I believe that this sort of explanation and the presence of a neutral third party gives children the sense that someone else is looking out for the parents and that the children can turn over that role, at least temporarily or partially. I found that some of the children were willing to have me say something to the parents and some not. I should also add that I screened families carefully for child abuse before accepting them for mediation.

Once the parents put together the ground rules of custody and the child had a physical calendar to look at there was usually a lessening of anxiety. Children need to know what to expect. Some find it hard to accept even small changes, like eating a new kind of cereal, much less the trauma brought about by the myriad of lifestyle changes divorce creates. Even children with robust temperaments require reasonable structure and need to know what to expect.

LS-S: *You've dedicated your career to helping families maintain the integrity of their parenting functions after divorce. How do you feel about the success you have achieved and your current work for the state of California?*

IR: I am delighted that *Mom's House, Dad's House* continues to be used as a text by attorneys, counselors, therapists, mediators, and parents and law schools. It's more popular now than it was when it was first published. After you put in six years writing a book, it's nice to have it be useful.

The first 15 years of my work in this area were focused on the bell of the normal curve. The population that fell within the bell appeared to be the people who could be strengthened and centered with a minimal amount of intervention. Now I have a chance to work with people who are more problematic. My interest is in researching and working with others who work with this population—understanding what it takes to work in the short-term, providing crisis intervention when needed, and using mediation, counseling, investigation and evaluation techniques. It's been wonderful to have the opportunity to approach my work from so many different angles and to expand it to reach different groups of people.

Words That Hurt, Words That Heal

In *Mom's House, Dad's House* Isolina Ricci provides alternative language to the generally pejorative terms society has assigned to divorce and divorced families. Here are some of her suggestions:

Negative Language	Positive Language
Visiting	Living with
I have children but they live with my spouse	I have a family
The children's parent left us	I have a family
The children are visiting their other parent	The children are at their other home
Broken home	Family, the home
Failed marriage	The marriage ended
Wife, husband, ex-	The children's parent
Custody, visitation	Parenting agreement
Child support	Contribution
Sole custody	Shared responsibility
Parent without custody	Second-home parent

Source: Ricci, I. *Mom's House, Dad's House.* (1980). Collier Books, NY. pp. 52, 172.

- Focus on Programs -
The Divorce and Remarriage Project at
Philadelphia Child Guidance Center

The Philadelphia Child Guidance Center is a well-established treatment, training and research institution. A division of the Department of Psychiatry at the University of Pennsylvania, the Center takes a family systems approach to helping individuals and their families. We spoke with Dr. Marion Linblad Goldberg, the Director of the Family Therapy Center and the Counseling Family and Remarriage Center at the Philadelphia Child Guidance Center, about the Divorce and Remarriage Project at the Center. This project was formerly the Divorce Project and was founded in 1978 under the direction of Dr. Salvador Minuchin.

The book, *The Difficult Divorce: Therapy for Children and Families* by Marla Isaacs, is a product of the Project's study of many families going through divorce and the development of clinical techniques to facilitate the process. It included a number of variables in its study, such as the relationship with the extended family, the type of custodial arrangement and the type of extended support. One interesting finding noted by Dr. Goldberg was that when asked to draw their families, children in joint custody arrangements drew both parents, while children in sole custody families drew the custodial parent only.

Dr. Linblad Goldberg added remarriage to the Divorce Project to meet the needs of a growing population of divorced and remarried or cohabiting families that needed support and clinical services. As she remarks, "Therapists in the 1990s cannot afford to be unfamiliar with the problems of remarriage, the natural aftermath of the increase in the divorce rate seen in the 1970s."

Statistics show that at present, only 50 percent of remarriages are successful. Dr. Linblad Goldberg maintains that this may reflect a lack of knowledge about how to make marriages "work." The Project, in focusing on remarriage, attempts to remedy this situation. It provides clinical services, training for mental health professionals, an Annual Workshop for remarried families in different stages of remarriage and is contracted to Pennsylvania's Children's Services Division to work on the Mental Health Family-Based Initiative.

The Project conducts research into the different stages and styles of remarriage and has as a goal the development of a model which can be used to train mental health workers with all levels of experience in working with remarried families. One aspect of the research into remarriage is the goal of creating a decision-making framework for the bachelor and master's level mental health workers in the Mental Health Family-Based Initiative so that when they enter clients' homes, they will be able to generate a plan for addressing the family's needs quickly. This involves deciding which unit of the family to address first, choosing appropriate interventions and having criteria by which to evaluate the efficacy of their interventions and change them as necessary.

Because people often do not experience their difficulties as being related to issues of remarriage, the intake staff at the Philadelphia Child Guidance Center screens clients for their marriage status and refers remarried couples to Dr. Linblad Goldberg's project. The Annual Workshop is a preventative service for remarried couples and mental health professionals at all stages of remarriage.

"The public knows so little about remarriage that couples often feel isolated in their problems, with one spouse often feeling trapped in an impossible situation," Dr. Linblad Goldberg explains. "A typical situation involves a couple in which the wife has not been married before and the husband has several children with a joint custody arrangement. Typically, the wife in this situation will feel powerless over events in the family, may be having difficulty establishing predominantly positive relationships with the children, who are threatened by the situation, and may be questioning her decision to marry her husband. In general, stepparents are Avis trying to be Hertz."

In the Annual Workshop couples are often reassured just to learn that their experiences are absolutely expectable and a normal stage in the process of creating the new marriage. One intervention used in the Workshop is to have the stepmother and the father reverse roles so that the father becomes the one talking about his children and the stepmother can relax her efforts in this area of the marriage. Carrying this subtle role reversal into the actual marriage helps to reduce tension in the family. Dr. Linblad Goldberg believes that people learn new concepts best in context and she tries to limit the workshops to 20 couples so that each couple has the opportunity to voice its difficulties and practice solutions.

In a successful remarriage of 17 years herself, Dr. Linblad Goldberg encourages couples in the very early stages of remarriage to attend her workshop and similar workshops and to make use of the new knowledge and understanding about remarriage that were not available before.

For more information, write: The Divorce and Remarriage Project, Attn.: Dr. Marion Linblad Goldberg, Philadelphia Child Guidance Center, Two Children's Center, 34th Street and Civic Center Boulevard, Philadelphia, PA 19104 or call (215) 243-2600.

Mediation vs. Litigation in Child Custody

Mediation is increasingly becoming the method of choice for handling divorces, and especially for resolving child custody issues. In several states there is legislation or pending legislation that requires the mediation of child custody before litigation over property can begin. California has a state-supported system of mediation (see interview with Dr. Ricci). Litigation requires an adversarial approach to deciding with whom the children will live. This approach promotes the idea that one parent is "bad" and should not have the children (is the loser) and the other parent is "good" and should have the children (is the winner). The parents communicate through their attorneys and hostility increases, sometimes leading to endlessly protracted litigation.

The Academy of Family Mediators defines mediation as:

Mediation is a family-oriented conflict resolution process in which an impartial third party assists the participants to negotiate a consensual and informed settlement. In mediation, whether private or public, decision-making authority rests with the parties. The role of the mediator includes reducing the obstacles to communication, maximizing the exploration of alternatives, and addressing the needs of those it is agreed are involved or affected. Mediation is based on principles of problem solving that focus on the needs and interests of the participants; fairness; privacy; self determination; and the best interest of all the family members.

Through its nonadversarial approach, mediation can empower family members and allow for the creation of a plan of parenting that best fits the family. The accompanying chart lists some of the differences between litigation and mediation in divorce and child custody disputes.

While parents are the primary parties in the mediation process, children are often also involved. Everett and Volgy (1989) suggest that there are four main reasons to involve the children in the process. These are: 1) to allow the children to talk with a neutral party about their fears and concerns regarding their parent's divorce; 2) to allow the mediator to evaluate each child's developmental level and needs so as to help the parents make informed decisions about living arrangements; 3) to use the evaluation of the children to help diffuse parental disputes and unrealistic demands, clearing the way for appropriate and flexible solutions; and 4) to provide support for the parents when they share the outcome of the custody decision with their children.

Everett and Volgy recommend that only experienced mediators participate in this final part of the process. The children should be seen alone as well as with their parents and should feel confident in the confidentiality of their conversations with the mediator.

Many mediators begin the process by focusing on settling the issue of child custody first. This approach has several benefits. First, it protects the children by providing for a less chaotic environment for the children, encouraging rapid resumption of parenting functions by both parents and helping the parents to recognize that their conflicts may be secondary to the goal of taking care of the children. Second, possession of the children is highly emotionally-charged for parents and helping them to work through their emotions and to feel that both are good parents (when appropriate) set the stage for better cooperation down the road, and for less acrimony when settling property disputes.

Gary Friedman, J.D. describes the mediator's position as one of "positive neutrality" in which both parents are understood at the same time. Addressing couples, he writes in his book *A Guide to Divorce Mediation* (1993): "Imagine yourself in a conflict with another person in which you both want the same object. You'll notice that the natural instinct is not to try to understand the other—otherwise the thinking goes, you'd be forced to weaken your position. My job is to understand both of you and to hold a perspective that includes both positions...The effort of positive neutrality is paradoxical, but in a productive way...to understand both members of a couple at the same time, I need to be deeply "subjective," trying to stand in both of their shoes as fully as I can. Ironically, I find that this effort at subjectivity creates for me an objectivity— the ability to see and understand each party's point of view without either one negating the other."

The mediator may at times need to empower a party who is not being realistic about his/her needs or to suggest alternative solutions for consideration if the couple does not work out a solution that is fair or appropriate. For example Everett and Volgy (1989) describe one couple who had done a lot of reading and had come reluctantly to the conclusion that the "correct" solution for the custody of their son was to alternate weeks with each parent. However, the mediator's clinical evaluation of the child suggested that more frequent visits with each parent during the week were required due to the child's immaturity and strong fears about his parent's separation. A graduated plan of visitation was agreed upon so that the family could slowly adjust to week long separations of each parent and the child. This solution clearly benefited the entire family.

In another case Everett and Volgy report using information about the child to help a father reduce his unrealistic demands for visitation. Again a plan for gradually increasing the previously uninvolved father's contact with his child was agreed upon to the satisfaction of both parents and to the benefit of the child. Friedman describes cases in which mediation was used to arrive at realistic and flexible child support agreements in situations where the mother would have agreed to taking less than she needed. In these situations the role of the mediator is to point out the consequences of possible decisions and to insist that both parties take responsibility for truly meeting their real needs.

Sources: American Academy of Family Mediators. Standards of Practice for Family and Divorce Mediation. Preamble, p.1. Berry, K. K. (1989) The mental health specialist as a child advocate in court. in Textor, M. (Ed.) *The Divorce and Divorce Therapy Handbook*. Jason Aronson Inc. Northvale, NJ. pp. 135-147. Everett, C. A. and Volgy, S. S. (1989). Mediating child custody disputes. in Textor, M. (Ed.) *The Divorce and Divorce Therapy Handbook*. Jason Aronson Inc. Northvale, NJ. pp. 123-134. Friedman, G. J. (1993) *A Guide to Divorce Mediation*. Workman Publishing, NY. pp. 26-31. Gardner, R. A. (1989) *Family Evaluation in Child Custody Mediation, Arbitration, and Litigation*. Creative Therapeutics. Cresskill, NJ. pp. 1-26. Hodges, W. F. (1991) *Interventions for Children of Divorce: Custody, Access, and Psychotherapy*. John Wiley and Sons Inc, NY. pp. 66-89. Neville, W. G. (1989) Mediation. in Textor, M. (Ed.) *The Divorce and Divorce Therapy Handbook*. Jason Aronson Inc. Northvale, NJ. pp. 103-122.

Differences Between Litigation and Mediation in Child Custody

Litigation	Mediation
Increases acrimony between parents	Decreases acrimony between parents
Potentially increases stress in family	Helps to decrease stress in family and promotes parenting
Decreases direct communication between parents	Increases direct communication between parents and family, paving way for later communication
Views divorce as a contest with winners and losers	Views divorce as a restructuring of family so that everyone wins to some degree
Promotes giving up decision-making powers to attorneys	Empowers couples to be responsible for their own solutions
Potentially relegates children's best interests to low priority	Places children's interests as one of the highest, if not the highest priorities
Facts are often distorted and spouses maligned as a means of retaliation, blocking the way for a positive resolution	Honesty in reporting facts, and efforts to reduce distortions are integral to mediation process
Women tend to win children and suffer significantly reduced incomes, placing the family at risk and depriving children of a potentially optimum lifestyle	Parents are helped to work though impasses to arrive at fair decisions regarding child support
Fathers with limited visitation feel they have "lost" their children	Parents work toward optimal visitation patterns considering parents' and children's needs

Sources: Berry, 1989; Everett and Volgy, 1989; Friedman, 1993; Gardner, 1989; Hodges, 1989; Neville, 1989

Second Chances:
A Dialogue with Judith Wallerstein, Ph.D.

The Child Therapy News *was fortunate to have the opportunity to talk with Judith Wallerstein, Ph.D. about her research with children of divorce and her new book,* Second Chances: Men, Women, and Children a Decade After Divorce *(co-authored with Sandra Blakeslee). Dr. Wallerstein is the founder and executive director of the Center for the Family in Transition in Corte Madera, California. She is an internationally-recognized authority on the effects of divorce on children, and has been a senior lecturer at the School of Social Welfare at the University of California at Berkeley for over 20 years. She is a fellow at the Center for Advanced Study in the Behavioral Sciences in Stanford, California. In addition to* Second Chances, *she is co-author with Dr. Joan Berlin Kelly of* Surviving the Breakup: How Children and Parents Cope with Divorce.

In addition to her vast knowledge of divorce and its effect on children, she demonstrates a deep compassion for and recognition of human nature that encompasses parents, children and the community. Her realistic outlook and wisdom are evident in her recent conversation with Senior Editor Laura Slap-Shelton, Psy.D.

Laura Slap-Shelton, Psy.D.: *In your book* Second Chances, *you speak of the winners and losers primarily as the adults. Do you ever consider the children to be winners in divorce?*

Judith Wallerstein, Ph.D.: I think the children are winners in divorced families where there was a high-conflict marriage and/or where they witnessed or experience abuse. Whether the children are winners or losers depends entirely on whether the divorce relieves the problems that occurred in the marriage. In a lot of families the marriage is broken, but the problems march on. Conflict between the parents is often exacerbated. Children can be winners only when the divorce serves to remove them from a harmful family situation.

LS-S: *You also talk about the opportunities as well as the dangers divorce creates for society. What are the opportunities?*

JW: I think there is a lot more opportunity to shape the kind of marriage that is suited to the needs of the couple than there used to be. There is more freedom to be one's own person. The hand of tradition has gotten much weaker, and it's partly because of divorce and the influence of divorce on marriage.

I'm writing a new book which is based on a study of happy marriages. People have higher expectations of marriage now. They want more, and a lot of people also realize that if they want more, they're going to have to give more. For people who have that kind of understanding there is an opportunity to have a more equal relationship between the man and the woman, as well as to have a better understanding of children's reactions to conflict between the parents.

LS-S: *What are the main psychological issues for children of divorce?*

JW: At the time of divorce, they are most frightened that no one is going to take care of them. They also experience a profound sadness about the loss of the family and previous relationships with family members. In our society, the nuclear family is responsible entirely for raising the children. We're not living in villages; maybe we'd be better off if we did. In our society it's the mother and father who are totally responsible for the child financially, emotionally and psychologically for a very long time.

Young adulthood gets more and more extended in America. When the parents divorce children wonder, "What's going to happen to me?", "Who's going to take care of me?" and "Who's going to protect me?" These questions persist at every developmental level, even to the point where they may wonder if either parent is going to help them through college.

Then come all the other reactions: "What's going to happen to my mom?", "What's going to happen to my dad?", "Who's going to take care of them?", "To what extent am I responsible for the divorce?", etc. All of these follow from the initial reactions of great anxiety and grief.

LS-S: *What would you recommend parents do to help reduce the level of anxiety in their children?*

JW: Almost everything they're not doing. Very few parents prepare their children for the divorce. They're embarrassed, they're ashamed, they're preoccupied, and a lot of children don't have the foggiest idea of what's happening to their family. They are left with a traumatic impression of how everything just suddenly came apart. It's a terrible preparation for life.

The parents must convey to their children that they've made a rational decision, that they're moral people, that they're very concerned about their children, and that they are going to make absolutely certain to continue taking care of their children.

LS-S: *One of the alarming findings in your book was the lack of support for these children to attend college.*

JW: I was shocked at this situation when I came across it in my group of affluent families. In this group of doctors, lawyers and business executives, only 10 percent of the children had help from their fathers after age 18. That's got to have a terrible chilling effect on the child's learning and motivation in high school.

This situation has not been remedied. Pennsylvania had a law that enabled a judge to order the father and mother to support a child in college when the family had the money to do so. The Pennsylvania Supreme Court reversed the law on the basis that if it couldn't order parents in intact families to send their children to college, it shouldn't order divorced parents to do so either.

To me that's sheer unadulterated nonsense because the situations of children in intact and divorced homes are not comparable. The amount of protection a child enjoys is much greater in an intact family. On a positive note, Massachusetts has gone the opposite way and agreed that support for college could be court ordered.

LS-S: *It is striking how powerless children of divorce feel even when asking for some basic assistance from the parents.*

JW: What can they do? I gave a lecture to third year Law students at the Law school at Berkeley on this subject. At the end of the class, a young woman came over to me and said, "Professor, you just gave me the most important lecture of my life." And I said, "How so?" She responded, "I never thought I had the right to ask my father to help me with my education." That's a terrible thing.

LS-S: *It seems that there should be a more precise way of awarding child support, a* *way that predicts future costs.*

JW: There are several issues with child support. One is that many families don't have court orders ordering child support. Secondly, one of the major scandals in American legal history has been the failure to enforce court orders when they exist. If you are in contempt of a traffic violation, you're going to be in trouble in most states. But if you are in contempt of a court order for child support, there was very little chance of being in trouble until quite recently. Even though there is better enforcement now, the latest figures I read indicated that of all child support orders, half are paid, one quarter are partially paid and one quarter are not paid at all.

LS-S: *How do you explain the lack of financial support by so many fathers?*

JW: In part there is simply a mentality of "If I don't have to pay I won't." On the other hand, many fathers really feel estranged from their children. It's one of the tragedies of divorce. And fathers tend to remarry a lot quicker than mothers. Once there are two families, it is economically and emotionally difficult to be a father in each one.

   Even if remarriage is not part of the picture, it is very hard to be a parent outside of a family. You don't see the kids every day. You lose touch with what they are doing. One of the major tragic effects of divorce is how hard it is for the father and children to maintain relationships.

LS-S: *In the best of all possible worlds, would you recommend joint or shared custody?*

JW: There's no across-the-board answer. Some people view joint custody as some-how "undoing" the divorce. While it does maintain fathers in their parenting role, it certainly does not remove the psychic effects of the divorce. Not everybody is able to handle a joint custody arrangement. The parents have to remain psychologically much closer than in a sole custody arrangement. They know a lot more about the former spouse's personal life; for example, when the former spouse has taken a lover. They also have to be in continuous contact, and for some people it makes it difficult to put closure on the divorce. Joint custody also doesn't guarantee an end to conflict and hostility between the parents.

LS-S: *So the children can still be at risk in joint custody.*

JW: If the parents aren't working well together, the children go back and forth between the two homes and are in a kind of no-man's land. They know that every time they leave mother's house she's furious, and every time they go back to father's house, he's furious.

   Joint custody is very beneficial for children in situations where the parents are working well together at parenting. It needs to be chosen voluntarily, however. One study indicated that about one in every five couples appears to be able to handle joint custody well. If the parents are willing to make sacrifices to maintain a protected environment for their child, that child feels loved and does well.

LS-S: *Another troubling and interesting finding that you discuss in* Second Chances *is the discovery of the "sleeper effect" of divorce on girls.*

JW: Yes. That's probably my most serious finding. In young adulthood when men and women are really seeking each other out and trying to make relationships, that's when all the ghosts arise from the divorce. All children of divorce suffer much more anxiety about being abandoned or being betrayed in relationships. But for girls there was a sleeper effect because so many of them seemed well-adjusted until they came to this stage of their development. Then they took a tumble. But the boys never looked good, so they never took a tumble.

LS-S: *How do you explain this phenomenon?*

JW: I think the girls felt very close to their mothers. There is a very close mother-daughter relationship when you are eight, or ten, and that's great. But it's not so great at ages 18, 19, and 20. That's when the experience of a good relationship with the father is very important, and many of these young women did not have that. Then there are the issues surrounding leaving the mother and the identity the girls have created for themselves on the basis of their mother's experience in relationships.

LS-S: *If girls and boys were brought up in sole-custody-by-father homes with little contact with the mother, would the picture reverse with boys generally looking better until early adulthood and girls having trouble all along?*

JW: I don't know. Girls need fathers and good father-child relationships just as boys do for different reasons and at different times in their lives. I think it's very important for girls to feel that their fathers find them important and attractive. That's very much part of the feminine identity. But on the other hand, I think a lot of those girls would feel that they have betrayed their mothers and that they're replacing their mothers by living with their fathers.

LS-S: *A very powerful metaphor in your book was what you described as the Medea syndrome. You use the myth of Medea and Jason to describe some parents who alienate their children from the other parent at great cost to the child.*

JW: I think that's inevitable to some degree. People go around saying, "Oh wouldn't it be nice if everyone getting divorced didn't get angry?" It's like saying, "Oh wouldn't it be nice if Bengal tigers would be nice house pets and not be carnivorous?" Divorce is about anger. It's pointless to say don't be angry or that if you are, don't let your kids see it.

We can help parents with the anger, but we certainly cannot stop it. Medea was a good mother. She only turns on her children to destroy them when she realizes that it's the only way to destroy Jason. That is what happens psychologically in some of these families where the parents are not able to cope with their anger.

LS-S: *It's a strong image.*

JW: It's an accurate image. This is not rational, and you cannot deal with it by saying you have to "make nice." We developed some interventions to try to help these people, but it's extremely difficult and it doesn't go away. We use a long-term intervention in which the therapist remains in the picture and continues to develop the kind of transference with the mother, father and children that keeps their emotions about each other in balance. But in many cases, once the therapist leaves the picture, the family goes back to square one. What organizes these people is the anger which is warding off the depression. That's exactly what happened with Medea.

LS-S: *In some families the limitations of the individual parent alone would be enough* *to contribute to difficulties in their children's lives and psychological functioning. How can this be understood?*

JW: I think there is no question that we need a lot of studies that compare divorced populations with married populations. The studies that have been done show much more psychopathology of a serious kind in the divorced population. There is much more narcissism, alcoholism and a higher frequency of psychiatric hospitalization. So you are looking at greater problems with mental health in this population even though there is certainly tremendous overlap between the two groups. There are also more serious problems in the ability to maintain relationships in the divorced population.

LS-S: *When doing the interviews it must have been difficult to observe the problems some of the children were having and not to become more involved. How did you handle this?*

JW: I didn't offer services unless I thought it was an emergency. When I saw an acutely depressed child or a suicidal child, I offered the appropriate services immediately. But by virtue of having contact with me, the children in the study developed a very positive view of the mental health world.

A whole group of them went into therapy when they reached their twenties and achieved very good results. The children kept in touch with me, and I was an important person to them. Although I didn't offer to be anybody's therapist, they knew that if they had an emergency they could call me, and they did. When they reached their twenties and wanted a therapist, they called me and asked who I'd suggest. I essentially ran a referral network that spanned the whole country. I even made a referral in Amsterdam. It was, and still is, extremely gratifying.

The Parental Alienation Syndrome

By Richard A. Gardner, M.D.

Starting in the late 1970s, in association with what can justifiably be called a custody litigation explosion, I began to see a disorder that developed almost exclusively in children exposed to and embroiled in custody disputes. Parental alienation syndrome refers to a disturbance in which a child is obsessed with unjustified and/or exaggerated deprecation and criticism of one parent and idolization of the other. It is as if the preferred parent can do no wrong and the nonpreferred parent can do no right. Such children have not merely been "brainwashed" or programmed by one parent to denigrate the other parent. The parental alienation syndrome does have a brainwashing component, but is much more inclusive. It incorporates not only conscious but subconscious and unconscious drives in the preferred parent that contribute to the child's alienation. Furthermore, it includes factors that arise with the child-independent of parental contributions-to foster the development of the syndrome.

Typically, the child is obsessed with "hatred" of a parent. (I put the word hatred in quotes because there are still many tender and loving feelings toward the parent that are not permitted expression.) The child speaks of the hated parent with every vilification and profanity in their vocabulary— without embarrassment or guilt. The vilification of the parent often had the rehearsed quality of a litany. With only minimal prompting, the record will be turned on and a command performance provided. One often hears phraseology identical to that used by the "loved" parent. (Again, the word loved is in quotes because there may also be hostility toward and fear of that parent, similarly unexpressed.) My experience has been that in about 80 to 90 percent of cases the mother is the favored parent and the father the vilified one; in the remaining 10 to 20 percent of cases the opposite is true. It is important to note that when the child's anger is warranted by bona fide abuse (physical, emotional, or sexual), the parental alienation syndrome concept does not apply.

The child may justify the alienation with years-old memories of minor altercations with the hated parent. Usually these are trivial and relate to experiences that most children quickly forget: "She used to say 'Don't interrupt,'" and "He used to make a lot of noise when he chewed at the table." Asked to give more compelling reasons for their hatred, these children are unable to provide them. Frequently, the loved parent will agree with the child that these professed reasons justify the ongoing animosity.

The hatred of the parent often includes that parent's complete extended family. Cousins, aunts, uncles, and grandparents with whom the child previously may have had loving relationships are now detested. Greeting cards are not reciprocated. Presents are refused, remain unopened, or even destroyed (generally in the presence of the loved parent.) When the hated parent's relatives call on the telephone, the child will respond with angry name-calling or quickly hang up. The rage of these children is so great that they become completely oblivious to the privations they are causing themselves. Again, the loved parent is typically unconcerned with the untoward psychological effects on the child of the rejection of these relatives.

Another symptom of the parental alienation syndrome is complete lack of ambivalence that characterizes normal parent-child relationships. In this syndrome the hated parent is viewed as all bad and the loved parent as all good. The hated parent may have been deeply dedicated to the child, and a strong bond may have been created over many years. The hated parent may produce photos that show clearly a joyful and healthy relationship of affection, tenderness, and mutual pleasure. But all these experiences appear to have been obliterated from the child's memory. When shown these photos, the child usually rationalizes the experiences as having been forgotten, nonexistent, or feigned: "I really hated being with him then. I just smiled in the picture because he made me. He said he'd hit me if I didn't smile."

The child may exhibit a guiltless disregard for the feelings of the hated parent. There will be a complete absence of gratitude for gifts, support (continued from page 13) payments, and other evidence of the hated parent's continued involvement and affection. Often these children will want to be certain the alienated parent continues to provide support payments, but at the same time will adamantly refuse to visit. Commonly they will say that they never want to see the hated parent again, or not until their late teens or early twenties. To such a child I might say: "So you want your father to continue paying for all your food, clothing, rent, and education—even private high school and college — and yet you still don't want to see him at all, ever again. Is that right?" The child might respond: "That's right. He doesn't deserve to see me. He's mean and paying all that money is good punishment for him."

Those who have never seen such children may consider this description a caricature. Those who have seen them will recognize the syndrome immediately, although some children may not manifest all the symptoms. The parental alienation syndrome is becoming increasingly common- a direct result, I am convinced, of social and legal changes underlying judicial decisions in custody disputes.

Let me review these changes briefly. First, in the replacement of the "tender years presumption" the best interests of the child became uniformly equated with the notion that custody determinations should be sex blind. Equating these two concepts, I believe, has caused considerable difficulty. I believe that in their desire to keep up with the seeming egalitarianism of the best interests of the child presumption, the courts have not been giving proper credit to the strength of the psychological bond in most families today (I am not predicting the future) between children and their mothers. And I believe that many women have responded to the threat of removal of their children by the utilization of maneuvers that have contributed to the development of the parental alienation syndrome in their children. Children, too, have been threatened by disruption of the mother-child bond. They have selected maneuvers that—although they may seem absurd—basically represent mechanisms of defense against the disruption of this bond. And the animosities engendered by these maneuvers have contributed to the increase in and intensification of custody litigation.

Second, the joint-custodial concept has contributed to an increase in the development of the parental alienation syndrome. In what becomes essentially a no-custodial arrangement, the children are used as ropes in a tug-of-war between the parents. These circumstances intensify the viciousness of the litigation, especially in cases where separated women— all too often at an economic disadvantage compared to men—program their children against their husbands in a desperate attempt to win the custody battle.

I believe that the utilization of the "stronger, healthy psychological bond presumption" that I have described would reduce the frequency of custody litigation and so help prevent the development of the parental alienation syndrome.

For example, let us envision a situation in which a couple has one child, a boy. During the first four years of the child's life, the mother remains at home as the primary child rearer and the father is out of the home during the day. When the child is four the mother takes a full-time job. During the day the child attends school and then stays with a woman in the neighborhood. At the end of the workday and over weekends both parents are involved equally in caring for the child. When the child is seven the parents decide to separate. Each parent wants primary custody. The father claims that during the three years prior to the separation, he was as involved as the mother in the child's upbringing; the mother does not deny this. The father contends that the court should make its decision solely on the basis of parenting capacity—especially as demonstrated in recent years—and claims that any custody decision taking his sex into consideration is sexist and is an abrogation of his civil rights. In the course of the litigation the child develops typical symptoms of the parental alienation syndrome. He becomes obsessed with hatred of his father and creates outlandish scenarios to justify his animosity. In contrast, he views his mother as faultless and all-loving. I believe that in this situation the child's psychological bond is strongest with the mother, and the symptoms of alienation are created by him in an attempt to maintain that bond. If the father had been the primary caretaker during the first four years of the boy's life and had shared equally in subsequent child rearing, then the child might well have the stronger, healthy psychological bond with the father. And if he did, I would recommend the father be designated the primary custodial parent.

If the stronger, healthy psychological bond were the central criterion, when the mother had been the primary caretaker, the father would hesitate to ask for custody. Accordingly, the likelihood of the mother's "brainwashing" the child and of the child's developing parental alienation syndrome would be obviated. Similarly, when the father had been the primary caretaker during the formative years, the mother would be discouraged from embarking on the custody litigation course. This would then obviate the brainwashing/parental alienation syndrome.

Reprinted with permission from *The Parents Book About Divorce* by Richard A. Gardner, M.D., Creative Therapeutics, Cresskill, NJ. 1991. pp. 264-268.

Research Findings in Child Custody

• In a study of 200 children of divorce in Hawaii, researchers found that preschool children were often told nothing before the divorce, fathers with higher levels of education and professional jobs were more likely
to have shared or sole custody, mothers with professional or managerial jobs were less depressed than statistically predicted and depression was a common response to divorce in parents and children.
Waldron, J., Ching, J. and Fair, P. (1986) A children's divorce clinic: analysis of 200 cases in Hawaii. *Journal of Divorce*, 9(3):111-121.

• An exploratory study of infants and toddlers and visitation patterns after divorce found that fathers who were more involved with early child care visited more often post-divorce, that a weak visitation pattern from the father led to some language delays and that the level of conflict before separation was related to the number of visits. However, the authors caution that these results are tentative and should not be used in court.
Hodges, W., Landis, T. et. al. (1991) Infants and toddlers and post divorce parental access: an initial exploration. *Journal of Divorce and Remarriage.* 16(3-4): 239-252.

• Parenting style is a predictor of child development for children of divorce. Parents who use an authoritative rather than authoritarian style tend to have children who have healthy peer interactions, decreased aggression, improved relationships with the parents, and a more positive attitude toward school.
Sorensen, E. and Goldman, J. (1990) Custody determinations and child development: A review of the current literature. *Journal of Divorce,* 13(4),p.63; Wallerstein, J. and Kelly, J. (1980) *Surviving the Breakup.* New York: Basic Books; Warshak, R. and Santrock, J.(1983) Children of divorce: Impact of custody disposition on social development. In Callahan, E. and McCluskey, K., Eds. *Life Span Developmental Psychology: Nonnormative Life Events* (pp. 163-241) New York: Academic Press.

• Sex- and age-related differences have been found to exist in response to remarriage by the sole custody parent who is the mother. Younger children respond better to remarriage by mother than preadolescent and early adolescent children. Boys tend to respond better to remarriage by mother than girls in terms of long-term adjustment.
Hetherington, E. (1990) Coping with family transitions: Winners, losers, and survivors. *Annual Progress in Child Psychiatry and Development.* pp. 221-241. Hetherington, Cox, and Cox (1985) Long-term effects of divorce and remarriage on the adjustment of children. *Journal of the American Academy of Psychiatry* 24:518-830.

• In Wallerstein's ten-year longitudinal study of 116 children of divorce, 50 percent of the children's divorced parents had a second divorce within 10 years of the first.
Wallerstein, J. and Blakeslee, S. (1990) *Second Chances: Men, Women, and Children a Decade After Divorce.* New York, Ticknor and Fields. p. 298.

• Fifty percent of the children in Wallerstein's ten-year study experienced ongoing anger between the parents.
(See above reference)

• Twenty percent of the children in Wallerstein's ten-year study experienced an enduring reduction in their standard of living and a significant discrepancy between the father's and the custodial mother's wealth.

(See above reference)

• Sixty percent of the children in Wallerstein's ten-year study felt rejected by one of the parents by self report.
(See above reference)

• Very few fathers in Wallerstein's ten-year study helped their children to obtain a college education even when they could afford to do so.
(See above reference)

• While boys have been found to suffer more from divorce than girls, especially when there is little contact with the father, Wallerstein reports a "sleeper effect" for girls, in which female children of divorce suffer significant emotional distress in late adolescence and early adulthood when they face the developmental task of establishing an intimate relationship with the opposite sex. At this juncture they become overwhelmed by fears of betrayal and choosing the wrong mate. This effect was not seen in the majority of boys in this study. Thus in the long-term, detrimental effects of divorce may be equal between girls and boys. Dr. Wallerstein speculates that this effect may be a sleeper effect only because studies tend not to examine children's subjective experiences of relationships.
(See above reference, pp. 56-64)

• Despite the increased assignment of joint custody arrangements, 90 percent of children are in the sole custody of their mother.
(See above reference, p. 17)

• A study by Professor Weitzman of Harvard University found that the average mother with minor children has a 73 percent reduction of standard of living as opposed to fathers, who experience on average a 42 percent reduction in standard of living. She suggests that this trend could lead to a society in which women become the underclass.
(See above reference)

• In a six-year follow-up study of 180 divorced families. Hetherington et. al. found that mothers with sole custody did not respond more negatively to "difficult" vs. "easy" children under the condition of low stress and stable maternal personality. However, the presence of personality problems or high levels of stress led to an increase in negative responses to difficult children. The combination of personality problems and stress led to increased levels of aversive behavior as compared to the presence of only one factor.
Hetherington, E. (1990) Coping with family transitions: Winners, losers, and survivors. *Annual Progress in Child Psychiatry and Development.* p. 225.

• Fathers and stepfathers followed a similar pattern to the mothers in response to difficult vs. easy children in Hetherington et. al.'s study, but fathers who had been remarried longer than two years, in contrast to non-remarried fathers and fathers remarried for a shorter time, were found to target girls more than boys for negative behavior.
(See above reference, p. 226)

• Difficult children and easy children differed in their ability to make use of support to cope with stressful situations. Under moderate levels of stress temperamentally easy children were able to make use of support and improve their problem-solving

ability while difficult children were not able to benefit from support.
(See above reference, pp. 226-227)

• Schools with defined rules, schedules, and a warm but authoritative stance serve
to buffer children of divorce and children in high conflict families. This is especially true for boys, children suffering multiple stressors and children with difficult temperaments.
(See above reference, p. 236-237)

• Conflict between parents, whether divorced or married, has been associated with
the behavior problems observed in children of divorce. Even if parents continue to
feel conflict in their relationship with each other, if they are able to cooperate in parenting the children, closer and more communicative relationships between noncustodial fathers and children are found as well as between mothers and children in non-
divorced families.
Camara, K. and Resnick, G. (1989) Styles of conflict resolution and cooperation between
divorced parents: Effects on child behavior and adjustment. *American Journal of
Orthopsychiatry.* 59(4):560-575; Emery, R. (1982) Interparental conflict and the children of discord and divorce. *Psychological Bulletin.* 92:310-330.

• In a study of 74 attorneys' and 43 judges' criteria for making custody decisions, it
was found that only half considered the wishes of the child to be among the most
important criteria for making the decision, and a majority reported that they did not
believe that the child's best interests were critical in making the custody decisions.
The authors consider this in part to be due to the ambiguity of the criterion of the
best interests of the child, and difficulty in knowing how to interpret the meaning of
the child's wishes.
Felner, R., Terre, L. et. al. Party status of children during marital dissolution: Child preference
and legal representation in custody decisions. *Journal of Clinical Child Psychology.* 14(1):42-48.

• A study of ten fathers with joint physical custody of the children found that the
fathers were highly available to their children. However, they experienced difficulty
with household management and adjustment to a new role.
Richards, C. and Goldenburg, I. (1986) Fathers with joint physical custody of young children:
A preliminary look. *American Journal of Family Therapy.* 14(2):154-162.

• In a study of 80 divorcing families with a custody dispute, support by extended family and friends was found to often include criticism and interference and led to an
increase in tension or conflict that was ultimately not supportive.
Johnston, J., and Campbell, L., (1986) Tribal warfare: The involvement of extended kin and significant others in custody and access disputes. *23rd Annual Conference of the Association of
Family and Conciliation Courts* (1985, Vancouver, Canada). Conciliation Courts Review. 24(1):1-
16.

• In a study of children five to eight and nine to twelve years old it was found that
visit frequency and visit regularity were associated with father-child closeness.
Measures of self esteem in the children were however more related to degree of
closeness with father, as gender and age.
Healy, J., Malley, J., and Stewart, A. (1990) Children and their fathers after parental separation.
American Journal of Orthopsychiatry. 60(4):531-543.

• When pairs of custodial and noncustodial parents were interviewed it was found
that custodial mothers interfered with noncustodial father's visits with their children
20 to 40 percent of the time. The level of hostility in mothers at the beginning of the

divorce proceedings was associated with less overnight visitation for noncustodial fathers three years later.

Braver, S., Wolchik, S., et. al. (1991) Frequency of visitation by divorced fathers: Differences in reports by fathers and mothers. American Journal of Orthopsychiatry. 61(3):448-454.

• Over the last ten years, the amount of time fathers spend with their children after divorce has increased 30 to 33 percent.

Kelly, J. (1993) Current research on children's postdivorce adjustment. No simple answers. *Family and Conciliation Courts Review.* 31(1):29-49.

• In a study of 517 adolescents aged 10 to 18 years, a complex relationship was found between types of custody arrangements, access to each parent, demographic, psychological and family process factors. It was found that dual-residence adolescents were on average better-adjusted than mother-resident and father-resident adolescents who were least well-adjusted for a variety of factors.

Buchanan, C., Maccoby, E., and Dornbusch, S. (in press). Adolescents and their families after divorce: Three residential arrangements compared. Journal of Research on Adolescence. in Kelly, J. (1993) Current research on children's postdivorce adjustment. No simple answers. *Family and Conciliation Courts Review.* 31(1):29-49.

Recent Journal Articles on
Child Custody

Arditti, J. (1992) **Factors related to custody, visitation, and child support for divorced fathers: An exploratory analysis.** Study of 125 mostly non-custodial fathers and the variables affecting their satisfaction with different aspects of custody arrangements. *Journal of Divorce and Remarriage.* 17(3-4):23-42.

Ayoub, C., Grace, P. et. al. (1991) **Alleging psychological impairment of the accuser to defend oneself against a child abuse allegation: A manifestation of wife battering and false accusation.** Discusses five groups of families in custody disputes in which there are counter allegations of abuse and psychological impairment. *Child and Youth Services.* 15(2):191-207.

Benjamin, M., Irving, H. (1989) **Shared parenting: Critical review of the research literature.** Review of 21 published studies on shared parenting. *Family and Conciliation Courts Review.* 27(2):21-35.

Bray, J. (1991) **Psychosocial factors affecting custodial and visitation arrangements.** Reviews and stresses importance of incorporating social-environmental factors in custodial decision-making to arrive at children's best interests. *Behavioral Sciences and the Law.* 9(4):419-437.

Camara, K., Resnick, G. **Styles of conflict resolution and cooperation between divorced parents: Effects on child behavior and adjustment.** Study of 82 families concluded that the level of cooperation between divorced parents is predictive of children's adjustment to divorce. *American Journal of Orthopsychiatry.* 59(4):560-575.

Cole, W.A., Bradford, J.M. (1992) **Abduction during custody and access disputes.** Controlled study of 20 cases of child abductions during divorce custody and access disputes. Findings indicate that abductors tend to be male and have psychiatric histories. *Canadian Journal of Psychiatry.* 37(4): 264-266.

Eastman, M., Moran, T. (1991) **Multiple perspectives: Factors related to differential diagnosis of sex abuse and divorce trauma in children under six.** Addresses the developmental impact of divorce and sexual abuse on children under age six. Case study provided. *Child and Youth Services.* 15(2):159-175.

Garrison, E. (1991) **Children's competence to participate in divorce custody decision-making. Special Issue: Child Advocacy.** Study of 144 children ages 9 to 14 found that 14-year-olds are as competent as 18-year-olds in having rational reasons for custodial preference, and that at younger ages reasoning is developmentally determined but does not affect the custodial preference. *Journal of Clinical Child Psychology.* 20(1):78-87.

Garwood, F. (1990) **Children in conciliation: the experience of involving children in conciliation.** Finds positive parental, professional and children's response to having children involved in conciliation program in Scotland. *Family and Conciliation Courts Review.* 28(1):43-51.

Geffner, R. (1992) **Guidelines for using mediation with abusive couples. Special Issue: Psychotherapy in independent practice: Current issues for clinicians.** Includes questionnaire that helps to identify abusive relationships. Stresses importance of protecting wife and children of batterers during time before actual divorce as incidence of murder increases during this period. *Psychotherapy in Private Practice.* 10(1-2): 77-92.

Glover, R., Steele, C. (1988-89) **Comparing the effects on the child of post-divorce parenting arrangements. Special Issue: Children of Divorce: Developmental and clinical issues.** Controlled study comparing children in single and joint custody arrangements with children of non-divorced families. Joint custody arrangements for children appeared to be as beneficial or more beneficial than single custody. *Journal of Divorce.* 12(2-3):185-201.

Hetherington, M. (1990) **Coping with family transitions: Winners, losers, and survivors.** Presidential Address at the Meetings of the Society for Research in Child Development (1987, Baltimore, MD). Study of 180 families including at least one child of four years or older at onset of study. Children from divorced families were able to be clustered into three groups: aggressive-insecure, opportunistic-competent, and caring-competent. *Annual Progress in Child Psychiatry and Child Development.* 1990:221-241.

Hodges, W., Landis, T. et. al. (1991) **Infant and toddlers and post divorce parental access: An initial exploration. Special Issue: The consequences of divorce: Economic and custodial impact on children and adults: II.** Evaluation of 45 children under three years for visitation/access patterns, attachment to the custodial mother and by mother's report to noncustodial father and psychomotor development. *Journal of Divorce and Remarriage.* 16(3-4):239-252.

Johnston, J., Gonzalez, R., Campbell, L. (1987) **Ongoing post-divorce conflict and child disturbance.** Study of 56 boys and girls ages 4 to 12 suggesting that at time of custody dispute extent of the child's involvement in the dispute and the amount of role reversal between parent and child predicts behavior problems. Two-and-a-half years following custody assignment an additional factor of degree of verbal and physical aggression between ex-spouses predicted behavioral problems in same children. *Journal of Abnormal Child Psychology.* 15(4):493-509.

Kalter, N., Kloner, A. et. al. (1989) **Predictors of children's post-divorce adjustment.** Examines 56 sole custody mothers and one of each mother's children using standardized measures to test six hypotheses predicting the child's development following divorce. Parental adjustment hypothesis provided best fit for the data. *American Journal of Orthopsychiatry.* 59(4):605-618.

Kaplan, L., Hennon, C., Ade-Ridder, L. (1993) **Splitting custody of children between parents: Impact on the sibling system.** Discusses dangers of split custody to the sibling system. *Families in Society.* 74(3):131-144.

Kelly, J. (1993) **Current research on children's post-divorce adjustment: No simple answers.** Findings include that the degree of parental conflict and not the divorce itself affects children's adjustment, and that of all the possible custody scenarios parents tend to be most satisfied with shared custody that is not court ordered. *Family and Conciliation Courts Review.* 31(1):29-49.

Lehner, L. (1992) **Mediation parent education programs in the California family courts.** Describes comprehensive parent education programs which are part of court-connected custody mediation services. Included are groups for highly litigious couples. *Family and Conciliation Courts Review.* 30(2):207-216.

Little, M. (1992) **The impact of the custody plan on the family: A five-year follow-up: Executive summary.** Review of 424 cases in which joint custody was assigned in California six years post-divorce found that follow-through on splitting the children's time equally between the parents was less than expected. *Family and Conciliation Courts Review.* 30(2): 242-251.

Peretti, P., DiVitorrio, A. (1993) **Effect of loss of father through divorce on personality of the preschool child.** Study of 66 children ages three to six who were living solely with mother. Some of the variables found in these children included increased guilt, depression, withdrawal, along with decreased sociability and self-esteem. *Journal of Instructional Psychology.* 19(4):269-273.

Renouf, E. (1991) **Impasses of divorce: Neither together nor apart.** Discusses an intervention for helping parents engaged in protracted custody disputes which involves counseling about the impasse in the divorce and mediation. *Australian and New Zealand Journal of Family Therapy.* 12(4):196-200.

Solomon, R. (1991) **A critical moment for intervention: After the smoke of the battle clears and custody has been won. Special Issue: The consequences of divorce: Economic and custodial impact on children and adults: II.** Articles discusses needs for special interventions for parents with custody in the critical period between the third and sixth month after custody has been awarded. *Journal of Divorce and Remarriage.* 16(3-4):325-335.

Sorensen, E., Goldman, J.(1990) **Custody determinations and child development: A review of the current literature.** Study of the criteria used by courts in making custody decision with aim of finding variables predicting best outcome for the children. *Journal of Divorce.* 13(4):53-67.

Wolman, R, Taylor, K. (1991) **Psychological effects of custody disputes on children.** Study of 95 children and their parents from 43 families yielded unexpected finding that contested children appeared to have less separation anxiety and greater internality of control than noncontested children. *Behavioral Sciences and the Law.* 9(4):399-417.

Periodicals Dealing with Divorce and Custody Issues

American Journal of Family Therapy
Bruner Mazel, 19 Union Square West,
New York, NY 10003
(212) 924-3344 Fax: (212) 242-6339
Published quarterly - Individuals: $38/yr.
 Institutions: $75/yr.

Children and Society
Whiting and Birch Ltd., P.O. Box 872, Forest Hill
London SE23 3HL England
Tel: 081-6990914 Fax: 081-6993685
Published quarterly - $90/yr.

Family and Conciliation Courts Review
Sage Publications, 2455 Teller Rd.,
Newbury Park, CA 91320
(805) 499-0721 Fax: (805) 499-0871
Published quarterly - Individuals: $44/yr.
Institutions: $96/yr.

Family Process
70 W. Allendale Ave., Suite D, Allendale, NJ 07401
(201) 235-8381 Fax: (201) 236-0954
Published quarterly - Ind.: $27/yr. Insts.: $44/yr.

Family Relations Journal of Applied Family and Child Studies
National Council on Family Relations
3989 Central Ave. NE, Suite 550
Minneapolis, MN 55421
(612) 781-9331 Fax: (612) 781-9348
Published quarterly - Ind.: $45/yr. Insts.: $75/yr.

Journal of Marriage and the Family
National Council on Family Relations
3989 Central Ave. NE, Suite 550
Minneapolis, MN 55421
(612) 781-9331 Fax: (612) 781-9348
Published quarterly - Individuals: $50/yr.
Institutions: $85/yr.

Journal of Divorce and Remarriage
Haworth Press
10 Alice St., Binghamton, NY 13904
(800) 342-9678 Fax: (607) 722-1424
Published quarterly - Individuals: $45/yr.
Institutions: $180/yr.

Journal of Family Psychology
APA Division of Family Psychology
750 First St. NE, Washington, DC 20002-4242
(202) 336-5600 Fax: (202) 336-5568
Published quarterly - Individuals: $40/yr.
Institutions: $80/yr.

Marriage and Family Review
Haworth Press
10 Alice St., Binghamton, NY13904
(800) 342-9678 Fax: (607) 722-1424
Published quarterly - Individuals: $38/yr.
Institutions: $160/yr.

Mediation Quarterly
Jossey Bass, 350 Sasone St., 5th Floor
San Francisco, CA 94104
(415) 433-1767 Fax: (415) 433-0499
Published quarterly - Individuals: $46/yr.
Institutions: $82/yr.

- Book Review -
Child Custody

By James C. Black and Donald J. Cantor

Custody decisions are to be made considering the "best interests of the child." This legal standard was established without clear guidelines or definitions. In a situation where one parent is clearly abusive, or neglectful, and the other is not, the decision is perhaps "easy." However, in many cases, neither parent is obviously inadequate. Child Custody, written from legal and psychiatric perspectives, traces the philosophical and historical roots of child custody issues, clearly defines different custody options and presents a developmental model for parent evaluation which identifies personality features most likely to promote healthy child development.

In the first part of the book, authors Black and Cantor trace historical and legal issues related to child custody. For much of this century, mothers were considered to be inherently better parents and were awarded sole or primary custody except in unusual circumstances. This was, however, a fairly modern perspective. The American legal system evolved from the British system with its roots in the sometimes conflicting philosophies of common law and parents patriae, with its goal of protecting "the Crown's subjects who were unable to protect themselves." Under English common law, the child was considered the property of the father and custodial rights followed.

During the early 19th century, the "tender age" doctrine emerged and prescribed that until an unspecified age children should be nurtured by the mother. The so-called "tender age" was defined differently by different states. "The age of five, 'tender' in Tennessee was considered 'tough' in New Jersey." However, the maternal preference gradually emerged as the superior principle and remained so through the third quarter of this century.

These changes in perspective emerged along with changes in the family structure. The English common law had its roots in the feudal order in which women were essentially considered chattel and children objects. With industrialization and its consequent gradual shifts in family roles, the view of children also changed to one in which the child was seen as a person rather than as a possession. Women "become more than chattels but less than equals...Women were deemed unfit for affairs of state but better with children."

With the women's movement and shift toward equality of men and women, the mother's "monopoly on nurturance has weakened and grows looser every day." Concomitant changes in child custody laws have occurred. While still a dominant philosophy, as women "ascend toward equality in economics and descend to it in custody matters, the maternal preference diminishes." The "best interests of the child" has emerged as the superior principle.

Black and Cantor list the five basic custody types:

1) Wherein one parent has sole custody and the other parent has rights of visitation. Here the custodial parent is the only parent legally vested with the authority to make the most important child-rearing decisions such as whether or not a medical procedure is appropriate, what school the child shall attend, or what religion the child should embrace. The child's time is divided between the custodial and non-custodial parent with the latter having generally only a small portion of the child's time. Visitation orders may, however, vary greatly with regard to the amount of time involved.

2) Wherein the child spends one-half of the time with each parent and where the parent the child is with has the sole legal custody of the child during the period of possession. Here the rights of both legal authority and possession are equally divided. This "divided" custody may not, however, be divided equally. Thus a variant of it is stated in Type 3.

3) Wherein the child's time is divided equally between the parents, but the parent the child is with has the sole legal custody of the child during the period of possession.

4) Wherein the child's time is divided equally between the parents but both parents retain full rights of custody all the time. Since each parent has a continuous, full legal right of custody, they are "joint" custodians, their "joint custody" being a legal concept that derives not from the time of possession, but rather from their equal, continuous right to make basic decisions of child rearing. It is still appropriate to label as "joint custody" an order like that in Type 5.

5) Wherein the child's time is divided unequally but where both parents retain, nonetheless, the equal, full and continuous right to make the basic decisions of child rearing.

After describing these basic custody arrangements further, Black and Cantor describe in detail the complexities of the divorce context, the custodial trial and other legal custodial issues. The discussion of these legal issues is clearly written for the lay person and is illuminating for the psychologist who wishes to understand their role in the complex custody process.

The authors then present a model for conducting custody evaluation. In conducting an evaluation, the authors recommend that the evaluator meet with each parent approximately four times. The evaluator meets with each child for one or possibly two individual interviews and collects relevant data from schools and other outside sources. Following this, each parent meets with the evaluator and the children to obtain information about parent/child interaction. The authors identify the types of information that should be collected and guidelines for how to use the information in making custody recommendations.

The authors present a developmental model for parent evaluation that focuses on five areas of healthy personality organization that foster positive child development. These include: 1) nurturance and empathy; 2) degree of personality separation and individuation; 3) impulse control; 4) reality testing; and 5) identity organization. Condensed, these characteristics "represent the capacity to emotionally invest in a child and put the child's needs before one's own, what is ordinarily considered love; the ability to foster independence and the child's unique personality; sufficient control over one's anger, aggression and sexual impulses to help one's child develop normal self-control; sufficient objectivity and clarity to help the child correctly assess the environment; and enough strength in one's personality to project a secure sexual identity and healthy values and beliefs." Strategies for evaluating parental strengths and weaknesses in each of the five areas are discussed in detail with descriptive, useful case examples. The parent's self awareness and capacity to improve parenting skills in any of these areas are also assessed.

Recognizing that there are no perfect solutions in custody situations and few, if any, perfect parents, the authors use the information collected during the evaluation process to arrive at compassionate recommendations that recognize both parents' strengths and weaknesses and are likely to represent the best interests of the child. The authors emphasize the need for conveying empathy and compassion to families who are contesting and suffering.

Child Custody. James C. Black and Donald J. Cantor. Columbia University Press, New York, NY. 1989. 250 pp.

Children's Books on Divorce:
An Annotated Listing

As the number of children with divorced parents has increased, several excellent books have appeared to address their concerns, fears and difficulties. Most of the books attempt to help children make sense of what is happening to the family, identify their feelings, and clear up some commonly-held misconceptions that children develop. The best books provide either a child model who learns to cope with the aspects of the divorce highlighted in the book, or provide information and exercises that help children take an active role in coping with the changes in their families. We have listed below some of the books currently available for children of divorce and their families.

All About Divorce by Mary Blitzer Field. The Center for Applied Psychology, Inc., King of Prussia, PA. 1992. Illustrated. 106 pp.
This Play-and-Read book is designed to encourage communication between parents and children aged 5 through 12 during this period of change. The sensitively-illustrated book not only offers honest answers to the most common concerns of children, but it also comes with a doll family and backdrop scenes to allow children to play out their concerns and written activities to help children express and share their feelings. The book also includes advice for parents, divorce "vocabulary" words for children, and the "Twenty Most Important Things Kids Must Remember About Divorce."

At Daddy's on Saturdays by Linda Walvoord Girard. Albert Whitman & Co., Morton Grove, IL. 1987. Illustrated. 29 pp.
This well-written book depicts the complex emotions and relationships between young Katie and her parents as Katie adjusts to her new relationship with her father who moves out of the home. It accurately describes the awkwardness of the situation and models positive adjustment including sharing feelings and recognizing that her father did not abandon her.

The Boys and Girls Book About Divorce by Richard A. Gardner, M.D. Bantam Books, New York, NY. 1970. Illustrated. 157 pp.
This classic book realistically explains all aspects of divorce to children. It discusses the divorce process, blame, anger, fears of abandonment, getting along with parents after divorce and seeing a therapist, among other topics. Recommended for ages nine and up, the book also includes an introduction for parents.

Break-up by Gianni Padoan. Happy Books, Milan, Italy. 1987. Illustrated. 22 pp.
Another delightfully illustrated book, Break-up presents the first-person account of a pre-teenage boy from the time his parents separate to the point when each parent has started a new relationship. The narrator is articulate about his feelings and presents a good role model for communicating feelings and fears to family and friends. This book is positive, presenting parents who communicate well with each other and maintain close contact with their son. As a result, it does not explore some of the more serious problems children of divorce face.

Dinosaurs Divorce: A Guide for Changing Families by Laurene Kransy Brown and Marc Brown. Joy Street Books, Little Brown and Co. Boston, MA. 1986. Illustrated. 32 pp.
A beautifully-illustrated book which provides basic information about divorce and

focuses on the experiences and feelings many children have when living with one parent at a time. It presents new experiences such as holidays, meeting their parents' new friends, and coping with step-parents. The book identifies the feelings, fantasies and misconceptions different situations engender and provides suggestions for coping. It is an upbeat book best suited for young and latency age children whose parents have maintained good parenting skills and are in regular contact with their children. A glossary of terms related to divorce is also presented.

The Divorce Workbook: A Guide for Kids and Families by Sally Blakeslee Ives, Ph.D.; David Fassler, M.D.; and Michele Lash, M.Ed., A.T.R. Waterfront Books, Burlington, VT. 1985. Illustrated. 145 pp.
This workbook is designed to help children through latency age to understand the cycle of marriage and divorce, identify their feelings and take action to get help for themselves. It includes pictures and quotes from children who have gone through divorce and plenty of room for young readers to write about and illustrate their own feelings. The book is especially effective in helping children to explore the variety of feelings brought on by divorce and in developing healthy coping techniques. The foreword includes useful ideas for parents, counselors, teachers and librarians.

The Kids' Book of Divorce: By, For and About Kids by Eric Rofes, Ed. Vintage Books, New York, NY. 1982. Illustrated. 122 pp.
This excellent book was written by 20 children (ages 11 to 14) who attended the Fayerweather Street School in Massachusetts. The book realistically describes the experience of living in a family through all stages of divorce. It includes book reviews by children and even a section on having a gay parent. This book should be "must" reading for divorcing parents as well as adolescents and teenagers living with the stresses of divorce.

My Life Turned Upside Down, But I Turned It Rightside Up by Mary Blitzer Field and Hennie Shore. The Center for Applied Psychology, Inc., King of Prussia, PA. 1994. Illustrated. 70 pp.
This novel book, written for children aged 5 through 12, tells the story of a young girl whose parents are divorced and how she handles the challenges of living in two places. On every other page, she tells us about a problem she had, and when the reader flips the book over, the next page tells how she solved it. Two sample pages read: I used to think that if I did everything Mom and Dad wanted me to do all the time, they would get back together...But I realized that the divorce had nothing to do with me, and that they are both happier now. Told with humor and sensitivity, this child's feelings and concerns echo those of most children of divorce. The activity of turning the book around to find solutions reinforces the message that children must take responsibility for their own well-being. This book will help facilitate the recognition of potential problems and stimulate practical solutions for the benefit of the entire family.

Please Come Home by Doris Sanford. Multnomah Press, Sisters, OR. 1985. Illustrated. 16 pp.
This book describes a young girl's struggle to cope when her father leaves following her parents' separation. She is plagued with feeling that the divorce is her fault and that no one understands her. But Teddy Bear, representing her inner self, teaches the young narrator to comfort herself and to understand why she is not responsible for the divorce. In the end, she prevails in her struggle to feel good about herself again. A lovely illustrated book for children aged 4 to 8.

Where Has Daddy Gone? by Trudy Osman. Ideal Publishing Co., Nashville, TN. 1989. Illustrated. 15 pp.

This simple story is "told" from the point of view of a young boy whose parents are separated and describes the painful feelings of sadness and longing that children experience when one parent moves out of the house. The story ends on a hopeful note with the boy continuing his relationships with his father and his mother with whom he stays as she begins to resume a satisfying life. When read with a parent or therapist, this beautifully illustrated book will evoke memories, questions and feelings about divorce for further discussion and clarification.

Why Are We Getting a Divorce? by Peter Mayle. Harmony Books, Crown Publishers, New York, NY. 1988. Illustrated. 28 pp.

This book's whimsical illustrations match the sense of humor the author brings to his sensitive treatment of this difficult topic. This book is appropriate for latency-aged children and young teens. It presents divorce as a fact of life and something that children can cope with although it is unpleasant. Children are encouraged to look at some of the positive aspects of living separately with each parent and are helped to understand that custodial arrangements are not based on the amount of love either parent has for the child. It also encourages children to avoid blaming either parent, to help more with household chores and to talk with parents about concerns and worries.

Organizations and Programs Related to Child Custody

Organizations
Academy of Family Mediators
1500 South Highway 100, Suite 355
Golden Valley, Minnesota 55416
(612) 525-8670
This group is a non-profit educational organization founded in 1981 to support professional and public mediation education. The Academy continues to develop and refine criteria for mediator training, education and ethical practice. General membership is $90.00 and includes quarterly newsletter Mediation News and quarterly journal Mediation Quarterly and discounted Academy conference registration. Practitioner membership is $120.00 and includes all of the general membership benefits in addition to listing in the Academy's National Referral Service. Other services include referral lists for clients, bookstore with an extensive collection of books for all audiences concerned with divorce, educational videotapes for sale, and sponsorship of Academy of Family Mediator-approved training.

American Association of Marriage and Family Therapists (AAMFT)
110 17th St. NW, 10th Floor
Washington, DC 20036
(202) 452-0109
Toll-Free Referral Service: 1-800-374-2638
Founded in 1942, this is a professional organization for the field of marriage and family therapy. AAMFT represents the professional interests of marriage and family therapists and facilitates research and the ongoing development of theory and educational programs. It develops standards for the training and practice of marriage and family therapy and sponsors local chapters.

Publications include Journal of Marital and Family Therapy, Family Therapy News, brochures and pamphlets on a variety of topics. Services include a toll-free referral service, which will send a list of qualified marriage and family therapists listed within the requested zip code area and the Consumer's Guide to Marriage and Family Therapy upon request.

Also, The AAMFT Research and Education Foundation which administers the following programs: The Family Impact Seminar, a monthly family policy seminar for staff from the U.S. Congress and Federal agencies; The Head Start Volunteer Initiative which recruits AAMFT members to consult with local Head Start agencies on such issues as working more effectively with families; and the "Listening to Families" videotape series, which is funded by the U.S. Department of Education and demonstrates family-centered approaches for human services providers; hosts an Annual National Conference and Summer Institutes.

Society of Professionals in Dispute Resolution
815 15th St. NW, Suite 530
Washington, DC 20005
(202) 783-7277
This is a membership organization for arbitrators and/or mediators in dispute resolution. The different membership levels range from $80.00 to $100.00 in cost. The organization provides a quarterly newsletter, *Society of Professionals in Dispute Resolution News*, publications, a Membership Directory, and ways for members to network. It holds an annual conference.

Programs
The Center for the Family
Director: Cheryl VanderWaal, M.S.W.
5725 Paradise Drive
Building B, Suite 300
Corda Madera, California 94925
(415) 924-5750

This is a nonprofit agency begun in 1980 by Dr. Judith Wallerstein, now its Senior Consultant, in order to help children of divorce and their families. Its ongoing programs include providing affordable clinical, preventative, educational and mediational services to over 350 families a year; research on divorce and those factors which contribute negatively and positively to the impact on children; training mental health practitioners, clergy, attorneys, judges, pediatricians, and educators who work with disrupted families; educating the public as to the best ways to cope with divorce; and working with social policy makers on matters concerning divorce and related issues.

Center for Mediation and Law
Director: Gary J. Friedman, J.D.
34 Forrest Street
Mill Valley, California 94941
(415) 383-1300

Provides private mediation and legal services as well as training in mediation. This group is primarily focused on lawyers as mediators.

Divorce Words and What They Mean

For many children, divorce and custody arrangements often bring confusing changes to their lives. Here is a list of words that children might hear during this time of change, with definitions they can easily understand.

Alimony - The money that one parent—usually the dad—pays the other parent after a divorce.

Alternating custody - When a child lives with one parent for a period of time and the other parent for another period of time.

"Broken home" - An old-fashioned term for families in which parents have divorced or separated. Few people use this expression anymore because in divorce nothing really "breaks."

Child custody - There are two types of custody. One has to do with decision-making power, such as where a child will go to school, and the other refers to the responsibility for the physical care and living arrangements of a child.

Child support - The money that one parent—usually the dad—pays the other parent to help take care of their children.

Court of law - A place where lawyers and judges work with parents to decide what's best for their children.

Custody arrangements - Rules about which parent is responsible for taking care of a child. Usually both parents help make important decisions like where the children will live and go to school, but the parent with custody has the final say.

Divorce - A process that married people go through to legally end a marriage.

Divorce decree - The document that says two people are no longer married.

Family therapist/psychiatrist/psychologist/social worker - A person who helps people sort things out when they're having problems.

Grounds for divorce - The legal reasons people get divorced.

Guardian - A relative, close friend or adult other than the parent who has custody of a child.

Judge - A person whose job is to help make fair decisions about a divorce.

Lawyer - A person whose job is to help parents understand the laws or rules about divorce. The lawyer can also represent children or parents in court.

Mediation - When parents try to agree on things about their divorce by working together rather than against each other. When they do this, they get another grownup called a mediator to help them. They still need to get a judge to write it all down. Many parents are happiest when they can work out their divorce in a friendly way.

Reconciliation - When parents who are separated decide to live together again.

Shared custody - When parents share equally in the responsibility of taking care of their children even though they are divorced.

Sole custody - When one parent cares for a child almost all of the time.

Visitation arrangements - Rules about when children will stay with each of their parents. There are many different kinds of arrangements that work for different families.

CHAPTER 4

Childhood and
Adolescent Depression:
The Internal Toll of Emotional Pain

"Steven was an 11-year-old child who showed signs of change in his behavior and feelings for at least one year before being seen by a psychiatrist. [Steven had] recurring thoughts that he wished he were dead and...plans to kill himself by either jumping off a roof or by hanging himself. He had withdrawn increasingly from friends and complained about being teased by his peers. Steven wished that he did not have to attend school and had been observed on several occasions to be crying in school. His academic work deteriorated from his previous outstanding performance to an average level of school achievement. Steven felt inadequate in his scholastic work and described feeling tired when he tried to complete homework. He had trouble falling asleep because he had dreadful thoughts of the next year when he would enter a different junior high school."
(*From* The Suicidal Child *by Cynthia Pfeffer, 1989, p.101*)

"Laura's depression deepened. And as it did, she became more defiant. She talked back to her teachers, cut classes, and refused to do her class work. After she got into a serious fight she was expelled. She ran away from home...and lived at a friend's house. Her friend's mother gave her drugs and alcohol...to get more money Laura stole from department stores—mostly clothing that she sold to friends. She was caught, put on probation, and sent home to her parents. She ran away again."
(*From* Understanding and Preventing Teen Suicide *by W. Colman, 1990, p.80*)

In these trying times there is no end of social problems and stressors that add to the burden of the family and the child. Increasingly, children are left on their own for longer periods of time, they are exposed to more violence both on television and in their communities, and they are exposed to drugs and alcohol. Their economic future may often seem bleak. And this listing represents only the external social conditions children must cope with. Add to this the stresses of normal growth and development and the conflicts that arise in families, and divorce, and it becomes apparent that there are many potentially negative and depressogenic experiences in the average child's environment.

Reynolds (1990) notes, "With approximately one out of six youngsters seen in psychiatric settings having a formal diagnosis of a depressive disorder, it is reasonable to view depression as one of the most prevalent and pervasive forms of psychopathology in this age group (children under 18 years)." Oster and Caro (1990) write, "Suicide has become the second leading cause of death for 15- to 24-year-olds." And yet only 30 years ago the mental health profession was not convinced that children have the developmental capacity to have depression. Now there are studies that indicate that depression is essentially the same for children as for adults, although its expression may be influenced by the developmental level of the child.

Depression may be understood as a syndrome, a collection of cognitions, emotions, and behaviors that together comprise a deleterious state of existence, at times so unbearable that it becomes deadly. There are many different etiological models of depression including psychoanalytic models, cognitive-behavioral models and family therapy models. There are also physiological and genetic contributions to be considered. In this chapter we focus on the cognitive-behavioral models and the treatment strategies which have been generated from these models. We interview Kevin Stark, Ph.D. of the University of Texas who discusses childhood depression and his work with children in different treatment settings. We also talk with Peter Lewinsohn, Ph.D. about The Oregon Adolescent Depression Research Project, his Integrative Model of Depression, and his and his colleagues' intervention for high school students, the Adolescent Coping with Depression Course.

Other featured topics include the observation of the play of depressed children, behavior indicators of possible depression, the assessment of suicidal risk in adolescents, and considerations of hospitalization for suicidal children. Our regular departments detail assessment tools, research findings, relevant periodicals, resources, journal articles and organizations related to childhood depression and suicide.

Depression *can* be effectively treated, and the evidence is that the earlier the intervention, the better the chance of avoiding relapse and the better the outcome for the child. We hope this chapter will stimulate new ideas and perhaps the creation of more intervention programs to help the increasing numbers of children who are coping with the overwhelming burden of depression.

–The Editors

Developmental Aspects of Childhood Depression: A Brief Review

by Laura Slap-Shelton, Psy.D.

Until fairly recently it was believed that children did not suffer from depression. Since the 1960s (Sandler and Joffee, 1965), increasing attention has been given to the appearance of depression in children. The 1970s and 1980s witnessed a dramatic increase in the study of childhood depression. Rawson and Tabb (1993) suggest three reasons for this development: 1) improved diagnosis and treatment of mood disorders in the adult population; 2) improved standardization of diagnosis standards for depression for children and adults; and 3) the development of many new assessment instruments for childhood depression, making both identification and evaluation of treatments possible. Despite these advances much remains to be understood about the developmental patterns of childhood depression.

Research has shown that childhood and adolescent depression is essentially the same as adult depression, although it may manifest itself somewhat differently depending on the age of the child (Reynolds, 1990; Hodges and Siegel, 1985; Kovacs and Paulauskas, 1984). What appears to be the same is the presence of many of the same symptoms across all age ranges. Thus the diagnostic criteria of the DSMIII-R for Major Depression and Dysthymia have held as valid for identifying depressed children. These DSMIII-R criteria (American Psychiatric Association, 1987) are listed in the accompanying chart on page 127.

Achenbach and Edelbrock (1983) found different clusters of depression symptoms in different age ranges with variations across sex. Children ages six through 12 were found to have a higher incidence of psychosomatic complaints and enuresis at the onset of their depression with the more adult-like symptoms of dysphoria, sleep disturbance and irritability following later. In the 12- to 16-year age group, the children have symptoms such as inability to tolerate routine, social withdrawal, temper tantrums, running away, and stealing (Achenbach and Edelbrock, 1983; Semrud-Clikeman, 1991).

Another finding was that in boys ages six to 11 suicidal talk was associated with other symptoms of depression while it was not for boys ages four to five. For girls ages six to 11 anxiety and feelings of persecution were associated with symptoms of depression. At ages four through five these factors did not appear as part of a depression factor for girls (Achenback and Edelbrock, 1983 in Kazdin, 1990). These behavioral signs that appear to be additional to the DSMIII-R diagnostic criteria are considered to be secondary reactions to depression (Lesse, 1983 in Semrud-Clikeman, 1991).

In another study hypersomnia was found to distinguish between age groups of depressed children with adolescents being significantly more likely to experience hypersomnia than children ages eight to 11 (Mitchell, McCauley et. al. 1988, Kovacs and Gastonis, 1989).

Prevalence rates for childhood depression also vary with age, with children ages one to six having significantly lower prevalence rates of major depression than children ages nine to 12 (Kashania, Ray, and Carlson, 1984 in Kazdin, 1990; Lefkowitz and Tesiny, 1985). Some studies show that once puberty begins the prevalence for depression increases for both boys and girls, but is greater for girls (Kazdin, 1990; Reynolds, 1985; Rutter et. al., 1970 in Kazdin, 1990). Adolescent girls have also been found to have more severe depressions than adolescent boys, and this difference increases with increasing age (Kandel and Davis, 1982 in Kazdin, 1990).

However, not all studies support these findings. For example, Lewinsohn et. al. (Lewinsohn, Hops, Roberts, et. al., 1993) did not find evidence that the difference in occurrence of depression in male and female adolescents increased with age for adolescents ages 14 to 18, although they did find greater severity of symptoms reported by female adolescents. They suggest that it will be important to find the point in time at which females begin to demonstrate greater depression than males. Lewinsohn et. al. (1993) also did not find evidence for an increase in the prevalence of depression for ages 14 to 18, suggesting that prevalence increases may level off in mid-adolescence.

Another parallel between adult depression and childhood depression has been shown in studies of the relationship between childhood depression and childhood suicidality. In her review of the literature, Pfeffer (1986) indicates that just as for adults, hopelessness is a major factor associated with suicidality in children and that this factor has a stronger correlation with suicidality than other depressive symptoms.

Kovacs (1989) makes the important point that whatever the effect of developmental stage on the manifestation of depression, depression almost always takes a toll on the ongoing developmental processes of the child. Thus she points out that major depression in children and adolescents slows their cognitive growth and in some areas appears to interfere with developmentally appropriate acquisition of verbal skills (Kovacs and Gastonis, 1988 in Kovacs, 1989). Decline in academic performance has been shown in adolescents by Bashir, Russell, and Johnson (1987 in Kovacs, 1989). Kovacs (1989) notes the need for studies of the impact of childhood depression on the development of social-competencies. Kazdin et. al. (1985a) provide evidence to indicate that depressed children have a lower level of social interaction and a lower level of nonverbal expressiveness.

As reduced social competency has been found to be associated with depression in childhood, social skills training is often included in cognitive-behavioral treatment of childhood depression. This raises the etiological question of which comes first, lack of social skills or affective interference in learning social skills. Stark (see interview in this chapter) indicates that depressed children often know what to do but don't do it because of depressogenic thinking and expectation.

Considerations such as these bring into light the importance of understanding the developmental level of the child being treated for depression. For example, Stark notes that for children, cognitive restructuring is more difficult than for adults. He has included an individual therapy treatment component in his larger treatment model to help with this aspect of the therapy. Stark (1987) noted that children had difficulty with self-monitoring when required to monitor over longer periods of time (Kendall, et. al., 1992). With young children it is important to know what behaviors are developmentally expectable and/or related to the temperament of the child so as not to over-diagnose or attempt to cure a child of normal development. When treating all children it is important to take into account the family and social environment, evaluating the level of cognitive and emotional resources the child has to cope with possibly aversive situations.

Finally, studies seem to suggest that while tricyclic antidepressants have been found useful in the treatment of both children and adults, the effectiveness of these medications (particularly Imipramine) in adolescents is not as great (Ryan, et. al. 1986, in Kazdin, 1990). Ryan et. al. (1986) suggest that their reduced effectiveness may be due to the presence of adolescent levels of sex hormones. The side effects of antidepressant medications are different in children than in adults and need to be carefully monitored.

While there are no clear-cut developmental syndromes of depression, there are developmental differences in the manifestation of depression in children and adolescents. These are manifested in symptom clusters, prevalence at different ages, and differences in severity across sex in adolescence. There is evidence that depression serves to alter the developmental course of children in its effects on social interaction and school performance. Understanding of developmental factors is vital in the treatment of childhood and adolescent depression.

Sources: Achenbach, L., Edelbrock, C. (1983) Manual for the child behavior checklist and revised child behavior profile. Burlington, VT: University Associates in Psychiatry. Hodges, K. and Siegel, L. (1985) Depression in children and adolescents. In Beckham, E. and Leber, W. (Eds.) *Handbook of Depression.* Homewood, IL: Dorsey Press. Kashani, J., Ray, J., and Carlson, G. (1984) Depression and depression-like states in preschool-age children in a child development unit. *American Journal of Psychiatry.* 141:pp.1397-1402. Kazdin, A., Esvedlt-Dawson, K. et. al. (1985a) Assessment of overt behavior and childhood depression among psychiatrically disturbed children. *Journal of Consulting and Clinical Psychology.* 53:pp.201-210. Kazdin, A. (1990) Childhood depression. *Journal of Child Psychology and Psychiatry.* 31(1):pp.121-160. Kendall, P., Kortlander, E., Chansky, T., and Brady, E. (1992). Comorbidity of anxiety and depression in youth: Treatment implications. *Journal of Consulting and Clinical Psychology.* 60(6):pp. 869-880. Kovacs, M. (1989) Affective disorders in children and adolescents. *American Psychologist.* 44(2):pp.209-215. Kovacs, M., Gastonis, C. (1989) Stability and change in childhood-onset depressive disorders: longitudinal course as a diagnostic validator. In Robins, L. and Barret, J. (Eds.), The validity of psychiatric diagnosis. pp.57-73. Kovacs, M. and Paulauskas, S. (1984) Developmental stage and the expression of depressive disorders in children: An empirical review. In Cicchetti, D. and Schneider-Rosen, K. (Eds.) *Childhood Depression: New Directions for Child Development.* San Francisco, CA: Jossey Bass. Lefkowitz, M. and Tesiny, P. (1985) Depression in children: prevalence and correlates. *Journal of Consulting and Clinical Psychology.* 53,pp.647-656. Lewinsohn, P.,Hops, H., Roberts, R. et. al. (1993) Adolescent psychopathology: I. Prevalence and incidence of depression and other DSMIII-R disorders in high school students. *Journal of Abnormal Psychology.* 102(1):pp.133-144. Mitchell, J., McCauley, E., Burke, P., and Moss, S. (1988) Phenomenology of depression in children and adolescents. *Journal of the American Academy of Child and Adolescent Psychiatry.* 27:pp.12-20. Pfeffer, C. (1986) *The Suicidal Child.* New York: Guilford Press. pp.68-72. Rawson, H. and Tabb, L. (1993) Effects of therapeutic intervention on childhood depression. *Child and Adolescent Social Work Journal.* 10(1):pp.39-52. Reynolds, W. (1990) Depression in children and adolescents: Nature, diagnosis, assessment, and treatment. *School Psychology Review.* 19(2):pp.158-173. Ryan, N., Puig-Antich, J. et. al. (1986) Imipramine in adolescent major depression: plasma level and clinical response. *Acta Psychiatrica Scandinavia,* 73, pp.275-288. Semrud-Clikeman, M. and Hynd, G. (1991) Review of issues and measures in childhood depression. *School Psychology International.* 12:pp.275-298. Stark, K., Reynolds, W., and Kaslow, J. (1987) A comparison of the relative efficacy of self-control therapy and behavioral problem-solving therapy for depression in children. *Journal of Abnormal Child Psychology.* 15:pp.91-113.

Indicators of Depression/Dysthymia

Symptoms	Major Depression	Dysthymia
Depressed or irritable mood	Yes	Yes
Marked diminishment of pleasure in daily activities	Yes	No
Significant weight loss or weight gain	Yes	Yes, but may be milder when not dieting
Insomnia or hypersomnia on a nearly daily basis	Yes	Yes
Psychomotor retardation or agitation on an almost daily basis	Yes	No
Fatigue or loss of energy on an almost daily basis	Yes	No
Feelings of worthlessness and/or excessive guilt on an almost daily basis	Yes	Low self-esteem
Decreased concentration, indecisiveness	Yes	Yes
Recurrent thoughts of death and/or suicidality	Yes	No, but feelings of hopelessness

(**Source:** American Psychiatric Association, DSMIII-R, (1987) pp.128-129; p.136)

An Interview with...
Kevin Stark, Ph.D.

Kevin Stark, Ph.D. has devoted his career to the study of childhood depression. Beginning with his important work at the University of Wisconsin he has developed and evaluated innovative treatment programs addressing the different aspects of depression. In this interview he shares his experience and some of the treatment tools he has developed to help children improve social and self-monitoring skills, identify and tolerate their emotions, and change their depressogenic thinking patterns. Dr. Stark demonstrates his keen understanding and feeling for depressed children and shows how the flexible application of cognitive and behavioral treatments can help to ameliorate their depression.

Laura Slap-Shelton, Psy.D.: *How did you come to focus your work on depression in children?*

Kevin Stark, Ph.D.: I did my dissertation on the treatment of depressed children in graduate school at the University of Wisconsin in 1983. My work then represented the second group treatment outcome study of depression in children. We tried to create a children's version of Lynn Rehm's self-control treatment program for depressed adults. I was fortunate at the time to have as my advisor Bill Reynolds, who had been doing research on childhood depression for a long time, and Nadine Kaslov who had been running Rehm's treatment groups for depressed adults at the University. Also, I had been studying Phil Kendall's treatment program for impulsive ADHD children and that helped me to translate the adult self-control program into a children's program.

LS-S.: *In what settings are you working at present?*

KS: I'm working with depressed children in a day treatment center and a residential treatment program. We've developed a milieu program along with treatment groups and individual therapy programs. We are trying to influence the family therapy that is provided as part of the residential treatment program, and hoping to be invited to run parent training groups. I've submitted a grant proposal to get back into running the groups in the schools, but traditionally my research has been conducted in the schools. In the future I would like to evaluate a continuum of care for the treatment of depressed kids—from school-based to the extreme of residential treatment, as well as following children from residential treatment back to the schools.

LS-S: *The terms "internalizing disorder" and "externalizing disorder" appear to have been developed fairly recently to help differentiate children with affective disorders from those with conduct and other types of disorders. Could you explain these terms?*

KS: Externalizing disorders are disorders where the child's symptoms are overt, and typically the child has a problem with acting out. The typical disorders in this group are ADHD, Conduct Disorder, and Oppositional Defiant Disorder. Internalizing disorders are disorders that are more subjectively experienced and less obvious to someone else, like depression and anxiety.

LS-S: *In terms of screening children for problems it would be easier to identify the children with externalizing disorders than those with internalizing disorders.*

KS: Yes. We find that the kids with internalizing disorders are not recognized in the schools as having a significant psychological problem. They're going unidentified. Often they're the kids who are very quiet, compliant, and don't cause any trouble. They really try extremely hard to be well-behaved and so they just go unnoticed.

LS-S: *Do you recommend group screenings for children in school to help with this problem?*

KS: I guess that would be ideal, but unfortunately schools don't have adequate counseling or psychological resources. If one were to screen children in grades four through seven s/he would end up with about five percent of the children having a diagnosable disorder.

LS-S: *And then you'd have to treat them.*

KS: Yes, and then the prevalence would increase from there. It actually increases with age. So in middle school and high school there would be even more identified children in need of treatment.

LS-S: *What signs should teachers be aware of in terms of identifying a child struggling with depression?*

KS: They need to watch for marked change in the child's mood and behavior, such as the child becoming suddenly sad and/or angry, withdrawn and dependent, with new complaints of difficulty concentrating, looking tired, sleepy, and wanting to go to the nurse's office.

LS-S: *The incidence rates for childhood depression are very high. Has it always been this way or are children more depressed now than they used to be?*

KS: I think that depression in children is increasing. I think it's due to greater stress in general through society and the new unavailability of parents. Parents are not only less able to provide emotional support for their children, but they simply don't have the time needed to teach their children how to cope with various difficulties in life. They're too busy with work. They come home and have to perform household duties. By the time they are done, the children are off to bed, and there's been no quality time spent with them.

In addition, children are experiencing more trauma now, especially violence-related trauma. We are finding a very high rate of abuse among kids who are depressed. Another problem is that children are not having the same kind of recreational and social experiences that we did. They're restricted to having to stay in the house after coming home from school, either because both parents are working or because it's simply not safe to go outside.

Quite a few young teens are experiencing this restriction of activity, along with being required to serve as a parental figure for their younger siblings. Their lives revolve around going to school and babysitting and that's it. They cannot get out of the house and they don't know how to parent. The parents either don't know how to parent or haven't been involved enough with their children because of a lack of time. This leaves the young teen alone to cope with poorly-disciplined younger children and it creates a negative emotional atmosphere which reverberates throughout the entire family. It's really sad.

LS-S: *When you work with the parents of children in this type of situation are they receptive to making changes?*

KS: They are usually genuinely concerned and want to make things better, but they're still limited by practical constraints such as not being able to afford a babysitter, having to work on Saturdays, not being able to leave work earlier, etc. They end up feeling stuck.

LS-S: *What do you do to help these families?*

KS: We try to do problem solving to identify relatives and/or neighbors who could help out, or with whom these parents can arrange babysitting exchanges. We like to try to load Saturday and Sunday with recreational activities for the children. We try to build in alternatives like allowing certain trusted friends to come over while the parents aren't there, more time allowed on the phone with their friends, and mini-vacations from babysitting duties. When possible, we help the parents to shift their work schedules so that they can take more of the child care responsibilities.

We help the parents with their parenting skills so that when they are home they do a good job and the younger siblings learn to be responsible and disciplined. We have the parents support the oldest child in his/her babysitting role by making it clear to the siblings that he or she is an authority when the parents are out and that they must listen to what he or she tells them. Finally, we try to identify safe recreational activities outside of the home where the babysitting child and the siblings can go. We try to build in as many supervised after-school activities as possible so the children can have safe social/recreational activities before having to come home.

LS-S: *Is working with the depressed child's environment in this way enough to relieve the child or do you also work with the child on an individual basis?*

KS: We usually also work with the depressed child individually because in most cases that child has begun to feel hopeless, angry and bitter. They often are engaged in acting out and attention-getting behaviors. We help them to develop better ways of coping with their situation and teach them how to express anger in more appropriate ways.

LS-S: *What theoretical model or models do you use when creating your treatment programs?*

KS: We use a very comprehensive cognitive and behavioral model that recognizes the mutual and reciprocal impact of cognitive, behavioral, affective and biological variables in the development of depressive disorders. In our treatment programs we focus most on the cognitive component, and draw on the work of Aaron Beck. We have found that the depressive cognitive triad (negative view of self, world and future)is associated with depressive disorders in children, and that we can differentiate depressed from anxious children based on their cognitive triad ratings.

We have also found that the automatic thoughts of depressed children are negative in nature. Their information processing is characterized by a negative distortion rather than by an actual deficit in information processing as we see in the externalizing disorders. An example would be the depressed 14-year-old boy who in seventh grade takes the SAT examination for Duke's gifted program, gets remarkably good scores, and yet still says that he's stupid. It's clear that he is not stupid but he still perceives himself as being inadequate.

LS-S: *What models influence the behavioral components of your treatment programs?*

KS: Behaviorally we are interested in social skill disturbances. We've evaluated Coyne's and Lewinsohn's models and have found support for both in that depressed children do experience social skill deficits as seen in their self-ratings and in teacher ratings. The deficit is not in lack of knowledge about social skills. They know what is appropriate and what is not appropriate. Their problem is that they know what to do, but they don't do it, or they know what not to do, but they do it anyway.

We found that this problem is linked to depressed children's cognitions about social interactions. In other words we found that these children often expect to be rejected or have some other negative output occur upon entry into social situations. They report being flooded with negative thoughts and experience heightened physical aversive arousal in social situations. So it seems that there's a real insidious cycle in which the children expect to have a negative outcome occur, react in an angry withdrawn style, and are flooded with negative thoughts and aversive arousal which confirms their expectations that the social situation is not going to work out well for them. It just keeps going around and around. In the meantime their behavior elicits negative feedback from others or serves to keep others at a distance.

LS-S: *What are the components of the groups you run for depressed children?*

KS: The treatment program with which we are currently experimenting involves running both individual and group therapy for depressed early adolescents. We have found that the more complex work of cognitive restructuring is best done individually because unlike in adults where it is a relatively easy process, it is very difficult for children and adolescents. We have also found that depressed early adolescents often have trouble relating to groups initially as they tend to be somewhat egocentric in their concerns. So we work on cognitive restructuring individually and then use the groups as a place to practice and reinforce the cognitive shifts achieved in individual therapy, as well as a place to build better interpersonal skills.

We typically begin with an "Affective Education Group" where the children learn to identify the behavioral, cognitive, and emotional cues to different emotions, and to recognize that there's a gradation of emotions in that things aren't always absolutely awful or absolutely great. We also use these groups to develop a sense of cohesion and trust. We use a lot of games that teach kids about emotions and the relationships between thoughts, feelings, and behavior, and in this context we have a lot of fun.

LS-S: *What kind of games do you use?*

KS: "Emotion Vocabulary" is one. In this game we put the names of emotions on cards and talk about how that emotion feels, how a person with that emotion would act, and when the last time was that the child felt that emotion. We then add in what the person with that emotion might be thinking. Then we move on to "Emotional Charades," "Emotional Pictionary," and "Emotional Statues." In the last of these one of the children is the clay and another child is the sculptor, and the sculptor has to shape the particular emotion on the other child. We have the kids play "Emotional Password" with teams, and "Emotional Expression," in which the children are asked to orally depict an emotion by making noises and not using words. These games are a great way to build trust and help the children become comfortable with disclosure, which are two basic group therapy skills.

LS-S: *What other group or groups do you run?*

KS: We have problem-solving groups where the children learn problem-solving skills and how to apply them to interpersonal as well as personal problems.

LS-S: *Do the children bring up their own situations in these groups?*

KS: Usually we have to start with contrived situations on cards for example, and once the kids have become more comfortable, we can usually have them bring in their own problems. If we're in the hospital we find out about problem situations the children are coping with from the staff. We also have a social skills group where the emphasis is on the acquisition of specific social skills with lots of role playing. We watch for what is going on interpersonally in the group and work with that.

LS-S: *What do you do with the families of the children in your current program?*

KS: We keep the families abreast of what's going on in the individual and group work with the children. They're getting the same treatment in in both situations plus they're learning how to use cognitive restructuring. The parents are taught how they can help their children acquire and master these skills. We teach family members conflict resolution to reduce the amount of anger and hostility in the household. We teach all family members how to use a more positive style of managing one another's behavior. We teach communication skills and we look for the structural elements in the family system which have led to the development of the child's depressogenic schemata and are currently maintaining the child's depression. We work hard at changing the things in the family that lead to the depressive thinking.

LS-S: *You mentioned that you're also doing some milieu therapy in the residential setting.*

KS: Yes. We try to create a solution-oriented environment, one that's preventative in nature, and also positive and problem-solving oriented. The milieu is designed to help the children learn to use problem-solving and to reinforce their efforts to apply problem-solving and other skills that are being taught in their therapies. It's a real positive environment.

LS-S: *How do you reinforce the children's use of new skills?*

KS: The children and staff have point sheets that have a preponderance of positive categories. The staff are taught to watch for appropriate and positive behaviors and to extinguish negative behaviors rather than in the typical program that is more reactive to negative behaviors. They socially reinforce appropriate behavior on a continual basis. For example they literally call out loud positives like, "Mark, I really like the way you're sitting there" or "John, that was an excellent job of asking for what you want."

Whenever an interpersonal conflict arises or any other problem or disturbance occurs in the milieu, problem solving is used to arrive at a solution. The staff teaches the entire process of problem solving: identifying the problem, generating possible solutions, consequential thinking, and implementation and monitoring the results of the solution. It's a systematic approach. We try to integrate what's happening in the family into the point system at the hospital through home notes and parent ratings of the child's behavior.

LS-S: *What purpose do the point sheets serve?*

KS: The children and staff both carry the point sheets so that the children are rating themselves at the same time as the staff. After the children achieve a certain level of agreement with staff, the staff stop carrying the sheets and the children become responsible for keeping track of their own points. If they continue to show a high level of improvement they switch to the identification of more personal therapeutic goals that they work toward. So we use this traditional point system to not just manage behavior, but to encourage kids to use and develop appropriate coping and social skills and to teach them how to monitor and evaluate their own behavior.

- Focus on Programs -
The Oregon Adolescent Depression Research Project

The Child Therapy News *was fortunate to have had the opportunity to talk with Peter Lewinsohn, Ph.D., one of the foremost researchers in the field of depression. He is the creator of the Social Learning model of depression (Lewinsohn and Shaw, 1969; Lewinsohn, Youngren, and Grosscup, 1979; Lewinsohn and Shaffer, 1971) which has served to stimulate much research and new models of treatment for the illness. Rather than restrict his interests to adults, Dr. Lewinsohn has delved into the study of adolescent depression with thoroughness and compassion.*

The Social Learning model of depression is derived from behavioral psychology theory. The model states that people become depressed when they have more negative than positive reinforcers from the environment. Over the years Dr. Lewinsohn and his colleagues have created the Integrative Model of Depression (Lewinsohn, Hoberman, Teri, and Hautzinger, 1985). This model takes into account the many variables that may cause and also lead to the treatment of depression. In this model antecedent "depression evoking events" occur which initiate a depressive episode to the extent that they interrupt positive interactions with the environment. The shift to less rewarding interaction patterns leads to a corresponding shift to negative affect which further interrupts the individual's ability to effectively and positively interact with the environment.

The second part of the model proposes that the inability to reverse the shift from positive to negative reinforcement increases the adolescent's state of self-awareness, making them prone to an increase in self-criticism, self-attribution for negative events, increased negative affect and behavioral withdrawal. The individual's normal protective, self-enhancing cognitive schema is disrupted and the individual experiences him or herself as failing to cope as effectively as s/he had before.

This cycle builds on itself, leading to a locked-in state of dysphoria and increased self-awareness, which maintain the depressive state (Clarke, G., Lewinsohn, P., and Hops, H., 1990). This model suggests that there are many factors which may lead to a depression, and that there are also different avenues of intervention which may be used to break the cycle and shift the individual back toward a positive interaction with the environment.

In the following interview Dr. Lewinsohn describes his research and treatment model and its implementation. He and his colleagues have made their treatment program available to other psychologists in the form of two manuals, one for running the adolescent groups, and one for running the parent groups, both of which comprise the Adolescent Coping with Depression Course.

Laura Slap-Shelton, Psy.D.: *Please describe the Oregon Research Institute (ORI) and the Oregon Adolescent Depression Project (OADP).*

Peter Lewinsohn, Ph.D.: The Oregon Research Institute is a not-for-profit research organization primarily involved with research into applied psychology. It was established in the early 60s and we now have approximately 30 research scientists. The projects supported by the Institute include research into depression, smoking, substance abuse, and community outreach to teach parenting skills. The Oregon Adolescent Depression Project is the title we have been using to distinguish our work from the other ORI projects.

LS-S: *Approximately how many high schools does the OADP work with in its research projects?*

PL: We have had two major projects over the years. One is the treatment outcome study in which we solicit referrals from any high school in the Eugene area, and we have done work in Portland also. We will take any adolescent and are interested in all of the high schools for this project. We also have done a large epidemiological study which involved 1,700 high school students, and in this study we had nine participating high schools.

LS-S: *Is the community interested in and responsive to the research that you are doing?*

PL: Yes, very, especially the high school counselors. The Public Mental Health Clinic here does not have the funding necessary to treat all of the people who need therapy but cannot afford the usual fee-for-service rates. We offer something that is not necessarily available in the community and it is free of charge.

LS-S: *How are the school counselors making use of your research findings and treatment programs?*

PL: My colleague Dr. Gregory Clarke has been using a modified version of our treatment program as an intervention tool for high schools. He presents a lecture on depression and another on suicide. As part of his presentation he administers a self-report depression inventory, telling the students that these are the symptoms of depression and they can find out if they are depressed. The students who report significantly elevated scores are offered a diagnostic interview, and if determined to have a clinical depression, are referred for treatment. For students who don't meet the full criteria for a diagnosis of depression, but who report enough symptoms to be at risk for depression we offer a course we call "Coping with Stress" as part of the school's curriculum.

LS-S: *That's wonderful. How has it worked?*

PL: Dr. Clarke has shown it to be reasonably successful. Our work always incorporates a very large outreach component because depressed kids don't usually get treatment. They don't seek it themselves and the parents don't necessarily know how depressed their children are. So there are a lot of depressed kids who don't get treatment, but when you ask them about how they are feeling they're quite willing to tell you and they are willing to participate if you have something useful to offer.

LS-S: *Are there studies that show that this kind of intervention for adolescents helps to prevents relapse in adulthood?*

PL: That was part of the design of our study. The treatment takes six to eight weeks, and then we follow people for two years post-treatment. During the follow-up period we have designed what we call booster sessions. We found that a relatively small portion of our kids relapse—approximately twenty to thirty percent, and it's hard to improve on that. We don't completely understand the reason, but the adolescents do not seem to relapse at the same high rates, often as much as 50 percent, that adults do.

LS-S: *How does your treatment work?*

PL: We call our treatment a cognitive behavioral intervention, and our program is called Coping with Depression. We use an educational format involving six to eight youngsters. Rather than therapists, we call ourselves leaders. The idea is that we teach people skills that they can use to over-come their depression. The format is highly structured, much like a regular high school class.

LS-S: *What are the components of your training program?*

PL: There are four main components. One component which others would call social skills we label "friendly skills." They include how to get along with people, and how to be nice to others and expect that they will be nice in turn. The second component is constructive thinking. Third, we work on identifying activities that will help reduce their depression, and fourth, we teach relaxation skills.

Another part of the program involves teaching conflict resolution skills with the parents. That's the part that is unique about our approach to adolescents. We try to help them and their parents to negotiate the kinds of conflicts that always exist between adolescents and parents—how late they can stay out, whether they can have the car, how much money they will get, chores, etc.

LS-S: *Are the parents directly involved in this part of the program?*

PL: Yes. We have a parent course. We see the kids twice a week for two hours each time and the parents once a week for two hours. Our goal is twofold. First, we want to make sure that the parents understand what we are teaching the kids so that they can support it, and the second is to give them conflict resolution skills training. We don't treat the parents as patients, and we do not attempt to diagnose them or identify their specific role in their child's problems. Our goal is to give them skills which will enable them to be as helpful as they can to their kids.

LS-S: *How does your social learning model of depression fit in with the treatment program?*

PL: We say that depression is a "life" problem, in that the quality of our interactions with our environment becomes exceptionally negative when we become depressed. We emphasize the quality of the person's interaction with his/her environment: how many good things and how many bad things happen, and how this effects his/her actions, thoughts, and feelings.

We use a tripartite model in which we view actions, thoughts, and feelings as influencing each other. We offer ways to intervene at each of these three levels. Treatment may occur by identifying problems in one area and working on changing those. This will influence the other areas. We teach more than any one person can use or need and hope that the person will find at least one way of dealing with depression that works for them. It's a social learning model. You learn how to become depressed, so you can learn to be undepressed. It is our goal to effect the quality of the individual's interaction with the environment so that more positive and less negative interactions occur.

LS-S: *How do parents react to being considered the environment for their depressed adolescents? Do they find it troubling?*

PL: Most of the parents with whom we work are glad that some help is going to be forthcoming for their kids. They are willing to involve themselves. But I should say there is a real limit to how much we involve them. This is not family therapy, for example. Ultimately it becomes clear to us that there is some conflict in the dynamics between the mother, father, and the kid. We try to understand this and work around it, but we do not attempt to alter the dynamics as would happen in family therapy.

LS-S: *What is the general prevalence rate according to your study of adolescent depression?*

PL: It is close to four percent. It is higher for girls than for boys. The rates we reported in the 1993 study suggest that the rates of depression for these adolescents is comparable to the rate for adults, which is very surprising to us. We expected that the rates for adolescents would be lower than the adult rates, because it has been assumed that the rate of depression increases with age until adulthood.

LS-S: *At what age does the rate increase for prevalence of depression drop off?*

PL: That's the $64,000 question. The adolescents in our study ranged from ages 14 to 18 and we did not see an increase. Dr. Garrison at the University of South Carolina studied a group of younger adolescents, ages 11 to 14, and she did not find a rate increase. So while everyone assumes that depression increases from adolescence to adulthood, when you look at any given study you find no evidence of that.

A related issue is at what age females begin to show a higher rate of depression than males. The ratio of depression for females vs. males is two to one. It's striking. There's fairly good evidence that it must come in quickly, probably between the ages of 12 and 14. This is probably related to the onset of puberty in girls.

LS-S: *What factors contribute to depression in girls?*

PL: In our studies we find that girls are higher on some of the areas that predispose people to depression like low self-esteem and negative body image. Girls have a much more negative body image after a certain point than boys do. One interpretation of the data is that girls are higher on the risk factor for depression than boys, but there is not a real consensus on that yet.

LS-S: *In one of your studies on suicide you find that previous suicide attempts are one of the best predictors of future attempts. Why is this so?*

PL: I think one could offer many hypotheses about this. One might be that when you make a suicide attempt you get a lot of attention. People who make suicide attempts are not getting enough attention or feel that they are not getting enough attention. The suicide attempt is a very powerful stimulus in terms of getting people in the environment to pay attention to you. That can be very reinforcing. So you might say that a suicide attempt is a very powerful way of manipulating or changing the environment so that it pays attention to you.

LS-S: *Your findings indicated that girls are more likely to make suicide attempts.*

PL: Absolutely. We are not very good at explaining the differences between the sexes in this area yet. It used to be said that girls made more attempts but that their attempts were not as lethal as the boys, but this is changing now. We are not finding any difference in lethality between the sexes just in numbers of attempts. It may well have to do with the greater severity of depression that girls have.

LS-S: *While depression is a large factor in suicide there are studies that indicate that adolescents with other disorders also can be suicidal. Is there an underlying depression in these cases?*

PL: Comorbidity is a big risk factor, over and beyond the fact that these disorders are often accompanied by depression. The level of risk is elevated for the kid who is depressed and who is having an anxiety disorder or has an attention deficit disorder or substance abuse problem.

   Another factor is that when we talk about kids with multiple disorders we are by definition talking about early onset of the disorders. In most disorders early onset suggests a more severe form of the illness. For example, people that develop diabetes early in life have a more serious type of diabetes than those that develop it later in life. So early onset indicates serious problems for the child or adolescent.

LS-S: *Just having to cope with such difficulties for a long period of time would lead to a greater chance of being tired of coping or from coping.*

PL: Exactly. These kids deal with a lot of things when most kids don't have to.

LS-S: *One final question concerns whether depression in children who have experienced a significant loss, such as the death of a parent or care taker is the same as depression which is not in reaction to a loss.*

PL: In our study early loss of a parent through death has never come through as a risk factor and there are many studies that do show it as a risk factor. My hypothesis is that the other studies don't control well for socioeconomic status. Lower SES kids are much more likely to lose a parent, especially the father. We control for this in our study. We find that it is the quality of the interaction between the child and the parent or primary caretaker that is important for these children.

An Integrative Model of Depression

Lewinsohn, Hoberman, Teri and Hautzinger (1985) have provided a comprehensive theoretical model of the etiology and maintenance of depression. The model below attempts to integrate the findings of recent epidemiological outcome studies (Zeiss et al., 1979) with the phenomenon of self-awareness that has been advanced by social psychologists (Carver and Scheier, 1982).

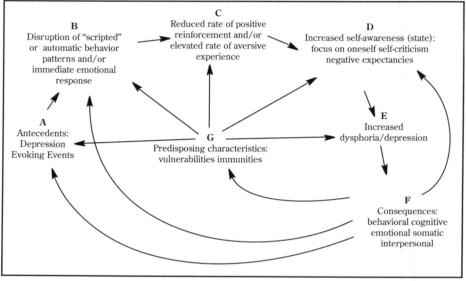

Reprinted with permission from the *Leader's Manual for Adolescent Groups: Adolescent Coping with Depression Course* by Gregory Clarke, Ph.D., Peter Lewinsohn, Ph.D. and Hyman Hops, Ph.D.

Age-Related Behavior Indicators of Possible Depression

In Infants:
- Excessive crying
- Failure to thrive
- Severe withdrawal
- Sleep disruptions

In Preschoolers:
- Temper tantrums
- Somatic complaints
- Brief durations of sadness
- Loss of interest in activities
- Disturbed play

In School-Age Children:
- Quiet and withdrawn behavior (head held down, poor eye contact, isolates oneself from peers in groups)
- Has few friends and avoids new friendships
- School refusal/phobia
- Becomes aggressive in reaction to perceived insult, or becomes angry for no apparent reason
- Draws pictures portraying the world as bleak
- Expresses intense anxiety, fear, despair in writing assignments
- Participates in class in arbitrary, idiosyncratic ways
- Decreased participation and avoidance of playground and gym activities or hyper-aggressive behavior in these situations
- Chooses exclusively books, music and movies about morose subjects
- Intense separation anxiety
- Longer periods of sadness
- Frequent trips to school nurse/many somatic complaints
- Sudden change in appetite, weight.
- Increased dependency
- Complaints of poor concentration
- Suicidality

In Adolescents:
- All behavioral signs for school-aged children listed above
- Increased fatigue
- Drug /alcohol use
- Loss of interest in family
- Loss of interest in future
- Antisocial behavior
- Sleep problems
- Excessive weeping
- Promiscuous behavior
- School failure
- Truancy

Sources: Rosenstock, J., Kraft, I., Rosenstock, J., et. al. (1986). Depression in Children. *Medical Aspects of Human Sexuality.* Oct. pp.18-31. Oster, G. and Caro, J. (1990). *Understanding and Treating Depressed Adolescents and Their Families.* John Wiley and Sons, Inc. Stark, K. (1994). Interview. *The Child Therapy News.* The Center for Applied Psychology, Inc. In Press.

Observing the Play of Depressed
and Suicidal Children

"The child attempted to jump off the balcony of the auditorium at school and repeated her suicidal behavior in play. Variations of jumping were repeated as she had dolls jump off roofs of houses, fall out of windows, and roll down hills." (Pfeffer, 1986, pp.199)

Observing the play of depressed and suicidal children often provides many clues as to the nature of their concerns, and the ways in which they are attempting to cope with internal and external pressures. As many psychotherapists have noted, play provides a window of opportunity for children to reconsider, re-enact, and hopefully resolve the troubling thoughts and experiences which preoccupy them.

Dr. Pfeffer (1986) notes four characteristics of play in suicidal children. The first she describes as play reflecting the process of separation and individuation. She reports that play in some suicidal children may appear developmentally below age level with content similar to the content of age-appropriate play seen in children working through separation issues. Themes of loss and retrieval, jumping, rescue, throwing and flying may be present.

A second characteristic play style for suicidal children is the reckless use of their bodies as play objects. This would involve jumping on and off furniture and engaging in obviously dangerous behaviors as part of normal play activities such as bike riding. The third characteristic she cites is the reckless use of toys, often including throwing and breaking of the toys. Dr. Pfeffer notes that the ego boundaries of these children are often diffused so that they lose a sense of themselves in their play and identify as both the actor and the object acted on.

Finally, these children sometimes repetitively engage in fantasies about superheros with an intensity that is not generally observed in normal play around this theme. At times these children may act as if they were a superhero, thus endangering their lives. One function of this type of play is to help the child cope with feelings of helplessness. Dr. Pfeffer describes one boy whose mother was dying of cancer. This child went about his neighborhood dressed as superman and jumped off of cars, and from fire escape to fire escape. He was hospitalized after trying to jump out of a school window.

Bereaved children may demonstrate their concerns and fears about the loss of a significant family member and death in general in play. Bowlby (1980, pp.276-285) describes a four-year-old girl and her siblings who were busy playing "London Bridge Is Falling Down" during the evening of her mother's death. Later, this little girl developed two games which she played with her father. In one she twirled around, lay down on the floor, and quickly stood up, saying, "You thought I was dead, didn't you?" In the other version she also twirled and lay on the floor. When her father gave the signal to get up (which included saying her mother's name) she didn't get up.

Bowlby cites another case in which a four-year-old girl, reacting to the changes in her family (including less availability of her mother and an older brother, resulting from her father's death a year earlier), suffered a regression in her play with other children, being less able to share and demanding more attention from adults.

An eight-year-old boy mourning his mother's death is described as engaging in play which became increasingly more violent. In one (game) a family was moving from one house to another. First the removal van was demolished; next the house was blown up and everyone was killed. In another (game) somebody in the family was ill. An ambulance came, but then the house was burned down and the ambulance burned up. In yet other play sequences the boy doll became destructive, and then, in an effort to control himself, became Superman. Then Superman became destructive (Bowlby, 1986, pp.328).

Play may be used to assess families of depressed children. Oster and Caro report on a psychodrama technique which may be conceptualized as a form of structured play called "family sculpting" (Constantine, 1978; Duhl, Kantor, and Duhl, 1973 in Oster and Caro, 1990). "Family sculpting" can be used as a means of assessing the families of depressed children. An example of this technique called "linear structuring" involves identifying a salient trait for the family and having the members place themselves along a line which is understood to go from high to low amounts of the trait. For example, a "powerline" may be created in which one end represents having almost total control over what happens in the family and the other having almost no control. Once the family has placed itself the therapist can explore this dynamic. The technique also serves to give the person feeling the least power opportunities to be heard. Another theme to be explored is closeness between family members. By having members find a representative distance from each other a visceral diagram of family relations can emerge.

Drawing exercises involving members of the family can also have both therapeutic and assessment value. Oster and Caro (1990) indicate that the addition of drawing to an assessment of families of depressed children helps to identify and disrupt maladaptive communication patterns and can serve to make concrete the goals of therapy and the needs of individual family members. By having the family draw individual pictures and also participate in group drawings the therapist is able to observe both individual perspectives and watch the dynamics of the family as it attempts to make decisions and work together on a project. They review a number of drawing techniques that can be used with families.

Finally, semi-structured and structured play can be used as a therapeutic intervention to teach social skills, identification of emotions, coping skills, and other aspects of behavior and cognition which have been identified as being related to depression in children (see interview with Kevin Stark, Ph.D. for some of the games used in his treatment program). Therapeutic games such as "The Talking, Feeling, and Doing Game" or "The Self-Esteem Game" provide the opportunity for the exploration of emotions and the learning of new coping, problem-solving and social skills. These games lend themselves to a variety of therapy groupings (individual, family, group) as well as to a variety of settings. While helping to teach and explore difficult areas, they can provide a sense of mastery for the participants as they come to gain skill and competence with the game itself.

Sources: Bowlby, J. (1980). *Attachment and Loss Volume III; Loss: Sadness and Depression.* Basic Books, Inc., New York. Oster, G. and Caro, J. (1990). *Understanding and Treating Depressed Adolescents and Their Families.* John Wiley and Sons, Inc. pp.63-79. Pfeffer, C. (1986) *The Suicidal Child.* Guilford Press, New York. pp.193-203.

Assessing Suicidal Risk in Adolescents
By Michael DeStefano, Ph.D.

Perhaps one of the most difficult and anxiety-provoking tasks confronting clinicians who work with adolescents is that of assessing the risk of imminent or potential suicide behavior. While the vast majority of adolescents who eventually make a suicide attempt or gesture provide verbal and behavioral signs beforehand, the risk assessment process is a complex task which requires the clinician to collect and synthesize data beyond the scope of a symptom checklist.

There is no typical "suicidal adolescent." There are a number of warning signs and areas of potential conflict or disturbance which collectively increase the potential suicide risk, yet there is no specific combination of behaviors or symptoms which will unerringly identify the teenager who will attempt suicide. Adolescents in turmoil, struggling with an overwhelming world, do not make the task a simple one.

While there are numerous indicators or "red flags" to which the clinician should attend, any particular adolescent may manifest many or only several of any combination of clinical warning signs. Undeniably, some of the behavior and symptoms carry more weight in the assessment, and significantly increase the risk of suicidal acts. However, it is the specific combination of factors, at a particular time in an individual adolescent's life, in the context of that teenager's history and current interaction with the assessor, upon which the ultimate treatment decisions must be based.

As in any therapeutic interaction of quality with adolescents, the assessment must be understood as an intervention—as a significant first step in establishing a working therapeutic alliance that begins the task of facilitating the adolescent's abilities to cope effectively with the circumstances of his or her life. The assessor should be able to convey a non-judgmental attitude, which can simultaneously communicate the serious concern for the adolescent's well-being, while promoting open discussion (within the limits of the adolescent's resistances and defenses).

However much discomfort such an assessment can provoke in the clinician, it is imperative that warning signs and indicators signal the need for further inquiry, and that direct questioning (e.g., "Do you have thoughts of killing yourself?") not be avoided when so much is at stake. Non-judgmental, direct inquiry can often allow for more open, genuine discussion of concerns by the adolescent, who may experience some relief at having an opportunity to speak about thoughts, feelings or behaviors to an empathic listener.

With these factors in mind, the following areas of clinical concern can provide an overview of significant data about which to inquire:

- **Significant changes in the adolescent's typical behavior**
- **Increasing school problems**
- **Tumultuous relationships/interactions with family members**
- **Increasing isolation from peers**
- **Preoccupation with themes of death, the afterlife, dying, escape and relief from problems**
- **Giving away possessions, writing wills or suicide notes**
- **Family history of suicide, psycho-pathology or abuse**
- **Actual or anticipated losses of family members, friends or status**
- **Feelings of despair, hopelessness or self-deprecation**
- **Exposure to the suicide of others**
- **Increasing impulsivity and difficulty controlling rage and frustration**
- **Affective lability or blunted emotions**
- **Rigidity and constriction of thought processes; idiosyncratic thinking;**

difficulty thinking of options
- History of or current substance abuse
- Statements, questions or threats made to others about death and suicide
- Presence of psychopathology (it must be noted that comorbidity of diagnostic categories is common, and increased degree of this may indicate higher risk)
  - mood disorders (unipolar and bipolar depression)
  - psychotic disorders, with impaired reality testing
  - conduct disorders (acting out; impulsive risk-taking; aggressive behaviors, often exacerbated by substance abuse; defiance masking despair)
  - borderline personality features

If suicidal thoughts or behaviors are indicated, the following should also be assessed:

- What is the adolescent's perceived intent—to die, or some other purpose?
- How recently has this occurred? How much planning has gone into the thought, decision or act?
- How preoccupied is the adolescent with suicide and death?
- What are the immediate and prior stresses contributing to the suicidality?
- Does the adolescent have a planned method? How available is that method? If s/he made prior attempts, what was used?
- How lethal does the teenager perceive the chosen method?
- Has the thought or plan been divulged to anyone? Have previous attempts been secretive or made public?
- Has there been prior treatment? How compliant was the adolescent and the family in following through with treatment and recommendations?
- How compliant is the adolescent in the current assessment?
- What effective coping skills are present? Are they decompensating?
- What support systems are available and able to be used by the adolescent?

Given a thorough assessment, the clinician must also recommend treatment options. The decision to seek hospitalization for an adolescent is a complex one, requiring the joint efforts of the family, the clinician and the adolescent. Several factors are of special salience when considering this option:

- Failure of previous outpatient treatment to resolve crises
- Presence of significant psychopathology, which increases the potential for impulsive, lethal acting out on the suicidal thoughts
- Significant intent to suicide plan with available methods
- Lack of a working alliance with the adolescent during the assessment
- Unavailability of family support for the adolescent
- Indications of strong anger, anxiety and little control over destructive acting out
- Presence of current unresolvable stress
- History of previous suicide attempts

When indicated by the severity of the adolescent's situation and the ineffectiveness of his/her current coping strategies, hospitalization can provide safety, support and further evaluation on a 24-hour basis. While the hospital can function as a sanctuary away from the external stresses, all therapeutic work should be targeted to resolving the current crisis, stabilizing the adolescent's affect, thinking and behavior, and organizing support systems, so that s/he can rejoin his/her world and continue therapeutic work on an outpatient basis.

Sources: Berman, Allan L. and Jobes, David A. (1991) *Adolescent Suicide: Assessment and Intervention*. Washington, DC: American Psychological Association. Oster, Gerald D. and Caro, Janice E. (1990) *Understanding and Treating Depressed Adolescents and Their Families*. New York: John Wiley & Sons. Weiner, Irving B. (1992) *Psychological Disturbance in Adolescence*. New York: John Wiley & Sons.

Considerations of Psychiatric Hospital Treatment for Suicidal Children

Psychiatric hospitalization is often the initial treatment of choice for suicidal children. Most hospital programs employ a multi-disciplinary treatment team which addresses the child's psychopathology and also begins to work with their often dysfunctional families to improve the child's environment before release from the hospital. Pfeffer (1989) notes that suicidal children who are hospitalized often display more dangerous suicidal behavior, have more extensive ego deficits, and a greater number of psychosocial stressors than non-hospitalized suicidal children.

Herein we have reprinted Dr. Cynthia Pfeffer's outline of the phases of inpatient treatment with suicidal children. She notes that it is important to recognize the disequilibrium in the child's family that results from the sudden removal of the child from the home. Helping the family to cope with this change, and to examine the stressors in and on the family unit is one of the first steps in developing a working relationship with the child and the child's family. Of obvious importance is the necessity of keeping the child safe from harm. Not only is this a function of managing the child in the hospital, but also of helping the family to recognize and accept the seriousness of the child's threats and the need to work with the hospital staff to help the child.

The process of treatment targets a variety of areas including addressing the suicidal wishes and their meaning, improving self-esteem, helping the child to manage anger and frustration, and improving social relationships and school participation and achievement. Dr. Pfeffer notes that a major cause of relapse for suicidal children is inadequate post-hospitalization treatment. Appropriate referrals for the child and the family are important in the final phase of treatment.

Goals and Some Interventions of Psychiatric Hospital Treatment of Suicidal Children

<u>Initial Phase</u>
Goal I: Adjust to hospital routine
Interventions:
1. Discuss child's and parents' responses to separation from each other
2. Explain hospital program to child and parents
3. Introduce child to peers and staff

Goal II: Develop therapeutic alliance
Interventions:
1. Interpret helping role of the hospital
2. State that the therapist, the child, and the parents will work together to solve problems

Goal III: Protect the child from harm
Interventions:
1. Emphasize the seriousness of the child's suicidal tendencies
2. Establish an agreement with the child to inform staff of suicidal urges or assaultive impulses
3. Emphasize that suicidal behavior is a poor way of coping with problems; discuss

alternatives
4. Observe the child's behavior at all times

Working-Through Phase
Goal I: Decrease suicidal tendencies and underlying conflict
Interventions:
1. Discuss alternative solutions to problems
2. Discuss child's unfulfilled wishes and outline acceptable compromise satisfactions

Goal II: Decrease depression
Interventions:
1. Talk with the child about many of the positive aspects of his or her situation
2. Discuss how the child can develop new supportive relationships to replace lost ones
3. Suggest ways to organize the day so that the child eats and sleeps regularly
4. Encourage the child to participate in hospital activities

Goal III: Enhance self-esteem
Interventions:
1. Compliment and reward child's accomplishments, skills, and appropriate autonomous behaviors
2. Suggest ways in which the child can behave independently and successfully
3. Support attempts to develop friendships
4. Help the child to accept his or her limitations or handicaps

Goal IV: Modify aggressive responses
Interventions:
1. Define alternative ways of responding to frustrations
2. Talk with child about being able to accept disappointment and to plan other ways of obtaining satisfaction
3. Remind child that it is unacceptable for anyone to be injured by the child and vice versa
4. Isolate the child during episodes of uncontrollable anger and allow a quiet period for the child to calm himself or herself
5. Provide rewards when the child can control angry feelings
6. Discipline child for uncontrollable aggressive behaviors

Goal V: Balance peer relationships
Interventions:
1. Support the child's participation in therapeutic group activities
2. Suggest ways to make friends and how to maintain friendships

Goal VI: Enhance school achievement
Interventions:
1. Reward appropriate classroom participation and academic success
2. Reward child's attempts to remediate learning problems
3. Provide school assignments that are of interest to the child
4. Provide help for the child to carry out independently chosen assignments
5. Use special education methods to decrease learning problems

Goal VII: Diagnose and treat neurophysiological disorder

Interventions:

1. Examine child, observe behavior, do an EEG
2. Use appropriate indicated medication

Goal VIII: Monitor responses to medication

Interventions:

1. Observe that child takes medication as indicated
2. Observe child for signs of medication-induced decrease in symptoms
3. Observe child for adverse medication side effects

Termination Phase

Goal I: Ameliorate child's suicidal tendencies

Interventions:

1. Talk with child about presence of suicidal feelings
2. Talk with child about death preoccupations and depression
3. Teach child to be able to recognize early signs of sadness, thoughts about death, and suicide
4. Talk with child about telling someone if suicidal tendencies occur

Goal II: Evaluate responses to discharge from the hospital

Interventions:

1. Talk to the child about leaving the hospital, loss of hospital friends, and memories of hospitalization
2. Talk to the child about going to a new living arrangement, whether it be return to home or setting away from home
3. Talk about need for continued treatment

Reprinted with permission from *The Suicidal Child* by Cynthia Pfeffer, 1986, Guilford Press, New York.

Models of Childhood Depression

There are many etiological models of depression, each of which makes its unique contribution to the understanding of this illness. Herein several of the current models of depression are detailed.

Psychodynamic Models of Depression

Early psychoanalytic writings emphasized the role of loss in creating depression (Abraham, 1912; Freud, 1917). Spitz (1946) studied children and infants evidencing depressive symptoms in relation to the absence of the mother or primary caretaker. This type of depression is called analytic depression. Later, Bowlby (1980) described depression as part of his study of attachment and loss. Oster and Caro (1990) note that the analytic explanation for depression in adolescence includes the breakdown of healthy narcissism which leads to lowered self-esteem.

The turning of anger inward, perhaps the hallmark of psychoanalytic thinking about depression, results from the inability to adequately handle feelings of anger and hostility directed toward family members, particularly parents, in the face of their not meeting up to earlier established ego ideals. In the analytic model, difficulties and traumas in early childhood development give rise to later depression, especially as further encounters with separation and individuation take place throughout adolescence.

Behavioral Models

Behavioral models focus on learning from the reinforcement provided by the environment (for more about behavioral models see interview with Dr. Lewinsohn in Focus on Programs). Behavioral models are often linked with cognitive models of depression, and features of both are used in cognitive-behavioral treatments.

Cognitive Models

The cognitive model which has influenced much thinking about depression is Beck's (1967) theory that cognitive distortions lead to depressogenic thoughts which then influence both the depressed individual's experience of them self and the environment. Beck introduced the idea of the cognitive triad as a hallmark of depressive thinking. The cognitive triad consists of negative views of the self, the world and the future. Children have been found to have negative cognitive distortions similar to the three highlighted by Beck's theory (Stark, 1990). Two other features of Beck's theory include the idea of schemas or systematic ways in which the person perceives the world, in this case ways governed by the cognitive triad, and the identification of different cognitive errors commonly made by depressed persons.

Seligman and Peterson's (1986) learned helplessness model suggests that people become depressed when they experience their actions on the environment as having no effect. In later extensions of this model hopelessness is addressed as a cause of depression (Kazdin, 1990).

Social skills deficits (Lewinsohn, Clarke, Hops, and Andrews, 1990) address the manner in which the depressed individual attempts to interact and be rewarded by the environment. Support for the role of social skills in causing depression is not entirely consistent, but the teaching of social skills to depressed children has been shown to be therapeutic (Kashani and Sherman, 1988). D'Zurilla and Nezu (1982, in Kazdin, 1990) have proposed interpersonal problem-solving skills deficits as being related to depression.

Another cognitive model, the self-control model of depression, has been proposed by Rehm (1986). In this model it is proposed that depressed persons have difficulty in one of three areas: 1) self-monitoring, which includes selectively attending to negative events and to the immediate rather than long term outcomes of their behavior; 2) self-evaluation in which depressed persons make inaccurate internal attributions of causation, and set too stringent criteria for identifying an experience as being positive; 3) self-reinforcement in which the depressed person has low rates of self-reward and high rates of self-punishment. This model has been incorporated into treatment programs for children (see Stark interview).

Family Models of Depression

Family therapy theorists view depression as occurring within the context of a family system. Different models focus on different aspects of family processes including Bowen's (Oster and Caro, 1990) focus on the degree of differentiation between family members; the structural model's (Minuchin, 1974 in Oster and Caro, 1990) focus on the relationship between generational units; the strategic model's (Madanes, 1981 in Oster and Caro, 1990) focus on the current communication patterns of the family members; and the solution-focused model's (Molnar and deShazer, 1987 in Oster and Caro, 1990) highlighting of the inherent ability of families to find their own solutions to problems within the family system.

Oster and Caro (1990) note that disturbed families have difficulty making the necessary adjustments to the changing homeostasis of the family brought on by the adolescent's move toward independence. As a consequence, these families attempt to maintain the homeostasis at a cost to the teenager. Often this results in the teenager becoming the symptomatic family member, allowing the family to focus on the "problem" child and avoid examining the underlying issues the family needs to address.

Davis and Sandoval (1991) note the following family characteristics as having been shown to be related to adolescent suicidality: higher rates of suicide in family, higher rates of medical and psychiatric illness in the family, increased economic stress in the family, and the adolescent's perception of the family as being high in conflict and low in supportive family interactions. Citing Aldridge (1984), Oster and Caro (1990) state that suicidogenic families are characterized by poor communication, unresolved issues of loss, dysfunctional boundary systems, poor ability to resolve conflict, and emotional problems in the family members.

Genetic Models of Depression

Studies (Kazdin, 1990) have shown that genetics play a role in depression. Twin studies have demonstrated a 65 percent concordance for identical twins vs. a 14 percent concordance for fraternal twins. Depression has been shown to be more prevalent in close relatives of depressed persons than unrelated persons. There is some evidence to suggest that people with depression beginning before puberty have a greater genetic contribution to their illness than those with later onset (Kashani and Sherman, 1988).

Biological Models

Biological models of depression focus on neurotransmitters. One area of research involves trying to understand the differences in the amount of several neurotransmitters in depressed vs. nondepressed populations. Another area of research is on the neuroendocrine system which is mediated by neurotransmitters (Kazdin, 1990). Pharmacological treatment for depression is derived from research in this area.

Sources: Abraham, K. (1912) Notes on the psychoanalytic investigation and treatment of manic-depressive insanity and allied conditions. K. Abraham (Ed.) *Selected Papers* (pp. 137-156).

London: Hogarth Press. Beck, A. (1967) *Depression: Clinical, Experimental, and Theoretical Aspects.* New York: Harper and Row. Bowlby, J. (1980) *Attachment and Loss III: Loss- Sadness and Depression.* New York: Basic Books. Davis, J. and Sandoval, J. (1991) Suicidal Youth. San Francisco: Jossey-Bass Publishers. Freud, S. (1917) Mourning and Melancholia. in *The Standard Edition of the Complete Psychological Works of Sigmund Freud* (Vol. 20). London: Hogarth Press. Kashani, J. and Sherman, D. (1988) Childhood depression: epidemiology, etio-logical models, and treatment implications. *Integrative Psychiatry.* 6(1),pp.1-21. Kazdin, A. (1990) Childhood depression. *Journal of Child Psychology and Psychiatry.* 31(1): pp.121-160. Lewinshon,P. Clarke, Hops, and Andrews, (1990) Cognitive-behavioral treatment for depressed adolescents. *Behavior Therapy.* 21,pp.385-401. Oster and Caro (1990) *Understanding and Treating Depressed Adolescents and Their Families.* New York: John Wiley and Sons, Inc. Rehm, L. (1986) A Self-control model of depression. In Coyne,J. (Ed.) *Essential Papers on Depression.* New York: New York University Press. pp.220-239. Seligman,M. and Peterson, C. (1986) A learned helplessness perspective on childhood depression: theory and research. In Rutter, M., Izard, C., Read, P. (Eds.) *Depression in Young People: Developmental and Clinical Perspectives.* New York: Guilford Press. pp.223-249. Spitz,R. (1946) Anaclytic depression. *The Psychoanalytic Study of the Child.* New York: International University Press. 2, pp.313-342. Stark, K. (1990) *Childhood Depression: School-based intervention.* New York: Guilford Press.

Selected Assessment Tools
for Childhood and Adolescent Depression

With the acceptance of childhood depression as a psychiatric diagnosis, a large number of assessment procedures were devised in the 1970s and 1980s. Assessment of depression is a multifaceted process involving not only diagnosis, but determination of severity, determination of the elements that comprise a given individual's depressive symptoms, evaluation of constructs related to depression such as self-esteem or social skills, and evaluation of recovery from depression after treatment.

Assessment measures for depression may be either self-report measures or structured or semi-structured interview formats. The latter often involve assessment for a number of psychiatric disorders and yield a diagnosis based on the criteria established by the Diagnostic and Statistical Manual of Mental Disorders. Some measures have a version which is administered to the parents of the child so that the child's self report and the parent's observations may be compared and others can be administered in groups. Behavioral observation is another less standardized form of assessment.

While not routinely used in the diagnosis of depression in children, biological markers of depression are being studied in children. There is some evidence to suggest that children, like depressed adults, also have increased levels of cortisol in their blood. Depressed adults have been found to have disturbed sleep patterns as evaluated by electrophysiological measures, but this has not been consistently demonstrated to be true of depressed children. Listed below is a sample of the wide variety of assessment tools now available for identifying depression in children and adolescents.

Self Report Measures

Children's Depression Inventory (CDI) [Kovacs (1979) University of Pittsburgh School of Medicine, Pittsburgh, PA] A frequently-used inventory consisting of 27 forced choice items identifying depressive symptomatology and the degree to which the child is experiencing the symptoms. A well-researched instrument with high internal consistency reliability and a moderate test-retest reliability, it has been demonstrated to differentiate children being seen in clinics from non-clinic groups of children. Validity studies have shown the CDI to correlate well with other measures of depression in children. Research suggests that a cut-off score of 19 can differentiate depressed and non-depressed clinical samples [Knight, Hensley and Waters (1988) and Carlson and Cantwell (1980) in Liddle and Spence (1990)]. Studies are available which allow for normative comparisons (Kazdin, 1990). There is no test manual including summarized normative data, and interpretive guidelines for the test. The CDI is appropriate for use with children ages 7-17.

Reynolds Child Depression Scale (RCDS) [Reynolds (1989) Psychological Assessment Resources, Odessa, FL] The RCDS, previously called the Child Depression Scale, is a 30-item self report scale that measures depressive symptomatology suggestive of clinical depression. Its items are presented in a four-point Likert Scale format, with the exception of one item consisting of faces with different expressions ranging from happy to sad. Normative data have been gathered from 1,600 children of heterogeneous backgrounds. High internal consistency and test-retest reliability have been demonstrated for the measure. The RCDS correlates well with other measures of depression in children. This measure can be given individually and in groups and is appropriate for children ages 8-12 years.

Reynolds Adolescent Depression Scale (RADS) [Reynolds (1986) Psychological

Assessment Resources, Odessa, FL] The RADS is a 30-item measure in a 4-point response format for adolescents. The items reflect the diagnostic requirements of the DSMIII for major depression and dysthymia. Normative data on 11,000 adolescents is presented in the test manual, and a cut-off score is provided. High internal consistency and test-retest reliability has been demonstrated for this test. It correlates well with other measures of depression in children. RADS is appropriate for adolescents aged 13 through 19.

Diagnostic Interview Measures
Schedule for Affective Disorders and Schizophrenia for School-Age Children (K-SADS) [Chambers, Puig-Antich, Hirsch, et. al. (1985) The assessment of affective disorders in children and adolescents by semistructured interview: test-retest reliability. *Archives of General Psychiatry.* 43. pp.696-702.] A much-used semi-structured and structured interview which is given separately to the child's parent and the child. Studies have shown this measure to reliably diagnose depressed children. K-SADS is appropriate for children aged six to 18 years.

Diagnostic Interview for Children and Adolescents (DICA) [Herjanic and Reich (1982) Development of a structured psychiatric interview for children: Agreement between child and parent on individual symptoms. *Journal of Abnormal Child Psychology.* 10. pp.307-324.] The DICA is a semi-structured and structured interview which permits current diagnosis as well as lifetime specification of diagnoses. Research has demonstrated the usefulness of this measure's ability to diagnosing depression in children. The DICA is designed for use with children ages eight to 17.

Measurements of Constructs Related to Depression
Matson Evaluation of Social Skills with Youngsters (MESSY) [Matson, Rotatari, Helsel (1983) Development of a rating scale to measure social skills in children: The Matson Evaluation of Social Skills with Youngsters (MESSY). *Behaviour Research and Therapy.* 21. pp.335-340.] This scale is used to identify children's social skills including initiating social interaction, responding to others, and making friends. Deficits in social skills have been shown to be related to depression in children, and a relationship between children's scores on the MESSY and depression has been shown (Helsel and Matson, 1984, in Kazdin, 1987). Children or adults can complete this scale.

Hopelessness Scale for Children [Kazdin, Rodgers, and Colbus (1986) The Hopelessness Scale for Children: Psychometric characteristics and concurrent validity. *Journal of Consulting and Clinical Psychology.* 24. pp. 241-245.] Derived from the Hopelessness Scale (Beck, 1978) this 16-item scale is a self report measure which evaluates the child's expectations of the future. This scale has been shown to correlate with suicidal ideation and behavior, as well as with diminished self esteem (Kazdin, Rodgers, and Colbus, 1986 in Kazdin, 1987.) This scale is appropriate for children ages six to 13.

Suicide Assessment Instruments
Child Suicide Potential Scale [Pfeffer (1986) *The Suicidal Child.* Guilford Press. New York. pp.186-188, 277-290] A comprehensive battery of nine scales developed for use in research but also useful in conducting a semi-structured interview with the child and the child's parents in order to assess the nature of the child's suicidality. At present formal scoring properties are being determined. Some studies have been

done on the reliability and validity of the scale but the psychometric properties of the scale are still being investigated. The nine scales are: Spectrum of Suicidal Behavior, Spectrum of Assaultive Behavior, Precipitating Events, General Psychopathology (Recent), General Psychopathology (Past), Family Background, Concept of Death Scale, Assessment of Current Ego Function, and Ego Defenses.

Suicidal Ideation Questionnaire (SIQ) [Reynolds (1989) Psychological Assessment Resources, Odessa, FL] This brief questionnaire can be administered in ten minutes and is designed to assess the frequency of suicidal ideation in adolescents from grades seven through 12. Its items are rated on a seven point scale. Studies have demonstrated the reliability and validity of this measure which is designed to be used as part of a larger assessment.

Suicidal Behavior History Form (SBHF) (Reynolds and Mazza,
Psychological Assessment Resources, Odessa, FL) The SBHF is a semi-structured interview presented in a four-page booklet format. The interview provides a systematic method of obtaining and documenting a client's history of suicidal behavior and ideation, and provides for assessment of current suicidal risk factors.

Suicide Intent Scale [Beck (1978) Center for Cognitive Therapy, Philadelphia, PA] This is a 12-item self report measure which is divided into the following sections: Circumstances related to the suicide attempt, Self Report, and Risk. This scale is designed to be used with other assessment measures in order to obtain a full clinical understanding of the patient.

Sources: Kazdin, A. (1990) Childhood depression. *Journal of Child Psychology and Psychiatry.* 31(1). pp.121-160. Kazdin, A. (1987) Assessment of childhood depression: Current issues and strategies. *Behavioral Assessment.* 9. pp.291-319. Liddle, B. and Spence, S. (1990) Cognitive-behavior therapy with depressed primary school children: A cautionary note. *Behavioural Psychotherapy.* 18. pp.85-102. Pfeffer, C. (1986) *The Suicidal Child.* Guilford Press. New York. pp.59-79,173-192. Reynolds, W. M. (1992) Depression in children and adolescents. Reynolds, W. M. (Ed.) Internalizing Disorders in Children and Adolescents. pp.149-253. Reynolds, W. M. (1990) Depression in children and adolescents: Nature, diagnosis, assessment, and treatment. *School Psychology Review.* 19(2). pp.158-173.

Research Findings on Childhood Depression

• In a study examining the relationship between childhood exposure to violent events and childhood depression, 223 six- to 12-year-old urban school children were examined. Of these, 57 children described violent events occurring to themselves, a relative or a friend, with the most common event being suicide either completed or attempted. These children were found to have higher scores on a measure of depressive symptoms. They also had more problems than the other children with low self esteem, weeping and worries about death or injury.
Freeman, L., Mokros, H., Poznanski, E. (1993). Violent events reported by normal urban school-aged children: Characteristics and depression correlates. *Journal of the American Academy of Child and Adolescent Psychiatry.* Mar. 32(2):pp. 419-423.

• A study of the effect of a short-term residential therapeutic intervention for childhood depression on 99 residential children ages eight to 12 years found support for the efficacy of the treatment in that after treatment there was a decrease in depression level as measured by the children's responses to the Reynold's Childhood Depression Scale. These children also had behavioral problems and learning disabilities.
Rawson, H. , Tabb, L. (1993). Effects of therapeutic intervention on childhood depression. *Child and Adolescent Social Work Journal.* Feb 10(1):pp.39-52.

• A study of depression in 1,710 randomly-selected high school students examined point and lifetime prevalences, one-year incidence (in 1,508 high school students), and comorbidity of depression with other DSMIII-R diagnoses. 9.6 percent of the adolescents met the criteria for a current disorder. More than 33 percent had experienced a disorder over their lifetimes. 31.7 percent of this group had experienced a second disorder. High relapse rates were found for all of the disorders especially unipolar depression (18.4 percent). Female subjects of all ages had higher rates of unipolar depression, anxiety disorders, eating disorders, and adjustment disorders than the male subjects. The male subjects had higher rates of disruptive behavior disorders.
Lewinsohn, P., Hops, H., Roberts, R. et. al. (1993). Adolescent psychopathology: I. Prevalence and incidence of depression and other disorders in high school students. *Journal of Abnormal Psychology.* Feb. 102(1):pp.133-144.

• In a study seeking to determine inclusion and exclusion criteria for the differential diagnosis of depression and anxiety in children, four criteria were found for depressive disorders. These are: feeling unloved, anhedonia, excessive guilt, and depressed mood. Symptoms describing worries were the best inclusion criteria for anxiety disorders, but the anxiety symptoms were better predictors of depression than anxiety in terms of diagnosis. The children studied were taken from an initial group of 740 fourth to seventh graders, and included 34 students diagnosed with depression and 30 students diagnosed with an anxiety disorder. There were 70 control students without either diagnosis.
Laurent, J., Landau, S., Stark, K. (1993). Conditional probabilities in the diagnosis of depressive and anxiety disorders in children. *School Psychology Review.* 22(1):pp.98-114.

• In a study of adolescent inpatient girls alcohol consumption was associated with the recent severity of suicidal behaviors in the subsample of girls who were diagnosed with major depression. Self-reported suicidal ideation was strongly predicted by depression severity and family dysfunction. Clinician-documented suicidal behavior and/or ideation was predicted by alcohol consumption and family dysfunction. The sample was composed of 54 psychiatrically disturbed female inpatients ranging from 13.9 to 18.4 years of age.

King, C., Hill, E., Naylor, M. et. al. (1993). Alcohol consumption in relation to other predictors of suicidality among adolescent inpatient girls. *Journal of the American Academy of Child and Adolescent Psychiatry.* Jan. 32(1):pp.82-88.

• In a study of 42 inpatient adolescents diagnosed with major depression, a relationship was found between the presentation of the depression and the amount of alcohol the adolescents consumed. Moderate to heavy alcohol consumption was associated with a previous history of dysthymia and increased severity of symptoms, particularly behavioral symptoms. The increase in behavioral symptoms was associated with poorer levels of adaptive functioning.

King, C., Naylor, M. Hill, E., Shain, B. et. al. (1993). Dysthymia characteristics of heavy alcohol use in depressed adolescents. *Biological Psychiatry.* Feb. 33(3):pp.210-212.

• The relationship between parents with depression and anxiety and their children was examined in a study of 214 children aged six to 23 years from 89 families. The findings indicated that children with one parent meeting the criteria for major depression were more impaired, had more psychiatric diagnoses, and received more psychiatric treatment than did children of parents with other psychiatric disorders and no psychiatric disorders.

Mufson, L., Weissman, M., Warner, V. (1992). Depression and anxiety in parents and children: A direct interview study. *Journal of Anxiety Disorders.* 6(1):pp.1-13.

• A study tested two hypotheses of how children of depressed mothers incur increased stress. The hypotheses were: 1) increased exposure of the children to stressful events and 2) the children contribute to increased exposure to stressful events because of increased interpersonal conflict. Fifty-three children of unipolar, bipolar, medically ill, and normal mothers were studied at six month intervals for three years. The study confirmed both hypotheses and called for further studies of interpersonal functioning in children of depressed mothers in order to decrease the children's risk of having depression.

Adrian, C., Hammen, C. (1993). Stress exposure and stress generation in children of depressed mothers. *Journal of Consulting and Clinical Psychology.* Apr 61(2):pp.354-359.

• A study identifying psychosocial risk factors associated with past suicide attempts in adolescents from ages 14 to 18 years was done. When current level of depression was controlled for the following risk factors were found to be associated with past attempts: previous psychiatric disorders, cognitions associated with depression, externalizing and internalizing behavior problems, poor coping, school problems, health problems and gender. The probability of having made an attempt increased significantly as a function of the number of risk factors. Female subjects had more risk factors than males and showed greater vulnerability to the risk factors.

Lewinsohn, P., Rohde, P., Seeley, J. (1993). Psychosocial characteristics of adolescents with a history of suicide attempt. *Journal of the American Academy of Child and Adolescent Psychiatry.* Jan 32(1) pp.60-68.

• Studies have shown that suicidal children may be classified as falling into two groups. One group has relatively stable ego functioning and becomes depressed in reaction to severe environmental stress. This group has suicidal ideation, threats or attempts but does not have assaultive ideas, threats, or attempts as part of their clinical description. The other group has both suicidal and assaultive components in their presentation. This group has ego deficits and is prone to identify with parental suicidal and assaultive behavior.

Pfeffer (1986). *The Suicidal Child.* Guilford Press. New York. pp.71-72.

• In a study of 481 children with symptomatic depression and 147 children with symptomatic depression and suicidal ideation, all ages 15 and under, it was found that suicidal ideation was associated with dysfunctional, hostile family relations, and with age in girls. Depression without suicide was associated with experiences of loss. Conduct disorders and additional psychiatric disturbances and emotional difficulties did not serve to distinguish these two groups of children. Behavioral differences such as withdrawal or impaired social relationships did not differentiate the groups and the authors pose this as an additional challenge for identifying suicidal children. Treatment for potentially suicidal children needs to address depression as well as family problems.

Kosky, R., Silburn,S., and Zubrick, S. (1986). Symptomatic depression and suicidal ideation: A comparative study with 628 children. *The Journal of Nervous and Mental Disease.* 174(9):pp.523-528.

• In a review of comorbidity of depression and anxiety in children the authors note that this condition is quite prevalent and treatment for children with both disorders needs to be flexible and to address the child's presenting symptoms rather than be oriented to classical definitions of the two illnesses. Components of recommended treatment for these children include affective education, enactive programming, addressing reinforcement difficulties, correcting cognitive distortions, and enhancing problem-solving skills. As many of these children have parents with depression and/or anxiety the therapist should be prepared to help the parents to learn more effective parenting techniques to cope with their children's problems.

Kendall, P., Kortlander, T., Chansky, E., Brady, E. (1992). Comorbidity of anxiety and depression in youth: Treatment implications. *Journal of Consulting and Clinical Psychology.* 60(6):pp.869-880.

- Book Review -
Understanding and Treating Depressed Adolescents and Their Families

By Gerald D. Oster and Janice E. Caro

Many clinicians struggle valiantly with assessing and treating depressed adolescents who are sad, hostile, lethargic, impulsive, oppositional, dependent, apathetic, acutely sensitive or near criminal in the scope of acting out. *Understanding and Treating Depressed Adolescents and Their Families* is an indispensable volume that offers a well-balanced presentation of theoretical considerations and concrete intervention strategies, individual and systems dynamics and assessment/diagnostic and treatment issues and alternatives for clinicians who work with depressed adolescents.

The authors do not write from a rigid theoretical bias. Instead, their continuing emphasis is on understanding the individual adolescent within the context of his or her family, and making informed treatment decisions based on that approach. In this regard, Oster and Caro provide a most useful framework for the task of adolescent assessment and treatment. Their approach has a striking respect for interpersonal dynamics within a family, and for the importance of developmental model for understanding adolescent behavior and depressive symptomatology.

The necessity of observing and understanding the symptoms and their roles in the family life cycle continually stressed. The fuller meanings or functions of the symptoms are most completely assessed in the context of their expression. Numerous case examples and intervention strategies highlight the authors' emphasis on the individual within the family system.

The book, while exploring a variety of treatment options, is stronger in its detailed examination of the assessment process. A well-written section on general assessment issues concerning adolescent depression (which interestingly begins with a focus on interviewing the family) is followed by a lengthy exploration devoted to the specific task of evaluation and clinically intervening with the suicidal adolescent. Both sections are replete with concrete clinical strategies concerning areas about which to inquire (often with specific examples of facilitation questions) and numerous case examples often with transcripts of salient interchanges during the evaluation. The authors wisely approach the assessment as a therapeutic intervention which can serve as a foundation for further therapy—not as simply an information-gathering session.

The authors write with the insight and experienced approach of seasoned clinicians, aware of the adolescent's frequently challenging resistance and attempts to thwart even well-intentioned therapists, and also of the reward in facilitating the teenager's movement toward healthy accomplishment and satisfaction. It is this attention to maintaining and strengthening the "fragile alliance" (of which John Meeks has so eloquently written) with the adolescent and the family which makes this book an invaluable resource for concerned clinicians.

—*Reviewed by Michael DeStefano, Ph.D.*

Understanding and Treating Depressed Adolescents and Their Families. Gerald D. Oster and Janice E. Caro. New York: John Wiley & Sons, Inc. 1990. 228pp.

Periodicals Likely to Contain Articles About Childhood Depression

Journal of the American Academy of Child and Adolescent Psychiatry
Williams and Wilkins, 428 East Preston Street, Baltimore, MD 21202;
(410) 528-4000.
Published bi-monthly. Individual - $90/yr., Institution - $165/yr.
Provides research and review articles on a variety of childhood and adolescent psychological disorders.

Child Welfare League of America
Transaction Publishers, Transaction Periodicals Consortium, Department 3092, Rutgers University, New Brunswick, NJ 08903; (908) 932-2280.
Published bi-monthly. Individual - $55/yr., Institution - $70/yr.
Explores methods for improving child welfare services and practice for for deprived, neglected, and dependent children and their families. Reports on innovative practice, new programs, and new strategies for program delivery.
Education and Treatment of Children
Pressley Ridge Schools, 530 Marshall Avenue, Pittsburgh, PA 15214;
(412) 321-6995.
Published quarterly. Individual - $35/yr., Institution - $70/yr.
The purpose of this journal is to disseminate information related to education and treatment services for children and youth. One of the primary criteria for the research articles is that they must be of practical use to professionals working with children.

Journal of Abnormal Child Psychology
Plenum Publishing Company, 233 Spring Street, New York, NY 10013-1578;
(212) 620-8000.
Published bimonthly. Subscription - $275/yr.
Provides theoretical, research and review articles on a variety of childhood and adolescent psychological disorders.

Journal of Affective Disorders
Elsevier Science Publishers B.V.P.O., Box 211, 1000 AE, Amsterdam, Netherlands.
United States and Canada: Post Office Box 882, Madison Square Station, New York, NY 10159; (212) 989-5800.
Published monthly. Individual - $98/yr., Institution - $705/yr.
Publishes papers on depression, mania, anxiety, and panic disorders. Interdisciplinary format brings together papers concerning biochemistry, epidemiology, psychodynamics, clinical studies, and all forms of treatment for affective disorders.

School Psychology Review
National Association of School Psychologists, 8455 Colesville Road, Suite 1000, Silver Spring, MD 20910; (301) 608-0500.
Published quarterly. Individual - $40/yr., Institution - $60/yr.
Official journal of the National Association for School Psychology. It contains articles on theory, research and opinion related to the practice of school psychology. Three of the four issues in each volume cover specific themes; the first covers general topics.

Special Services in the Schools
Haworth Press Inc., 10 Alice Street, Binghampton, NY13904; (800) 342-9678.
Published quarterly. Individual - $36/yr., Institution - $45/yr.
This journal is designed for education professionals involved in the assessment, treatment, and the making of both preventive and intervention programs for children with special needs. It also addresses issues of administration of schools and programs.

Resources for Depressed and Suicidal Children

There are a number of books, both fiction and nonfiction, about depression and suicide for children from the early teens and up. For younger children, there are books which deal with death and loss, as well as books explaining feelings, self-esteem and various behavior problems. Because this represents a wide range of topics these books are not individually listed here.

As suicide has become a nationally-recognized problem for teenagers, a number of videotapes, films and pamphlets have been directed to this age group. In addition, many states and school systems have created manuals for the implementation of programs which address teen suicide. A sampling of these is listed below.

Books - Nonfiction

Colman, W. (1990) *Understanding and Preventing Teen Suicide*. Chicago: Children's Press. 112pp. Ill. This book discusses the phenomenon of teen suicide from a variety of perspectives, and includes a list of warning signs, a good discussion of the importance of therapy, and a list of common questions and answers. It is written in clear, simple prose, and illustrated with photographs.

Gordon, S. (1985) *When Living Hurts*. New York: Yad Tikvah Foundation. This is a book which provides suggestions for coping with the emotions surrounding depression and suicide, such as anger and hopelessness.

Gootman, M. (1994) *When a Friend Dies: A Book for Teens About Grieving and Healing*. Minneapolis: Free Spirit Publishing. 107pp. This is an elegantly-written guide through the grieving process which uses brief passages and quotes of teens. It includes issues specifically relevant to teenagers as well as general information about grieving. The Appendix includes a list of some organizations and inspirational quotations. The small size of the book makes it easily portable.

Levinson, N. and Rocklin, J. (1992) *Feeling Great: Reaching Out to Life, Reaching into Yourself Without Drugs*. California: Hunter House, Inc. 98pp. Ill. This book combines a friendly "users guide" to the brain, body and emotions, with suggestions on how to experience good feelings as well as tolerate those that are not so good. Some chapters discuss the importance of sound nutrition, exercise, relaxation, having a "good cry," etc., in a positive yet realistic manner. The Appendix presents a comprehensive listing of organizations which address many of the problems teenagers experience.

Myers, I. and Myers, A. (1982) *Why You Feel Down and What You Can Do About It*. New York: Scribner's. This book discusses family problems, peer pressure, and other problems and discusses getting help when needed. It is designed for adolescents.

Newman, S. (1991) *Don't Be S.A.D.: A Teenage Guide to Handling Stress, Anxiety, and Depression*. New Jersey: Julian Messner. 121pp. Ill. This book presents first person vignettes by teenagers and young adults who struggled with stress, anxiety and depression. These vignettes are followed by a discussion of the issues at hand and coping strategies. The Appendix includes a comprehensive list of organizations which address many of the problems teenagers face and books for further reading.

Toma, D. and Biffle, C. (1992) *Turning Your Life Around: David Toma's Guide for*

Teenagers. New York: HarperCollins. 211pp. Ill. This comprehensive book guides readers through reflections on their families and the individual problems they face in a one-on-one dialogue with David Toma. Exercises are integrated into the chapters to allow for further self exploration. A chapter is devoted to depression. The Appendix presents a comprehensive listing of relevant organizations.

Books - Fiction

Arrick, F. (1971) *Tunnel Vision.* New York: Bradbury Press. The story of how the family and friends of a 15-year-old boy who has committed suicide cope with his death. For grades 6 and up.

Bridges, S. (1982) *Notes for Another Life.* New York: Bantam Books. The story of two teenagers coping with significant family problems.

Cleaver, V. and Cleaver, B. (1975) *Grover.* New York: New American Library. Describes the confusing emotions and thoughts of a child whose seriously-ill parent commits suicide. For grades 5 and up.

Ferris, J. (1983) *Amen Moses Gardenia.* New York: Farrar, Straus, and Giroux. The story of a girl who suffers with depression while coping with an alcoholic father and a boyfriend who is not as serious as she had hoped.
Grades 7 and up.

Hale, J. (1972) *The Owl's Song.* New York: Doubleday. This book tells the story of a Native American boy who copes with suicide and alcoholism. Grades 7 and up.

Madison, W. (1979) *Portrait of Myself.* New York: Random House. The story of a 15-year-old girl struggling with issues of self esteem. She is rejected by the teacher she likes most and attempts suicide. Grades 7 and up.

Terri, S. (1972) *The Drowning Boy.* New York: Doubleday. The story of a boy who considers suicide in response to stressful life events but realizes that he doesn't want to die. Grades 6 and up.

Pamphlets

"About Suicide Among Young People." Chaning L. Bete Company Inc. South Deerfield, MA 01373.

"Grief After Suicide." Mental Health Association in Waukesha County, Inc., 414 West Moreland Blvd., Room 101, Waukesha, WI 53186.

"Suicide: We Are All Victims" and "Suicide: A Teenage Tragedy." Publications Service, Family Service America, 11700 West Lake Park Dr., Milwaukee, WI 53224.

School District and State Suicide Manuals

California: *Suicide Prevention Program for California Public Schools.* (1987) 260 pp. (ISBNO-8011-0682-6) California State Department of Education, Public Sales, P.O. Box 271, Sacramento, CA 95802-0271.

Colorado: *Handbook: Suicide Prevention in the Schools.* By Ruof, S., Harris, J., Robbie, M. Special Education, Weld BOCES, P.O. Box 578, La Salle, CO 80645-0578.
Florida: *Youth Suicide Prevention: A Guide for Trainers of Adult Programs.* (1989)

ERIC/CAPS Publications, 2108 School of Education, University of Michigan, Ann Arbor, MI 48109-1259.

Indiana: *Youth Suicide: A Comprehensive Manual for Prevention and Intervention.* 132 pp. By Barrett Hicks, B. National Educational Service, P.O. Box 8, Bloomington, IN 47402.

Videotapes and Films
"Why Isn't My Child Happy?" 110 minutes. Neurology, Learning and Behavior Center, South 500 East, Suite 100, Salt Lake City, UT 84102; (801) 532-1484. This new video is the first to deal directly with childhood depression as a clinical problem facing perhaps 10 percent of all children and adolescents. Dr. Sam Goldstein, a noted psychologist and lecturer on childhood psychological disorders, presents information on causes, warning signs, diagnosis, and treatment of childhood depression. The video features interviews with depressed children and families as well as a round table discussion of the topic.

"Adolescent Suicide: A Matter of Life and Death." 39 minutes. American Personnel and Guidance Association, 2 Skyline Place, Suite 400, 5203 Leesburg Pike, Falls Church, VA 22041; (703) 823-9800. Presents vignettes on many of the stressful situations adolescents face such as family problems, death of friend or family, teenage pregnancy, joblessness, academic suspension.

"Depression: Blahs, Blues, and Better Days." 20 minutes. Directions Unlimited, 8271 Melrose Ave., Los Angeles, CA 90046. This film explains the difference between depression and "the blahs" and presents normal and abnormal reactions to life crises.

"Keeping Your Teenager Alive: Theory, Prevention and Treatment of Adolescent Suicide." 110 minutes. Vidcam, Inc., 6322 Kings Pointe Rd., Grand Blanc, MI 48439; (313) 694-0996. Carl Tishler, Ph.D. discusses teenage accidents and suicide, and depression and treatment factors for working with adolescents.

"Too Sad to Live." 60 minutes. Massachusetts Committee for Children and Youth, 14 Beacon St., Suite 706, Boston, MA 02108. This film presents four studies of depressed and suicidal teens. Davis and Sandoval (1991) recommend it for mental health professionals and guidance counselors.

"Young People in Crisis." 30 minutes. EXAR Communications, 267B McClean Ave., Staten Island, NY 10305. This video presents young people in a variety of painful situations. It is narrated by Dr. Pamela Cantor and suggestions for intervention and adequate problem solving are presented.

Source: Davis, J. and Sandoval, J. (1991) Suicidal Youth: School-Based Intervention and Prevention. San Francisco: Jossey-Bass. pp.201-223.

- Video Review -
"Why Isn't My Child Happy?"

A unique and comprehensive clinical video, "Why Isn't My Child Happy?" uses the latest information on childhood depression and its treatment to explain clinical concepts. The format is that of a lecture at a parents' focus group by child psychologist, Dr. Sam Goldstein. Dr. Goldstein is a warm and caring clinician with in-depth knowledge of childhood depression and the children who have depression. Underlying all the information he provides is the strong message that parents need to talk with their children, to be involved, and to take their role as parents seriously. Toward the end of his discussion he presents a guideline for parents in the form of an acronym: P: Prepared, A: Available, R: Re-attribute, E: Emphasize strengths, N: Never quit, T: Take care of yourself.

Dr. Goldstein breaks down the complex web of research about depression into easily assimilated blocks of information. For example, he explains the difference between the externalizing and internalizing disorders in terms of the parents' reaction to their children. The children with externalizing disorders cause annoyance in their parents, while the children with internalizing disorders tend to cause more of a sense of being worried. Having established this, he continues to define depression in terms of three categories: 1) emotions and cognitions, 2) affect, and 3) symptoms. He explains these concepts clearly, and later in the video describes the essential symptoms needed to make a diagnosis of depression.

In discussing cognitions he highlights the child's locus of control. Depressed children tend to have an external locus of control; hence, they cannot own either their successes, which they tend to devalue, or their failures which they may blame on others or about which they may feel helpless. He notes the high co-morbidity of depression with other psychiatric disorders, especially anxiety, and provides the useful rule of thumb that when depressed, children look back and devalue, and when anxious, they look ahead and worry. He includes the feeling that no one really loves them and thoughts that life would be better without them as two other common cognitions of depressed children. In terms of emotions he lists unhappiness, inability to experience pleasure, hopelessness, guilt, and anger.

Risk factors for depression are different for boys and girls. For depressed boys Dr. Goldstein notes that research has found risk factors that include: above average number of health problems in infancy; boys who are overly dependent on their mothers at age five; boys overly dependent on their parents at age nine; early parental discord; and signs of anxiety. For girls he notes that research has identified the following risk factors: being raised by older parents; being raised in large families; being more anxious and not popular at age nine; having low status in the family; and growing up with families with more than an average number of stressful life events. Unfortunately he does not mention or discuss the higher rate of depression in females.

Dr. Goldstein recommends psychotherapy as the treatment of choice for childhood depression, and discusses his cognitive-behavioral approach to treatment. Two of his major areas of focus in the sessions are to help the child to internalize his or her locus of control and to become better at generating and implementing different solutions to their problems. He reports that medication for depression is helpful for a minority of depressed children, but does not appear to have more than a placebo effect for the majority of children with depression. He provides an interesting description of some of the research in this area.

Clinically, this video is more focused on pre-adolescent children. Throughout the video, sequences of discussions with a depressed boy and his family and a depressed girl are interspersed to help illustrate the concepts and to provide a better feel for the experience of the depressed child. The reactions of the boy's family members to his depression help to highlight the difficulties families face as they attempt to understand their child's changed behavior, as does the parents' narration of the steps they took to realize that professional consultation outside of the school was needed.

Also interspersed throughout the video are "man-on-the-street" interviews with several people. These interviews are interesting in that the particular people interviewed are more knowledgeable about childhood depression than one might expect. They serve to highlight the societal aspects of depression, the universality of the experience, and the need for parents to set aside time for their children.

Overall, this video is an excellent didactic tool, useful for training therapists and for educating parents, teachers, and community organizations about depression in children.

"Why Isn't My Child Happy?" 110 minutes. $49.95. Neurology, Learning and Behavior Center, South 500 East, Suite 100, Salt Lake City, UT 84102; (801) 532-1484.

Recent Journal Articles on
Childhood Depression

Ball, J., Archer, R., Gordon, R., French, J. (1991). **Rorschach depression indices with children and adolescents: Concurrent validity findings.** *Journal of Personality Assessment.* Dec. 57(3): pp.465-476. Presents evidence that the Exner Rorshach Depression Scale alone does not appear to have diagnostic validity for children, and should not be used without other measures of depression.

Harris, F., Ammerman, R. (1986). **Depression and suicide in children and adolescents. Special Issue: Health promotion in children: A behavior analysis and public health perspective.** *Education and Treatment of Children.* 9(4): pp.334-343. This article notes the association between childhood depression and parental depression as well as child abuse and neglect, and social and academic problems. It reports that parent training and social skills training are two promising behavioral interventions to prevent suicide and depression in children.

Jensen, P., Ryan, N., Prien, R. (1992). **Psychopharmacology of child and adolescent major depression: Present status and future directions.** *Journal of Child and Adolescent Psychopharmacology.* 2(1): pp.31-45. Reviews current knowledge of psychopharmacology of childhood depression, noting parallels to the history of the development of adult medication treatment for depression, and suggests that future research needs to include multi-site, longitudinal studies which address the problems of previous studies.

Kashani, J., Ray, J. and Carlson, G. (1984). **Depression and depression-like states in preschool-age children in a child development unit.** *American Journal of Psychiatry.* 141:pp.1397-1402. This study indicated that using DSMIII criteria children ages one through six have a significantly lower rate of depression than children ages nine to 12.

Kazdin, A. (1990). **Childhood depression.** *Journal of Child Psychology.* 31(1):pp.121-160. This is another excellent and thorough review of depression in childhood. It covers assessment, diagnosis, prevalence, etiological models and treatment. The author concludes with a consideration of the importance of considering treatment of depressed children as more than a downward extension of adult treatments, and in particular suggests that a focus on the family is particularly relevant to treatment of childhood depression.

Kazdin, A. (1989a). **Evaluation of the pleasure scale in the assessment of anhedonia in children.** *Journal of the American Academy of Child and Adolescent Psychiatry.* 28:pp.364-372. This paper indicates that as for adults, childhood depression is related to diminished pleasure, decreased pleasurable activities, and an increase in stressful events.

Kazdin, A., French, N., Unis, A. et. al. (1983). **Hopelessness, depression, and suicidal intent among psychiatrically disturbed inpatient children.** *Journal of Consulting and Clinical Psychology.* 22. Presents an important study indicating that as for adults, suicidal risk is more correlated with hopelessness than depression. Depression and low-self esteem also were shown to correlate with hopelessness.

Keller, M., Beardsless, W., Lavori, P. et. al. (1988). **Course of major depression in non-referred adolescents: a retrospective study.** *Journal of Affective Disorders.* 15:pp.235-243. This study indicates that dysthymia in children may be a precursor of later major depression and that major depression in children is often a chronic disorder.

Larsson, B. (1992). **Psychological issues in the assessment and treatment of depression in children and adolescents.** *Scandinavian Journal of Behavior Therapy.* 21(1):pp.3-18. This review article brings to light the need for more clarity about the effect of pharmacological treatment in children and for more treatment studies, noting that the majority of treatment studies in the literature refer to group treatments in school settings.

Lefkowitz, M. and Tesiny, E. (1985). **Depression in children: prevalence and correlates.** *Journal of Consulting and Clinical Psychology.* 53:pp.647-646. This study is one of several that finds no sex differences in prevalence of depression in children ages six to 12.

Mezzich and Mezzich (1979). **Symptomatology of depression in adolescence.** *Journal of Personality Assessment.* 43:pp.267-275. This study indicated that depression is more prevalent among adolescent girls than boys.

Puig-Antich, J. and Weston, B. (1983). The diagnosis and treatment of major depression in children. *Annual Review of Medicine.* 34:pp.231-245. This report indicates that Imipramine is effective in treating childhood depression as long as the dose is high enough to maintain a steady-state plasma level.

Reynolds, W. (1990). **Depression in children and adolescents: Nature, diagnosis, assessment, and treatment.** *School Psychology Review.* 19(2):pp.158-173. This is an excellent review of depression in children and adolescents covering the areas of assessment, psychotherapeutic intervention, and new directions in research. The article discusses the need for school psychologists to become familiar with this body of knowledge.

Reynolds, W., Stark, K. (1987). **School-based intervention strategies for the treatment of depression in children and adolescents.** *Special Services in the Schools.* 3(3-4):pp.69-88. This article describes the components of intervention strategies for childhood depression as they may be applied in the school setting. The results of group treatment studies are discussed, and suggest that interventions in the school can have a therapeutic effect.

Ryan, N., Puig-Antich, J. Cooper, T. et. al. (1986). **Imipramine in adolescent major depression: plasma level and clinical response.** *Acta Psychiatrica Scandanavica.* 13:pp 10-15. This study indicates that depressed adolescents do not respond as well or in the same way as prepubescent children and adults to treatment with Imipramine.

Semrud-Clikeman, M., Hynd, G. (1991). **Review of issues and measures in childhood depression.** *School Psychology International.* 12(4):pp.275-298. This is a good review article discussing many of the assessment tools available for childhood depression as well as other issues related to assessment.

Wilson, H., Staton, R. (1984). **Neuropsychological changes in children associated with tricyclic antidepressant therapy.** *International Journal of Neuroscience.* 24:pp.307-312. This study indicated that treatment of depressed children ages five-and-a-half to 16 resulted in improved neuropsychological and intellectual functioning.

CHAPTER 5

Violent and Aggressive Children: Society's Responsibility, Therapy's Challenge

"It was the wave of the hand from a 10-year-old boy with a Botticelli face and Dennis the Menace bangs that brought Elizabeth Alvarez to her death...The boy, Jacob Gonzales, wheeled around a bank parking lot on the banana seat of a pink bicycle he had stolen and looked for a robbery victim. His accomplice, Damien Dorris, a 14-year-old drug dealer who owed the neighborhood kingpins $430.00, lay in wait near the automated teller machine...But Mrs. Alvarez refused to hand over her $80.00, so Damien shot her in the head with a .22 caliber pistol."*

"Cynthia Kierstedt's 15-year-old son, big as a linebacker, foolish as a child, was hand- cuffed to the wall of a Brooklyn police station house. He had just been arrested in the killing of a man who delivered candy bars...Ms. Kierstedt cried and hollered at Shaul to give her a reason, but he just hung his head."**

"The country is facing a crisis of violence among young people unlike any before, crim- inologists say. Even as overall violent crime has leveled off since 1990 and the number of teenagers has declined, arrests of people under 18 for violent crime rose 47 percent from 1988 to 1992, according to the Federal Bureau of Investigation."*

As we researched and wrote this chapter, we were both heartened and discouraged by the wealth of information on violent and aggressive children. While the increase in youth violence is a depressing and frightening commentary on the state of youth and society, we are encouraged by the massive effort by professionals from many dif- ferent fields to stem the tide of aggression at all levels.

The problem of aggression in children needs to be addressed at both the micro or individual level, and the macro or community/societal level. Individual children become aggressive in reaction to a variety of factors including overly harsh punish- ment, abuse, witnessing violence, deprivation, etc. However, the environment which provides such experiences must also be considered as a factor. Many of the children who become aggressive are caught in a larger pattern of community violence and media glorification of violence. *Violence and Youth: Psychology's Response: Vol. 1* reports the following key ideas when it comes to poverty and aggression:

Many social science disciplines, in addition to psychology, have firmly established that poverty and its contextual life circumstances are major determinants of violence.

Rates of poverty are high in each of the ethnic minority groups.

Despite public stereotypes,...socioeconomic inequality—not race—facilitates higher rates of violence among ethnic minority groups.

Because of the significant number of programs and resources available to therapists and other professionals working in the area of violence prevention, one goal of this chapter is to present listings of these resources. Thus we have expanded our resources, organizations, and conferences sections, and have included a list of curricula related to youth violence and aggression.

One important preventive program is the FAST Track program. This program is now being run at four different sites across the country. It provides prevention and intervention by working with individual children who have been identified by the first grade as having problems with aggression, as well as providing training and consultation designed to reduce aggression at the class and school levels. *Child Therapy Today* interviews Kenneth Dodge, Ph.D., one of the psychologists implementing FAST Track, and a leading researcher in childhood aggression.

We also speak with Ronald Slaby, Ph.D., who wears many hats in his work with aggressive youth. As a member of the Commission on Violence and Youth, he has had the opportunity to interact directly with the public on this issue, and as Senior Scientist at the Education Development Center he works on the development of several programs and curricula for aggressive children.

With the goal of promoting increased involvement in the effort to counteract the growing tide of aggression in children we have reprinted the section entitled, "How Can We Intervene Effectively?" from *Violence and Youth: Psychology's Response, Volume 1*. We have also included an article about guns and youth which details the magnitude of the problem, organizations addressing the issue, and promising approaches to solving this enormous problem.

We review the significant research on aggressive children, which has led to a better understanding of the cognitive process that characterizes the thinking of aggressive children and the STAR curriculum created by the Center to Prevent Handgun Violence, as well as two videos designed to educate children about violence.

The increase in childhood and youth violence reflects a society that has been unable to nurture, support, and protect its children. The realities that many aggressive children must cope with are daunting and overwhelming. Efforts to reach these children before they become aggressive adults are of paramount importance and should be the concern of all mental health professionals.

As always, crisis brings with it opportunity. As therapists we have the opportunity to share our knowledge not only with individual children, but with society at large. It is our hope that the ideas and resources presented in this chapter will contribute to this effort.

—The Editors

*New York Times, *Vol. CXLIII, No. 49,698, May 16, 1994, page 1*
**New York Times, *Vol. CXLIII, No. 49,697, May 15, 1994, page 1*

Children, Adolescents and Firearms

By Beth Jacklin

The prevalence of firearms in adolescents' lives is at an all-time high. Fortunately, many federal and state agencies, national groups, and grassroots organizations are addressing the issue with a multitude of promising approaches.

MAGNITUDE OF THE PROBLEM

To intervene effectively, an individual or agency must clearly discern exactly where, how, and to whom firearm violence occurs so that prevention and intervention strategies will be appropriately designed and implemented. Statistics illustrate the magnitude of the firearm problem in a variety of ways. One may study mortality and morbidity numbers in the United States; the difference between rates in the United States as compared to those in other developed countries; rates of African American males killed by guns as compared to white males; children's accessibility to guns; psychological trauma; or even financial figures related to the cost of firearm injuries.

Firearm Mortality and Morbidity Rates in the United States

Firearm injuries are the second leading cause of death in the United States for all children and adults 10 to 34 years of age. In the United States in 1990, an adolescent between the ages of 10 and 19 was unintentionally shot every 19 hours; committed suicide with a gun every 6 hours; and was intentionally killed with a gun every 3 hours. In 1989, in core metropolitan counties, firearm homicide was the leading cause of death for all children 15 to 19 years of age. From 1985 to 1990, the firearm homicide rate for children 19 and under increased 114 percent. Although it is difficult to find data on morbidity, the Centers for Disease Control and Prevention (CDC) reports that for every firearm fatality in 1985, 7.5 nonfatal firearms injuries occurred.

U.S. Firearm Rates Compared to Other Developed Countries

Compared to every other developed country, the rate of firearm homicide in the United States is enormous. The homicide rate in the U.S. among males 15 to 24 years of age was 21.9 deaths per 100,000 in 1987. This is 4.4 times higher than the rate of the developed country with the next highest homicide rate for the same population. (In 1987, Scotland had 5.0 deaths per 100,000.)

In 1987 in the U.S., 4,223 homicides occurred among males 15 to 24 years of age. Three-quarters of these homicides resulted from the use of firearms. The combined data from 14 other developed countries reached a total of 398 homicides among males ages 15 to 24—less than one-quarter of these homicides were committed with firearms.

Firearm Rates of African American Males as Compared to White Males

Firearm injuries are the leading cause of death for African American males aged 15 to 19. In 1990, firearm homicide rates for African American males 15 to 19 years old were 11 times the rate among white males.

When comparing African American and white mortality rates, however, it is essential to note that the relationship between race, socioeconomic status, and violence is quite complex. Studies have found that socioeconomic status more accurately predicts rates of violence than race. When socioeconomic status is considered, the difference between African Americans and the general population, both as victims and perpetrators, becomes quite small.

Firearm Accessibility

Mortality statistics only begin to describe the extent to which firearms are present in the lives of many adolescents. In November 1991, the Journal of the American Medical Association reported on a study that found that 1 out of 20 high school students (5 percent) had carried a firearm in the last month. A 1993 Harris Poll found that 15 percent of the 2,508 children surveyed in grades 6-12 said that they had carried a handgun in the last month.

Many children have access to guns at home. Estimates suggest that half of the homes in the United States contain one or more firearms. In 1990, experts calculated that 1.2 million elementary-aged, "latchkey" children lived in a home with a firearm. The most common reason handgun owners give for owning a firearm is self-defense. A study in the New England Journal of Medicine, however, found that in King County, Washington, guns kept at home were involved in the death of a stranger. These deaths included suicide, homicides, and unintentional fatal shootings.

In 1990 in the United States, 451 adolescents (10 to 19 years of age) were unintentionally killed with a firearm. Not surprisingly, a study of unintentional handgun shootings among children ages 16 and under found that such incidents usually occur when the children are unsupervised.

Psychological Trauma

Adding to the tragedy of firearm injuries and deaths is the psychological toll that is taken on the perpetrators, the victims, their families, and those who witness violence. Witnesses to violence are at high risk for psychological disturbances as well as later involvement in violence either as a victim or perpetrator. Even in infancy, clear associations have been found between exposure to violence and posttraumatic symptoms and disorders. A recent survey of American children 10 to 19 years of age found that 39 percent of them knew someone personally who had been killed or injured from gunfire.

Financial Costs

Additionally, the community and society as a whole suffer serious financial impact. A 1988 study of a regional trauma center in San Francisco found that the average cost of initial hospitalization per firearm patient was $6,915. Taxpayers paid 85.6 percent of this cost. Another study conducted in the mid-1980s found that the average cost of initial and subsequent hospitalizations for firearm injuries was $14,982. In this study, the public paid 80 percent of the cost of treating the gunshot wounds.

ORGANIZATIONS ADDRESSING THE ISSUE

Fortunately, a variety of potentially effective points of intervention exist and a range of activities are currently being conducted at many levels. Federal and state agencies, professional associations, and national and grassroots organizations are all identifying ways their constituencies can reduce firearm injuries and deaths.

Federal and State Agencies

At the federal level, the report entitled *Healthy People 2000: National Health Promotion and Disease Prevention Objectives*, developed by the United States Department of Health and Human Services, defined 18 objectives related to prevention of violent and abusive behavior. Three of these objectives concern firearms, specifically firearm accessibility as a point of intervention.

Healthy People 2000 states that "although the question of restricting firearm ownership and usage is contentious...few argue that adolescents should have unsupervised access to firearms or other lethal weapons. Fewer still argue that adolescents should be permitted to carry loaded firearms or other lethal weapons at school or on the city streets." The Centers for Disease Control and Prevention are currently tracking baseline data and delineating strategies to address each of the Year 2000 objectives.

Over the past five years, state public health departments have become more involved in the firearms issue. They are now supporting initiatives at the state level, many of which follow recommended CDC strategies.

Professional Associations

Professional organizations such as the American Academy of Pediatrics (AAP) and the American Psychological Association (APA) are also making the problem a priority. The AAP held a forum on firearms and children in 1989, where its membership recommended that, in the short-term, gun manufacturers and retailers develop and sell gun safety devices. For the long-term, the AAP advocated that legislative bans be placed on various firearms and the public be made aware of the prevalence of childhood gun injuries. Currently, many pediatricians are working to carry out these recommendations.

The Commission on Violence and Youth was created in 1991 by the APA to review current and past research on youth violence. After a review of the literature and a series of hearings, the commission released a report in August 1993 entitled *Violence and Youth: Psychology's Response* (see article in this chapter "Violence and Youth").

The commission recommended many specific action steps to be taken by APA members and concerned others, including parents, health care providers, educators, state and local agencies, the armed services, the Federal Communications Commission, and the U.S. Civil Rights Commission. The report noted that "violence is not a random, uncontrollable, or inevitable occurrence. Many factors, both individual and social, contribute to an individual's propensity to use violence, and many of these factors are within our power to change."

National Organizations

A national leader in this area is the Center to Prevent Handgun Violence, which educates the public about the dangers of handgun violence and accessible loaded handguns. Center programs work primarily with students, the entertainment industry, and pediatricians. In collaboration with the AAP, the Center has developed a protocol for pediatricians to use when speaking with parents about the risks of keeping a gun in the home, as well as dangers of community gun violence. Its school-based program, *Straight Talk About Risks*, is a curriculum for children in grades pre-K to 12 and covers gun safety, violence depicted on television, emotions, and anger management.

Community-Based Organizations

Community-based organizations across the country are working to prevent youth violence. One such group, Teens on Target (TNT), a grassroots organization in Oakland, California, was established in 1988 after two junior high school students were shot in school. TNT was founded on the assumption that young people can address the problem of gun violence better than adults. Each year an Oakland teacher and a San Francisco Trauma Foundation staff member educate a group of high school students on gun violence. The students develop their leadership skills, then become violence prevention policy advocates, peer educators, and mentors for middle and elementary school students.

PROMISING APPROACHES

The agencies and organizations mentioned above are all examples of efforts that focus on preventing firearm injury and death. Individuals and organizations working to prevent firearm violence choose and develop strategies that are specifically appropriate for them to use, depending on what aspect of the problem they would like to address. Interventions can be categorized into three basic types: educational, legal, and technological/environmental. Clearly, a comprehensive approach that includes a combination of strategies is most like to result in a reduction of firearm violence.

Educational Interventions

Educational programs are often carried out in schools, community-based organizations, and physicians' offices. They emphasize the prevention of weapon misuse, the risks involved with possession of a firearm, and the need for conflict resolution and anger management skills. Programs may also include firearm safety instruction (defined as either how to act safely around firearms or how to avoid situations involving firearms), public information campaigns, counseling programs, or crisis intervention hotlines.

Legal Interventions

Legal measures strive to limit access to firearms—the number and type of people eligible to own or possess firearms, as well as the types of firearms that can be manufactured, owned, and carried. Federal law prohibits the sale of guns to minors but does not regulate the possession of guns by minors. Currently, minors may legally possess and carry an unconcealed handgun in 37 states.

Each year a large number of firearm-related bills are proposed in Congress and state legislatures. In June 1993, the Youth Handgun Safety Act of 1993 (S. 1087) was introduced into the United States Senate. If passed, it would prohibit "the possession of a handgun or ammunition by, or the private transfer of a handgun or ammunition to, a juvenile."

Concerning state activities, one example is what the Florida, California, and Wisconsin state legislatures have done. They each passed laws requiring gun owners to keep guns stored or locked to deter accessibility to minors, and requiring investigation and prosecution if a minor is injured with a gun that is not properly locked or stored. Whatever legal intervention Congress or a community implements, the enforcement of the legal measure is critical to its success.

Technological/Environmental Interventions

Firearm design requirements are both a technological and a legal intervention. Unlike most other products in the United States, firearms are manufactured without regulatory standards. Firearm standards that have been proposed include designing guns to be less concealable; producing guns with trigger safeties and loading indicators; and regulating the appearance of toy guns as well as actual handguns made of plastic. Design of ammunition is also being explored, since bullet shape, consistency, and composition determine the severity of a gunshot injury.

Environmental and technological measures are based on the premise that automatic protections are more effective than those requiring specific action by individuals. Environmental interventions include those approaches that change the institutions and structures that surround children. For example, the reduction of violence on television could positively affect cultural norms about violence (analogous to the reduction of television's portrayal of smoking).

Schools are also exploring the use of such measures as metal detectors and dress codes to try and reduce the ability of students to conceal weapons.

CONCLUSIONS

Educational, legal, technological, and environmental interventions are all tools used to form violence prevention initiatives. The statistics concerning children and firearms tell the current epidemiological story, while the many organizations and institutions addressing the issue illustrate the commitment and energy available to intervene.

It is time now to fund, implement, and carefully evaluate more of the existing firearm violence prevention strategies to determine which will effectively reverse the current trend and ensure the safety of all children.

Beth Jacklin is Technical Assistance Coordinator at Education Development Center, Inc. in Newton, Massachusetts. This article is reprinted with permission of the author from Options, *Adolescent Violence Prevention Resource Center, Volume 2, Spring 1994.*

Violence and Youth:
How Can We Intervene Effectively?

The plethora of intervention programs designed to address violence in children and adolescents highlight the need for a systematic approach to intervention and for the evaluation of the effectiveness of these efforts. We have reprinted here the recommendations for intervention made by the American Psychological Association's Commission on Violence and Youth as published in their report, Violence and Youth: Psychology's Response, *Volume I. The report in its entirety is available, free of charge, from the American Psychological Association, Public Interest Directorate, 750 First St. NE, Washington, DC 20002-4242.*

The urgent need to prevent further destruction of young lives by violence has led to a proliferation of antiviolence interventions for children, youth, and their families. Many of these interventions were created primarily for service delivery, without scientific underpinnings or plans for outcome evaluation. Some are targeted at perpetrators of violence, others at their victims, and still others at bystanders who may play a pivotal role in condoning or preventing violence. Some are preventive, and others seek to ameliorate the damage already done. Some are targeted toward changing individuals, and others seek to change the systems and settings that influence behavior, such as the family, peers, schools and community.

Those programs that have been evaluated and show promise include interventions aimed at reducing risk factors or at strengthening families and children to help them resist the effects of detrimental life circumstances. Few programs, however, have been designed to evaluate the direct short-term and long-term effects of intervention on rates of violence; most concentrate instead on assessing the program's effects on risk factors or mediators of violence. Many potentially effective psychological interventions have been developed and are currently being investigated, but most have been too recently implemented to have appropriately long-term evaluation data to judge their effects on rates of violence.

Characteristics of Effective Programs

Effective intervention programs share two primary characteristics: (a) they draw on the understanding of developmental and sociocultural risk factors leading to antisocial behavior; and (b) they use theory-based intervention strategies with known efficacy in changing behavior, tested program designs, and, validated, objective measurement techniques to assess outcomes. Other key criteria that describe the most promising intervention approaches include:

• **They begin as early as possible to interrupt the "trajectory toward violence."** Evidence indicates that intervention early in childhood can reduce aggressive and antisocial behavior and can also affect certain risk factors associated with antisocial behavior, such as low educational achievement and inconsistent parenting practices. A few studies have included 10- to 20-year follow-up data that suggest these positive effects may endure. Some of the most promising programs are interventions designed to assist and educated families who are at risk before a child is even born.

• **They address aggression as part of a constellation of antisocial behaviors in the child or youth.** Aggression usually is just one of a number of problem behaviors found in the aggressive child. Often the cluster includes academic difficulties, poor interpersonal relations, cognitive deficits, and attributional biases.

• **They include multiple components that reinforce each other across the child's everyday social contexts: family, school, peer groups, media, and community.** Aggressive behavior tends to be consistent across social domains. For this reason, multimodal interventions that use techniques known to affect behavior and that can be implemented in complementary ways across social domains are needed to produce enduring effects.

• **They take advantage of developmental "windows of opportunity:" points at which interventions are especially needed or especially likely to make a difference.** Such windows of opportunity include transitions in children's lives: birth, entry into preschool, the beginning of elementary school, and adolescence. The developmental challenges of adolescence are a particular window of opportunity, because the limit-testing and other age-appropriate behaviors of adolescents tend to challenge even a functional family's well-developed patterns of interaction. Also, antisocial behaviors tend to peak during adolescence, and many adolescents engage in sporadic aggression or antisocial behavior. Programs that prepare children to navigate the developmental crises of adolescence may help prevent violence by and toward the adolescent.

Primary Prevention Programs

Prevention programs directed early in life can reduce factors that increase risk for antisocial behavior and clinical dysfunction in childhood and adolescence. Among the most promising of these interventions are:

• "Home visitor" programs for at-risk families, which include prenatal and postnatal counseling and continued contact with family and child in the first few years of life. In a 20-year follow-up of one such program, positive effects could be seen both for the at-risk child and for the mother.

• Preschool programs that address diverse intellectual, emotional, and social needs and the development of cognitive and decision-making processes.

Although these results indicated improvements in factors that have been associated with violence, there is no way to tell from the findings if the programs actually had an effect on the incident of violence. Only when outcome measures include an assessment of the frequency of violent behaviors can we determine the validity of these or any programs as violence-prevention efforts.

School-based primary prevention programs for children and adolescents are effective with children and youth who are not seriously violence-prone, but these programs have not yet been demonstrated to have major effects on seriously and persistently aggressive youth. Evaluations of such school-based programs show they can improve prosocial competence and reduce at-risk behavior among youth who are not seriously violence-prone by promoting nonviolent norms, lessening the opportunity for and elicitation of violent acts, and preventing the sporadic violence that emerges temporarily during adolescence. The programs teach youth how to cope better with the transitional crises of adolescence and offer them behavioral alternatives and institutional constraints to keep sporadic aggressiveness within socially defined bounds.

Primary prevention programs of the type that promote social and cognitive skills seem to have the greatest impact on attitudes about violent behavior among children and youth. Skills that aid children in learning alternatives to violent behaviors include social perspective-taking, alternative solution generation, self-esteem enhancement, peer negotiation skills, problem-solving skills training, and anger management.

Secondary Prevention Programs for High-Risk Children

Secondary prevention programs that focus on improving individual affec-

tive, cognitive, and behavioral skills or on modifying the learning conditions for aggression offer promise of interrupting the path toward violence for high-risk or predelinquent youth. To the extent that development is an ongoing process, programs that target learning contexts, such as the family, should produce the most enduring effects. On the other hand, programs for youth already showing aggressive behavior have not been successful when the programs are unfocused and not based on sound theory. Furthermore, because most interventions have been relatively brief and have emphasized psychoeducational interventions, it is not known whether they would be effective with seriously aggressive or delinquent youth.

Programs that attempt to work with and modify the family system of a high-risk child have great potential to prevent development of aggressive and violent behavior. A growing psychological literature confirms that family variables are important in the development and treatment of antisocial and violent behavior. For example, in a study of adolescents referred to juvenile court for minor infractions, an intervention that used a family-therapy approach to identify maladaptive family interaction patterns and provide instruction for remedial family management was successful in reducing recidivism rates and improving family interactions for up to 18 months after treatment. Sibling delinquency rates were also reduced.

Interventions that aim to prevent or treat violence within the family have been shown to be of great value in preventing the social transmission of violence. Modes of transmission within the family may include direct victimization and witnessing abuse of other family members. Both the parent-perpetrators of child abuse and the child-victims require treatment to change the current situation and to help avert long-term negative consequences for the victim and for the family. Physical abuse of children and adolescents, and other patterns of domestic violence, may be effectively treated with family-centered approaches to intervention.

Interventions to prevent and treat sexual violence by and against children and adolescents are of critical importance because of the potential long-term effects of such victimization. Victims of sexual violence are at increased risk for future victimization and may develop a constellation of problems ranging from low self-esteem to posttraumatic stress disorder (PTSD).

• Many programs have been created to prevent sexual victimization (e.g., "good touch/bad touch" programs for young children). Although these programs have been shown to affect children's knowledge, awareness, and skills, little is known about whether they actually affect the child's behavior in an abuse incident or not.

• Individual treatment that involves the parents (or the nonoffending parent, if the sexual violence is intrafamilial) and includes behavioral techniques is one approach that has been found to be effective for children with PTSD symptoms.

• Youthful offenders are highly likely to reoffend if they go untreated, whereas treatment with multimodal approaches (i.e., addressing deficits in cognitive processes, family relations, school performance, and peer relations) has shown great promise in reducing the rate of recidivism for both sexual and nonsexual offenses among these youth.

The concept of "diversion programs" to keep high-risk or redelinquent youth out of the juvenile justice system has great merit, and there is evidence that diversion programs with strong grounding in psychological theory can have a positive effect on recidivism rates. In one such intervention, youth 12 to 16 years old who had been referred to juvenile court were diverted to a program in which each had close contact with a trained volunteer 6 to 8 hours per week for 18 weeks. The intervention included behavioral contracting, child advocacy, help to obtain access to community resources, and involvement in the community. The contacts between the student volunteer and the youth took place in the youth's home, recreational settings, or other convenient locales.

Carefully controlled and large-scale evaluations of the diversion program have shown that the intervention reduced recidivism among participants up to 2 years after the point of intake. Diversion programs are favored in many jurisdictions because the crowded, poorly supervised conditions of many juvenile facilities expose predelinquent youth who are referred to the courts for minor infractions to more experienced and violent youth, putting them at risk for victimization and potentially socializing them to adopt a criminal trajectory. In most jurisdictions, however, the diversion programs do not have scientific grounding and encompass little more than vaguely formulated counseling programs; the overall effectiveness of such programs has not been demonstrated.

Treatment Programs

Several promising techniques have been identified for treating children who already have adopted aggressive patterns of behavior. These include problem-solving skills training for the child, child management training for the parents (e.g., anger control, negotiation, and positive reinforcement), family therapy, and interventions at school or in the community.

For youth who have already shown seriously aggressive and violent behavior, sustained, multimodal treatment appears to be the most effective. Such psychological treatment consists of carefully designed and coordinated components involving school, parents, teachers, peers, and community, often coordinated around family intervention. By the time youth with antisocial behavior are referred clinically, their dysfunction often is pervasive and severe, and multiple counterinfluences need to be brought to bear to achieve significant impact. Research has demonstrated that adolescents with aggressive, antisocial, or delinquent behavior can improve with such treatment. Although long-term outcome data are not available, existing data show the improvements are maintained at least up to 1 year.

• **Interventions with gang members, a small but significant number of whom are among the most seriously violent and aggressive youth, also must be multimodal, sustained and coordinated.** Such interventions should combine and coordinate current and past approaches to intervening with gang youth, including social control methods (i.e., surveillance, incarceration, probation), "gang work" methods (i.e., building relationships between gang members and social workers who help gang members abandon delinquency and adopt conventional ways of behavior), and "opportunities provision" methods (i.e., jobs programs, educational development). Because ethnic minorities make up a large proportion of gangs and gang membership, the importance of cultural sensitivity in these gang interventions cannot be overemphasized.

Societal Interventions

The partnership between police and community represented by community policing may play a pivotal role in reducing youth violence. Although the effect of community policing on youth violence has not been evaluated, community policing is believed to have great potential, making the officer's role one of preventing problems, not just responding to them.

Interventions can mitigate the impact of children's continued and growing exposure to violence in the media. Some successful or promising approaches include:

• Empowering parents to monitor their child's viewing;
• Helping children build "critical viewing skills" or develop attitudes that viewing violence in the media can be harmful;

• Working with the Federal Communications Commission to limit the amount of dramatized violence available from viewing by children during the "child viewing hours" of 6 am and 10 pm; and

• Working with the media to better inform and educate children in strategies for reducing or preventing their involvement with violence.

Design and Evaluation of Intervention Efforts

Intervention programs would be carefully designed to fit the specific needs of the target group. Program design must take into account significant differentiating factors identified in psychological research as relevant to an intervention's success. Chief among these factors is the need for interventions to be linguistically appropriate and consonant with the cultural values, traditions, and beliefs associated with the specific ethnic and cultural groups making up the target audience. The gender, age, and developmental characteristics of participants are other factors that must be carefully considered in the design of any intervention.

Improvements in evaluation techniques have been a major contributing factor in the development of scientific approaches to antiviolence interventions with children and adolescents. Evaluations identify the relative strengths and weaknesses of an intervention and the direction of the effects. In addition, programs vary in their breadth of impact, and it is critically important to document whether or not an intervention has a broad impact (e.g., across multiple social domains, multiple problem behaviors, or both) or a more focused impact (e.g., altering use of one substance but not others and improving social competence but not altering at-risk behaviors).

In addition to evaluation's role in identifying promising interventions, an important reason for evaluation programs is that even well-designed programs may have no effect, or, occasionally, adverse outcomes. Programs may be ineffective for a variety of reasons, such as poor staffing, weak interventions (i.e., interventions unlikely to affect behavior, such as information and education materials only), lack of cultural sensitivity, departures from the intended procedures while the interventions are still in effect, and lack of administrative support. As well, the potential for iatrogenic (treatment-caused) effects must also be acknowledged in psychosocial interventions.

- Focus on Programs -
The FAST Track Program

Kenneth Dodge, Ph.D., psychological researcher and clinician, has devoted his career to studying and working with aggression in children. Having received his doctoral degree in Clinical Psychology from Duke University and worked on the faculty of Indiana University in Bloomington, and the University of Colorado in Boulder, he is now a professor of psychology at Vanderbilt University in Nashville. At Vanderbilt he is a member of the Conduct Problems Prevention Research Group which is implementing a primary and secondary intervention program called FAST (Families And Schools Together) Track. FAST Track has as its focus working with aggressive and potentially aggressive children.

In our interview Dodge indicated that he has had a lifelong interest in children, and a particular interest in conduct problems in children from disadvantaged backgrounds. He cited his upbringing on the South Side of Chicago and being a "witness to teenage gang activity and some modest degree of violence" as one of the experiences which may have stimulated his interest in aggressive children, long before aggressive and violent children became the focus of national attention.

Dodge is the author and co-author of numerous papers on the subject of aggressive and conduct-disordered children in which he has attempted to delineate some of the internal cognitive factors leading to aggressive behavior, as well as some of the environmental factors. In this interview he talks about the FAST Track Program and his research findings.

Laura Slap-Shelton, Psy.D.: *Please explain what the FAST Track program is and what its goals are.*

Kenneth Dodge, Ph.D.: The FAST Track program is a research study, an attempt to develop, implement and evaluate a comprehensive program to prevent conduct disorder. It is funded by The National Institutes of Mental Health and the Department of Education, and is being implemented at four different sites nationally. In addition to Nashville, Tennessee the other sites are Seattle, Washington, Durham, North Carolina, and rural areas of Central Appalachian Pennsylvania.

The intent is to study children from a diverse range of backgrounds. This research population provides diverse ethnic groups, who are for the most part of lower socioeconomic status. It also enables us to study regional effects and urban versus rural differences.

LS-S: *How does the program work?*

KD: There are two different features or hierarchical levels to the program. The first is a universal primary prevention program. We have randomly assigned schools in each of the four areas to receive the intervention. The primary intervention involves working with all of the children at a grade level in a classroom curriculum that is designed to teach children social cognitive skills and behavioral self-control.

This is the called the PATHS (Providing Alternative THinking Strategies) Program. We supplement the PATHS curriculum with consultation with the teachers around behavior management. We work with the schools as a whole, even with the principals, so the first level is a program designed to enhance social competence in all of the children in the schools receiving the intervention with the goal of preventing conduct problems.

LS-S: *Are the school personnel receptive to learning new ways of handling disciplinary problems and working with children labeled as "troublemakers?"*

KD: Yes. We've had to work with them closely, over time, and I can't say that everyone's been perfectly receptive, but by and large they have recognized the problem, and they have bought into the overall goal of long-term preventive intervention. We respect the fact that the teachers and other school personnel are working extra hours at times in order to participate in the program. We pay the teachers for their time, for coming to weekly workshops or supervision sessions.

LS-S: *What is the second part of the program?*

KD: The second part is more intensive work that is directed toward high-risk children. The children are identified at the beginning of first grade. Some children within each school are targeted as high risk for conduct problems. They receive intensive services based on a theoretical developmental model which addresses the combination of family and child factors that might lead to conduct problems.

One of the services provided in the high-risk program is weekly parent training in behavior management. The parents come to a weekly group meeting of five or six parents. The groups are led by our staff and are designed to teach behavior management techniques and methods of praising, motivating, and positively interacting with their children.

While the parents are meeting in the parent group, the children are in another room in the same school building engaged in a child social skills training group, also led by our staff. Again the groups consist of five or six children. They engage in games and activities designed to teach problem- solving, emotion regulation, and behavioral self-control in a highly- structured curriculum.

LS-S: *How do you help the parents translate the sessions into action at home?*

KD: We follow the sessions with bi-weekly home visits. This enables us to individualize the program and get to know each family on a one-on-one basis.

A third component of the intensive program is that each high-risk child receives academic tutoring in reading skills three times a week. The addition of this component is based on the idea that being able to read at grade level is a buffer against the development of conduct problems. That is, academic problems may lead to conduct problems or they may co-occur with conduct problems.

LS-S: *Is this because academic problems lead to frustration and feelings of failure?*

KD: Yes, because for children who are having academic difficulties, school is no longer a desirable place to be. There may be ostracism by teachers and/or peers, and lack of motivation or interest in school. In the long run, these kids are more likely become disenfranchised from school, drop out, and then move toward juvenile delinquency and conduct problems.

LS-S: *How far into the future will these children be followed in the study?*

KD: We plan to follow them for 12 years.

LS-S: *How do you identify the high-risk children to be included in the study?*

KD: We look for behavior problems in kindergarten, as rated by teachers and parents. The schools in which we are working are already serving children from high-risk areas: children from high-violence crime neighborhoods, schools that have high rates of school drop-out, high rates of poverty—not suburban schools. Initially, we screen for the children by conducting individual structured interviews with the teachers. We have them evaluate each child in their classroom. We follow that up with telephone or in-home visit interviews with the parent. In order to be selected as high-risk, the child needs to meet criteria on each of the evaluations. The children who are selected display aggressive behavior problems in both settings.

LS-S: *What is the cut-off for including children in the program?*

KD: Approximately the top 10 percent of children with behavior problems within a school are selected for the FAST Track program.

LS-S: *What are some of the techniques you are using to teach conflict resolution and problem-solving?*

KD: In the small groups, everything becomes an opportunity to try to teach different skills. For example, when we have a snack we collaborate with the children in order to decide who's going to hand out the cups, hand out the napkins, pour the drinks, hand out the cookies, etc. The children have to cooperate and collaborate, and sometimes that takes a long time. That's one way that we teach certain skills in the context of daily activities.

In terms of a curriculum, we teach children to recognize and identify emotions. We go through about 25 different emotions, from happy, sad, angry and afraid to jealous, humiliated and so on. We teach the words that go with the emotions, what faces might express the emotions, and what circumstances might lead to those emotions. We talk with them about what experiences they have that might lead them to feel a particular way.

In the first year we focus on understanding emotions. Later we link that understanding to behavior by saying that while it's okay to feel emotions, it's not okay to engage in whatever behavior they wish. We also teach the kids methods of controlling their behaviors.

LS-S: *How do you do that?*

KD: The method we use is based on a stop light. We teach the children to identify when they're having a problem. For example, a child might know he is having a problem because his heart is racing, or he feels something horrible, or he's confused. Once he knows he is having a problem, he needs to go to the red light and calm down. At the beginning we literally have the children go to a red light—it might be a red circle on the floor, or on their desk that they touch. We make it as concrete as possible. We teach them to take some deep breaths, count to 120, whatever works best to calm them down. Then we have them say what the problem is, so that they can learn to verbalize the problem that they're experiencing. It might be that someone stole their pencil, or that the teacher humiliated them.

Then they go to the yellow light to think about what to do. Here we teach and practice problem-solving skills to generate both multiple solutions and high quality solutions. In the 2nd, 3rd, and 4th grades we increase the complexity of the problem-solving step by having the children envision in their minds the consequences of various behaviors. They might say, "Well, one thing I could do is threaten the other kid by telling him that if he doesn't give me the pencil back, I'll hit him over the head." Then we try to teach them to anticipate what would happen if they did that, what the consequences would be of hitting their peer over the head. When they're ready they go to the green light where they try out a solution to see how it works. Then we help them to evaluate the solution's success.

We have the teachers use the stop light model in the classroom, and we use it in our parent groups so everyone involved in the FAST Track program learns this technique. We find that it is useful to parents in their own behavior management of their children; helping the parents to respond effectively and thoughtfully to their children's behavior is very important because we know that harsh discipline contributes to aggressiveness in children.

LS-S: *In some of your studies you have the children paired with popular nonaggressive children. Would you explain that part of the program?*

KD: We do have a peer pairing component in which the high-risk children learn and practice concrete behavioral skills like turn-taking, cooperation, and complimenting, with a more popular peer. We go to the classroom once a week, we take the child out of the classroom with a selected peer, go to another room and they engage in a task for about 15 minutes. The high-risk child has been primed, ahead of time, to cooperate or do something in a skillful way with us watching. Not only does this provide practice in social skills, but it also offers the high-risk child an opportunity to form a friendship with a well-adjusted peer. So far we've found that this works very well in first grade when the skills are very concrete and the kids are very happy to come out of the classroom and to participate. We haven't done it in third grade and beyond because we feel much more hesitant to take children out of the classroom.

LS-S: *What program components are you adding for the higher grades?*

KD: When the children reach fourth grade, we will add a mentoring component. Research shows that it is quite important for child development during this period to have a same sex, same gender adult role model with whom the child can connect. We will continue with the parent and children groups. An additional focus will be on the transition to middle school. We have a component that involves explicitly helping the children with the skills needed to make that adjustment.

LS-S: *Is there a group in middle school yet?*

KD: Not yet. The oldest children are currently in third grade.

LS-S: *Have the data you have collected up to this time demonstrated that the program is already reducing aggressive behaviors in the high-risk children?*

KD: We've been able to evaluate the first cohort of children at the end of first grade and again at the end of second grade, and the second cohort at the end of first grade. Based on the evaluations to date we have found a reliable modest level of success in bringing about proximal changes in short-term outcomes. We hope this will lead to long-term positive outcomes.

LS-S: *What do you mean by proximal?*

KD: Well, for example, compared to our randomly-assigned control group, the intervention group is performing more skillfully on our independent test of social cognitive skills, problem-solving skills, and emotional understanding. So they're learning the skills that we are trying to teach. Second, direct observations of the children on the playground indicate that they're displaying fewer aggressive behavior problems compared to the control group.

Third, in terms of peer sociometric interviews the intervention group is more well-liked than the control group, and peers are a tough group to please. The differences between the intervention and control groups are at a modest level. I don't mean to say that every intervention child has fewer aggressive behavior problems than every control child, but on average these findings are consistent across the four geographic sites. If they hold up over a long period of time, we hope and expect that they will lead to long-term outputs that are really important.

LS-S: *I'd like to switch our focus and ask about some of the theoretical aspects of your research. Your studies indicate that both a hostile attributional bias and an intention-cue detection deficit are part of the perceptual bias that lead children to engage in aggressive behavior. Would you explain these two concepts?*

KD: The intention-cue detection deficit is an error that a child makes in interpreting another's intentions. Usually that happens in a negative outcome provocation situation. For example, a child might be standing in line in the hallway at school and another child comes running and bumps in to the child from behind. The running child's intentions may be hostile or benign. If the target child misreads the other child's intention as being hostile he or she is more likely to react in an aggressive manner to the incident.

Children who make errors in reading other's intentions have a hard time relating effectively. We assess intention reading by presenting children with videotapes of sample social interactions like the one I described. We ask them to imagine being one of the children in the video, to watch about 30 seconds of the videotape, and then watch a provocation. After that we ask them what is the intention of the peer provocateur. We have found that aggressive children as a group are less skilled than non-aggressive children in accurately interpreting the intentions of others.

The hostile attributional bias is a particular kind of error that children make in assessing the intentions of others. Aggressive kids rarely make the error of assuming that the other child was prosocial or benign, when in fact the child was hostile. They're very good at recognizing hostility when it occurs. Instead, their bias is toward assuming that others are being negative and hostile in ambiguous cases and also in cases where it's clearly not true.

LS-S: *Another interesting aspect of your research is the idea that aggressive children tend to rely more on their cognitive organizations or schemas in interpreting behaviors than nonaggressive children.*

KD: Yes. The theory is that these children have had negative experiences in early life that are stored in memories or world views, what we call schemas about the way the world operates. For these children the expectation is that the world behaves in negative, hostile ways. When they see some negative outcome cues like being bumped from behind, they immediately assume that the peer must have been hostile, because that fits the child's world view.

LS-S: *Will FAST Track become a nationally-available program like Head Start?*

KD: We see it as a logical follow-up to Head Start. Head Start is a preschool program generally directed toward all children in poverty. Some of the children will emerge from that kind of program still in need of more intensive kinds of services because they're at particular risk and that's where this program might pick up.

LS-S: *What is the cost of the program?*

KD: The estimated cost for the first grade year, which is the first year, is about $5,000 per child. In subsequent years the cost goes down per child because we're not doing as much tutoring, etc. That's expensive, there's no doubt about that. On the other hand, these are the highest-risk children, and we believe that a high proportion of these children would end up incarcerated, or school dropouts or in special education for behavior problems without the intervention. Given that the cost of incarcerating one child for one year is approximately $50,000.00, FAST Track will be cost-effective if it reduces the rate of incarceration, say, from a half to a quarter of the kids who go through the program. It's a matter of paying more money now to save much more money later.

For more information about FAST Track, write: Department of Psychology and Human Development, Peabody College, Vanderbilt University, Nashville, TN 37203, Attn.: Kenneth A. Dodge, Ph.D., or call (615) 322-7311.

Highlights From an Interview with...
Ronald Slaby, Ph.D.

Ronald Slaby, Ph.D. is a Senior Scientist at the Education Development Center in Newton, Massachusetts and a Lecturer at Harvard University. As a psychologist who has devoted his work to the problem of aggressive youth, he has made contributions at many levels including research, program and curriculum development, writing, and teaching. As a member of the American Psychological Association's Commission on Violence and Youth, he contributed to Volume 1 of its report, *Violence and Youth: Psychology's Response,* and to five chapters of Volume 2 which is to be published in August of this year.

Dr. Slaby recently represented the Commission at a press conference in Washington, DC, which lead to a media blitz with hundreds of news articles and TV stories about the issue. This generated calls from police, lawyers, teachers, congressmen, foundations, community leaders, and mental health professionals seeking more knowledge about what can be done to counteract the alarming increase in youth generated violence. In our interview he noted that Janet Reno was observed to have "Violence and Youth: Psychology's Response" with her when testifying in Congress on violence and television.

Slaby reported that he is preparing a book on violence prevention for young children with three other professionals. The book will be titled *Early Violence Prevention Tools for Teachers of Young Children*, and will be published by the National Association for Education of Young Children.

In addition, a curriculum for middle school children entitled *Aggressors, Victims, and Bystanders* is in final revision at present and will be published by the Education Development Center. This curriculum takes the approach of studying the "habits of thinking" of middle school children that put the children at risk for involvement in violence. Such habits include egging on other children to fight, beliefs about the importance of fighting, and beliefs about how and whether it is "okay" to stop fighting.

With the large number of curricula now available for violence prevention and intervention programs, *Child Therapy Today* asked Dr. Slaby what criteria are important in selecting a curriculum. He suggested that the psychologist or school professional ask the following questions:

1) Has the curricula been evaluated and demonstrated effectiveness? Does it provide for evaluation?
2) Is the curricula an ongoing program with materials and implementation procedures?
3) Is the curricula based on strong connections to theory and research?

Slaby sees the violence prevention curriculum as "building a bridge between our two most important bodies of knowledge: scientific evidence of what happens in controlled settings, and wisdom generated from implementation of interventions by practitioners." He says, "If we can connect evidence with wisdom we have the makings of a successful program."

Another of Slaby's unique contributions is to teach the first college-graduate level course on violence prevention. His course, taught at Harvard University, is called "Preventing Violence in America." He reports that his classes always consist of students and professionals from a variety of disciplines and occupations including lawyers, physicians, corrections officers, and divinity school students. He feels that his course provides a strategy for integrating the different perspectives and information bases on issue of youth violence.

Using his Habits of Thought Model he addresses how children can be approached from a variety of professional perspectives, as well as parenting perspectives. Another goal of his course and other work is to "clean up the toxins of violence in society and/or help children to dissociate themselves from these toxins." Slaby stated that some people feel that it is up to the government to solve this problem, but that this solution has many pitfalls. It is preferable to involve the community at every level in this effort.

One particular "toxin" that Slaby has addressed is television. The Commission's report states that, "There is absolutely no doubt that higher levels of viewing violence on television are correlated with increased acceptance of aggressive attitudes and increased aggressive behavior." While one would expect that there is more violence in adult prime time programming, the statistics indicate otherwise. While on average there are five to six violent acts per hour occurring during prime time viewing, there are *20 to 25 violent acts per hour* occurring on children's Saturday morning television programs.

In the interview, Slaby noted that this programming actually teaches children to laugh at violence by playing laugh tracks (often adult laugh tracks) during the violent activity. He noted that when children confront real violence they do not find it funny, and try to withdraw as much as possible from such activities. Exposure to violence in a positive context has been found to significantly affect a child's perception of it. For example, the Commission's report cites a study in which a significant relationship was found between exposure to television violence at age 8 and antisocial acts 22 years later. Some of the effects of the culture of violence include desensitization to violence, and increased mistrust of others related to a fear of becoming a victim.

Yet another hat that Slaby wears is being on an Advisory Group to the Joint Center for Political and Economic Studies in Washington, DC. This Advisory Group is funded by the Pew Foundation and is writing a paper on television violence which will serve as a guide for the funding of television programming. Slaby is also proactively involved with positive television programming for children and is a consultant to the popular public television program, "Shining Time Station."

For more information about Dr. Slaby's upcoming publications and the Education Development Center, contact the Center at 55 Chapel St., Newton, MA 02174; (617) 969-7100.

Working with Aggressive Children:
Avoiding Cyclic Interactions

In an article by Nicholas Long (1991) which was written as a tribute to Fritz Redl, former Chief of the Children's Research Branch of the National Institutes of Mental Health (NIMH), and a pioneer in work with aggressive children, a number of useful suggestions for working and training staff to work with aggressive children are provided. We summarize them here as they speak to the difficulty of therapeutic work with clients who are often less than receptive to the "help" that is being offered them.

The essence of Long and Redl's message is that to work successfully with aggression in others, it is imperative to know one's own experience of aggression and its effects on one's own affects and behaviors, as well as to understand the cyclic, dynamic nature of aggressive behavior.

Long presents the Aggressive Conflict Cycle Paradigm as a means of conceptualizing the aggressive child or adolescent's internal experience. In this paradigm he begins with the aggressive individual's self concept, noting that "'never trust or need adults' is the basic assumption of the highly aggressive student's power struggle."

The first component to set off the cycle is a Stressful Event which sets off the next component, Feelings. Here Long notes that aggressive students find certain affects intolerable and therefore react to them by attempting to disavow them in a variety of dysfunctional ways. They also are often not able to distinguish between their feelings and their behavior. For example, Long notes that while it is healthy to be angry in certain situations it is not healthy to violently attack the person who may have caused the anger. While it is healthy to feel sadness at the loss of a friend or family member either due to a death, a change of residence, or because of neglect by the person, it is not healthy to withdraw from all other people.

The Feelings stage leads to the observable behaviors that cause others to assess the individual as aggressive. Behaviors designed to make the source of painful unacceptable affect go away may include hitting, fighting, breaking rules, running away, stealing, using drugs, and other activities that bring the child or adolescent into direct conflict with the therapist and with the individual's environment. These behaviors lead to the final stage in the cycle, the stage which enables the cycle to snowball, and that is the reactions of others to the child or adolescent.

Aggressive behavior in others inevitably arouses counter-aggressive feelings and actions in ourselves. Long writes, "One of the amazing concepts of interpersonal relationships is that students in stress can actually generate their feelings, and at times, their behavior in others." The more negative and punitive the response of the therapist or helping other, the more likely the aggressive child is to become further burdened by unacceptable, painful emotions, and to become even more hostile, and primitive in reaction to the Stressful Event. In addition, the Stressful Event has now has generated a second Stressful Event—negative response by others. If the therapist is drawn into the client's aggression cycle, the chances are that a power struggle will occur and escalate. Therefore, it is the therapist and staff who must act responsibly in order to stop the cycle rather than fuel it.

To change the situation into one in which the children or adolescents can learn to improve their coping skills, it is important for the therapist to provide "I" messages about their experience or what they will do, rather than "You" messages, either in negatively describing the child's behavior or ordering the child to engage in another behavior. This keeps the therapist from directly engaging in the child's cycle.

It is important to see beyond children's behavior to the needs that they are experiencing, and to help them make the connection between their feelings and their behavior. From this point, a connection between the Stressful Event and children's feelings can be made, and alternative ways to process and respond to the event discussed.

Long suggests seven steps needed to break the Aggressive Conflict Cycle and makes suggestions for changing it into what he calls a Coping Cycle. To break the cycle it is important to:

1. View conflict as a normal part of human experience.

2. View conflict as a product of the aggressive child's perceptions, and as being neither good or bad.

3. Understand that when in conflict or stressed the aggressive child tends to be overwhelmed by his/her affect.

4. Understand that the affect will generally drive the child's behaviors.

5. Recognize that these behaviors will lead to more negative consequences for the child or adolescent and are therefore self-destructive, even if they are also destructive to others.

6. Recognize the effect of the child's behavior on the therapist or care provider and avoid mirroring or in other ways joining in the hostile behaviors.

7. Avoid creating a new Stressful Event in the form of a power struggle.

Source: Long, N. (1991) What Fritz Redl taught me about aggression: Understanding the dynamics of aggression and counteraggression in students and staff. *Residential Treatment for Children and Youth.* 8(4), pp.43-55.

Information Processing and Aggressive Children

Researchers on aggression in children have come to a consensus on some of the key features of the way these children think. Following an information processing model, they have been able to identify the ways in which the information processing of aggressive children differs from adaptive children.

Dodge (1993) breaks down the cognitive tasks of problem-solving into the following stages: 1) Encoding, 2) Mental representation, 3) Response access, 4) Response evaluation and selection, and 5) Enactment. Problems at each of these stages have been found in aggressive children, although not all of these children have problems with all of the stages. Akhtar and Bradley (1991), in a review article which makes use of Dodge's model, report that aggressive children:

- **Often fail to encode all relevant environmental cues**
- **Are biased to assign hostile intentions to their social partners**
- **Generate fewer and less effective solutions for problematic situations**
- **Pursue inappropriate social goals**
- **Experience deficits in the enactment of many social behaviors**
- **May display a degree of egocentrism in evaluating the social environment's response to their behavior.**

We will review each of these items in terms of Dodge's model. In terms of encoding relevant environmental cues, aggressive children have been found to attend more often to hostile acts directed towards themselves (Dodge, 1993, p. 564). While this pattern may have arisen as an adaptive defensive pattern, it serves to increase the likelihood that the child will misidentify situations as hostile when they are not.

Dodge (1993) includes in the heading of "mental representation" a variety of functions including attributions of causation and intent, social perspective taking, and moral reasoning and the meaning of an event on the child's sense of self-worth. Many studies (Nasby et al. 1979; Guerra and Slaby, 1989; Wass, 1988) have supported the finding that aggressive children are more likely to assign hostile intent to another's actions than nonaggressive children. This bias predisposes the child to react aggressively (Dodge, 1980, in Dodge, 1993).

However, aggressive children are more likely to make hostile attributions when they are directly involved in the action as opposed to when they are merely observing their peers. Thus hostile attribution is associated more with reactive aggression than proactive aggression (Dodge, 1993). Dodge describes this problem as "intention-cue detection deficit." Intention-cue detection deficit has been shown to be independent of intelligence or general skill at cue detection (Dodge, 1993). Interestingly, depressed children have also been found to misinterpret the intentions of others as being hostile, but attribute blame for the hostility to themselves.

Response access includes the ability of the child to generate effective and adaptive responses to different situations. Aggressive children tend to generate more atypical responses to difficult situations and to be more inflexible in their ability to generate alternative responses. Dodge (1993) reviews a number of studies in which the response of aggressive children to specific situations have been evaluated. For example, in response to friendship or peer entry dilemmas aggressive children are more likely to generate responses that are "verbally coercive, physically aggressive, or bizarrely irrelevant to the task" (p. 568).

Response evaluation and selection includes functions determining the moral value of a proposed response, the degree to which the response will bring about the desired outcome, the degree to which the response may be subject to approval or disapproval by others, and effect of the response inter- and intra-personally (Dodge,1993). Aggressive children and adolescents have been found to identify fewer possible outcomes, to assign a more positive value to aggressive behavior than other children, and to underestimate the amount of disapproval their actions will generate. They tend to expect more positive outcomes from aggressive behavior than nonaggressive children and adolescents (Dodge, 1993; Slaby and Guerra, 1988, Boldizar et al., 1989). Whereas reactive anger was found to be more associated with the stage of Mental Representation, proactive, or instrumental aggressive behavior was found to correlate more with the characteristics of the aggressive individual's Response Evaluation phase. The Enactment phase has to do with the carrying out of the chosen response. There is not as much research in this area of processing for aggressive children (Dodge,1993; Akhtar and Bradley, 1991). Although aggressive children engage in behaviors which are deviant, it is not clear if these result purely from a deficit in knowledge of how to carry out a behavior or if the behaviors reflect earlier stages of processing as described above.

Dodge (1987, 1993) and Huesmann (1988) conceptualize aggressive children as containing knowledge bases or mental structures that are applied to the majority of the behaviors in which the child engages. Huesmann speaks of aggressive scripts learned early in childhood. The child may learn these scripts from direct experience or from witnessing the aggressive behaviors of others. Cues related to the event in some way are likely to elicit the previously learned scripts for aggressive behaviors. Huesmann (1988) writes:

The likelihood that a child will access a script for specific aggressive behaviors is certainly dependent on how many relevant cues are present in the environment at recall time. Theoretically, the most important cues are characteristics of the environment (even seemingly irrelevant ones) that are identical with those present when the script was encoded. However, other cues for general aggressive behavior (e.g. guns) may also trigger the recall of specific scripts for aggressive behavior even if they were not associated with the scene at encoding. (p. 21)

Dodge (1993) reports on studies which indicate that aggressive children tend to depend more their own knowledge bases in interpreting situation than nonaggressive children, and that children with a high number of aggressive constructs engage in fighting more often than children with fewer aggressive constructs [(Stromquist and Strauman (in press) as reported in Dodge (1993)].

Sources: Akhtar, N. and Bradley, J. (1991) Social information processing deficits of aggressive children: present findings and implications for social skills training. *Clinical Psychology Review.* 11, pp. 621-644. Boldizar, J., Perry, D. and Perry, L. (1989) Outcome values and aggression. *Child Development.* 60, pp. 571-579. Dodge, K. (1993) Social-cognitive mechanisms in the development of conduct disorder and depression. *Annual Review of Psychology.* 44, pp. 559-584. Dodge, K. and Tomlin, A. (1987) Cue utilization as a mechanism of attributional bias in aggressive children. *Social Cognition.* 5, pp. 280-300. Huesmann, L. (1988) An information processing model for the development of aggression. *Aggressive Behavior.* 14, pp. 13-24. Nasby, W., Hayden, B., DePaulo, B. (1979) Attributional bias among aggressive boys to interpret unambiguous social stimuli as displays of hostility. *Journal of Abnormal Psychology.* 89, pp. 459-468. Wass, G. (1988) Social attributional biases of peer-rejected and aggressive children. *Child Development.* 59, pp. 969-992.

Coping with Aggressive
Children in the Classroom

"Dealing with aggression in the classroom is one of the most difficult tasks that confronts a teacher. It requires both strength and sensitivity...Strength is determined by how well a teacher can control and regulate disruptive students, whereas sensitivity is reflected in the teacher's perception of the cues signaled by these students."

In *Student Aggression*, Goldstein, Harootunian and Conoley provide a model of the factors important to a teacher's handling of aggressive students, and ways that teachers can be helped to make effective decisions in handling violent or aggressive behavior in the classroom. Their ideas on this topic are summarized here, and their book is highly recommended for professionals working in school settings.

As managing the aggressive student becomes more of a daily reality for school teachers, there is more of a need for professionals working with the teachers to understand and provide support and guidance to teachers managing aggressive behavior in their classrooms. There are several factors which make the sudden aggressive act of a student or students one of the most difficult challenges a teacher can face. Grant and Secada (1990) point out that there will be an increasingly larger difference between teacher and student backgrounds in the coming years and suggest that cultural differences will contribute to teacher's difficulties in coping with aggressive students.

Teaching involves more than simply providing students with information. Doyle (1986) points out that the classroom situation is one which requires management skills because of the many different levels and types of activity that occur in it. He describes the dimensions of the classroom environment as including: multidimensionality of events, simultaneity of events, immediacy of events, unpredictability of events, the "public" nature of teaching, and the history of the particular classroom. All of these factors influence how a teacher will decide to respond to an aggressive action on the part of a student.

Harootunian and Yarger (1981) report that teachers evaluate the success of their efforts more on the degree of student involvement than on the actual amount of information imparted. While student violence was a negative factor in teachers' self evaluations, its absence was not a positive factor. Thus student violence impacts quite negatively on a teacher's opinion of his or her success as a teacher. This potentially creates a situation in which a teacher may feel powerless and make decisions based on a desire to retain control rather than address the core of the situation.

Goldstein, Harootunian, and Conoley (1994) suggest that decision making is an important, if not pivotal, aspect of teaching which plays a critical role in how a teacher handles an aggressive student. The decisions teachers make about how to handle the aggressive student will depend to a large extent on the teacher's implicit and explicit understanding of the student, the situation, and their ability to resolve the situation. For example, Brophy and Rohrkemper (1980b) found that teachers who believed that aggressive students had the ability to stop engaging in violent behavior at will were more likely to have low expectations for promoting change in the student's behavior and used punishment-related strategies rather than interventions which promote long term change.

The teacher characteristics which would lead to sound decision-making when coping with aggression in the classroom are:

1) Remaining calm in the face of a crisis

2) Listening actively without becoming defensive and authoritarian
3) Avoiding win-lose situations
4) Maintaining a problem solving approach

One way role for psychologists to help teachers develop and/or maintain these qualities when coping with the aggressive student is to help them make their implicit assumptions explicit. By making the teacher's assumptions explicit, the teacher has an opportunity to develop a wider variety of coping strategies, and a better sense of when and with whom certain strategies are likely to be most effective and useful. Part of making assumptions explicit involves the process of learning more about the aggressive student. The following questions are useful in helping teachers to make decisions based on a fuller and more conscious understanding of the student and the situation:

1. Who is the person? (identify)
2. What does the person want? (intention)
3. What does the person know? (knowledge)
4. What does the person know how to do? (competence)
5. What is the person trying to do? (action)
6. How is the person trying to do it? (style)

Another series of questions they suggest helps the teacher evaluate how the student acts (more techniques to help teachers make their assumptions about aggressive students and situations explicit may be found in *Student Aggression*):

1. Like all other students in some ways.
2. Like some other student in some ways.
3. Like no other students in some ways.

When a teacher intervenes he or she must simultaneously evaluate the outcome for the class as a whole and for the individual or individuals who are being disruptive. Hunt (1971) suggests that it is important to know a student's "accessibility channel" in deciding on the best approach. The four channels he proposes are: 1) cognitive orientation; 2) motivational orientation; 3) values orientation; and 4) sensory orientation. Understanding students in this way allows for the planning of interventions which have a chance of impacting meaningfully on the student or students, as well as creating a classroom situation which will discourage such students from acting aggressively. It is also useful for teachers to have an understanding of the developmental level of their students, although this may not directly impinge on the immediate decisions made.

Finally, teachers need to be able to evaluate the effects of their interventions. Psychologists are in a unique position to help teachers develop effective ways of monitoring the level of aggressive activity on the part of a student or students.

Sources: (as found in Goldstein, Harootunian, and Conoley, 1994, pp. 171-195): Brophy, J. and Rohrkemper, M. (1980b) *Teacher's specific strategies for dealing with hostile aggressive students.* (Research Series No. 86). East Lansing, MI: Institute for Research on Teaching. Michigan State University. Doyle, W. (1986) Classroom organization and management. In M.C. Wittrock (Ed.) *Handbook of Research on Teaching.* New York: Macmillan, 3rd Ed. pp. 392-431. Goldstein, Harootunian, and Conoley (1994) *Student Aggression*, New York: Guilford Press. pp. 171-195. Grant, C. and Secada, W. (1990) Preparing teachers for diversity. In W. R. Houston (Ed.). *Handbook of Research on Teacher Education.* New York: Macmillan. pp. 403-422. Harootunian, B. and Yarger, G. (1981) *Teachers' conceptions of their own success.* Washington D.C.: ERIC Clearinghouse on Teacher Education.

Selected Assessment Tools for Aggressive Children

There are several approaches that may be taken in assessing aggressive children. When interested in arriving at a standard DSMIII-R diagnosis, there are several commonly-used personality inventories and structured interviews for children such as the Child Behavior Checklist (Edelbrock and Achenbach, 1984), the Schedule for Affective Disorders and Schizophrenia for School-Age Children (Chambers, Puig-Antich, Hirsch et al. 1985), the Diagnostic Interview for Children and Adolescents (Herjanic and Reich, 1982), and others.

The DSMIII-R diagnoses most often considered are Conduct Disorder and Oppositional Defiant Disorder. However, aggressive behaviors can be observed in reaction to a variety of emotional and psychological disturbances including depression, anxiety, Attention Deficit Hyperactivity Disorder, and a variety of dissociative disorders. Thus, in order to fully understand the nature of a child or adolescent's behavior, it is often most helpful to not only test in order to arrive at a diagnosis, but to evaluate what situations lead the child in question to engage in aggressive behavior, as well as what environmental factors support aggressive interaction with others as a reasonable strategy.

Dodge and Murphy (1984) endorse a three-step procedure for the assessment of aggressive children. The first step involves identifying the child as being aggressive. The second step involves identifying the social situations that are problematic for the child, and the third step involves identifying the social skills deficits that the child demonstrates when involved in the problematic situations. Dodge et. al. (1985) write, "The outcome of this three-step procedure will be a two-dimensional profile, in which the situational contexts of a child's social incompetence are identified along the first axis, and the component skill deficits are identified along the second axis. Such a detailed assessment could provide the clinician with a basis for social skills training of the individual child."

With greater attention being focused on children with aggressive behaviors it is expected that an increasing number of scales and measures will be seen in the coming decade. Below we have listed a sampling of assessment tools that draw on the identification of the child and adolescent's behaviors.

Conners Parent and Teacher Rating Scales (CTPS and CTRS) [Conners (1969, 1989,1990) and **Manual for Conners' Rating Scales**. North Tonawanda, New York: Multi-Health Systems, Inc.] The CTPS and CTRS are widely-used instruments which can be administered in a relatively brief amount of time. Two of the subscales included in these measures are Conduct Disorder and Antisocial. Both the CTPS and CTRS come in short and long forms. The items consist of descriptions of behaviors which the rater is asked to evaluate in terms of how much the child has been bothered by the behavior in the past month. The tests have been shown to have good reliability and validity on a number of dimensions.

Interpersonal Problem Solving Analysis [Marsh, D. (1982) The development of interpersonal problem-solving among elementary-school children. Journal of Genetic Psychology. 140:pp.107-118.] In this procedure, children are presented with two situations and are asked to imagine themselves in the situation. Seven questions are asked following the presentation of each story. The questions include, "What is the problem?", "If you were to solve this problem what would be the goal?", and "What do you think the best solution would be?"

The Perceived Competence Scale for Children (PCSC) [Harter, S. (1982) The Perceived Competence Scale for Children. Child Development. 53:pp.87-97.] The

PCSC was developed as a self-report measure of perceived competence for children grades 3 through 9. A parallel Teacher's Rating Scale can be administered with the child scale. The test consists of 28 items which evaluate perceived competency in three separate categories: 1) Cognitive competence, 2) Social competence, and 3) Physical competence. The questions are presented in a structure alternative format so as to avoid the over endorsement of socially desirable traits. The test demonstrated good reliability and validity.

Preschool Behaviour Questionnaire (PBQ) [Behar and Stringfield (1974) A behavior rating scale for preschool children. Developmental Psychology. 10: 601-610.] This questionnaire was designed to identify social-emotional problems in young children. It has 30 items which fall into three factors: 1) Hostility/aggression, 2) Anxiety/fearfulness, and 3) Hyperactivity/distractibility. It has been found to have high inter-rater and test-retest reliability (Behar, 1977), and good external validity for preschool and grade one children (Rubin, K., Moller, L., and Emptage, A., 1987).

Taxonomy of Problematic Social Situations for Children. (TOPS) [Dodge, K., McClaskey, C., and Feldman, E. (1985), Situational approach to the assessment of social competence in children. Journal of Consulting and Clinical Psychology, 53(3):pp. 344-353. Available from Kenneth Dodge, Vanderbilt University, Nashville, TN (see Focus on Programs).] TOPS is an empirically-developed measure of children's social competence based on their responses to specific situations, requiring some level of social skill for successful mastery. The TOPS instrument contains 44 situations, grouped into one of six mutually-exclusive categories. These categories include: 1) Peer Group Entry, 2) Response to Peer Provocations, 3) Response to Failure, 4) Response to Success, 5) Social Expectations, and 6) Teacher Expectations. TOPS can be used as part of a clinical evaluation. Teachers and parents are asked to rate, on a scale of one to five, how likely the child will be to respond inappropriately to the situation. It was found to successfully differentiate rejected aggressive children and adaptive children.

Sources: Dodge, K., McClaskey, C., Feldman, E. (1985) Situational approach to the assessment of social competence in children. *Journal of Consulting and Clinical Psychology.* 53(3):pp. 344-353. Harter, S. (1982) The Perceived Competence Scale for Children. *Child Development.* 53:pp. 87-97. Rubin, K., Moller, L., and Emptage, A. (1987) The Preschool Behaviour Questionnaire: A useful index of behaviour problems in elementary school-age children? *Canadian Journal of Behavioural Science.* 19(1):pp. 87-100. Slaby, R. and Guerra, N. (1988) Cognitive mediators of aggression in adolescent offenders: 1. Assessment. *Developmental Psychology.* 24(4):pp. 580-588.

Recent Research Findings on Aggression in Children

• Using Kenneth Dodge's (1986) information processing model of social problem solving and interaction, researchers reviewed studies of aggressive children. They found that a**ggressive children as a group have information processing deficits** at all stages of Dodge's model. Difficulties include: 1) failing to encode all relevant environmental cues; 2) having a bias toward hostile interpretation of other's intentions; 3) generating fewer and low quality solutions to problem situations; 4) pursuing inappropriate social skills; 5) having difficulty in performing social activities; and 6) egocentric thinking in interpreting the environment's response to their behavior. The authors stress that individual aggressive children may have difficulties at one or more stages and that interventions such as social skills training need to be targeted to the child's particular strengths and weaknesses.

Akhtar, N. and Bradley, J. (1991). Social information processing deficits of aggressive children: Present findings and implications for social skills training. *Clinical Psychology Review.* 11(5):pp. 621-644.

• In a study of the parent-child relationships of aggressive, withdrawn, and sociable children, it was found that **withdrawn girls and aggressive boys perceived less support in their father-child relationships than did other children.** The mothers of aggressive and withdrawn children and the fathers of aggressive children perceived less support in their parent-child relationships than did other parents. Sociable children and their parents tended to have a higher agreement about the level of support within their relationships.

East, P. (1991). The parent-child relationships of withdrawn, aggressive, and sociable children: Child and parent perspectives. *Merrill Palmer Quarterly.* 37(3):pp. 425-443.

• **A study examining the validity of the Human Figure Drawing Test (HFDT) to differentiate aggressive and nonaggressive 3- to 5-year-olds (n=32) failed to support the efficacy of the HFDT as a valid discriminator of aggressive from nonaggressive children.** The children were categorized as aggressive or nonaggressive by teacher ratings on the Child Behavior Checklist. Two methods were used to evaluate the HFDT results. The children's drawings were scored using seven measures of the Koppitz system, and additionally were evaluated clinically by ten clinical judges. Neither method led to a valid differentiation of the two groups of children.

Norford, B., Barakat, L. (1990). The relationship of Human Figure Drawings to aggressive behavior in preschool children. *Psychology in the Schools.* 27(4):pp. 318-325.

• In a study of the relationship between mothers' beliefs about how social skills should be taught and their preschool aged child's behavior, it was found that **mothers of the aggressive children in the study endorsed highly directive strategies in teaching social skills, but were more accepting of maladaptive behaviors than mothers of children with average social adaptation.** Mothers of withdrawn children were more likely to endorse highly directive strategies and coercive enforcement of social rules than mothers of the children with average social adaptation.

Rubin, K. and Mills, R. (1990). Maternal beliefs about adaptive and maladaptive social behaviors in normal, aggressive, and withdrawn preschoolers. *Journal of Abnormal Child Psychology.* 18(4):pp. 419-435.

• In a study of the relationship between the attributional style of mothers and the level of aggression in their children it was found that **mothers with a lack of per-**

sonal control were more likely to have aggressive children than mothers with a sense of personal responsibility and an internal attributional style. The study involved 61 mothers and their children ages four to 13. A life-style questionnaire was used to evaluate the mothers and the Health Examination Survey (W. Wells, 1980) was used to evaluate the children's level of aggression.

Keltikangas-Jarvinen, L. (1990). Attributional style of the mother as a predictor of aggressive behavior in children. *Aggressive Behavior.* 16(1):pp. 1-7.

• In a study of the validity of teacher's identification of aggressive children, it was found that the **teacher's ability to identify popular, aggressive, and socially withdrawn children was validated by self-report, peer sociometric nominations and ratings, and behavioral observation measures.** The three groups of students were drawn from a pool of 780 fourth graders.

Ollendick, T., Oswald, D., and Francis, G. (1989). Validity of teacher nominations in identifying aggressive, withdrawn, and popular children. *Journal of Clinical Child Psychology.* 18(3):pp. 221-229.

• A review of literature on learning disabilities and aggressive and anti-social behavior in children concluded that **learning disabilities may worsen aggressive behavior and that conduct disorders predispose children to a variety of problems including academic problems.** It could not be concluded that learning disabilities lead to aggressive or delinquent behavior.

Cornwall, A. and Bawden, H. (1992). Reading disabilities and aggression: A critical review. *Journal of Learning Disabilities.* 25(5):pp. 281-288.

• In a study examining the relationship between verbal ability and aggressiveness in 53 physically abused children, ages 6 to 14 and living in a residential treatment center, it was found that the **highly aggressive children were more significantly deficient in reading and expressive language skills, and required more speech-language services than the other children.**

Burke, A., Crenshaw, D. et. al. (1989). Influence of verbal ability on the expression of aggression in physically abused children. *Journal of the American Academy of Child and Adolescent Psychiatry.* 28(2):pp. 215-218.

• In a study of 43 families with aggressive boys in grades 2 to 6, a time-limited social learning family therapy model was evaluated. **The boys in the families receiving this treatment demonstrated gains in positive behaviors at home and school, empathy, family cohesion, problem-solving efficiency, and positive family relationships relative to a waiting-list control group.** At a 9 to 12 month follow-up, the gains were still maintained.

Sayger, T. Horne, A., et. al. (1988). Social learning family therapy with aggressive children: Treatment outcome and maintenance. *Journal of Family Psychology.* 1(3):pp. 261-285.

• A study of the social networks of aggressive children and matched control nonaggressive children indicated that **aggressive children did not differ from their peers in terms of membership in a social cluster or in being isolated or rejected from their social network.** The aggressive children tended to affiliate with other aggressive children and within their social network were as likely as nonagressive children to be identified by their peers as a best friend and having friendship choices reciprocated. The study evaluated behaviors in school of 695 boys and girls in two cohorts of fourth and seventh graders.

Cairns, R. and Cairns, B. et. al. (1988). Social networks and aggressive behavior: Peer support or peer rejection? *Developmental Psychology.* 24(6):pp. 815-823.

• In a study of classroom environments and the behavior of children, it was found that c**lassrooms with low achieving environments had higher rates of children identified as aggressive and/or withdrawn than classes with high achievement or mixed levels of achievement environments.** Children in poor-behavior classroom environments had higher rates of children identified as withdrawn than in the average behavior environments. The study was conducted at the end of the first grade with 609 children and their teachers.

Werthamer-Larsson, L. et. al. (1991). Effect of first-grade classroom environment on shy behavior, aggressive behavior, and concentration problems. Special Issue: Preventive Intervention Research Centers. *American Journal of Community Psychology.* 19(4):pp. 585-602.

• **A study of the effectiveness of Trazodone (TRZ) in treating two oppositional defiant boys ages 7 and 8 and one 9-year-old boy with conduct disorder and oppositional defiant disorder, found significant improvement in behavior 7 to 10 days after treatment was started.** TRZ is a serotonin reuptake inhibitor and its effectiveness in treating aggressive children suggests a possible role for serotonin deficiency in the etiology of aggressive behaviors.

Ghaziuddin, N. and Alessi, N. (1992) An open clinical trial of Trazodone in aggressive children. *Journal of Child and Adolescent Psychopharmacology.* 2(4):pp.291-297.

• In a study of the relationship between aggression and socialization in preschoolers it was found that the **preschoolers with aggressive behaviors at the beginning of the study showed a significant delay in interpersonal awareness and perspective taking skills.** By the end of the study, although they had caught up to their peers in these abilities, their aggressive behaviors remained.

Minde, K. (1992) Aggression in preschoolers: Its relation to socialization. Journal of the *American Academy of Child and Adolescent Psychiatry.* 31(5):pp.853-862.

• In a retrospective study of the long-term effects of child abuse and neglect on criminal behavior in men it was found that **men who had been abused as children were three times more likely to engage in violent criminal acts as adults than nonabused men.** Specific types of childhood abuse were correlated to the types of violence the adults inflicted on others, and the two were isomorphic, supporting the cycle of violence hypothesis.

Dutton, D. and Hart, S. (1992) Evidence for long-term specific effects of childhood abuse and neglect on criminal behavior in men. *International Journal of Offender Therapy and Comparative Criminology.* 36(2):pp. 129-137.

- Book Review -
Aggression in Our Children:
Coping with it Constructively

By Henri Parens, M.D.

What are the roots of aggression, and at what point does it become destructive? Is it ever constructive? Dr. Parens and his colleagues present a theory of aggression which answers both questions, and drawing on research and current developmental and psychoanalytic theory, provides sound guidance for parents, caretakers, and therapists concerned especially with the raising of young children. In this book the authors succeed in distilling and translating a large body of theory and research into a understanding and compelling discussion of how to help children channel their aggressive strivings. By anticipating the questions and concerns of parents, the book achieves a supportive and dialog-like quality.

Parens has studied aggression in young children in naturalistic settings for over 20 years. He and his colleagues carefully documented the behaviors of children as they observed them in interactions with parents and peers and attempted to make sense of the children's different types of aggressive behaviors. They state that aggression is not one unitary category but rather consists of different types of behaviors all having "one common feature: They are an attempt to control, act upon, and master ourselves and our environment, including the people within it. These aggressive behaviors seem to be propelled by inborn mechanisms, or by an inner 'force' that motivate them." (p. 6).

Dividing aggression into two broad categories, they define "nondestructive aggression" as including "assertive, nonhostile, self-protective, goal-achieving, and mastery behaviors." They view these behaviors as being inborn and as operating and developing from birth on. "Hostile destructiveness" on the other hand, is the second type of aggression, and is the type of aggression that has lead to the shocking increase in youth crime.

Parens et. al. include hate, rage, bullying, torture, and vengefulness in the list of behaviors characterizing this type of aggression. Hostile aggressiveness is not present from birth, but is generated by a self-protective mechanism that seeks to cope with "the experience of excessive unpleasure (excessive pain or distress)" (p. 7). The role of hostile destructiveness is to eliminate the source of the excessive pain. While not innate, the capacity for hostility is present in infants, and is, the authors claim, part of the human psyche. All of us must cope with feelings of hostility and ambivalence towards loved ones and towards society. How this coping occurs, what levels of hostility are present, and how they are discharged have their roots in the earliest years of our lives in our first interactions with the caretaking environment.

Therefore, one of the major and most important tasks that parents of young children have is to help in the regulation of this hostility both externally, by controlling the child's environment to prevent the child from experiencing unusually high levels of frustration and emotional and physical pain, and internally, by helping the child process and manage aggression.

The body of the book discusses seven areas of parent-child interaction which can promote nondestructive aggression, and minimize destructive hostility. These areas are: 1. Dealing constructively with the child's experiencing excessive unpleasure; 2. Recognizing the need for and allowing children sufficient and reasonable autonomy and exploratory/ learning/practicing activity; 3. Setting limits constructively; 4.

Teaching children how to express and discharge anger and hostility in reasonable and acceptable ways; 5. Handling the child's rage reactions and temper tantrums in growth-promoting ways; 6. Helping the child cope with painful emotional feelings such as anxiety and depression; and 7. Optimizing the parent-child relationship (pp. 20-21).

All of these areas of parenting are discussed with clarity and empathy for both the parent and the child. Many useful guidelines and suggestions are given. The behaviors are well-illustrated with descriptions of children observed in the course of research, making recognition of the every-day traumas and conflicts of young childhood immediately accessible to those who have or work with children. One of the most appealing aspects of the book, and one which makes it a great book for sharing with clients, is its respect for the importance of the young child's experience and the parents' task of guiding the child through the trials of growing up.

Aggression in Our Children: Coping with it Constructively by Henri Parens, M.D. in collaboration with Elizabeth Scattergood, M.A., William Singletary, M.D., and Andrina Duff, M.S.S. North Wales, New Jersey: Jason Aronson, Inc. 1993, 197 pp. plus index.

- Curriculum Review -
Straight Talk About Risks (STAR):
A Curriculum for Preventing Gun Violence

The STAR curriculum is designed to help reduce the number of deaths and injuries children sustain from gunshot wounds. Gun violence is now a leading cause of death for children and adolescents, and it accounts for 12 percent of all premature deaths. Pediatric trauma centers are reporting dramatic increases in the number of gunshot victims they are treating on a daily basis, and many pediatricians have become involved in the creation of prevention programs as a result of their experiences. While STAR is focused on reducing gun related death and injuries, its comprehensive program does much more than preach about gun use.

The authors of this prevention curriculum incorporate the elements which, in general, have been shown to increase the effectiveness of prevention efforts. Thus students are taught skills that can be used outside of the classroom, such as decision-making skills, conflict resolution skills, and skills for refusing peer pressure. The program incorporates activities stressing self-reflection and role play of the individual student's typical coping mechanisms and emotions.

The students are asked to set goals for personal and societal change and are supported in their efforts to reach these goals. In accord with this, they are helped to build leadership skills with which they can interact with peers and community members. Finally, the classroom work of the STAR program is supported by parents and the broader community.

Evidence for the STAR program's effectiveness comes from a pilot implementation in Dade County, Florida. In the first two years of the program's implementation, a one third reduction in gun injuries and deaths in school-aged youth was observed. In the face of increasing gun-related injury rates for other populations, the creators of STAR report that at least some of the drop in school-age gun-related accidents was due to the STAR program. Furthermore, stringent evaluation of the program's effects is currently underway.

The STAR curriculum is divided into four sections: Pre-K to Grade 2, Grade 3 to Grade 5, Grade 6 to Grade 8, and Grade 9 to Grade 12. Each section contains a variety of exercises and activities which are appropriate to the particular age group. This allows for the learning experiences of the curricula as a whole to grow developmentally so that the child has the experience of understanding the main themes of the program from each developmental level. Each level of the curricula contains a bibliography and videography of resource materials, some of which are directly incorporated into the teaching sections.

For the Pre-K to Grade 2 levels, there are a number of exercises and games that teach safety, the importance of rules, recognizing what is a toy and what is not (i.e. guns are not toys), conflict resolution, and other related topics. In addition to participating in games and discussion, role play is also used. One unit, called "The Crayon Game," begins by giving the children a crayon and telling them to "start" without any further information. After allowing a few minutes of exploration the teacher is to discuss how not knowing the rules made it hard for the children to know what to do. This is followed by a Traffic Role Play in which the children pretend to drive a car with no other rule than a walking speed limit. After they walk around for a short time the teacher leads a discussion on the importance of traffic rules and safety rules.

For the third to fifth graders, the emphasis focuses more on the nature of guns, the emotions that draw people into violent situations, and grief. There is further work on conflict resolution and more direct discussion of guns and gun-related accidents. The students are helped to make up skits called "actos" to dramatize some of the things they are learning and to share that learning with others. They are also helped to distinguish between fantasy violence such as seen on television and in movies and real violence. One project involves making a bulletin board with news articles about real events.

For the sixth to eighth graders, further work on conflict resolution is built into the curriculum. The emphasis shifts to an exploration of their own reactions to media images and peer pressure, and to helping them comprehend the longterm and final nature of gun violence as it effects family, friends, and community. At this level facts are presented, the nature of anger explored, and the concept of triggers discussed. One exercise called "The Ketchup Game" has the children divide into two groups and imagine that one group has carelessly splattered ketchup on the other. They are asked to role-play their reactions and then identify the verbal and nonverbal responses of the angry "victims." Situations are presented involving what to do when a friend discloses that they have obtained guns as potential solutions to their problems.

For the ninth to 12th graders, the themes of the previous years are further developed. They are asked to write papers and explore their thoughts about gun use and gun violence. Videos and guest speakers are used to enhance their level of involvement, and they are encouraged to participate in the school and greater community by conducting poles on violence and guns, creating a "Student Speak-out," writing letters, etc.

The support for the implementation of this program is excellent. The Center to Prevent Handgun Violence recommends that local school districts be invited by state agencies to participate in the STAR program. Regional training sessions are provided over a two- to three-year period. The sessions accommodate approximately 75 people and last six hours. It is recommended that a multi-disciplinary team from the local schools participate in the training. This would include teachers, guidance counselors, parent advocates, and others.

Straight Talk About Risks (STAR): A Pre-K through Grade 12 Curriculum for Preventing Gun Violence. (1992) Washington, D.C.: Center to Prevent Handgun Violence. 1225 Eye St. NW, Room 1150, Washington DC 20005; (202) 289-7319 or 10951 W. Pico Blvd., Room 204, Los Angeles, CA 90064; (310) 475-6714. Cost for curriculum and video is $13.90. Estimated cost of implementation range: $40,000 to $60,000 to serve approximately 150 educators.

- Video Reviews -

"Sweetwater and June"
"Guns and Teens"

There are many videos and films available to help children and adolescents learn and talk about anger and violence. Some of the films are presented in an educational "news special" format, and others are more like regular films or videos which tell a story. We review one of each type here. "Sweetwater and June" is a docudrama telling an authentic story of a night in the life of two gang members. "Guns and Teens," presented in a news format, interviews families and teens who have been affected by gun accidents. When presented with class discussion, videos of each type present an engaging and meaningful way to bring youth into an ongoing dialogue about anger, violence, personal choice and larger social issues.

"Sweetwater and June" tells the story of two African-American teenagers, Sweetwater, aged 16, and June, aged 15, whose lives come to tragic ends as a result of their participation in gang activity. It is poignant and well-acted. The drama of the characters is left to speak for itself and the video avoids lecturing or moralizing. Conclusions as to the meaning of the story, the kinds of choices the characters had and made, the effectiveness of the juvenile criminal system and the safety of the community are left to the viewer, thus offering opportunity for a lively group discussion.

The action takes place one night in an urban area when Sweetwater, June's mentor in the gang, and June decide what to do that evening. They carjack a woman's car at gunpoint, engage in a drive-by shooting at a gang member's house, and are arrested. Realistically enough, the police arrive at the scene of the shooting 45 minutes after a neighbor calls. Once processed in the detention center, June is released in the custody of his mother. In the meantime the rival gang members are plotting revenge. When June and his mother return to their apartment building they are gunned down in a drive-by shooting.

The action returns to the detention center where Sweetwater, who has a longer police record, is now in a group therapy session. He becomes involved in a fight and is put back in his "box," the cement cubicle where the teens are individually held. Not long after, the detention center personnel come to tell Sweetwater, yelling from the hallway, that his buddy and his buddy's mother have been killed. They make no effort to discuss this with him.

A dialogue between Sweetwater and his neighbor begins through the walls. Initially, Sweetwater takes the news lightly, saying it was June's fault for "not watching his back." His neighbor, however, won't let him off the hook, and eventually Sweetwater connects with his guilty feelings about June's death. As his neighbor goes on about ways out of their life situations, Sweetwater becomes increasingly depressed, responding to the ongoing chorus of, "What are you going to do?" Later he is found dead, hanging in a rope made of the sheets in his cubicle. The action of the story stops here, and the main events are briefly presented again in a kind of memory sequence of the night that led to so many tragedies. The Leader's Guide, a small pamphlet, has a list of learning objectives for preteens and teens, and a good list of discussion questions. Some of the discussion questions include:

"Why are older gang members viewed as role models for male youth?" "What family situations lead individuals to gang membership? Could this be avoided?" "Ultimately,

Sweetwater committed suicide. Why did he do it in detention rather than outside of custody?" "Who are some positive role models in the community that youngsters can look to for positive guidance?"

The producer and writer of "Sweetwater and June," Peter Adams, is an authority and speaker on the subject of gang membership, and is committed to preventing youth from joining gangs. His video will make a significant contribution to the education of youth and the prevention of gang violence.

"Sweetwater and June." (1992) Written and Produced by Peter Adams. Karol Video, A Division of Karol Media. P.O. Box 7600. Wilkes-Barre, PA 18773-7600; (800) 526-4773. Videocassette, 30 minutes. Leader's Guide included.

"Guns and Teens" does not focus on one type of violence or one type of person or child. Its makers have skillfully interviewed victims of accidental shootings, families, and professionals who work with the victims in different capacities. The fragility of the human body and the finality of death are two strong messages that the video shares with its viewers.

Two teens who are partially paralyzed are shown, and a physical therapist underscores the difficulties which will follow them throughout the rest of their lives as handicapped persons. The anger and sadness of the families is brought home as one father points out that his son will never walk again, whereas the teen who shot the gun will be out of jail in a few years, and will have forgotten what he has done.

Other families who lost children in accidental shootings are interviewed. One father who was accidentally shot in the neck when his son's gun misfired is interviewed, along with his son. The video takes the viewer into the morgue where a pathologist describes his job, bringing the viewer to the area in which bodies are stored, numbered, and essentially nameless. The vulnerable nature of the human body, with its three thin layers of skin serving as the main protective shield for the organs contained within, is brought home by a man who is interviewed in a firing range.

While "Guns and Teens" is part of the Center to Prevent Handgun Violence's Curriculum (appropriate for Grades 6 to 12) it stands on its own as a direct and honest testimony to the destructive force and the dangerous and unpredictable nature of gun use.

"Guns and Teens." Center to Prevent Handgun Violence, Dade County, Florida, Public Schools Youth Crime Watch of Dade County. Distributed by Center to Prevent Handgun Violence, 1225 Eye Street, NW, Suite 1100, Washington DC 20005; (202) 289-7319.

Resources for Aggressive Children and Adolescents

Books - Fiction
Aborn, A. (1994) *Everything I Do You Blame on Me!* King of Prussia, PA: The Center for Applied Psychology, Inc. Ill. 112 pp. Ages 6-12. This book presents the humorous and sensitive story of the transformation of Eddie, a young boy who sometimes thinks his name is "Cut It Out, Eddie!" He has difficulty managing his anger at home and school, but with effort, learns to control his anger, thereby earning the name "Steady Eddie." The story is addressed to the child reader, and represents Eddie's firsthand account of his behaviors, his experience in the different stages of his therapy, the solutions he learns and how he implements them.

Garden, N. (1986) *Peace, O'River.* New York: Farrar-Strauss-Giroux. Grades 7 and up. This story describes a teenage girl's efforts to cope with class difference, internal conflict, and school violence as well as the accidental death of a friend.

Hogan, P. (1980) *Sometimes I Get So Mad.* Milwaukee: Raintree Children's Books. Ill. Grades 2 to 4. This book tells the story of how Karen comes to learn how to deal with her anger positively. Karen makes friends with a popular older child and finds herself ignored and left behind at times. The story is well told and presents a common childhood theme.

Myers, W.D. (1988) *Scorpions.* New York: Harper Row. Grades 6 to 9. This story of an urban family in trouble and three boys struggling with the issue of gang involvement covers issues including peer pressure, decision-making, anger, violence and gun use.

Rhoads Mauser, P. (1982, 1987) *A Bundle of Sticks.* New York: Aladdin. Grades 5 to 7. This book tells the story of an 11 year old boy who must cope with a school bully and his father's disappointment in his unwillingness to fight. He learns a self defense technique and comes to develop respect for himself and his own beliefs.

Richardson, J. *Bad Mood Bear.* New York: Barron's. 27 pp. Ill. Preschool. This beautifully illustrated book tells the story of a young bear whose irritable and angry behavior, resulting from his staying up too late the night before, becomes a problem for his family and friends. When Bear finally exhausts the patience of his parents he takes a nap and awakes feeling better, makes amends, and decides to be a "Good Mood Bear." The simple language and familiar situations make this book particularly appropriate for preschool children.

Simon, N. (1974) *I Was So Mad!* Morton Grove, Illinois: Albert Whitman and Company. 34 pp. Ill. Ages 6-12. This book accurately and empathically presents the many types of situations that make children angry. It presents different children describing the situations that make them mad. The book ends by showing that even parents get mad, and that anger is a normal part of life. The closing pages include a song (with musical score) that the father of one of children sings when he gets angry.

Books - Non-Fiction
Marsano, W. (1985) *The Street Smart Book.* New York: J. Messner. Grades 3 to 5. This book describes dangerous situations urban children are likely to confront and suggests ways to avoid and/or handle the situations. It provides examples of chil-

dren coping with different situations.

Landau, E. (1990) *Teenage Violence.* Englewood Cliffs, New Jersey: J. Messner. Grades 6 and up.

Berger, G. (1989) *Violence and the Media.* New York: Watts. Grades 5 and up. This book discusses the effects and roles of media portrayals of violence.

Lagone, J. (1984) *Violence! Our Fastest Growing Public Health Problem.* Boston: Little Brown. Grades 7 and up. This book discusses the increasing violence in this country, its individual and cultural roots, and ways to decrease it.

Videotapes

"Lollipop Dragon's ABC's of Self-Esteem." (1990) Three filmstrips and accompanying audiocassettes (12 minutes each). Teacher's Guide. Society for Visual Education. 55 E. Monroe St., Suite 3400, Chicago, IL 60603; (312) 849-9100. Grades pre-K to 3. The three film strips are entitled "Autonomy: Getting To Be Me," "Belonging: Getting Along With Others," and "Competence: Getting Better All The Time." Issues covered include understanding individual differences and conflict resolution skills.

"Tell 'Em How You Feel." (1986) Videocassette or 16mm film. 18 minutes. Teacher's Guide. From Gary Mitchell Film Co., distributed by Coronet/MTI, 108 Wilmot Road, Deerfield, IL 60615; (708) 940-1260. Grades 4 to 6. This film teaches methods to cope with anger effectively and ways in which to be assertive in getting needs met.

"Gunplay: The Last Day in the Life of Brian Darling." (1990) Videocassette. 30 minutes. Study Guide. From HBO Project Knowledge. Home Box Office, Inc., 1100 Avenue of the Americas, New York, NY 10036; (212) 575-5611. Grades 4 and up. This production tells the story of the tragic accidental shooting of 10-year-old Brian Darling by a friend who was showing him his father's handgun. The handgun had been bought as a reaction to increasing crime in the neighborhood.

"Learning To Say No." (1989) Videocassette. 30 minutes. Teacher's Guide. Sunburst Communications. 30 Washington Ave., Pleasantville, NY 10570; (914) 747-3310. Grades 5 to 8. This video teaches assertiveness skills as an alternative to aggressive behaviors.

"Guns and Teens." Videocassette. 52 minutes. Can be used with STAR Curriculum (see Curriculum Review). Center to Prevent Handgun Violence. 1225 Eye St. NW, Suite 1100, Washington, DC 20005; (202) 408-1851. This video presents the stories of teens and their families who have been effected by gun shot accidents. It realistically portrays the drastic changes in the lives of teens who have been incapacitated by bullet wounds (see Video Review).

"Dealing With Anger." (1988) Videocassette or 16mm film. 25 minutes. Teachers Guide. Salenger Educational Media, 1635 12th St., Santa Monica, CA 90404. Grades 7 and up. This production explores anger, its different causes, and coping skills for managing it.

"Guns: A Day in the Death of America." (1990) Videocassette. 50 minutes. From

HBO Project Knowledge. 1100 Avenue of the Americas, New York, NY 10036-6737; (212) 575-5611. Grades 7 and up. Discusses the high frequency of gun deaths in the United States and presents the situations leading to several such deaths and repercussions for family, friends, and community.

"Bad Girls." (1990) Videocassette. 48 minutes. Teacher's Guide. From NBC News. Distributed by Coronet/MTI Films and Video. 108 Wilmot Rd., Deerfield, IL 60615; (708) 940-1260. Grades 7 and up. Deborah Norville interviews teenage girls who have been arrested for violent crimes and the professionals who work to help them in this news documentary.

"Sweetwater and June." (1992) Videocassette. 30 minutes. Teachers Guide. Produced by Peter Adams. Distributed by: Karol Video, a division of Karol Media, P.O. Box 7600. Wilkes-Barre, PA 18773-7600; (800) 526-4773. Grades 7 and up. This video tells the realistic story of a tragic night when two teenage gang members engage in activities which lead to the murder of one, and the suicide of the other (see Video Reviews).

Source: *Star Talk About Risks: A Pre-K through grade 12 Curriculum for Preventing Gun Violence.* (1992). Center to Prevent Handgun Violence, 1225 Eye St. NW, Room 1150, Washington, DC 20005.

Selected Journals
Addressing Aggression in Children

Aggressive Behavior
John Wiley and Sons, Inc., 605 3rd Ave., New York, NY 10158; (212) 850-6000. Bimonthly, $396/yr. Multidisciplinary journal devoted to experimental and observational analysis of conflict in humans and animals.

Behavior Therapy
Association for the Advancement of Behavior Therapy, 15 W. 36th St., New York, NY 10018; (212) 279-7970. Quarterly. Individual $55/yr.; Institution, $110/yr. Interdisciplinary journal presenting treatment research concerning theory, methodology, clinical and ethical issues.

Child Abuse and Neglect
Pergamon Press, Journals Division, 660 White Plains Rd., Tarrytown, NY 10591-5153; (914) 524-9200. Bimonthly, $575/yr. Provides international multidisciplinary forum on all aspects of child abuse with emphasis on prevention and treatment.

Journal of Family Violence
Plenum Publishing Corporation, 233 Spring St., New York, NY 10013-1578; (212) 620-8000. Quarterly, $140/yr. Academic and scholarly journal providing a discussion of the psychology of family violence.

Journal of Social and Clinical Psychology
Guilford Publishers, Inc., 72 Spring St., 4th Floor, New York, NY, 10012; (212) 431-9800. Quarterly. Individual, $35/yr.; Institution, $99/yr. Covers research, theory, and practice in the growing interface of social and clinical psychology.

Personality and Social Psychology Bulletin
Sage Publications, Inc., 2455 Teller Rd., Newbury Park, CA 91320; (805) 499-0721. Bi-monthly. Individual, $60/yr.; Institution, $189/yr. Publishes theoretical articles and empirical reports of research in all areas of personality and social psychology.

Residential Treatment for Children and Youth
Haworth Press, 10 Alice St., Binghamton, NY 13904; (800) 342-9678. Quarterly. Individual, $36/yr.; Institution, $90/yr. Provides forum for those in the field of residential treatment including discussions of practice and perspectives on current issues and developments in the field.

Social Cognition
Guilford Publishers, Inc., 72 Spring St., 4th Floor, New York, NY, 10012; (212) 431-9800. Quarterly. Individual, $35/yr.; Institution, $90/yr. Examines the role of cognitive process in the study of personality, development, and social behavior.

Recommended Journal
Articles on Childhood Aggression

Bell, C., and Jenkins, J. (1990). **Preventing black homicide. The State of Black America.** *National Urban League,* pp. 143-155. Discusses violence in lower economic status communities and its prevention.

Dishion, T., Patterson, G., Stoolmiller, M. and Skinner, M. (1991). **Family, school, and behavioral antecedents to early adolescent involvement with antisocial peers.** *Developmental Psychology.* 27: pp. 172-180. This study describes some of the factors that lead early adolescents to choose involvement with antisocial peers.

Dodge, K., Bates, J., and Pettit, G. (1990). **Mechanisms in the cycle of violence.** *Science.* 250:pp. 1678-1683. In this prospective study of 309 children, further evidence is presented that physical abuse is a risk factor for later aggression and that abused children tend to acquire deviant patterns of social information processing which mediate the aggressive behavior.

Dodge, K., McClaskey, C., Feldman, E. (1985). **Situational approach to the assessment of social competence in children.** *Journal of Consulting and Clinical Psychology.* 53(3):pp. 344-353. Describes the development of the Taxonomy of Problematic Social Situations for Children, and identifies six types of situations which can be used to differentiate aggressive and adaptive children.

Huesmann, L. (1988). **An information processing model for the development of aggression.** *Aggressive Behavior.* 14:pp. 13-24. This paper describes a comprehensive model of aggression indicating that children learn aggressive scripts early in life both through enactive and observational processes. The author describes how aggressive behavior is elicited.

Kemph, J., DeVane, C. et al. (1993). **Treatment of aggressive children with Clonodine: Results of an open pilot study.** *Journal of the American Academy of Child and Adolescent Psychiatry.* 32(3):pp. 577-581. The authors found that clonidine, a medication which effects the neurotransmitter, gamma-aminobutyric acid (GABA) was effective in treating 15/17 aggressive children. The authors suggest that GABA blood plasma levels may be correlated with childhood aggression.

Kennedy, R. (1982). **Cognitive-behavioral approaches to the modification of aggressive behavior in children.** *School Psychology Review.* 11(1):pp. 47-55. This is a good review article of various cognitive-behavioral interventions available for the treatment of childhood aggression.

Patterson, G., Narrett, C. (1990). **The development of a reliable and valid treatment program for aggressive young children. Special Issue: Unvalidated, fringe, and fraudulent treatment of mental disorders.** *International Journal of Mental Health.* 19(3):pp. 19-26. This article describes the development of a successful in-home parent-training program to treat aggressive young children.

Quiggle, N., Garber, J. et. al. (1992). **Social information processing in aggressive and depressed children.** *Child Development.* 63(6): pp. 1305-1320. This study showed that while depressed and aggressive children share a hostile attributional bias, aggressive children were more likely to report that they would engage in aggressive behavior and that they would be comfortable in engaging in this behavior.

Schneider, B. (1991). **A comparison of skill-building and desensitization strategies for intervention with aggressive children.** *Aggressive Behavior.* 17:pp. 301-311. In a study of 41 institutionalized aggressive children, ages 7 to 13 treated with either desensitization strategies or social skills training both methods were found to reduce aggressive behavior as observed on the playground. Neither intervention affected teacher ratings of the children's behavior in the classroom.

Slaby, R. and Guerra, N. (1988). **Cognitive mediators of aggression in adolescent offenders: 1. Assessment.** *Developmental Psychology.* 24(4):pp. 580-588. This study identified the cognitive mediators associated with aggressive behavior in adolescents. Findings include that aggressive adolescents are more likely to solve social problems by defining problems in hostile ways, setting hostile goals, and not taking in all of the relevant information.

Stromquist, V. and Strauman, T. (1991). **Children's social constructs: Nature, assessment, and association with adaptive versus maladaptive behavior.** *Social Cognition.* 9(4):pp. 330-358. This study provides evidence that children's internal social constructs are consistently associated with their behaviors, with antisocial and unlikable-trait constructs associated with anti-social behavior.

United States Congress: House Select Committee on Children, Youth, and Families. **Children and guns: Hearing before the Select Committee on Children, Youth and Families, House of Representatives, 101st Congress, first session.** United States Printing Office. June 15, 1989. Washington, DC.186 pp. Report on the toll that guns have on children's health.

Weiss, B., Dodge, K., Bates, J., and Pettit, G. (1992). **Some consequences of early harsh discipline: Child aggression and a maladaptive social information processing style.** *Child Development.* 63:pp. 1321-1335. This article describes a controlled study of children with parents who admitted to using harsh punishment methods. It provides evidence that harsh punishment leads to aggressive behavior in children and that this is mediated by the children's development of maladaptive social information processing patterns in response to the punishment.

Organizations Dealing with Aggression in Childhood

The following is a sampling of member programs of the National Network of Violence Prevention Practitioners.

Building Conflict-Solving Skills
Kansas Child Abuse Prevention Council, 715 SW 10th St., Topeka, KS 66612; (913) 354-7738. Goals are to decrease child abuse and neglect by educating elementary and middle school students, their parents, and teachers about conflict-solving skills.

Community Youth Gang Services Project
Community Youth Gang Services, Inc., 144 S. Fetterly Ave., Los Angeles, CA 90022; (213) 266-4264. Goals are to reduce the level of gang violence perpetrated by youth gangs in the city and county of Los Angeles and to educate and mobilize communities in an effort to provide alternatives to gang membership.

Conflict Management/Mediation Program
University of Missouri System, 3166 Santiago Dr., Flourissant, MO 63033; Missouri Department of Health, 600 Monroe St., Box 570, Jefferson City, MO 65102; (314) 837-1038; (314) 751-6365. Goals are to train student mediators in more than 100 elementary, middle, and secondary schools throughout the state.

Conflict Resolution Resources for Schools and Youth
The Community Board Program, 1540 Market St., Rm. 490, San Francisco, CA 94102; (415) 552-1250. Goals are to empower students with non-violent skills and approaches for peacefully resolving the conflicts they encounter.

ESR National Conflict Resolution Program
Educators for Social Responsibility, 23 Garden St., Cambridge, MA 02138; (617) 492-1764. Goals are to provide training, curriculums, and ongoing support to educators that enable them to help students prevent violence, deal effectively with differences, appreciate diversity, and manage and resolve conflict creatively.

Gang Intervention Program Youth Development, Inc. (YDI)
1710 Centro Familiar SW, Albuquerque, NM 87105; (505) 873-1604. Goals are to curb gang violence; build self-esteem, self-respect and decision-making skills; and to promote community mobilization.

Outreach and Tracking Program
Old Colony YMCA, 15A Bolton Place, Brockton, MA 02401; (508) 584-1100. Goals are to provide advocacy and support services through positive role models to at-risk adolescents, holding them accountable for their behavior while teaching problem-solving and decision-making skills.

PACT Violence Prevention Project
Contra Costa County Health Services Department, 75 Santa Barbara Rd., Pleasant Hill, CA 94523; (510) 646-6511. Goals are to stimulate the development of violence prevention activities in community organizations, schools, city and county government and neighborhood groups.

Positive Adolescent Choice Training (PACT) Program
Wright State University, School of Professional Psychology, Ellis Human

Development Institute, 9 N. Edwin C. Moses Blvd., Dayton, OH 45407; (513) 873-3492. Goals are to reduce actual or potential involvement of youth as perpetrators or victims of acts of violence.

Resolving Conflict Creatively Program (RCCP)
163 Third Ave., #239, New York, NY 10003; (212) 260-6290. Goals are to provide effective instruction in conflict resolution and intergroup relations in grades K-12 in the New York City Public Schools.

Second Step: A Violence Prevention Curriculum
Committee for Children (CFC), 172 20th Ave., Seattle, WA 98122; (206) 322-5050. Goals are to reduce impulsive and violent/aggressive behavior in children and to increase their level of social competence.

Straight Talk About Risks (STAR)
Center for Prevent Handgun Violence, 1225 Eye St. NW, Suite 1150, Washington, DC 20005; (202) 289-7319. Goals are to reduce the risk of handgun violence through research, legal action, education and community outreach programs.

Targeted Outreach: Gang Prevention/Intervention
Boys and Girls Clubs of America, 771 First Ave., New York, NY 10017 (212) 351-5906. Goals are to identify youth at risk of delinquency and/or gang involvement, mainstream them into a youth development program, and, through networking and referral, arrange for needed support services.

Teen Dating Violence Program
Austin Center for Battered Women, P. O. Box 19454, Austin, TX 78760; (512) 928-9070. Goals are to provide support groups for boys and girls on teen dating relationships and nonviolent problem-solving.

Teens on Target
Youth ALIVE, c/o Summit Medical Center, South Pavilion, 2nd Fl., 350 Hawthorne Ave., Oakland, CA 94609; (510) 450-6225. Goals are to reduce violent injuries and deaths to youths, to generate youth-driven community and school-based violence prevention programs, and more.

Violence Prevention Project
Department of Health and Hospitals, 1010 Massachusetts Ave., 2nd Floor, Boston, MA 02118; (617) 534-5196. Goals are to reduce interpersonal violence among adolescents through education, training, mass media campaigns, clinical services, etc.

Washington Community Violence Prevention Program
Washington Hospital Center, 110 Irving St. NW, Room 4B-46, Washington, DC 20010; (202) 877-3761. Goal is to reduce the rate of homicide and intentional injury among adolescents through primary and secondary prevention.

There are two core sites of the **Children's Safety Network Resource Center.** The CSN National Injury and Violence Prevention Resource Centers are located at the National Center for Education in Maternal and Child Health, Georgetown University, 2000 15th St. N., Suite 701, Arlington, VA 22201-2617; (703) 524-7802 and at the Education Development Center, Inc., 55 Chapel St., Newton, MA 02158-1060; (617) 969-7100.

CHAPTER 6

Attention Deficit Disorder: "The Most Common Behavioral Disorder in American Children"

Allen has been racing around the playground for 15 minutes during a raucous game of kickball. When the ball is kicked toward him, instead of throwing it to first base, he begins dribbling it and runs toward the nearby basketball court. A boy on the opposing team shouts, "Oh no, there he goes again. What a jerk." Allen is then tackled by several boys and saved from undue damage by the school bell...

Allen appears not to have heard the teacher giving directions and looks at the math sheet with an expression of confusion. He waves his hand frantically, and when the teacher shakes her head, "No," he blurts out, "But I don't know what I'm supposed to do." Reluctantly and with an expression of exasperation, the teacher approaches Allen and gives him the directions. He begins to work on the problems but after less than a minute, he raises his hand again.

> – *From* Understanding and Treating Attention Deficit Disorder.
> *1986. p. 9. New York: Pergamon Press.*

Allen goes on to complete most of the problems, but only after poking another child with an eraser and being moved to a seat next to the teacher where he receives continuous supervision.

This sort of scenario is experienced by three to five percent of children in this country, as many as three and one half million children, on a daily basis. This means that almost every classroom in the country can expect to have one or two children with ADD. It is no surprise that this disorder made the cover of Time magazine, which labeled it "the most common behavioral disorder in American children."

Until 1992, ADD was not recognized as a handicapping condition necessitating proper educational placement or intervention by the public school system. Due in part to the work of advocacy groups like Children and Adults with Attention Deficit Disorders (CH.A.D.D.), children with ADD are now entitled to proper educational accommodation and placement. Fortunately, most children with ADD respond well to interventions within the regular classroom setting. How this can be accomplished is the subject of much new and ongoing research.

In this chapter, we interview Harvey Parker, Ph.D., an expert on ADD and the co-founder of CH.A.D.D., for an update on the current understanding of ADD. With the recognition of ADD as a handicapping condition came the release of research monies for the study of effective school-based treatments, and *we* explore two different types of intervention and research programs in this chapter. In an interview with George DuPaul, Ph.D. of Lehigh University, an exciting new consultation program designed to help school districts come up to speed in working with these children is discussed. Timothy Wigal, Ph.D., Assistant Director of the University of California at Irvine's innovative school for children with ADD and public school intervention program describes some of the methods his program uses in working with ADD children, as well as an important national research study on the treatment of children with ADD.

One of the underplayed dramas revolving around ADD is the tremendous effort and cooperation of thousands of parents of children with ADD and the therapists working with them. Advocacy groups like CH.A.D.D. have helped to change the laws so that children with ADD can receive the proper care and support within the public school system. On this subject, we have included Dr. Parker's description of the steps taken to having ADD included as a handicapping condition in the public school system.

Some experts claim that ADD can be traced to ancient times. The diagnostic nomenclature for this disorder has frequently changed, and this year brings yet more new criteria with the Diagnostic and Statistical Manual of Mental Disorders-Fourth Edition's (DSM-IV). We list these new criteria, explain diagnostic changes, address the assessment of ADD in the schools, and provide a description of many of the rating scales and some of the more specialized evaluation tools available for assessing ADD. Assessment is an ongoing project and must be incorporated into every successful behavior intervention program. The basics of psychosocial and medication interventions in the schools are reviewed, and a chart highlighting developmental issues is also provided.

It is clear that the roles of clinical and school psychologists will be expanded and altered as we come to grapple with the complex, interdisciplinary nature of effectively intervening to help children with ADD. ADD touches every aspect of a child's life, and impinges on family, school, and peer interactions, as well as academic and life achievement. It is our hope that this chapter will serve to point us all in the direction of cooperation with the other professionals and nonprofessionals who are involved in the child's treatment, as well as highlight new possibilities for creating a happier childhood and future for the ADD child.

A Brief Overview of Attention Deficit Disorders and the New DSM-IV Diagnostic Criteria

Despite the continuing controversy (Gardner, 1987) as to the existence of Attention Deficit Disorders (ADD) and their causes and cures, the scientific community has reached consensus on the basics of ADD. ADD is characterized by a collection of problems which impair the child and adolescent's ability to regulate their own behavior. The key areas of difficulty that characterize ADD are inattention and distractibility, impulsivity or difficulty in controlling behavior, difficulty with rule-governed behavior leading to the need for increased levels of feedback from the environment, hyperactivity or overarousal, and difficulty in maintaining a consistent level of performance (Barkley, 1992; Goldstein and Goldstein, 1990).

Inattention refers to difficulty in maintaining a focus on activities for the necessary amount of time needed to complete them. Children and adolescents with ADD have difficulty in maintaining attention on tasks that they perceive as being too long, tedious, and repetitive. Barkley (1992) writes, "Such activities might involve completing school assignments or homework, doing lengthy household chores, or attending prolonged lectures."(p.3) Parents and teachers observe inattention in the form of the child who shifts from activity to activity without completing them, and the child who appears to not be listening or daydreaming.

Distractibility is now believed to be secondary to inattention. In other words, as the child's attention shifts, the child focuses on different salient aspects of the environment. Goldstein and Goldstein (1990) write, "Thus attention and distractibility problems combine to negatively affect their ability to remain on task."(p.8)

Impulsivity or difficulty in controlling behavior refers to acting before thinking and difficulty in delaying gratification or working toward long-term goals. These children may appear not to learn from the consequences of their actions as they repeat the same impulsive behaviors despite their understanding of what is expected of them. This can set up a negative interaction cycle between the child and the parent or teacher who feels that the child's behavior is oppositional (Goldstein and Goldstein, 1990). Children and adolescents with ADD often opt for short-term rewards even when these are smaller than proffered long-term rewards. Thus, in planning interventions, short-term rewards are often used as secondary reinforcers. The negative aspects of this problem are seen in greater risk-taking behavior. Barkley notes that, "...people with ADD are more accident-prone, have greater difficulty managing money and credit, and engage in more use of both legal and illegal substances than do others." (p.5-6)

Related to impulsivity is **difficulty in executing rule-governed behavior.** This problem manifests as an inability to carry out instructions and follow rules. Children with ADD often need frequent reminders of what the task is or what the rules are in order to do well. They respond to increased levels of positive feedback and immediate mild negative responses about their behavior. When their difficulty with rule-governed behaviors is not recognized by the parent and teacher significant punitive behaviors from the adult may result in negative consequences for the child such as school failure (Barkley, 1992).

Hyperactivity or **overarousal** refers to the excessive motor movement observed in children and adolescents with ADD. This may appear in the form of fidgeting in their seats, drumming fingers or feet, handling objects unrelated to the activity, pacing, and extreme emotional states of short duration. These behaviors are often irritating to parents and teachers, and disruptive to peer relationships.

Finally, children and adolescents with ADD exhibit **extremes of variability in**

their performance. Children and adolescents with ADD will have some periods in which they work well and appear to need no assistance. These periods are then followed by a return to symptomatic behavior. To the outside observer it may look as if children are just being lazy because they have demonstrated the ability to do the task. It is important that this dysregulation of output be recognized as part of the disorder and not an indication of a negative personality trait (Barkley, 1992).

While the etiology of ADD is not fully understood, it is believed to be primarily a genetically-determined disorder and there is evidence that it involves mild brain abnormalities relating to the connections between the prefrontal area of the brain and the limbic system and/or the brain stem. Goldstein and Goldstein (1990) characterize ADD as a dysfunction of the attention system that comprises these brain connections. They write: "A disorder in the mechanism for setting the level of the system would produce situations where the subject was always set on a high or low degree of concentration; a high or low degree of restlessness and impulsivity; a high or low degree of motor activity. The system that was working ineffectively might produce responses that were variable and unpredictable. A poorly functioning center might sometimes produce an appropriate and sometimes an inappropriate level of concentration, restlessness, motor activity, or impulsivity." (p.46)

Barkley, drawing on the same data about brain functions and ADD, has put forth a theory of ADD which characterizes the basic impairment as being one of poor response inhibition. In his foreword to DuPaul and Stoner's book on classroom interventions for ADD, he describes the types of neuropsychological difficulties resulting from poor delay of response as including among others, impaired functioning of working memory, impaired ability to access relevant past experiences, impaired ability to conceive of future outcomes, and difficulty in the use of internal speech to bring about self-regulation and goal-directed behavior.

An interesting aspect of Barkley's theory is his understanding of the impact of poor response delay on affective responding in those with ADD. He theorizes that those with ADD are not able to separate affect from fact do to a lack of response delay. This results in emotionally over-reactive responses to situations, behavior that appears self-centered, and less objectivity in the analysis of situations. He cites the need for further research in this area (Barkley, 1992).

ADD affects three to five percent of children in the United States and may contribute to as much of 40 percent of clinic child referrals in this country. Boys with ADD outnumber girls with this disorder 3:1 in the community, and in the clinics by as much as 6:1. With ADD's inclusion as a handicapping disorder and better identification of children with ADD, schools are now facing the need to accommodate these children whose behaviors are often highly disruptive to the classroom effectively. About 80 percent of children with ADD perform below their academic potential, with about 20 to 30 percent of these children evidencing true learning disorders.

In addition, children with ADD are at risk for other comorbid disorders. For example 40 percent of children and 65 percent of adolescents with ADD are also diagnosable with Oppositional Defiant Disorder (ODD). Approximately 25 percent of children and adolescents with ADD demonstrate antisocial behaviors and Conduct Disorder. This group of children and adolescents is particularly at risk for illicit drug use and delinquent behavior. Evidence of significant difficulty in relating to peers has also been documented, as these children have difficulty in executing appropriate social skills even when they are knowledgeable about the skills. In addition, adolescents with ADD are also more vulnerable to depression.

Despite the current surge of renewed interest in ADD, it is a disorder which can be traced back to ancient times (Goldstein and Goldstein, 1990). During the twentieth century many labels and definitions of the disorder have come and gone.

Twentieth century terminology has included "defect in moral control, post-encephalitic disorder, hyperkinesis, minimal brain damage, minimal brain dysfunction, and hyperkinetic reaction of childhood" (Goldstein and Goldstein, 190). Current diagnostic changes have revolved around delineating the disorder according to whether the symptom of inattention exists with or without the symptom of hyperactivity.

The new DSM-IV diagnostic criteria now distinguish three types of ADD: ADD predominantly characterized by hyperactive symptoms, ADD predominantly characterized by symptoms of inattention, and ADD with a significant number of both kinds of symptoms. It divides the symptoms of Attention-Deficit/Hyperactivity Disorder into two categories: Inattention and Hyperactivity-Impulsivity. The number of symptoms in either category determines the type of ADHD the child or adolescent (or adult) has. The symptoms, as adapted from the DSM-IV, are listed in the accompanying chart.

In order to meet the general criteria for ADHD some symptoms must have been present before the age of seven, some impairment must be observed in at least two settings, and there must be evidence of clinical levels of impairment in social or academic functioning. The child or adolescent with the combined type of ADHD has six or more symptoms of inattention and six or more of the symptoms falling under hyperactivity and impulsivity. The child with six or more symptoms of inattention, but fewer than six symptoms of hyperactivity and impulsivity, has the predominantly inattentive type of ADHD, and the child with six or more symptoms in the hyperactive/impulsive grouping has the predominantly hyperactive-impulsive type of ADD. For all types, the symptoms must have been present for the previous six months.

It used to be believed that ADD is a disorder that children outgrow. Evidence now clearly demonstrates that 50 to 65 percent of children with ADD can expect to continue to experience difficulties as adults (Barkley, 1992). While some symptoms such as hyperactivity and inattention have been observed to improve as children with ADD reach adolescence, 70 to 80 percent of these children will not have improved to the point that they are equal to their peers. A significant number of adolescents with ADD are behind their peers academically and are at risk for substance abuse and antisocial behavior. Thus it is important that services and support be made available throughout the entire educational process. The long-term effects of ongoing treatment are still being investigated (see the interview with Timothy Wigal, Ph.D. in this chapter). New interventions and types of medications are also be investigated. While a great deal has been discovered about ADD, it is clear that the last chapter has not yet been written.

Sources: American Psychiatric Association: *Diagnostic and Statistical Manual of Mental Disorders, Fourth Edition.* Washington, DC, American Psychiatric Association, 1994. pp.78-85. Barkley, R. (1992) *ADHD in the Classroom: Strategies for Teachers- Program Manual.* New York: The Guilford Press. Barkley, R. (1994). *Foreword.* in DuPaul, G. and Stoner, G. (1994) *ADHD in the Schools: Assessment and Intervention Strategies.* New York: Guilford Publications. Gardner, R. (1987) *Hyperactivity, The So-Call Attention-Deficit Disorder, and the Group of MBD Syndromes.* Cresskill, New Jersey: Creative Therapeutics. Goldstein, S. and Goldstein, M. (1990) *Managing Attention Disorders in Children: A Guide for Practitioners.* New York: John Wiley and Sons, Inc.

SYMPTOMS OF ADHD

Inattention
1. Poor attention to detail and careless mistakes as seen in schoolwork and other activities
2. Poor sustained attention during activities and tasks
3. Often appears not to be listening when directly spoken to
4. Poor follow through and completion of tasks
5. Difficulty in organizing work and activities
6. Often avoids or expresses dislike of tasks requiring sustained attention
7. Often loses things necessary for tasks or activities such as books, toys, assignments, etc.
8. Often appears easily distracted by extraneous stimuli
9. Often forgetful in routine activities

Hyperactivity
1. Often fidgets or squirms in seat
2. Often leaves seat at inappropriate times
3. Often runs or climbs excessively or at inappropriate times, or if an adolescent, may feel restless frequently
4. Difficulty in quietly engaging in leisure pursuits
5. Often appears to be "on the go" or driven to activity
6. Often talks excessively

Impulsivity
1. Often answers questions before speaker finishes asking
2. Difficulty in waiting for one's turn in activities
3. Often interrupts conversations and activities of others

Assessment of Attention Deficit Disorder

The assessment of ADD in children and adolescents has been well documented and described (Barkley, 1990; DuPaul and Stoner, 1994; Goldstein and Goldstein, 1990; Parker, 1992). Assessment for ADD is multidimensional and takes place in the school, home, and the psychotherapist's office. The steps generally taken for a complete assessment of ADD are as follows:

1. **School or home report of behavioral problem eventually resulting in involvement of school psychologist or psychologist**
2. **Screening via brief interviews with parents and teachers in order to determine if the child's problem may be ADD and whether further assessment is advisable**
3. **Gathering records of academic and medical history**
4. **Evaluating in the school and at home via teacher- parent- and (for adolescents) self-rating scales, behavioral observation, and further interviews**
5. **Psychometric testing for ADD and related problems such as learning disabilities and conduct disorders as well to gain a better understanding of the child's learning style**
6. **Interpretating and sharing of the results with child, parents, and relevant school personnel**
7. **Developing of a treatment plan**
8. **Implementation and ongoing evaluation of the treatment plan**

Each part of the assessment process provides valuable information not only about the child's behavioral, academic, and emotional functioning, but also about the types of interactions in which the child engages with significant others. There are four types of assessment procedures involved in this process: interviews, rating scales, behavioral observation, and standardized psychological tests. We will review each briefly.

Interviews provide a wealth of knowledge about the child's behavior in his or her environment, and also serve to initiate the creation of the treatment team by involving parents and teachers from the beginning stage of the treatment process. Parker (1992, pp. 35-38) suggests that parent interviews should include:
1. Documentation of the presenting problems including age of onset, duration and intensity, and troublesome situations
2. Documentation of developmental and medical history. This may be best done with a semi-formal structured interview such as the one provided by Barkley (1990, 1992)
3. Documentation of the family including the family's socio-economic and cultural situation, and parental and sibling history of stress and adjustment.
4. Documentation of the parents' perception of their child's educational history and experience
5. Documentation about the child's peer relations

Teacher interviews should include (Parker, 1992; DuPaul and Stoner, 1994):
1. The kinds of problems in the child the teacher has observed
2. The kind of situations that appear to increase and decrease problematic behaviors
3. The interventions the teacher has tried already and how successful they

have been
4. How the child is doing academically including how the child does in each
   subject and the accuracy and amount of work the child produces
5. Under what conditions the child appears to work most efficiently
6. What the child's peer relations are

Child interviews need to be reassuring and nonjudgmental. It is important that the child or adolescent understand that the information s/he provides will be helpful in better understanding the child and his/her needs. Various projective techniques such as Incomplete Sentences or The Children's Apperception Test may be used to add structure to the session. In general, the interviews should provide the child with the opportunity to talk about his/her perceptions of how s/he is doing, his/her problems, and his/her concerns. Clinical interviews should include (Goldstein and Goldstein, 1990; Parker, 1992):
1. A discussion of the child's understanding of why s/he is being seen and what
   areas of difficulty s/he is experiencing
2. A discussion of the child's perceptions of interactions with family, friends, and
   teachers
3. A discussion of how the child is doing in school
4. A discussion of how the child is feeling; i.e. what the child worries about, feels
   sad and happy about, etc
5. Observation of the child's behavior during the interview
6. Explanation of further testing if it is to follow the interview.

There are a number of **rating scales** available for the assessment of ADD. Some of the more well-known scales are listed in the accompanying Assessment Instruments section. Many of these scales may be found in Russell Barkley's (1991) clinical workbook for ADD. The rating scales provide additional opportunities to gain information from parents, teachers, and children, and are useful in arriving at a diagnosis. Many of the rating scales have items derived from the diagnostic criteria described in the Diagnostic and Statistical Manual of Mental Disorders-Revised- III (DSM-R III). Most of the commonly-used rating scales have normative data and are psychometrically sound. The rating scales take relatively little time to administer and score, and are excellent tools to be used in the ongoing evaluation of the child as treatment progresses as well as the initial assessment.

Behavioral observations of the child or adolescent can be instrumental for gathering information needed to create and implement behavioral interventions in the home and school. There are several behavioral rating systems currently in the literature (see below). The types of information collected include how much time the child remains on task in various school situations, the number of times the child fidgets, and the number of appropriate and inappropriate interactions the child has with the teacher or with peers.

Standardized psychological testing is an important part of the diagnosis of children and adolescents with ADD. This kind of testing provides information about the child's learning abilities, provides a means of differential diagnosis, and if neuropsychological tests are incorporated into the evaluation, allows for the evaluation for neurologically-based difficulties which may coexist with ADD. The testing involves a standardized intelligence test, an achievement test, and personality testing. Neuropsychological tests may be incorporated or if there are complicating factors suggestive of organic brain dysfunction, a neuropsychological test battery may be used.

Once the assessments have been made the task of integrating the test findings ensues. DuPaul and Stoner (1994) suggest that the following questions be used to help organize the test data:

1. What is the number of the child's ADD symptoms?
2. What is the frequency of the symptoms?
3. What are the age of onset and chronicity of the symptoms?
4. Do the problem behaviors occur across settings?
5. Is there functional impairment in academic, social, or emotional areas?
6. Could other factors be causing the ADD-like symptoms?

It is important that the presence of coexisting disorders such as a learning disability, Conduct Disorder, and Oppositional Disorder or depression be evaluated so that a comprehensive and appropriate treatment plan can be devised.

Planning a treatment intervention for hyperactive and inattentive behaviors requires the identification of specific target behaviors and strategies for those behaviors. Consideration needs to be given to who will be implementing the strategies and under what conditions, as well as to what strategies would work best for the child or adolescent. Further discussion of treatment strategies can be found in the article on interventions for ADD.

Implementation of the treatment plan requires collecting baseline data and consultation with the teachers or parents who will be involved in the treatment, as well as preparing the child or adolescent and teaching them the techniques such as self-monitoring that they will be using. In addition to behavioral interventions, the child or adolescent may also use an adjunct treatment such as psychotherapy. Medication is likely to be an important part of the child's treatment. Ongoing assessment of the child's progress, as well as the teacher and parent's success in applying the strategies, and the degree to which the parties involved are experiencing meaningful, beneficial changes for the child or adolescent are necessary in order to evaluate the effectiveness of the overall treatment as well as components of the treatment.

Sources: Barkley, R. (1990) *Attention Deficit Hyperactivity Disorder: A Handbook for Diagnosis and Treatment.* New York: Guilford Publications. Barkley, R. (1991) *Attention-Deficit Hyperactivity Disorder: A Clinical Workbook.* New York: Guilford Publications. DuPaul, G. and Stoner, G. (1994) *ADHD in the Schools: Assessment and Intervention Strategies.* New York: Guilford Publications. Goldstein, S. and Goldstein, M. (1990) *Managing Attention Disorders in Children: A Guide for Practitioners.* New York: John Wiley and Sons. Parker, H. (1992) *The ADD Hyperactivity Handbook for Schools.* Plantation, Florida: Impact Publications, Inc.

Selected ADD Assessment Instruments

ADD Rating Scales

Child Behavior Checklist (CBCL) Parent's Form and Teacher's Form and the Child Attention Profile (CAP) [Achenbach and Edelbrock (1983). Available through T. M. Achenbach, Ph.D., University Associates in Psychiatry, Department of Psychiatry, University of Vermont, 1 South Prospect St., Burlington, VT 05401] The CBCL consists of 118 items for the Teacher's Form and 113 items for the Parent's Form. It has separate scoring profiles standardized for sex at ages 6-11 and 12-16. The CBCL provides ratings of eight factors: Anxious, Social Withdrawal, Depressed, Unpopular, Self-Destructive, Inattentive, Nervous-Overactive, and Aggressive, as well as two global ratings of internalizing and externalizing behaviors. The Inattentive and Nervous-Overactive scales have been found to identify children with ADD. Two advantages of the CBCL are the conformity of the parent and teacher forms making test results easily comparable, and its ability to identify affective disorders, thereby helping in differential diagnosis. The CBCL is widely used and has a solid normative and psychometric base.

The Child Attention Profile (CAP) consists of 12 items drawn from the CBCL-Teacher's form and is a convenient way for teachers to evaluate the presence and degree of hyperactivity and inattentiveness in children. It can also be used to help differentiate ADD children with hyperactivity from those without hyperactivity. Normative data is available including suggested cut-off scores that help to distinguish ADD+H from ADD-H children.

Conners Teacher Rating Scale (CTRS) - 39 and 28, and Conners Parent Rating Scale (CPRS) - 93 and 48, Abbreviated Symptom Questionnaire (ASQ-T) [Conners, K. (1969, 1989, 1990) Multi-Health Systems, Inc., 908 Niagara Falls Blvd., North Tonawanda, NY 14120-2060] These Conners scales have been widely used and have reliable and valid normative data. An advantage of the Conners scales is that they provide norms for children as young as three years old. A Hyperactivity Index can be derived from the short forms of the parent and teacher's scales. The long form of the teacher's rating scale yields five factors: Day-dreaming-Inattentive, Hyperactivity, Conduct Problems, Anxious-Fearful, and Sociable-Cooperative. The long form of the parent's rating scale yields the following factors: Conduct Disorder, Anxious-Shy, Restless-Disorganized, Learning Problem, Psychosomatic, Obsessive-Compulsive, Antisocial, and Hyperactive-Immature. One drawback of the Conners tests is that the parent and teacher's forms do not have the same factors, which slightly complicates the comparison of the child's teacher's and parent's ratings, an important component of ADD assessment.

The ASQ-T consists of the 10 items which compose the Hyperactivity Index Score discussed above. The tests are in a Likert scale format, and are easy to score. A manual provides a good test description, normative and psychometric data, scoring instructions, and a guide to interpretation.

The ADHD Rating Scale [DuPaul, G. (1991a) Parent and teacher ratings of ADHD symptoms: Psychometric properties in a community-based sample. *Journal of Clinical Child Psychology,* 20:pp. 245-253] This scale consists of 14 items derived from the DSMIII-R criteria for a diagnosis of ADD. The rater is asked to determine the severity of the problem behavior rating it from "Not at all" to "Very much." Normative data exists for parent and teacher's ratings and is divided by sex and age from six to twelve years. Two factors are assessed, Inattention-Restlessness and

Impulsivity-Hyperactivity.

The School Situations Questionnaire (SSQ) and the Home Situations Questionnaire (HSQ) [Barkley, C. (1987,1990) Can be obtained from Russell Barkley, Ph.D., Department of Psychiatry, University of Massachusetts Medical Center, 55 Lake Avenue North, Worcester, MA 01655. Also published in Barkley (1990) and Parker (1992)] The SSQ and HSQ were designed to help assess where and to what degree a child or adolescent is exhibiting ADD problem behaviors. The SSQ has 12 items and the HSQ has 14 items. Norms for the SSQ exist for children ages four to 11, and for the HSQ for children ages 4-18. These scales are useful in developing treatment plans. The HSQ has been found to be sensitive to parent training and medication effects and is useful in monitoring the child's progress. Both measures discriminate ADHD children from normal children. The SSQ and HSQ both tend to confound ratings of conduct problems with ADHD.

School Situations Questionnaire-Revised (SSQ-R) and Home Situations Questionnaire-Revised (HSQ-R) [DuPaul and Barkley (1992a) Situational variability of attention problems: Psychometric properties of the revised home and school situations questionnaires. *Journal of Clinical Child Psychology.* 21:pp. 178-188. Test and norms published in Barkley (1990)] This revised version of the SSQ is designed to assess problems with attention and concentration in the school setting and does not confound conduct problems with ADHD symptoms. It has eight items and normative data for children ages six to 12. Like the SSQ-R, the HSQ-R also provides a more refined evaluation of those situations in which attention and concentration are problematic. It has 14 items and normative data for children ages six to 12. Both questionnaires have established reliability and validity.

Rating Scales for Related ADD Problems

Academic Performance Rating Scale (APRS) [DuPaul, Rapport, and Perriello (1991) Teacher ratings of academic skills: The development of the Academic Performance Rating Scale. *School Psychology Review,* 20:pp. 284-300] This scale was developed to help assess the productivity and accuracy of the child's classroom work. Consisting of 19 items, it has established reliability and validity. It provides five scales including a Total Score, Learning Ability, Academic Performance, Impulse Control, and Social Withdrawal. As it takes approximately five minutes to administer, many consider it to be a good test for use in following a child's progress in therapy.

Conflict Behavior Questionnaire (CBQ) [Robin and Foster (1989) *Negotiating Parent-Adolescent Conflict: A Behavioral Family Systems Approach.* New York: Guilford Publications] The CBQ is designed to measure the level of conflict and quality of communication between adolescents and their families. It has been found to be useful in assessing the degree of stress in families with ADHD teens. The test consists of parallel questionnaires, one to be completed by the adolescent, and the others to be completed by the parents. The resulting scores are pooled to yield two scales: Appraisal of the Adolescent or Parent and Appraisal of the Dyad. This measure has been found to be useful in discriminating distressed and nondistressed families and the results have been found to correlate with behavioral observation of interaction patterns in families with ADD adolescents (Barkley, 1990, p.315).

Issues Checklist for Parents and Teenagers (IC) (Robin and Foster (1989) *Negotiating Parent-Adolescent Conflict: A Behavioral Family Systems Approach.* New

York: Guilford Publications) The IC was developed to assess the areas and intensity of conflict between adolescents and their parents. It consists of 44 items listing the types of conflicts and having the test taker evaluate frequency and intensity for each item. Adolescents and parents each take the test. The adolescent fills one out for each parent who is actively involved in the family system. The scale yields three scores: the quantity of conflictive issues, the general intensity of anger, and weighted average anger-intensity level and frequency of issues.

Child Behavior Checklist-Youth Self-Report (CBCL-YSR) [Achenbach and Edelbrock (1987) *Manual for the Child Behavior Checklist-Youth Self-Report.* Burlington, VT: University of Vermont, Department of Psychiatry] The CBCL-YSR is adapted from the original CBCLs and is a self-report measure for adolescents ages 11-18. While it does not evaluate ADD directly, it is useful in assessing for the emotional and behavioral problems associated with ADD during adolescence. The test has satisfactory reliability and validity.

Behavior Observation Systems
Restricted Academic Situation Coding Sheet [Barkley (1991) *Attention-Deficit Hyperactivity Disorder: A Clinical Workbook,* New York: Guilford Publications] This behavioral coding system is designed to assess children and adolescent's behaviors while they are engaged in individual academic work either in the clinic, at school or at home. The child's behaviors are coded every 30 seconds for 15 minutes while s/he is working on his/her task. The behaviors coded are: off task, fidgeting, vocalizing, playing with objects, and out of seat.

The Teacher-Student Behavior Coding System [Saudargras, R. and Creed, V. (1980) State-event classroom observation system. Knoxville, TN: University of Tennessee, Department of Psychology; DuPaul and Stoner (1994) *ADD in the Schools: Assessment and Intervention Strategies.* New York: Guilford Publications, pp. 56-58] This coding system allows for recording of teacher and student behaviors so that their interactions can be better understood. Criteria include: teacher approaches student engaged in on-task behavior, teacher approaches student engaged in off-task behavior, student approaches teacher in appropriate manner, student approaches teacher in inappropriate manner. In addition the quality of the interactions is recorded as either positive, negative, or other.

Computerized Continuous Performance Tests
The Gordon Diagnostic System (GDS) [Gordon, M. (1983) Gordon Systems, Inc. P.O. Box 746, DeWitt, NY 13214] The GDS is a self-contained instrument which does not require the psychologist to own or have access to a personal computer. It contains three tests: The Delay Task measures impulse control, the Vigilance Task measures sustained attention, and the Distractibility Task measures sustained attention in the presence of extraneous stimuli. Normative data are available.

The T.O.V.A. (Greenberg, L. Universal Attention Deficits, Inc. 4281 Katella Ave., Los Alamitos, CA. 90720) This is a computerized instrument that is available for IBM, Apple, and Macintosh systems. It contains a number of tests of vigilance and sustained attention, and is well normed. It is often used to monitor medication effects.

Sources: Barkley, R. (1990) *Attention-Deficit Hyperactivity Disorder: A Handbook for Diagnosis and Treatment.* New York: Guilford Publications. Barkley, R. (1991) *Attention-Deficit*

Hyperactivity Disorder: A Clinical Workbook. New York: Guilford Publications. DuPaul, G. and Stoner, G. (1994) *ADHD in the Schools: Assessment and Intervention Strategies.* New York: Guilford Publications. Parker, H. (1992) *The ADD Hyperactivity Handbook for Schools.* Plantation, Florida: Impact Publications, Inc.

DEVELOPMENTAL ASPECTS OF ADD

Attention Deficit Disorders manifest themselves in different ways at different ages. Symptom descriptions, statistics, and assessment and treatment suggestions according to age group are listed below.

Age Group	Symptom Description	Significant Statistics
Preschool (3-5 years)	May have been overly active and irritable as infant. Problematic behaviors: impulsive, fearless, noncompliant, not responsive to verbal warnings of punishment or promise of reward, excessive moodiness, highly variable behavior. May have language problems and difficulty with toilet training. Difficulty adapting to preschool.	60 to 70% of children later diagnosed with ADD had some symptoms as preschoolers.
School Age (6-10 years)	Symptoms of hyperactivity, impulsive and/or inattention significantly greater than those of peers. Classroom/school difficulties include behaviors that disrupt class, incomplete school and homework assignments, peer rejection, and learning problems.	80% - academic underachievement 20-30% - learning disability 40% - Oppositional Defiant Disorder 20-35% - Repeat a grade in school 52% - poor motor coordination 46% - accident-prone 45% - enuresis
Adolescence (10-Adulthood)	Adolescents with ADD are at higher risk for academic and behavior problems than peers. They tend to feel sad, may question their ability to finish school and have concerns for their future. If not addressed, earlier negative interpersonal patterns may be entrenched.	70% of children with ADD continue to have ADD in adolescence 50% - Conduct Disorder 58% - have failed one grade 30% - subsatnce abusers 35% - high school dropouts

DEVELOPMENTAL ASPECTS OF ADD

Age Group	Assessment	Treatment
Preschool (3-5 years)	Difficult to sort out ADD symptoms from developmentally normal behavior. Symptoms should be intense and chronic. Need to assess: Are problems due to immaturity? Are classroom expectations realistic? Are classroom rules clear?	Parent education/training; home-preschool notes; modify preschool classroom and structure, vary activities.
School Age (6-10 years)	Multi-instrument assessment with teacher and parent ratings; behavioral observation; psychometric testing, especially with academic problems; ongoing evaluation of treatment effects	Behavior modification; cognitive-behavioral; adjunct therapies: tutoring, social skills; medication; parent education/training.
Adolescence (10-Adulthood)	Check school record to obtain reliable history; involve in assessment with self-rating scales; obtain behavioral ratings from multiple teachers and look for consistencies across profiles	Same as above; involve in identifying treatment goals, methods, reinforcers; family therapy; support groups.

Sources: Barkley, R. (1990) *Attention-Deficit Hyperactivity Disorder: A Handbook for Diagnosis and Treatment.* New York: Guilford Publications. DuPaul, G. and Stoner, G. (1994) *ADHD in the Schools: Assessment and Intervention Strategies.* New York: Guilford Publications. Goldstein, S. and Goldstein, M. (1990) *Managing Attention Disorders in Children: A Guide for Practitioners.* New York: John Wiley & Sons, Inc.

An Interview with...
Harvey Parker, Ph.D.

Harvey Parker, Ph.D. is an international expert on Attention Deficit Disorders. He is the cofounder of CH.A.D.D. (Association of Children and Adults with Attention Deficit Disorders) and at present serves as the organization's Treasurer. Dr. Parker has written numerous books and workbooks for children, parents, teachers, and mental health professionals who have and/or work with ADD including The ADD Hyperactivity Workbook for Parents, Teachers and Kids *and* The ADD Hyperactivity Handbook for Schools, *and he has spoken extensively on the subject. He is CEO of Specialty Press, Inc. which publishes and sells books, assessment tools and other items which promote the health and welfare of those with ADD.*

In addition to his work for those affected by ADD, Parker is the Director of Counseling Care Center, a multidisciplinary private practice in Plantation, Florida. In this interview, he discusses the new diagnostic criteria for and types of ADD presented in the DSM-IV, describes the founding of CH.A.D.D., and shares his extensive knowledge about the assessment and treatment of children with ADD.

Laura Slap-Shelton, Psy.D.: *How did you become interested in working with children and adolescents who have Attention Deficit Disorder (ADD)?*

Harvey Parker, Ph.D.: In the late 1960s, when I was a teacher in New York City, I noticed some of the children in my class had problems with hyperactivity and inattention. When I entered graduate school in 1971, I took a special interest in trying to better understand the problems of such children. This led to my specializing in studying and working with children with ADD.

LS-S: *How did you come to form Children and Adults with Attention Deficit Disorder (CH.A.D.D.)?*

HP: In 1987 I met with a parent of a child who was hyperactive. Her child attended the local preschool, and we met at the school one day and basically decided that it would be a good idea to share information about hyperactive children with other parents in the community. We put an advertisement in the local newspaper about a support group starting that would provide information about ADD to parents. We had three consecutive monthly meetings in early 1987, and each meeting grew in size.

We weren't prepared for the 100 people the first meeting attracted. We had expected ten to 15 people. At the second meeting the number of attendees doubled. Some parents from neighboring counties found out about these meetings and asked if they could run their own. From there we formed chapters, and other parents from around the state began to learn of us. We produced a local newsletter which eventually reached people throughout the country. At this time Carol Lerner, a speech and language pathologist, stepped in to help form and develop the organization.

LS-S: *How big is CH.A.D.D. today?*

HP: Today CH.A.D.D. has close to 600 chapters, and 27,000 members in the U.S. and abroad.

LS-S: *How many children have ADD and how is ADD defined?*

HP: Three to five percent of children have ADD. The definition and sometimes the name of the disorder we are calling ADD has changed over the years. The DSM-IV has changed the definition again by officially identifying three types of ADD. The first type is Attention Deficit Hyperactivity Disorder, predominantly Inattentive-Type. Then there's Attention Deficit Hyperactivity Disorder, predominantly Hyperactive-Impulsive-Type, and there's Attention Deficit Disorder, predominantly Combined Type. So over the years we've recognized that ADD is not a unitary one-dimensional construct.

The disorder itself is manifested by symptoms of inattention, hyperactivity, and impulsivity which are chronic and pervasive in at least two settings, either work, school, or home. Although all children exhibit these characteristics from time to time, those children who are inattentive, hyperactive, or impulsive and fit this diagnostic criteria exhibit these symptoms to a greater degree than is found in the normal population of children of like age. In addition, these symptoms must have begun prior to the age of 7, must have lasted more than six months, and must not be the result of any other mental or physical illness.

LS-S: *How do you differentiate between an impulsive/aggressive child or adolescent and one with ADD?*

HP: They overlap a lot. Aggression is not the same disorder as ADD, so when you have a child who is aggressive, that's another problem. However, the overlap is significant. For example, the disorder which we call Oppositional Defiant Disorder overlaps about 60% with ADD in clinic populations. Many children with ADD have symptoms of defiance, refusal to obey requests, oppositional behavior, and some aggression. Those children who are severely aggressive, break the rules, defy authority, run away from home, and steal have a Conduct Disorder. The overlap between children with Conduct Disorder and children with ADD is about 30% in clinic populations. ADD doesn't cause aggression, although it can cause impulsive/aggressive outbursts.

LS-S: *What does ADD look like in the classroom?*

HP: Children with ADD in the classroom can be one of two types. As we said, they can be of the hyperactive-impulsive variety, which is characterized by restlessness, excessive fidgeting, inability to remain seated, and difficulty with self-control, such as raising the hand before speaking, often blurting out answers to questions before they've been completed, difficulty playing quietly, often talking incessantly, often interrupting or intruding on others, things of that nature.

Children or adolescents who are inattentive without showing hyperactivity will have problems paying attention. They are often passive, quiet, and may be hypoactive (underactive). They often will lose things, be forgetful, and they show signs of excessive tension, worry, or passivity.

Children with the combined type of ADD, which is very hyperactive and inattentive together, might have trouble completing schoolwork, trouble organizing their desks, drop things on the floor because of their fidgeting, misplace assignments, and lose homework that they may have completed at home but can't find in their book bag. They are distractible and distracting to others in the classroom as they often blurt out answers, and in general can be very disruptive to the classroom setting.

LS-S: *Do these children tend to do better on the playground or in gym class than in the regular classroom?*

HP: For the most part they do. School is not the best environment for the ADD child. On the playground, where there are fewer rules, these kids bump into regulations and expectations less frequently. There's no tremendous need for attention-paying on the playground, so they have less trouble.

However, despite the reduced expectations, these children often run into significant problems because they get carried away easily. They become overly enthusiastic during positive times and when they're enjoying themselves they get over exuberant. When they're annoyed or upset they get overly angry or overly upset. Either way, their behavior feels intrusive to other children, and their impulsivity leads to social ostracism. The child with the inattentive type of ADD also has more social problems on the playground than the average child. These children are more "laid back" and more on the periphery of the social scene, so they get left out.

LS-S: *So in addition to behavioral and academic areas, social skills represents another area that children with ADD must work at.*

HP: Yes. That's where a lot of children have trouble, especially as they grow into adolescents.

LS-S: *Is it likely that a child with ADD who does not receive treatment will become more involved in antisocial behaviors as an adolescent than the young child who does receive intervention?*

HP: There are a couple of variables that are associated with outcome in terms of antisocial conduct in children who have ADD. One is early detection and early intervention. Another is a family history of Conduct Disorder with mothers or fathers who have had a history of Conduct Disorder. A third variable is the presence of learning difficulties or limited intellectual ability. Related to this, those children who come from less-involved families and who give less attention to treatment could also have a greater likelihood of Conduct Disorder. A fourth variable is aggression. Those children who exhibited high levels of aggression at a very young age have a greater likelihood of exhibiting antisocial behavior or Conduct Disorder later on.

LS-S: *How would you evaluate a child suspected of having ADD?*

HP: There's no single test to identify a child with ADD. The process of making the diagnosis often involves the collaboration of several professionals and the use of a number of interviews and tests, as well as behavioral observations of the child. Often, the process begins with a referral to a pediatrician, or from a pediatrician to a mental health professional, or from a school to a pediatrician or mental health professional who interviews the child and the parents. The parents frequently give a fairly consistent history of problems with the child's behavior and/or attention span which dates back to age three or four, that is, the preschool years.

The parents are often given rating scales to complete to measure the child's hyperactivity, inattention, social development, impulsivity, and emotionality, and teachers are also given rating scales to evaluate those factors in the classroom. A detailed history is taken of the child's development both at home and at school to determine whether there's been consistency in the child's behavioral pattern. Direct observations are made by professionals in the classroom to determine to what degree that child exhibits inattention, hyperactivity, or impulsive behavior as compared to other children in the classroom. The child may undergo some psychological testing to determine the existence of any comorbid or correlated condition such as a learning disability, anxiety disorder, depression, or conduct and oppositional disorders. The child is also interviewed to determine his/her self-perception, emotionality, and thoughts about ability to function at school, at home, and socially.

For problems of a severe emotional nature, referral to a psychiatrist may be indicated. If there are correlated problems of a neurological nature, such as a tic disorder or possible seizure disorder, then referral may be made to a pediatric neurologist for consideration and for assistance with diagnosis. So the diagnostic process involves a collaborative information-sharing process making use of information from multiple sources, and multiple procedures involving interviewing and psychological and medical testing.

LS-S: *In terms of the psychological evaluations, are there any tests that are particularly useful?*

HP: The primary instruments are rating scales. Some of the more commonly-used scales include the Conners Teachers and Parents Rating Scales, the ADD-H Comprehensive Teacher Rating Scale, the ADHD Rating Scale, and the Child Attention Profile, along with the Home Situation Questionnaire and School Situation Questionnaire. There are psychological tests such as the Wechsler series of tests, and academic achievement tests such as the Woodcock-Johnson Test for Achievement or the Wide Range Achievement Test-Revised, which help to measure learning ability in case a learning disability is suspected. There are a number of computerized tests on the market called continuous performance tests, some of which are the T.O.V.A. and the Gordon Diagnostic System. These tests are designed to objectively measure inattention, impulsivity, alertness, and reaction time as well as consistency of performance across time in these areas.

LS-S: *How do you see the role of the psychologist who's seeing the child individually for ADD, and the interface between the therapist and the school?*

HP: The psychologist in the school and the physician have to work together with the parents to form a team approach, and the parents have to basically coordinate that team approach. In the optimum situation between the psychologist and the school, the relationship begins with the evaluation process. The psychologist should contact the school to interview the teacher either by telephone or in person, and have the child's teacher(s) rate the child's behavior. School records should be obtained and, if needed, previous teachers of the child contacted.

Psychologists should, if they have time, do direct observation in the classroom, or arrange for a school official to possibly do some direct observation. The school should be informed of the results of the psychological evaluation and any recommendations, and a meeting should ensue with the psychologist, parents, teacher(s) and, hopefully, the medical personnel involved to discuss a treatment plan both for home and school. Then the psychologist and the parent should work together with the teacher to construct an accommodation plan within the school to enable the child to improve his/her academic performance.

In September 1991, the U.S. Department of Education issued a memorandum stating that ADD could be considered a handicapping condition and that accommodations could be made in the classroom to help these kids. Since then there have been a number of school districts that have instituted screening methods for ADD in special education classes and then provided accommodations for regular education so that they could return to the regular classroom.

The psychologist needs to see what supports are in the school and to work with the parents and the teacher to see that those support systems are implemented in the classroom, to evaluate whether the accommodations are working effectively, and to modify accommodations as appropriate.

LS-S: *At what point would a child with ADD be considered for a special education class?*

HP: We've looked at this issue by having a team of researchers look into what percentage of children with ADD would require a regular classroom setting and what percentage would require special education. We found that 80 percent of kids with ADD could benefit from having regular education and 20 percent may need special education services of one sort or another. Half of that 20 percent would have already been eligible for special education services on the basis of a coexisting condition, either a learning disability or an emotional handicap, so that left 10 percent of "pure" ADD children who would need special education.

Of that 10 percent we estimate that a very small number, only 1 in 1000, would need a full-time special education setting to manage their ADD, whereas the remainder would be able to succeed in a resource program in conjunction with regular education. Those children with ADD who need special education would likely need it because they have extreme symptoms with high degrees of hyperactivity or impulsivity and signs of coexisting problems such as learning disabilities and/or emotional difficulties. Children with only ADD but with very severe symptomatology would also be included in this last group.

LS-S: *There are many schools for children with ADD and learning disabilities. Even if the child could do well in a regular classroom, is there any benefit that they would receive from going to one of these small private schools?*

HP: There very well may be. Not every school district is up-to-speed in terms of its knowledge of how to manage these children. Some school districts have a combination of children with special needs in special education classes, and sometimes the child with ADD is put into classrooms with children who have more serious emotional impairments. This is not the best placement for some ADD children. In those districts where public school interventions don't seem to be working well, either because the teachers aren't trained or the programs haven't been implemented, private schools specifically geared toward these children do a better job.

LS-S: *At what point should medication be considered for children with ADD?*

HP: I think medication should always be considered. Medication should not be seen as a last resort. The benefits of medication must always be evaluated against the risks. A child with ADD, whether it be severe or even mild, should always be considered a candidate for possible medical intervention. The more severe the characteristics, the more weight should be placed on medicine, because it's likely that with those children who have more severe cases, other methods of intervention have already been tried unsuccessfully.

The child with moderate or mild ADD may first try counseling and/or behavioral management systems such as token economy systems, self-monitoring systems, and accommodations in the classroom. However, we must always evaluate those strategies to see if they're working effectively. In many cases a trial of medication may be used to see if it will help to optimize the results of the other interventions. So I think medication should be in the minds of anyone treating a child with ADD as either a way of drastically improving behavior, learning, and attention, or as a way of optimizing other treatment results.

LS-S: *How would you evaluate the effects of medication? Would that be the psychologist's or the teacher's job?*

HP: I think it involves everyone. One of the problems we've had is that the children are too easily put on medication without a comprehensive evaluation. When that happens, there's no team approach. Instead, a medical doctor says, "Try this," and the parent doesn't have access to enough education about the medication and or the disorder itself. In those cases most parents stop the medication after a short period of time because they're not really aware of what the medicine is doing, and they don't like the idea of their child being on medication.

When you start with a comprehensive assessment, you have team development, and you have very well-informed parents. Everyone is working together to evaluate the results of the medicine. Evaluation comes in the form of behavior rating scales, re-taking of psychological tests to determine whether effects of medication are within what we expect, anecdotal reports from the school, additional direct observation to compare previous behaviors with behaviors while taking medication, and the child's report of the effects of the medication including any side effects s/he may be experiencing.

LS-S: *What kind of side effects do children have to contend with if they're on Ritalin® or another stimulant?*

HP: The main side effects are appetite suppression, stomach aches or headaches, lethargy, sadness, and mild dysphoria. Some children experience a rebound effect in the late afternoon at the time the medication leaves the bloodstream. At this point their ADD symptoms may temporarily worsen. Some children may develop tic-like behaviors. There is a controversy about whether these tics are actually side effects or symptoms of an underlying tic disorder.

LS-S: *In your experience, do antidepressants work as well as stimulants?*

HP: The effectiveness of antidepressants depends on the target behavior. Stimulants are the first-line medicines to be used because they've been around the longest, they're the safest, and they have the most beneficial track record. While they work best to improve attention span and hyperactivity, they have less of a positive effect on mood. If you have a child or adolescent who has depression and mood fluctuations as well as hyperactivity and inattention as the targets of treatment, you might choose an antidepressant. Antidepressants probably have a less positive effect on attention and impulsivity than do stimulants. There are also a number of significant side effect with the antidepressants such as dry mouth, constipation, some possible dizziness, blurred vision, and some cardiac irregularities, so they need to be used cautiously with supervision of the prescribing physician.

LS-S: *While the targets of treatment for ADD in schools are usually behavioral, one of the goals of treatment is to allow ADD students to achieve academically at their potential. Is there a correlation between improvements in behavior and academic performance?*

HP: Typically, we find that there is. There's clearly a relationship between academic performance and stimulant usage, but the relationship between learning and achievement scores and medication treatment is less clear.

LS-S: *One of the classroom interventions mentioned in* The ADD Hyperactivity Handbook for Schools *is the Peer Teaching Intervention. How does that work?*

HP: The Peer Teaching Intervention is based upon the key role motivation plays in helping children pay attention. The more one-to-one experience a student with ADD can have with a teacher, whether it be a peer teacher or a regular teacher, the more the likelihood that his/her learning or academic performance will improve.

There are two components to this intervention. The student with ADD can be either the teacher or the recipient of peer tutoring. Being the recipient in a one-on-one teaching experience makes it likely that the ADD child will stay on track more consistently than he/she would while participating in a group learning experience. If the ADD child is the provider in the peer teacher experience he or she hopefully will experience increased self-esteem, feelings of accomplishment, as well as gain a sense of satisfaction from helping others. Academically this gives the child a sense of mastery over a subject area.

LS-S: *How would this be implemented?*

HP: This would be an accommodation, and it would be specified in an accommodation plan devised by the psychologist, teacher, and parents. In the plan the teacher would write that the child will receive peer tutoring from another student in the class in a subject area where they're having difficulty or that the ADD child who is excelling in a specific area would be able to provide peer teaching or tutoring to another child.

LS-S: *How might a token economy system be implemented in a classroom in which many of the children are not going to be part of the economy?*

HP: We have a system called the Goal Card Program, which we've used clinically for years. It involves a token economy system in which the teacher rates the child on a scale from one to five on behaviors such as paying attention in class, keeping desk and notebook neat, completing work in school, completing homework, and cooperating with others.

Children with ADD often require more positive and/or negative feedback than is normally provided in the classroom. Again, the token economy serves as a method of providing additional structure to the child in terms of feedback about their behavior and performance in the classroom. Young children are rated in every period of the class, several times during the class period, just in the morning and the afternoon, or even once a day. By working together with the teacher and the parents, the token economy serves to structure the school environment and provides a motivational incentive for the child to be more conscious of his/her attitudes and behavior and more focused on classroom goals.

LS-S: *Does this work with the older kids as well?*

HP: It works well with middle school and elementary school age children. High school students with ADD respond better to contracts than to token systems.

LS-S: *Are children with ADD aware that their behavior is different from that of other* *children? Is there a motivation to change their behaviors because of the negative consequences they're experiencing?*

HP: It depends. With those children who are predominantly hyperactive and impulsive, the chances are that the natural negative reponses they encounter will not be motivating because they usually don't take responsibility for their behavior. These children and adolescents are more likely to externalize and blame others for their behavior rather than to see it as a result of their own difficulties.

We try to explain ADD to the children—what it means to have ADD and how they can help themselves. We give them material to read at their level with the hope that they will gain more insight and through that insight become more motivated to change, to try to control themselves and to take responsibility for ways that they can get help.

On the other hand, those children with the ADD and little hyperactivity are more anxious about their behavior and about events around them. They are more interested in developing methods that will help them, so they can become more instrumental in their own therapy. As kids with either type of ADD get older, they are more willing to look into themselves and to face their issues because they realize that their future success depends upon becoming more successful in handling their problems.

LS-S: *Many of the parents of ADD kids are coping with ADD themselves. Is it helpful to have parents "coach" their child or adolescent?*

HP: I believe that's the most important part of this puzzle, having the parents involved and serving as coaches for their children. Parents who never give up on their kids, who always look for ways to provide assistance for their children, who seek alternative interventions, and stand by their children as advocates in the classroom, playground, with peers, and within the family unit, will have children who, despite these difficulties, will have a better chance of succeeding. There's no question that as children grow they come to understand and appreciate the support and loyalty and efforts by their parents. The child learns the values which guide the parents in their supportive role: values of good education, hard work, responsibility, self-caring and self-esteem.

LS-S: *I'm sure that CH.A.D.D. goes a long way with helping parents stay with this difficult task.*

HP: That's the mission of CH.A.D.D.: to give parents the education and information they need. There are local chapters that hold monthly support meetings for that purpose. Parents don't always come to every meeting every month, but when they need support, they come.

LS-S: *Now that there is more public awareness of ADD, is there a trend to overdiagnose this disorder?*

HP: There's no question that there is greater awareness of ADD today than there was when we started in 1987. ADD still accounts for 40 percent of all referrals in child guidance clinics and mental health practices. However, there's also no question that ADD still remains a highly underdiagnosed disorder in this country. This means that there are a lot of children with ADD who have not reached the appropriate mental health setting to receive an accurate diagnosis. That doesn't mean that there aren't children for whom the ADD diagnosis will become an overly inclusive diagnosis which masks other significant problems. Diagnosticians have to keep in mind that although ADD is getting a lot of attention right now, other conditions can mimic ADD and they must take care to give the appropriate diagnosis.

ADD as an Educational Disorder:
The Legal Issues

By Harvey C. Parker, Ph.D.

For a long time no one seemed to have the answers to help students with ADD in a school setting. Daily reports of poor school performance created heartache and misery for ADD children and their parents, who faced each new school day with the discouraging thought that it would offer no more hope than the day before. Unfortunately, most teachers didn't know what to do with these inattentive, hyperactive children who took up much of their day with poor behavior and even poorer work. For the most part, teachers never had any training in their undergraduate education programs about attention deficit disorders and probably had received little, if any, ADD related in-service training during their teaching career. Books about ADD were not readily available five or six years ago and those that were had been written more for health care professionals and parents than for teachers. With an average of one to two ADD children in every classroom and with teachers unaware of how to reach them, ADD children were in trouble and their parents and teachers knew it.

One of the reasons so few educators knew about ADD was because for many years ADD had not been considered a handicapping condition in our nations' public schools. No mention of ADD or its cardinal symptoms of inattention, impulsivity, and hyperactivity could be found in the Education of the Handicapped Act (EHA; PL 94-142) or in its reauthorized form, the Individuals with Disabilities Education Act (IDEA; PL 101-476). ADD was not considered, in and of itself, a disabling condition, despite the fact that many ADD children experienced substantial problems in school.

Parents Advocate for ADD

Fueled by concern and desperation, parents of ADD children began to meet and organize support groups. The ADD parent support group movement had unprecedented growth between 1987 and 1991. With a strong conviction to find help for their children and to secure a place for them in our country's educational system, parents like Sandra F. Thomas, Mary C. Fowler, JoAnne Evans, Bonnie Fell, Michael and Fran Gilman, Ellen Kosh, Carol Lerner, Pamela Murray, Debra Maxey, Nancy Cornish, Nancy Eisenberg, Tom Phelan, Judy Mitchell, Judy Leonard, Mary Jane Johnson, Jean C, Harrison and many others, worked tirelessly to develop support groups and to spread information about ADD throughout their communities and around the country.

One parent support group, CH.A.D.D., Children With Attention Deficit Disorder, started in 1987 by myself, Fran Gilman, and Carol Lerner took off like a rocket in south Florida. Within six months three chapters of CH.A.D.D. had started and within a year we were planning our first national conference in Orlando with over 20 chapters formed. As of March 1992, there are almost 300 CH.A.D.D. chapters around the country offering information and support to parents. Similarly, other ADD support groups, like Debra Maxey's HAAD (now part of CH.A.D.D.) in Virginia, Pamela Murray's ADDAG in Colorado, Nancy Eisenberg's ADHD Association of Texas, Judy Mitchell's ADD-IN in Massachusetts, to name just a few, have significantly influenced attitudes about ADD in their states.

Starting in 1989, parents began to tell members of the United States Congress stories of heartache and discouragement in trying to get educational help for their ADD children. Their timing was right because the Education of the Handicapped Act, which became law in 1975, had to come before the legislature for reauthorization.

While considering the reauthorization of PL 94-142 the United States Senate became aware that children with ADD were not receiving a free appropriate public education as the law required. Attempting to remedy this situation, the Senate Committee on Labor and Human Resources passed a bill in November 1989 which added ADD to PL 94-142 under the definition of specific learning disability (SLD). While categorizing ADD children within the definition of learning disabled looked like a workable solution to members of the Senate, ADD experts knew that this step would not only be technically inaccurate, but would not help the majority of ADD children, since they do not have learning disabilities.

In order to be considered eligible for special education services, a learning disabled child must show a significant discrepancy between tested mental ability and academic achievement. The SLD child must be underachieving relative to his ability level. Since most ADD children did not have academic achievement problems in school, they would not have been eligible to receive services under the SLD category. The Senate's remedy would have been a solution in name only, with little practical benefit to most ADD children who needed special help. Trying to apply an SLD definition to ADD children would not work.

In the Spring of 1990 the U.S. House of Representatives' Committee on Education and Labor was also considering their EHA reauthorization bill. Sandra F. Thomas, Mary C. Fowler, and Dr. James Swanson prepared testimony which was heard by the Subcommittee to recognize, as the Senate did, that ADD children were being denied a free appropriate public education. They were also made aware of the fact that ADD and SLD were different disorders. The drawbacks of the Senate Bill, which was passed six months earlier, became evident. Taking this testimony into consideration, the House passed a bill which would have included ADD in EHA as a handicapping condition under the existing category of Other Health Impairments. By doing so, ADD children would have a better chance of receiving help if needed.

As soon as the House bill was passed in May 1990, opposition to the ADD language in the bill was heard from a number of education-related groups. These groups opposed the inclusion of ADD as a special education disability. They created enough uncertainty about the issue to cause a joint House and Senate conference committee to meet to discuss the issue further and arrive at a consensus as to what should be done. To resolve the controversy, the conference committee decided to ask the Department of Education to issue a public Notice of Inquiry which would provide Congress with the widest possible range of advice on the issue.

DOE Policy Memorandum on ADD

Nearly 3,000 responses to the Notice of Inquiry were submitted to the Department of Education by parents and professionals. In May 1991 the Office of Special Education and Rehabilitative Services (OSERS) provided a summary of these responses to Congress. Overall, the Department found that there was a great deal of confusion as to how ADD children were being understood and taught in schools.

With the Notice of Inquiry responses in mind, the Department of Education sought to clarify to state departments of education whether ADD children could be eligible for special education services. OSERS announced that, "Children with ADD may be considered disabled solely on the basis of this disorder within the Other Health Impaired category in situations where special education and related services are needed because of ADD." (OSERS News Update, March-April 1991, p. 2). On September 16, 1991 the U.S. Department of Education more fully explained its policy on ADD in a memorandum to chief state school officers. This memorandum, included in its entirety in Appendix A, was signed by the Assistant Secretaries of the Office for Civil Rights, and the Office of Elementary and Secondary Education. The memorandum was far reaching in its content and emphasized state and local education agencies' responsibility to address the needs of children with attention deficit disorders both within general and special education. Dr. Judy Schrag, Director of Special Education Programs, received a standing ovation from parents, educators, and health care professionals at the CH.A.D.D. conference in Washington, DC when she announced the new ADD policy clarification.

Policy Memorandum Emphasizes Regular Classroom Accommodations: The new policy memorandum pointed out that state and local education agencies should offer protections to ADD students even if such students were found *not* to be eligible for services under Part B of IDEA. The Department encouraged such education agencies to take necessary steps to make accommodations within the classroom to meet the needs of students with ADD in the regular education setting and emphasizes that education agencies must consider the provisions of Section 504 of the Rehabilitation Act of 1973 in doing so.

Section 504 is a federal law which requires public school districts to provide a free appropriate public education to every "qualified handicapped person" residing within their jurisdiction. The Office of Civil Rights (OCR) is the federal agency within the Department of Education that enforces Section 504. OCR has ruled that ADD children are "qualified handicapped persons" under Section 504 if their ability to learn or to otherwise benefit from their education is substantially limited due to ADD.

Thus, regardless of whether an ADD child meets eligibility guidelines to receive federally funded special education programs (under IDEA), Section 504 guarantees the ADD child the right to receive a free appropriate public education.

The policy memorandum emphasizes the important role that teachers in regular education have in providing help to ADD students: "Steps also should be taken to train regular education teachers and other personnel to develop their awareness about ADD and its manifestations and the adaptations that can be implemented in regular education programs to address the instructional needs of these children" (p. 7).

The Department felt that through the use of appropriate adaptations and interventions in regular classes, many of which may be required by Section 504, that local education agencies will be able to effectively address the instructional needs of many children with ADD.

Policy Memorandum Clarifies that ADD Can Fall Under "Other Health Impaired" Category: With respect to special education, the memorandum indicated that children with ADD may be considered disabled solely on the basis of this disorder within the "other health impaired" category: "The 'other health impaired' category includes chronic or acute impairments that result in limited alertness, which adversely affects educational performance. This, children with ADD should be classified as eligible for services under the 'other health impaired' category in instances where the ADD is a chronic or acute health problem that results in limited alertness, which adversely affects educational performance." (p. 3)

The policy memorandum also stated that children with ADD are also eligible for services under Part B (IDEA) if the children satisfy the criteria applicable to other disability categories. For example, children with ADD are also eligible for services under the "specific learning disability" category or Part B if they meet criteria and under the "seriously emotionally disturbed" category of Part B if they meet criteria for that category.

Furthermore, it was made clear that state and local education agencies are obligated to evaluate the possible need for special education services for children with a prior medical diagnosis of ADD and for those children who are suspected of having ADD.

ADD Centers Funded

The Department of Education's action reinforces the notion that the educational needs of children with ADD must be addressed in our nation's schools, both within regular and special education. In an effort to determine how this could best be done, Congress recently funded an ADD Resource Center at the University of Kentucky to search throughout the country for promising practices that currently exist to educate ADD children. Understanding that educators know little about attention deficit disorders, Congress also authorized funding to establish four ADD centers to collect, synthesize and distribute information about ADD to schools. Additionally, in the fiscal year 1992 House Appropriations Committee report, the committee indicated that $1,500,000 should be used for the funding of projects that develop new inservice and preservice training for special education and regular classroom teachers in order to address the needs of children with attention deficit disorders.

The pleas of parents have been heard. Thanks to new changes in policy at the federal level, children with ADD will have a better opportunity to receive a free and appropriate public education.

Reprinted with permission from Harvey C. Parker, Ph.D. (1992) *The ADD Hyperactivity Handbook for Schools.* Plantation, Florida: Impact Publications, Inc. pp. 117-124.

Classroom Interventions for ADD Children

With the addition of Attention Deficit Disorder as a handicap, and better identification of children and adolescents with ADD, there is increasing interest in creating programs that will accommodate these students in the regular classroom. A number of behavioral and cognitive-behavioral interventions have been described for this purpose and studies have shown that when well-designed and correctly implemented, these interventions serve to improve the children's behavior and help in improving their school performance.

DuPaul and Stoner (1994) stress the importance of having clearly designed interventions which are based on the child's behavioral data and have well-defined, child appropriate behavioral goals. Studies have shown that it is important to individualize treatments to fit the personalities and/or predilections of the children being helped.

Secondary reinforcers play a key role in successful interventions. As ADD can be perceived as a problem with motivation and attending to rules, the use of reinforcers which are particularly salient to the child or adolescent in question will give treatment more salience and meaning for the child. It is better to use reinforcers that involve choosing of a preferred activity rather than receiving concrete items, especially with older children. Involving the student and, when appropriate, the parents, in the constructing of a list of rewards to be used in treatment encourages greater involvement by the student and the family, in addition to increasing the chance of choosing meaningful reinforcers.

When targeting behaviors for interventions it is important to define them in terms of positive and productive outcomes. For example, the goal of having a child sit still is not necessarily a productive one (see interview with DuPaul for an explanation of the "Deadman's Rule"), although it might bring some relief to the teacher. A more important goal that would encourage motoric stillness on the part of the child would be the completion of a certain amount of schoolwork (i.e., 10 math problems) in a specified period of time. It is important to link behavioral and academic goals so that the true interests of the child are being addressed.

Behavioral interventions focus on providing external feedback to the child at a greater rate than would be provided in the average classroom environment. There are two basic principles which underline the various types of behavioral interventions based on contingency management. One is to provide children with ADD with more frequent feedback about their behavior in the form of reinforcement for positive behaviors. The second is to judiciously use mild reprimands to help keep the child on task and aware of the behavioral goals to which s/he has agreed. Reinforcement schedules need to be fairly frequent at the beginning of the interventions and can be decreased as the child makes progress. Reprimands need to be brief, focused on the behavior, nonemotional, and should directly follow the misbehavior (Abramowitz and O'Leary, 1991; DuPaul and Stoner, 1994; Parker, 1992).

Another consideration in the use of contingency based systems is the concept of response cost. Research has shown that having a mild penalty in the form of a loss of a privilege or token increases the effectiveness of these interventions. DuPaul and Stoner (1994) recommend that to avoid discouraging the child by creating too much emphasis on punishment, teachers should 1) highlight the positive reinforcement aspect of the program, 2) not take away points or tokens at a rate more frequent than one per minute, and 3) avoid reducing a child's tokens or points to below zero.

Token economy systems have been used effectively with children who have ADD. As a classroom intervention this system works efficiently, and has the advantage of being able to be tied into behavior management efforts at home as well. A caveat is that behaviors generated by the token economy will not necessarily generalize to different situations. It may be necessary to expand the program as the child encounters new difficulties. It is important for the child to have a clear idea of the behavioral goals and rewards. Goals should be listed in clear language, and the economy system kept simple. The following steps are generally taken to implement a classroom token economy for a child with ADD (DuPaul and Stoner, 1994; Parker, 1992):

1. Identify the target behaviors and situations. Once this has been done through the evaluation, discuss the target behaviors with the child and explain the concept of a token economy system.

2. Select the type of secondary reinforcers or tokens. These may be actual poker chips, stickers placed on a chart, or less tangible rewards such as a favored activity. Involve the child in determining a list of rewards.

3. Determine the number of tokens or rewards to be gained for achieving or maintaining the target behavior or goal.

4. Determine how frequently tokens may be exchanged for the predetermined rewards. This should occur on at least a daily basis and can be more frequent, particularly at the beginning of the program. Determine if the system will include the loss of tokens for a behavior.

5. Assess the impact of the program in terms of the child's behaviors to determine if new target behaviors are needed or if previous targets can be faded.

6. Fading of the program should be done gradually.

Other contingency-based interventions include behavioral contracting, in which the child and teacher agree on the target behaviors and the rewards as well as how and when the target behavior will be evaluated. This works better with older children who can better understand the concept of a contract, and who may be able to adhere to the agreement despite the lower frequency of reinforcement.

Home-school contingency programs can be highly effective as they involve the parents more directly, increase the importance of school behaviors, and increase the pool of possible reinforcers (DuPaul and Stoner, 1991; Parker, 1992; Pfiffner and Barkley, 1990). There are several types of home-school programs that may be created. Parker (1992) describes "The Goal Card Program" which involves selecting five target behaviors. The teacher rates these behaviors on a scale of one to five, either once or several times a day depending on the needs of the child. The parents review the card each evening and the child must bring it back to school. A reward system is established.

Once the child has demonstrated success he or she is asked to fill out his/her own Goal Card and his/her ratings are compared to the teacher's. Once the child has established success at this level the program is slowly faded, but teachers and parents continue to positively reinforce goal behaviors even after the Goal Card is no longer used. In general these programs work best when they are well planned, the reinforcers are meaningful to the child, and the treatment team carries through on the agreed intervention.

DuPaul and Stoner (1994, p.116) list the following as components of a home-school contingency plan for children with ADD:

1. Daily and/or weekly goals are stated in a positive manner.

2. Both academic and behavioral goals are included.

3. A small number of goals are targeted at a time.

4. The teacher provides quantitative feedback about student performance.

5. Feedback is provided by subject or class periods

6. Communication is made on a regular basis (either daily or weekly).
7. Home-based contingencies are tied to school performance. Both short-term and long-term consequences are employed.
8. Parental cooperation and involvement are solicited prior to implementation.
9. Student input into goals and contingencies is solicited, particularly with older children and adolescents.
10. Goals and procedures are modified as necessary.

Self-management strategies specifically target the student's learning to monitor his/her own behaviors. Because the student is asked to develop internal coping strategies, these interventions are described as cognitive-behavioral. While considerable attention has been given to the behavioral strategies in the past, interest in developing effective self-management strategies is increasing. Self-management strategies include self-monitoring, self-reinforcement, and self-instruction. Different systems can be set up to address behavioral and academic goals. Behavioral goals such as hand raising to answer questions and refraining from off-task behaviors can be monitored by having children record the number of times they achieve the behavioral goal.

There are several devices available that can be used to cue children to evaluate their behavior at regular time intervals. Signaling devices and systems such as Gordon's *The Attention Training System*, electronically administers a point every 60 seconds, and can also be controlled by the teacher from a module on her desk. *The Listen, Look, and Think Program* provides a continuous play tape that can be used as a signaling tape and self recording materials for the child. *The MotivAider* is a vibrating device that can be worn by the child and programmed to signal the child at various intervals.

Parker (1992) presents self-monitoring classroom protocols for attention, hand writing, productivity, and social skills, among other areas. DuPaul and Stoner (1994) state that self-reinforcement, which includes self-monitoring, may be the most effective form of self-management intervention. Self-reinforcement involves the use of secondary reinforcers and initial guidance in achieving accuracy in self-evaluation.

As in the later stage of the Goal Card Program described above, children practice self-monitoring by comparing their self-evaluation to the teacher's ratings. When both have demonstrated accuracy in self-rating the teacher's ratings are faded. This sort of intervention is useful for older children and adolescents and also can be the second phase of an intervention which begins with a contingency-based treatment.

Self-instruction involves having the child or adolescent learn to verbally remind him/herself of the steps s/he needs to follow. For example, s/he is asked to internally say to him/herself, "Stop, look and listen." Parker (1992) incorporates this type of intervention into some of his self-monitoring protocols. The success of self-instruction has been inconsistent and more research is needed to refine the techniques for use with children who have ADD (Fiore, et. al. 1993). Problems include its failure to generalize and a lack of understanding of what in the procedure serves to create improved behavior (DuPaul and Stoner, 1994).

In addition to specific intervention strategies, psychologists can help teachers to establish classroom environments which will enhance the learning experience of the student with ADD. These strategies include (Parker, 1992):
1. Having well-defined rules.
2. Having predictable routines for repetitive classroom activities.
3. Helping the student with ADD to maintain external organization (i.e., keeping the desk organized).

4. Giving clear and deliberate directions.
5. Optimizing placement of the child in the classroom.
6. Maintaining a good level of stimulation in class.
7. Planning ahead for transitions (such as from resource room to the regular classroom).
8. Providing frequent praise.
9. Helping the child or adolescent with ADD establish reasonable work goals.

To conclude, there is growing evidence that children often do best when they receive medication therapy along with behavioral or behavioral cognitive treatment. The successful intervention will involve close teamwork on the part of the psychologist, teacher, child, family, and physician. While the effort of assessing the child or adolescent and setting up and evaluating the intervention program may seem large, the student's potential gains provide excellent reinforcement for all involved.

Sources: Abramowitz, A. and O'Leary, S. (1991) Behavioral interventions for the classroom: Implications for students with ADHD. *School Psychology Review.* 20:pp. 220-234. DuPaul, G. and Stoner, G.(1994) *ADHD in the Schools: Assessment and Intervention Strategies.* New York: Guilford Publications. pp. 96-134. Fiore, T., Becker, E., Nero, R. (1993) *Research summary on education interventions for students with ADD.* Research Triangle Institute, ADD Intervention Center. Parker, H. (1992) *The ADD Hyperactivity Handbook for Schools.* Plantation, Florida: Impact Publications. pp. 125-208. Pfiffner, L. and Barkley, R. (1990) "Educational Placement and Classroom Management" in Barkley, R. (1990) Ed. *Attention Deficit Hyperactivity Disorder: A Handbook for Diagnosis and Treatment.* New York: Guilford Publications. pp. 498-539.

- Focus on Programs -
The Lehigh University Regional Consulting Center for Adolescents with Attention Deficit Disorder

George DuPaul, Ph.D. has devoted his work to helping children with ADD through research, clinical and school interventions, and by sharing his knowledge with others. He currently is an Associate Professor of School Psychology at Lehigh University in Bethlehem, Pennsylvania, and has written numerous publications related to assessment and intervention for children and adolescents with ADD including his recently-published text, ADHD in the Schools: Assessment and Intervention Strategies, *co-authored with George Stoner, Ph.D. This book furthers his efforts to bring appropriate treatment for ADD into the schools.*

In another such effort Dr. DuPaul has worked with Edward Shapiro, Ph.D., Professor and Coordinator of the School Psychology program at Lehigh University, to create a consultation program that is unique in both its scope and its focus on young adolescents. In his interview with Senior Editor Laura Slap-Shelton, Psy.D., DuPaul discusses the Lehigh University Regional Consulting Center for Adolescents with Attention Deficit Disorder as well as some guidelines for in-school interventions.

Laura Slap-Shelton, Psy.D.: *To begin, our readers will be interested in the history of the Lehigh University Regional Consulting Center for Adolescents with Attention Deficit Disorder (LU-CCADD) program.*

George DuPaul, Ph.D.: LU-CCADD was originally devised by Lehigh University's Dr. Edward Shapiro. As coprincipal investigators on this project, we are funded by a three-year grant from the U.S. Department of Education. The program is designed to develop and disseminate a model for consulting with school personnel who are working with early adolescents who might have Attention Deficit Disorder. This primarily includes teachers, school psychologists, and guidance counselors.

In the first two years of the project, we have consulted with approximately 50 to 60 school districts in Eastern Pennsylvania and Western New Jersey with regard to a variety of potential services for kids who might have ADD. Some of these services include designing ways for teachers to help these kids in the classroom, helping districts work with physicians in medication management, designing social skills training and parent training programs, and providing further inservice training to teachers.

LS-S: *Why are you targeting the early adolescent population?*

GD: Dr. Shapiro and I believe that this has been a neglected age group relevant to ADD. Most of the research on ADD has been focused on elementary school students. There is only a handful of studies in the literature relevant to nonpharmacological intervention for older children. Early adolescence is such a key transitional phase. The peer group is starting to become more influential than the family, the child must adjust to multiple teachers instead of just one, and the level of teacher support and flexibility in dealing with the problems of ADD kids tends to decrease.

In addition, the level of complexity and independence that is expected academically increases. This is the time when kids are beginning to be exposed to sex, drugs, and rock and roll. And children with ADD, with all their impulsivity, tend to gravitate in this direction. We hope to affect the long-term outcome for ADD kids by working through the schools to target children at this key transitional period.

LS-S: *The program operates on three levels of intervention. What is the first level?*

GD: The first level involves a two-day inservice. Each school district will send at least two, usually three, representatives to a two-day inservice where we cover background information about Attention Deficit Disorder, focusing primarily on intervention strategies, but also including methods for assessment and factors of which school personnel need to be aware regarding medication.

Most training programs for school personnel in ADD stop here. The unique feature of our project is that we go beyond education to a second level, which involves a fairly intense period of on-site consultation in each of the school districts. Our two graduate student assistants go out to the school district for up to 30 hours total of on-site time. They work with one or more individuals from the school district on the areas that the district personnel feel are most important. Some districts have teachers who don't know anything about ADD. Other districts might use us to help facilitate one or more meetings with area physicians about information relevant to both diagnosis and medication management. This level two consultation is usually conducted within a two-month period.

LS-S: *What does the third level of intervention involve?*

GD: The third level is made up of two components. The first is to promote ongoing connections between our group and the districts. To do this we have several district follow-up periods in which we obtain information from districts about what was valuable to them about the program, and to provide further consultation by phone if necessary. The follow-up data we are getting is quite positive. We are finding that the districts are not only using the information that we've given them with regard to specific students when we were there, but are also applying similar procedures to other students. That is exactly what we are trying to accomplish. We are very encouraged to see this ripple effect.

The other part of the third level is that we provide districts with the opportunity to receive advanced training in Attention Deficit Disorder. We have experts from across the country come in and talk about issues relevant to adolescents with ADD. This year we focused on intervention strategies, with a different speaker for each strategy area. Each district that participates with us is allowed to send one representative free of charge to the Institute, and of course other people can attend for a fee. We plan on sponsoring another Summer Institute next year.

LS-S: *Are the districts finding that implementing interventions for their students with ADD is cost-effective?*

GD: The project itself is free to the district. Our intent is to give the districts the kind of information that will successfully maintain these students in the regular classroom. So far there have been no reports of extra cost.

LS-S: *In what year of your grant are you?*

GD: Our third year will start in October. We will focus on disseminating this consultation model on a national basis. We've already been contacted by several sites. Our goal is to explain how our model works and to work with different groups to help them set up regional consultation centers. Again, our goal is to help facilitate appropriate treatment strategies in the schools for as many students with ADD as possible. Along these lines, we are also in the process of developing a manual of procedures and a videotape that will help interested parties to set up their own consultation programs.

LS-S: *Are you hoping to extend this project?*

GD: Yes. We would like to create a national-level consultation program. This involves developing regional teams that would be available to work with groups across the country. Rather than focusing on school districts, we would work with the consultation agencies, and they, in turn, would work with their school districts. We hope we will be successful in getting funding for this expansion of the consultation project.

LS-S: *Is your group involved in research also?*

GD: Yes. I'm just finishing up a research project on class-wide peer tutoring with elementary school students as an intervention for ADD which looks promising. Within the context of the consultation project, we've collected some pilot data on a self-management intervention for middle school kids. We hope to obtain a research grant to conduct controlled research in this area.

LS-S: *Do you feel that self-management is the next step in terms of working with ADD children in the schools?*

GD: Yes. I think it has a lot of promise. The type of self-management approach that we try to promote involves initially creating a strong connection to contingencies and then a gradual move away from the external contingencies to an exclusive reliance on self-evaluation and self- reinforcement. Past studies in this area have been too quick in trying to achieve exclusive reliance on self-evaluation and reinforcement. We would like to promote a much more gradual move that may occur across school years. The difficulty with teaching ADD children self-management is that we are dealing with a disorder that is most likely biologically-based. For some children, even external contingencies are not always enough to bring about consistent change. We need to do more work in this area.

LS-S: *When creating behavioral management programs for children how do you include academic goals in the treatment strategy?*

GD: If you target academic productivity and/or accuracy on seat work, for example, such that if a certain amount of work is done correctly and the child receives reinforcement, you affect not only the child's academic performance but his/her behavioral control as well. This is because a child can't be doing his/her work and misbehaving at the same time. That seems to be the better approach than to target staying in the seat or not talking out of turn.

When I am working with groups, particularly with groups of teachers, I always use the Dead Person Rule, devised by Linsley. It simply states that if a dead person can do a particular behavior, then that behavior is not a good target behavior. For instance, you often see behavior management programs rewarding a child with a token for sitting still for a certain number of minutes. Could a dead person do that? Yes, s/he could sit still and earn a token. However, a dead person cannot complete ten arithmetic problems in 15 minutes. That involves an active response from the child, and is a much more appropriate and productive goal. The child probably is going to sit still while doing those problems, but, quite frankly, if s/he needs to stand

up while doing them, I don't see the difficulty in him/her doing that. This emphasizes our ultimate goal—to have these kids *actively* make academic gains.

- Focus on Programs -
ADD Program at the Child Development Center
University of California at Irvine

Timothy Wigal, Ph.D. is the Assistant Director of the well-established educational and research ADD program and a professor at the University of California at Irvine. Working with the founder of the program, James Swanson, Ph.D., Wigal has been involved in the school programs and in the conducting research on school-based interventions for ADD. Formerly at the University of Texas, Wigal has been working with children who have ADD for over seven years and has published scientific articles on the subject of ADD in childhood. In this interview with Senior Editor Laura Slap-Shelton, Psy.D., he describes some of the methods his program uses in working with ADD children as well as an important national research study on the treatment of children with ADD.

Laura Slap-Shelton, Psy.D.: *What kind of ADD research and programs are you working on at the Child Development Center?*

Timothy Wigal, Ph.D.: We have a clinical program, a year-round day treatment program which has academic and social skills components, and a research program.

LS-S: *How does the school interventions program work?*

TW: Over the last 12 years we have developed an education and treatment program on campus. More recently we have exported it to local area elementary schools where we use a behavior modification program based on a token economy system with reinforcement, response-cost, and time-out procedures.

LS-S: *How many children are in the campus classroom?*

TW: We use the school program to develop and refine our treatments. We have three classrooms which cover grades kindergarten through fifth, with 15 kids in each. Traditionally, the kids in the on-site classrooms are those who are on the verge of being expelled from school, or who have already been expelled. We work with the local school districts on Individual Education Plans (IEPs) with the goal of transitioning the students back into their regular school placements within a year's time. Sometimes the child is with us for longer than a year, sometimes less, but the program is designed for a year.

LS-S: *How well do the children adjust to the token economy system in the program?*

TW: Very well. We introduce the children to a structured behavioral program, and when they are ready, we fade it so that they can make the transition into self-monitoring and self-evaluating.

LS-S: *How do you teach the students to monitor and evaluate their own behavior?*

TW: We have them keep track of their points. They can earn or lose points during every module they work in during the day. The modules include all of the areas found in regular schools with the addition of a social skills group. We call out points on a 20-minute interval from when the children first enter the program. This might sound like it would make for a very loud and raucous classroom, but at any one time we're taking in only a few new kids. At the same time we are transitioning a few out. We use teacher's assistants, or a behavior specialists as we call them, to help with the point delivery system.

LS-S: *How long does it take the children to learn to monitor their behavior, and what are the target behaviors?*

TW: There are five or six areas that we monitor, such as compliance and staying on task. Depending on each kid's ability, it takes a few weeks or months to learn the system and start keeping track of their own points. Once they've had some practice we begin looking for matches between the child's and the behavior specialist's calculation of points.

LS-S: *How are reinforcers used in this system?*

TW: The children can graduate through different levels which have different reinforcers and privileges. Each week the group can earn a special outing such as a trip to the beach. On a daily basis, we have found that the strongest reinforcer is free time on the computer.

LS-S: *How successful has the transition back to regular school been for these children?*

TW: Some kids transition very well, while others need a little help. For the kids who need it, we will provide a behavior specialist who goes out to the regular classroom and continues to work the program for six to twelve additional weeks to help the child get back into the swing of things. Generally, this also involves training the teacher in better classroom management skills which are actually beneficial to all of their students, but necessary for the child who is having trouble with ADD.

LS-S: *Are the teachers receptive to this kind of training?*

TW: Generally they are. That's because we have worked this program from the district level on down and the administrators like the program. There is significant concern in California about ADD because there is not enough money to place all of the children diagnosed with ADD in special education classes. This program makes it possible for these kids to remain in the regular classroom to everyone's benefit. If there is a teacher who doesn't want an assistant in his/her classroom we place the child with a different teacher. In other words, we look for a good transition placement in which the teacher is interested in helping the child and working with us.

LS-S: *Does your program have a parent training component?*

TW: Yes. All of the parents of the children in the day treatment program are required to go through a six-week parent training course at the time of their child's admission. We also provide outpatient parent training modules for the parents of children who are not in the program, but are receiving treatment, or are on the waiting list for the program. The parent training program is also very behaviorally based. We teach parents to do daily report cards at home and a lot of home-based reinforcement using rewards that the parent and child create together such as having pizza or extra time watching television.

LS-S: *What has your experience been with the increased prevalence of ADD in boys over girls?*

TW: We see three or four boys for every girl. This may reflect bias in the referrals because aggressive behaviors are most likely to be seen in boys, making them more likely to be identified as having problems in the classroom or at home. More girls may have problems primarily with inattention. It's harder to see the inattention, especially in the younger kids. Nevertheless, the bias towards males having this disorder is significant.

LS-S: *Are there any theories that account for this yet?*

TW: There are several genetic theories being considered. We're involved with a study that is investigating the role of dopamine by taking blood samples and looking at the number of repeats on a given gene that codes for a particular dopamine subtype receptor. However, I don't know of a good sex-linked theory.

LS-S: *Many of these children have parents with ADD. How does that affect the children?*

TW: At least half the time the child's problems are similar in type to either the mother or father's or both. In addition, the parents of children with ADD are also at risk for alcohol and drug abuse and trouble with the law. Somewhat fewer are at risk for depression. Poor parenting doesn't lead to ADD, but we think that it makes this condition worse. So in our parent training classes our goal is always to help these parents learn better parenting skills. Some of them have adequate parenting skills to deal with normal kids, but not with these kids. Some of them don't have adequate skills to deal with kids at all.

In general, we find that parents are not consistent enough. Children with ADD need a lot of consistency and structure because internally they are in a kind of chaotic situation. They don't time things well. They're not sure how long they have to be in the classroom because five minutes seems like an hour to them, and yet at other times an hour goes by in five minutes. We've all had that kind of experience, but these kids have it on a daily basis.

LS-S: *What kind of research is your program doing?*

TW: One of our research projects is part of a National Institute of Mental Health (NIMH) investigation of different treatments for ADD. The study is being run at six different sites, including University of California at Berkley, University of California at Irvine, Duke University, the University of Pittsburgh, Columbia University and the University of Montreal in conjunction with Schnieders Children's Hospital on Long Island. Each of the sites has an expertise in a particular area of treatment for ADD. Our expertise is in school interventions. Pittsburgh is the expert in the summer treatment programs, Columbia in medication treatment and assessment, and Duke provides the expertise in parent training. The protocols for each aspect of the intervention are determined by using the protocols of the expert site. It took a lot of work and many meetings in Washington to work out the details of the protocols.

LS-S: *How is the research set up?*

TW: There are four treatment groups. The first is a stimulant medication group in which the children receive Ritalin®, Dexadrine® or Cylert®, depending on which works best for each child. The second group, which is the group we are running, is the psychosocial-only group. They receive parent training, social skills training, a summer treatment program which is similar to the school program we just discussed, and in the first 12 weeks of school they receive support from the behavioral specialist in their regular classroom.

During the summer we introduce behavioral principles and set up a school-home system with daily report cards. This way both the parents and the child are prepared for the beginning of school, and the parents are able to administer a behavioral system by working with the child's teacher. Our hope is that even after the behavioral specialist is finished, the parents and teacher will continue the program for the entire school year. The third group is a combination group in which the children receive stimulant medication and all of the psychosocial interventions the second group receives. Finally, the fourth group is our community control group. We assess the children in this group and refer them to another helper/provider in the community.

LS-S: *So the control group is still receiving treatment?*

TW: It's not ethical not to provide treatment for the fourth group of children who certainly need some form of intervention. The research inclusion criteria specify children between the ages of seven and nine years or basically second and third graders. Another restriction for the study is that the children must meet the DSM-IV criteria for ADHD-mixed type. We do the assessments and make the referrals. We will also periodically check up on them over the next two-year period and bring them back in for regular assessment to mark their progress.

LS-S: *Is your group involved in any other research?*

TW: Yes. One project is to study how parents of children with ADD interact with that child and how their interactions affect the other children in the family. We're taping the parents with their children and analyzing problematic patterns of interactions the parents have with their children.

Another project involves testing new kinds of drugs and new kinds of drug delivery systems to see if children with ADD will respond to different types of amphetamines. One example is a stimulant that doesn't cross the blood brain barrier. Another is a medication that has a very slow release based on osmotic pumping principles and would be superior in terms of dosing to even the slow-release forms of Ritalin® and Cylert®.

We do medication assessments in our regular clinical program in order to evaluate learning, memory and other cognitive abilities as well as behaviors. This is important because behavioral improvement without improved academic performance is not the treatment goal. Medication may help a child to sit still, but he may be completely spaced out because he's suffering from what we call cognitive toxicity. In other words, he's on a such a high level of the drug that he can't concentrate or pay attention. We will routinely do a double blind medication assessment on all of the kids. The children are given several different levels of medication and we assess them with behavior rating scales and computer-based tests. On the assessment end, we (including the parents and teachers) do not know which dose the child is on at any particular time during the evaluation.

LS-S: *Should this evaluation be done for every ADD child who is on medication?*

TW: Yes.

LS-S: *But the reality is that this is not done for most children?*

TW: The stereotypical ADD child is seen by a pediatrician who doesn't have much training in ADD, if any. The doctor says, "Let's try this," and then asks the mother's opinion as to whether there is any behavior change. I think most kids are on dosages that are too high, or they're on medication when it's not helping them. We are not antimedication, but we want it to be used to the benefit of the child.

For example, Ritalin® is a valuable drug for treating ADD. Last year we did a review of all the reviews of treatment studies of Ritalin® ever done, going back to 1937. There's very good evidence that this is a safe drug. It doesn't have long-term side-effect problems, and the short-term benefits are there. You get temporary improvement of activity levels, attention, impulsivity, and even an associated featured of increased compliance and decreased aggression, and decreased negative social interactions and increased work in terms of both accuracy and amount completed. But there is no evidence of long-term benefits. Once the kid is off medication all the benefits are lost.

LS-S: *The behaviors come back?*

TW: Yes.

LS-S: *And how about learning?*

TW: In most cases stimulant medication doesn't last more than a year or two. In most cases it stops before two years and there don't seem to be any residual effects for learning. In other words, they benefited when they were on it, but when you take them off there is no improvement in academic achievement. It falls back to the previous level. This is probably due to the fact that medication is given to most kids without any associated behavioral program. But medication should be given in the context of a behavioral program, and this is not usually done, even though it is often recommended.

LS-S: *Another problem is that there are few long term studies on the effect of behavioral interventions at this point.*

TW: Actually, this NIMH study we are doing is going to be *the* long term study because we are going to follow these kids for five years, and we hope to be able to follow them for the next 20 years. So this is going to be the largest, best characterized, and best followed sample that probably will ever be done, because there's not going to be this kind of money available for this sort of study of children with ADD in the future.

LS-S: *What would you recommend to the individual psychologist who is working with children with ADD?*

TW: I would say look at some of the things that have been written by people like Russell Barkley on parent training, and encourage the child's parents to become involved in groups like CH.A.D.D. It's important to think of terms of getting the parents to take responsibility for getting the right treatment for their child and for being involved in the treatment itself. It's also important to make sure the children receive proper medication assessment. The practitioner may want to speak with some of the centers where this sort of research is being done to get some advice as to how to set up the child's treatment program.

Schools will also need to make changes with the new interpretation of Public Law 94-142. Parents need to be active about saying, "We want help for these kids." School psychologists are going to have to do more than assess. They're going to have to start implementing treatment programs in order to accommodate all these ADD children.

Pharmacotherapy for Children and Adolescents with ADD

Medication is one of the major treatment modalities for children with ADD. Safer and Krager (1988) report that over 750,000 children or more than two percent of school-aged children and adolescents are currently taking psychostimulant medications annually (DuPaul and Stoner, 1994). Of all the medications used in the treatment of childhood emotional and behavioral problems, the psychostimulants have been studied the most. Although there was a period in which their safety and effectiveness were challenged, they are now widely accepted as an important aspect of treatment for many children and adolescents (and, increasingly, adults) with ADD. Other psychotropic drugs such as the tricyclic antidepressants are used also, especially if the stimulant medications do not produce the desired results.

One of the most important and often overlooked aspects of including medication in a child or adolescent's treatment is the need for ongoing evaluation of its effectiveness. All too often, a physician may prescribe stimulant medication without involving the family and school in a systematic or even primitive assessment procedure. DuPaul and Stoner (1994) recommend that a systematic evaluation of the child's response to the medication at three dose ranges (low, medium, and high) be conducted so that optimal medication levels are reached. This is particularly important with the stimulant medications because children vary to a great extent in their reactions to and rate of metabolizing of this medication (DuPaul and Barkley, 1990).

An important role for the school psychologist or treating independent psychologist is to help in developing and implementing a monitoring system to evaluate the drug's effects on the child (DuPaul and Barkley, 1990). In order to evaluate changes in the child's behavior while on the medication it is important to have collected substantial baseline data. This is normally done in the initial evaluation of the child with teacher and parent ratings of behavior and academic performance and when possible, behavioral observations. The same rating scales or a subset thereof should be used to evaluate the child or adolescent at each dosage with particular interest given to which, if any, dosage improves the child's academic work. The minimal dosage at which real improvement is observed serves as the optimal dose for the child and this information needs to be shared with the prescribing physician.

In addition to evaluations of the child's behavior and academic work, systematic recording of the child's reaction to the drug is important. Barkley (1991) and Parker (1992) provide forms which allow for a comprehensive but quick recording of this type of information. Once the optimal dosage is determined, evaluation of the medication's effect on the child is continued with periodic administration of rating scales and observations. Residual academic problems can then be evaluated by the teacher and psychologist and appropriate additional treatment or support added to the child's program.

The drugs most often used in the treatment of ADD fall into three categories: amphetamine-based stimulants, nonamphetamine-based stimulants, and antidepressant drugs (see chart). Ritalin® or methylphenidate is the most often prescribed medication for children with ADD and is a non-amphetamine-based stimulant. Approximately 66 to 75 percent of children respond positively to Ritalin® and five to ten percent do not (Barkley, 1991). Studies have shown that Ritalin® and the other stimulant medications positively affect attention, hyperactivity, impulsivity, and to some degree academic work. The child's improved behavior leads to improved family interactions and to improved self-esteem for the child (Barkley 1991; DuPaul and Barkley, 1990; DuPaul and Stoner, 1994, Goldstein and Goldstein, 1991).

Thus far, studies of children taking stimulant medication have not been able to demonstrate significant changes on standardized tests such as achievement tests and intelligence tests. This may be due to the short-term nature of the studies and to the insensitivity of many of the tests used in the studies to fluctuations within a particular grade at school. Long-term studies of children taking these medications are needed to assess overall improvement in academic achievement.

Studies have shown that children who tend to respond best to stimulant medication are children with more significant inattention problems, children with high-quality relationships between themselves and their mothers, and children with higher levels of restlessness, poor motor coordination, and absence of emotional disorder (DuPaul and Barkley, 1990).

How the stimulants affect the brain to bring about behavioral change is not completely understood at this time. One theory is that they affect the catecholamine neurotransmitters in the brain, especially dopamine, and that ADD may represent a dopamine deficiency. Another theory is that they enhance communication between the frontal lobes of the brain and the limbic regions. In terms of brain function, studies have indicated that the stimulants appear to decrease fluctuations in attention and arousal and thereby increase inhibitory brain responses while at the same time increasing the brain's sensitivity to reinforcement (DuPaul and Barkley, 1990).

There are a wide range of possible side effects that stimulant drugs can produce in children. These include loss of appetite/weight, insomnia, irritability, increased crying, tics, headache, stomach ache, sadness, dizziness, dark circles under eyes, fearfulness/anxiety, social withdrawal, and drowsiness. For most children, the side effects will be mild, and most children do not experience all or even many of the side effects.

One side effect which must be taken seriously is the development of tics, as this sometimes turns into a full-blown Tourette's Syndrome which is irreversible. At this time researchers have been unable to determine if the stimulant medication alone creates Tourette's Syndrome or if it unmasks a predisposition to this illness. Approximately one percent of children taking stimulants develop tics (DuPaul and Barkley, 1990). Therefore, an important contraindication for the prescription of stimulant medication is a history of tics in the child or the child's family. Other contraindications for stimulant treatment include hypersensitivity or allergy to the medication, a history of seizures, glucoma, hypertension, and hyperthyroidism.

The two other most commonly prescribed stimulant medications are pemoline or Cylert® and dextroamphetamine or Dexedrine®. Cylert® has the advantage of having a longer lasting effect than Ritalin®, but it also has the disadvantage of taking four to six weeks to reach its maximum effectiveness. An additional concern with Cylert® is its possible negative effect on liver function. Thus periodic evaluation of liver enzymes is a necessary part of the ongoing monitoring of children on this medication.

Dexedrine is the only stimulant medication that can be safely administered to children between the ages of three and six (Goldstein and Goldstein, 1992). In terms of duration of effect Dexedrine® is approximately the same as Ritalin®. Dexedrine® may cause delays in overall growth and may more frequently produce sadness as a side effect than the other stimulants (Goldstein and Goldstein, 1992). All three stimulant medications have approximately the same response rate in terms of effectiveness (Barkley, 1977b).

One final consideration in the use of stimulants is that for children who have ADD without hyperactivity there is a slightly lower response rate. These children may do better on lower doses of the medication than children with ADD and hyperactivity. Some of these children tend to be anxious, and this would be an indication that caution should be taken in prescribing stimulant medication (Parker, 1992).

The next category of medications used in the treatment of ADD in children is the tricyclic antidepressants including imipramine (Tofranil®), desipramine (Norpramine®) and amytriptyline (Elavil®). These drugs are useful for children who do not respond to stimulant medication, who experience too many or too severe side effects from stimulant medication, or who, in addition to ADD, are suffering from significant depression and low self-esteem. While these medications have been shown to produce behavioral effects similar to the stimulants (DuPaul and Stoner, 1994, Pliszka, 1991) they take longer to become effective and have the potential to affect cardiac functioning. Careful medical monitoring of young children on tricyclics is necessary. Side effects include constipation, dry mouth, elevated blood pressure, confusion, and, to a less common degree, stimulation of manic behavior and inducement of seizures (Parker, 1992).

Aside from the stimulants and antidepressants the use of clonidine or Catapress® has been recently demonstrated to be effective for children with ADD who have a tic disorder or Tourette's syndrome and for children with ADD who are severely overactive and aggressive (Parker, 1992). For some children in this later group the combination of Ritalin® and Clonidine® works best (Parker, 1992). The major side effect of Clonidine® is drowsiness and this wears off as the child gets used to the medication. It also may increase appetite, improve sleep, and facilitate growth. It may take four to six weeks before this medication's effects on the child's behavior are observed.

While medication is an important part of treatment for many children and adolescents with ADD, it has not been demonstrated to produce effects that last once it is discontinued. Also, recent studies have shown that the combined treatment of medication and cognitive-behavioral interventions work best for many children and adolescents.

Sources: Barkley, R. (1991) *Attention-Deficit Hyperactivity Disorder: A Clinical Workbook.* New York: Guilford Publications. pp. 93-100. Barkley, R. (1977b) A review of stimulant drug research with hyperactive children. *Journal of Child Psychology and Psychiatry.* 18:pp.137-165. DuPaul, G. and Barkley, R. (1990) "Medication Therapy" in Barkley (1990) ed. *Attention Deficit Hyperactivity Disorder: A Handbook for Diagnosis and Treatment.* New York: Guilford Publications. pp.573-612. DuPaul, G. and Stoner, G. (1994) *ADHD in the Schools: Assessment and Intervention Strategies.* New York: Guilford Publications. pp. 135-170. Goldstein, S. and Goldstein, M. (1990) *Managing Attention Disorders in Children: A Guide for Practioners.* New York: John Wiley and Sons. pp. 221-266. Parker, H.(1992) *The ADD Hyperactivity Handbook for Schools.* Plantation, Florida: Impact Publishers, Inc. pp. 83-104. Pliszka, S. (1991) Antidepressants in the treatment of child and adolescent psychopathology. *Journal of Clinical Child Psychology,* 20, pp. 313-320.

DuPaul and Barkley (1990, pp. 592-594) list the **major considerations that need to be made in prescribing stimulant medications for children with ADD.** Many of these apply to the prescription of the other medications as well. They are summarized as follows:

1. **Adequate psychological and physical evaluations of the child must have been made**
2. **Age of the child**
3. **Previous treatments attempted**
4. **Severity of child's behavioral problems**
5. **Family's ability to afford medication**
6. **Parents' ability to comply with medication program**

7. Parents' attitude toward medication
8. Presence of delinquent sibling or drug abusing family member
9. History of tics or psychosis in child
10. Is child highly anxious, depressed, or prone to somatization?
11. Is physician willing to be thorough in evaluating dosage and monitoring child?
12. Child's attitude toward taking medication

MEDICATIONS FOR ADD

CLASS	Stimulants	Antidepressants	Antihypertensive
GENERIC NAME	Methylphenidate Dextroamphetamine Pemoline	Imipramine Desipramine Amytriptyline	Clonidine
COMMERCIAL NAME	Ritalin® Dexedrine® Cylert®	Trofanil® Norpramine® Elavil®	Catapress®
EFFECTS	Improves behavior, attention, academics; decreases aggression	Improves behavior and attention; helpful when affective problems are present, decreases aggression	Helps severely overactive, aggressive children; reduces activity level and aggression
SIDE EFFECTS	Mild insomnia, appetite reduction, rebound effect, stomach aches, headaches, tics	Constipation, elevated blood pressure, confusion, precipitation of mania or seizures (rare), dry mouth, cardiac irregularities	Drowsiness, improvement in sleep, improvement in appetite, low blood pressure, headache, dizziness
COUNTER-INDICATIONS	Tics, Tourette's Syndrome, psychosis	Heart disorders or abnormalities	

Sources: Barkley, R. (1992) *ADHD in the Classroom: Program Manual.* New York: Guilford Publications. Parker, H. (1992) *The ADD Hyperactivity Handbook for Schools.* Plantation, Florida: Impact Publishers.

Recent Research Findings in ADD

• In a study designed to corroborate earlier findings on the effectiveness of correspondence training for managing ADD, Paniagua and Black found that **positive reinforcement given upon successful inhibition of target behaviors resulted in a decrease in the levels of inattention, overactivity, and conduct disorders.** Three procedures were used with a total of eight subjects: 1) "reinforcement-set-up-on-promises" in which the therapist displayed the reinforcer contingent upon each subject's promise to inhibit target behaviors and delivered the reinforcer when the promise was fulfilled; 2) "reinforcement-of-corresponding-reports" in which the therapist reinforced the subject's true reports of target behaviors inhibited; and 3) "reinforcement-of-fulfillment-of-promises" in which the reinforcer was delivered after the subject fulfilled a promise to inhibit target behaviors. The researchers noted that the effectiveness of specific reinforcers varied with subjects (some preferring activities, others tangible rewards), and stressed the importance of careful selection and revision of reinforcers for individual children.

Paniagua, F.A., Black, S.A. (1990). Management and prevention of hyperactivity and conduct disorders in 8-10 year old boys through correspondence training procedures. *Child & Family Behavior Therapy,* 12:pp. 23-56.

• A study using a single-subject design demonstrated the effects of variable doses of medication and behavioral treatments on two boys, ages 10 and 11 involved in a summer treatment program. By independently and jointly manipulating pharmacological and behavioral treatments during an 8-week program, the researchers found that 1) **the assessment of medication dose response must occur within the context of differing "doses" of behavior therapy** (e.g. one boy performed as well academically with behavior modification as with medication) and 2) **difficult-to-manage children, who fail to respond sufficiently to either behavior modification or medication alone, can be effectively managed with combined treatments involving potent "doses" of both interventions.**

Hoza, B., Pelham, W.E., Sams, S.E., Carlson, C. (1992). An examination of the "dosage" effects of both behavior therapy and methylphenidate on the classroom performance of two ADHD children. *Behavior Modification,* 16:pp. 164-192.

• In a study of 42 children diagnosed with ADHD between the ages of 7 and 11, Horn and his colleagues found that **combining behavioral parent training with child self-control instruction resulted a significantly greater proportion of improvements in some behaviors,** according to parent reports. The training consisted of 12 weekly 90-minute training sessions involving the principles and application of social learning and behavior modification techniques for the parents and the learning of rehearsed problem-solving and relaxation techniques for the children. Gains made by the subjects at post-test were not maintained at follow-up according to teachers' reports.

Horn, W. F., Ialongo, N., Greenberg, G., Packard, T., Smith-Winberry, C. (1990). Additive effects of behavioral parent training and self-control therapy with attention deficit hyperactivity disordered children. *Journal of Clinical Child Psychology,* 19:pp. 98-110.

• Hinshaw and Melnick presented case studies of two ADHD children, ages 9 and 10, who were treated with a combination of behavioral, cognitive, and pharmacological interventions. The authors used two training procedures considered to be effective adjuncts to behavioral and pharmacologic treatments: reinforced self-evaluation and group instruction in anger control and management. They concluded that **cog-**

nitive procedures can be very effective if they are used as an adjunct to behavioral strategies and suggest that future research concentrate on discovering "the optimal combinations of strategies" rather than on which interventions are most effective for children with ADHD.

Hinshaw, S.P., Melnick, S. (1992). Self-management therapies and attention-deficit hyperactivity disorder: Reinforced self-evaluation and anger control interventions. *Behavior Modification,* 16:pp. 253-273.

• In a study examining the relative effectiveness of behavior modification and cognitive training implemented with and without medication, Hall and Kataria found that **for tasks involving sustained attention there was a trend toward better performance when behavioral and cognitive interventions were combined with medication, but the combination of cognitive intervention and medication was the only intervention that significantly improved subjects' abilities to delay impulsive responding.** Their study involved 21 children, ages 6 to 12, who were clinically diagnosed with ADHD and randomly assigned to three treatment groups: behavior modification, cognitive training, or control.

Hall, C.W., Kataria, S. (1992). Effects of two treatment techniques on delay and vigilance tasks with attention deficit hyperactive disorder (ADHD) children. **The Journal of Psychology,** 126:pp. 17-25.

• In a case study involving two boys, ages 9 and 10, diagnosed with ADHD, it was found that **self-instructional training, involving both conceptual and concrete training, is an effective way to teach children both general problem-solving skills and task-specific strategies, and may result in improvement in self-control, hyperactivity, and school grades.** Conceptual training consisted of self-instructions which were general statements independent of the specific task requirements (e.g., "What do I have to do first?"). During concrete training, verbalizations were specific to the mathematics, spelling, and reading worksheet requirements (e.g., "I have to multiply 7 and 4 and carry the 2").

Guevremont, D.C., Tishelman, A.C., Hull, D.B. (1985). Teaching generalized self-control to attention-deficient boys with mothers as adjunct therapists. *Child and Family Behavior Therapy,* 7:pp. 23-27.

• Erhardt and Baker describe case studies of family-based behavioral interventions involving two preschool boys diagnosed as having ADHD, from which they conclude that **parent training alone was insufficient to normalize the behavior of children with ADHD.** It was demonstrated, however, that such training did help decrease targeted child behavior problems (although these gains did not generalize beyond the targeted behaviors), increased the mothers' confidence in their children's management abilities, and helped the mothers to develop more appreciative views of their children's positive qualities.

Erhardt, D., Baker, B.L. (1990). The effects of behavioral parent training on families with young hyperactive children. *Journal of Behavior Therapy & Experimental Psychiatry,* 21:pp. 121-132.

• **In a study comparing the relative effectiveness of a response-cost program alone and in conjunction with a directed-rehearsal procedure, researchers concluded that the findings were ambiguous regarding whether the combination provided additive benefits beyond response-cost alone.** The study involved two boys diagnosed with ADHD and enrolled full-time in a self-contained public school classroom. The response-cost program was implemented by using a commercially available electronic apparatus that displays cumulative points earned according to a fixed-interval reinforcement schedule.

DuPaul, G.J., Guevremont, D.C., Barkley, R.A. (1992). Behavioral treatment of attention-deficit hyperactivity disorder in the classroom: The use of the Attention Training System. *Behavior Modification,* 16:pp. 204-225.

• Dubey, O'Leary, and Kaufman **compared parent behavioral training and Parent Effectiveness Training (PET)** with a group of 44 parents of 32 boys and 5 girls, ages 6-10, who were hyperactive and exhibited problem behaviors in the home. Their results indicated that, while both treatment methods proved effective in reducing hyperactivity, problem severity, and daily problem occurrence, and both resulted in sustained improvement at a nine-month follow-up, the **behavior modification program effected more change than did PET** on several measures. In addition, the researchers found that group training effectively improves parents' competence for handling their hyperactive children's problem behaviors.
Dubey, D.R., O'Leary, S.G., Kaufman, K.F. (1983). Training parents of hyperactive children in child management: A comparative outcome study. *Journal of Abnormal Child Psychology,* 11:pp. 229-246.

• In a study by Chase and Clement **the effects on academic performance (task accuracy and number of items completed) of methylphenidate and self-reinforcement, alone and in combination,** were compared. The six boys studied, ages 9-12 and diagnosed with ADHD, **demonstrated greatly improved performance when the two treatments were combined, slightly improved performance with self-reinforcement alone, and no improvement with methylphenidate alone.**
Chase, S.N., Clement, P.W. (1985). Effects of self-reinforcement and stimulants on academic performance in children with attention deficit disorder. *Journal of Clinical Child Psychology,* 14:pp. 323-333.

• In a study of 30 children, half of whom were clinically diagnosed as hyperactive (12 boys and 3 girls, ages 6-13), Braud found that **both electromyographic (EMG) biofeedback and progressive relaxation exercises were effective in reducing EMG-defined muscular tension and problem behaviors in hyperactive children.** The greatest behavioral benefits were in aggression and emotionality (i.e. irritability, explosiveness, impulsivity, and low frustration tolerance). Medicated and nonmedicated subjects equally reduced tension levels, but nonmedicated children made greater behavioral gains.
Braud, L.W. (1978). The effects of frontal EMG biofeedback and progressive relaxation upon hyperactivity and its behavioral concomitants. *Biofeedback and Self-Regulation* 3:pp. 69-89.

• An assessment of the relative short-term efficacy of multicomponent cognitive-behavioral therapy (CBT), which included child, parent, and teacher components, vs. teacher-only CBT found that **the only significant post-intervention difference was the multicomponent group made greater gains in decreasing off-task/disruptive behavior.** At a six-week follow-up, the researchers found no significant differences among the two treatment groups and the control group. The study included a total of 36 students at three suburban schools.
Bloomquist, M.L., August, G.J., Ostrander, R. (1991). Effects of a school-based cognitive-behavior intervention for ADHD children. *Journal of Abnormal Child Psychology,* 19:pp. 591-605.

• **A study to compare the effectiveness of three different family therapy approaches,** involving 64 adolescents (ages 12-17) with ADHD and their parents, **resulted in only slight improvements in communication, conflicts, anger intensity, and school adjustment with no significant differences among the**

three treatment groups, according to clinical measures. The first treatment group included only the mothers, who received training in child behavior management techniques, the second group included both mothers and children, who received "problem solving and communication training," while the third group participated in "structural family therapy" involving both mothers and children. The authors concluded that the study confirmed the need for long-term multi-modal interventions as opposed to short-term therapy approaches.

Barkley, R.A., Guevremont, D.C., Anastopoulos, A.D., Fletcher, K.E. (1992). A comparison of three family therapy programs for treating family conflicts in adolescents with attention-deficit hyperactivity disorder. *Journal of Consulting and Clinical Psychology,* 60:pp. 450-462.

• In two related experiments (involving 16 children, ages 7-9 years, attending a remedial summer program) designed to **compare the effects of teacher encouragement to either no feedback or reprimands in reducing students' off-task behavior, researchers found significantly lower off-task rates with reprimands than with no feedback or encouragement.** The effects of encouragement were inconclusive, but it was postulated that it may be more effective if used to support on-task behavior.

Abramowitz, A.J., O'Leary, S.G., Rosen, L.A. (1987). Reducing off-task behavior in the classroom: A comparison of encouragement and reprimands. *Journal of Abnormal Child Psychology,* 15:pp. 155-163.

• Using a single-subject design, Abramowitz and O'Leary examined the effects of immediate and delayed reprimands delivered contingently for off-task behavior to a group of four first- and second-grade boys in a laboratory school classroom for hyperactive children. **Immediate reprimands yielded much lower rates of interactive off-task behavior (any behavior that involved two or more children attending to one another) than did delayed reprimands, but reprimand timing did not affect the rates of noninteractive off-task behavior (any behavior neither appropriate to the task nor categorized as interactive).**

Abramowitz, A.J., O'Leary, S.G. (1990). Effectiveness of delayed punishment in an applied setting. *Behavior Therapy,* 21:pp. 231-239.

• In a study of three hyperactive boys, ages 10 and 11, each of whom was exposed to six possible combinations of methylphenidate dose and reprimand "intensity" (defined by the timing of the reprimand), it was found that **all three were off-task most during the delayed-reprimand/placebo condition (the teacher delivered reprimands approximately 1 minute following onset of off-task behavior),** but optimal conditions varied for each subject. The results suggest that a simple behavioral intervention can be as effective as medication for some children with ADHD, while for others medication can obviate the need for intense behavioral intervention. In response to pharmacotherapy and behavior therapy, individual differences appear to be the rule.

Abramowitz, A.J., Eckstrand, D., O'Leary, S.G., Dulcan, M.K. (1992). ADHD children's responses to stimulant medication and two intensities of a behavioral intervention. *Behavior Modification,* 16:pp. 193-203.

Recent Journal Articles on ADD

Platzman, K., Stoy, M., Brown, R., Coles, C., Smith, I., and Falek, A. (1992) **Review of observational methods in attention deficit hyperactivity disorder (ADHD): Implications for diagnosis.** *School Psychology Quarterly,* 7:pp. 155-177. This review article on different observational methods concludes that classroom behavioral observations are more effective than clinic-based observations in identifying children with ADHD. The three behaviors which served to discriminate ADHD children from control children were off-task behavior, excessive motoric activity, and negative verbalizing.

Satterfield, J., Hoppe, C., and Schell, A. (1982) **A prospective study of delinquency in 110 adolescent boys with attention deficit disorder and 88 normal adolescent boys.** *American Journal of Psychiatry,* 139:pp. 795-798. In this article the investigators found that intervention significantly reduced the amount of delinquency found in adolescent boys.

Fiore, T., Becker, E. and Nero, R. (1993) **Educational interventions for students with attention deficit disorder. Special Issue: Issues in the education of children with attention deficit disorder.** *Exceptional Children.* 60(2):pp. 163-167. This article reviews the research findings on nonpharmacological interventions focusing on behavioral management, academic instruction, home-school collaboration, and comprehensive programming. The authors underline the need for more research, better addressing the daily issues faced by teachers, and the need for comprehensive educational programs for children with ADD.

Burcham, B., Carlson, L., Milich, R. (1993) **Promising school-based practices for students with attention deficit disorder. Special Issue: Issues in the education of children with attentional deficit disorder.** *Exceptional Children.* 60(2):pp. 174-180. In this study treatment teams consisting of parents, teachers, researchers, and health care personnel developed criteria for assessing the efficacy of different interventions in the school. The criteria they report included 1) schools having systematic and comprehensive training programs, 2) administrative support, 3) a variety of interventions available, and 4) recognition of ADD as a disorder.

Faraone, S., Biederman, J., Lehman, B., Spencer, T. (1993) **Intellectual performance and school failure in children with attention deficit hyperactivity disorder and in their siblings.** *Journal of Abnormal Psychology.* 102(4):pp. 616-623. This study found that children with ADHD were more likely to demonstrate academic and intellectual impairment as well as greater emotional difficulty than the control group. Siblings of ADHD children also demonstrated more intellectual impairment than siblings of the control group providing convergent evidence for regarding ADD as a familial disorder.

McCain, A. and Kelly, M. (1993) **Managing the classroom behavior of an ADHD preschooler: The efficacy of a school-home note intervention.** *Child and Family Behavior Therapy.* 15(3):pp. 33-44. This single case study of a five-year-old boy used an ABAB design to evaluate the effectiveness of the school-home note intervention. They demonstrated that the child improved in the areas of attention, disruption, and excess activity when this intervention was in place.

Pelham, W. (1993) **Pharmacotherapy for children with attention-deficit hyper-**

activity disorder. *School Psychology Review.* 22(2):pp. 199-227. This article reviews basic and new information about stimulant medications and their use in the classroom, details a cost and time effective method of evaluating drug response, and describes the important role of the school psychologist in helping to set up an ongoing evaluation system of the child's response to the drug as well as behavioral interventions.

Carlson, C. and Bunner, M. (1933) **Effects of methylphenidate on the academic performance of children with attention-deficit hyperactivity disorder and learning disabilities.** *School Psychology Review.* 22(2):pp. 184-198. This review article finds support for short-term improvement in classroom performance but did not find support for sustained achievement over months or years.

Pelham, W., Carlson, C., Sams, S., and Vallano, G. (1993) **Separate and combined effects of methylphenidate and behavior modification on boys with attention deficit-hyperactivity disorder in the classroom.** *Journal of Consulting and Clinical Psychology.* 61(3):pp. 506-515. This study indicated that while both behavioral and pharmacological treatments had significant impact on the 31 boys with ADD in their study, the medication had a greater impact, and also enhanced the amount of improvement in children receiving behavioral treatment. Children who responded well to one of the interventions tended to respond well to the other as well.

Hoza, B., Pelham, W., Milich, R., Pillow, D. (1993) **The self- perceptions and attributions of attention deficit hyperactivity disordered and nonreferred boys.** *Journal of Abnormal Child Psychology.* 21(3):pp. 271-286. This study found that boys with ADD were more likely than controls to take responsibility for social success and less likely to take responsibility for social failure. Other findings suggested that perceptions of self-worth were not different between the two groups when internalizing symptomatology was taken into account.

Pennington, B., Grossier, D., Welsh, M. (1993) **Contrasting cognitive deficits in attention deficit hyperactivity disorder versus reading disability.** *Developmental Psychology.* 29(3):pp. 511-523. This interesting study provides evidence that ADD and reading disability are two distinct disorders relating to executive function impairment and phonological processing impairment, respectively. Children with both disorders were found to have profiles most similar to children with reading disabilities and their ADD symptomatology was considered to be a secondary problem.

Hakola, S. (1992) **Legal rights of student with attention deficit disorder.** *School Psychology Quarterly.* 7(4):pp. 285-297. This article discusses the role of federal agencies in enforcing special education laws for children with ADD, and provides a model policy for ensuring proper services and procedures, as well as a case example.

Alessandri, S. (1992) **Attention, play and social behavior in ADHD preschoolers.** *Journal of Abnormal Child Psychology.* 20(3):pp. 289-302. This study used videotape recordings of preschool children in the classroom and found differences between ADHD preschoolers and the control group. Differences included less overall play and more sensory motor play in the ADHD group as well as less competent behavior with peers.

Gordon, M., Thomason, D., Cooper, S., and Ivers, C. (1991) **Nonmedical treatment of ADHD/hyperactivity: The Attention Training System.** *Journal of School Psychology.* 29(2):pp. 151-159. This study reported on the implementation of a response cost-based classroom management system for six children. Five children clearly benefited from the intervention but the effects of training faded after the intervention was withdrawn.

Atkins, M. and Pelham, W. (1991) **School-based assessment of attention deficit-hyperactivity disorder.** *Journal of Learning Disabilities.* 24(4):pp. 197-204. This article describes the components of school-based assessment stressing the importance of multiple measures, as well as the relationship between assessment and intervention.

Resources for ADD

There is such a wealth of resources for ADD that it would be impossible to list them all. Herein we feature a recommended selection of books, videotapes and games.

Fiction

Galvin, M. (1988) *Otto Learns About His Medicine.* New York, NY: Magination Press. The story of Otto, a fidgety car, who has trouble paying attention in school and visits a special mechanic who prescribes medicine to help control his behavior.

Gehret, J. (1990) *Eagle Eyes.* Fairport, NY: Verbal Images. This sensitive story shows how Ben and his family come to understand, work with, and even appreciate Ben's unique way of being. Ben uses nature to help understand his ADD.

Moss, D. *Shelley the Hyperactive Turtle.* Rockville, MD: Woodbine House. This story of Shelley empathically describes the problems he has in effectively engaging with the world, and follows Shelley as he and his parents learn that he has ADD. He receives medication and treatment, and a realistic picture of his improvement, along with the reassuring message of his parents' ongoing love for him. Ages 3-7.

Shapiro, L. (1993) *Sometimes I Drive My Mom Crazy, But I Know She's Crazy About Me.* King of Prussia, PA: The Center for Applied Psychology, Inc. This amusing and sensitive book describes the experiences of a boy with ADD and the efforts he and his family make to work together. It introduces the concepts of behavioral therapy in the home and at school, medication treatment and parent support, as well as providing behavior charts and information for parents and educators. Ages 5-8.

Shapiro, L. (1994) *Jumpin' Jake Settles Down: A Workbook to Help Impulsive Children Learn to Think Before They Act.* King of Prussia, PA: Center for Applied Psychology, Inc. This humorous story and activity book follows the antics of Jake, an impulsive frog, who learns to think before acting. It teaches cognitive techniques, new behaviors, and organizational skills in a way that will appeal to most children. Ages 5-10.

Non-fiction

Barkley, Russell A. (1990) *Attention-Deficit Hyperactivity Disorder.* New York: Guilford Publications. A 750-page textbook divided into three major sections including diagnosis, assessment and treatment, covering such diverse treatments as family therapy and social skills training. Includes a review of parent, teacher and multi-informant rating scales.

Barkley, Russell A. (1991) *Attention-Deficit Hyperactivity Disorder: A Clinical Workbook.* New York: Guilford Publications. The companion volume to Dr. Barkley's groundbreaking text contains forms for clinical interviews with children and adolescents, rating scales for ADHD adults, home and school questionnaires, the Children's Atypical Development Scale, and much more.

DuPaul, G. and Stoner, G. (1994) *ADHD in the Schools.* New York: Guilford Publications. Addressing school-related problems associated with ADHD such as academic underachievement, noncompliance with classroom rules, and problematic peer relationships, this concise volume is specifically designed to meet the needs of school professionals.

Goldstein, M. and Goldstein, S. (1990) *Managing Attention Disorders in Children.* New York: John Wiley & Sons. Drawing on their current work with ADD children, the authors have compiled this practical guide to the history, diagnosis and treatment of ADHD.

Gordon, M. (1991) *ADHD/Hyperactivity: A Consumer's Guide.* DeWitt, NY: GSI. Dr. Gordon has simplified the ADD identification and treatment process into 30 basic principles, which can be easily understood and remembered by parents and teachers.

Neuville, M. (1991) *Sometimes I Get All Scribbly.* La Crosse, WI: Crystal Press. Written by the mother of a child with ADHD, this book presents an intimate look into the hearts and home of a family struggling with the disorder.

Parker, H. (1992) *The ADD Hyperactivity Handbook for Schools.* Plantation, Florida: Impact Publications. This comprehensive workbook provides easy to understand descriptions and strategies for assessment, behavioral intervention, medication therapy, and classroom interventions, as well as providing worksheets, resource listings, and explanations of how to work within the schools.

Parker, H. (1988) *ADD Hyperactivity Workbook.* Plantation, Florida: Impact Publications. This best-selling workbook is an invaluable resource for anyone trying to help ADD children. Includes a section of basic facts as well as activities, stickers, behavioral contracts, rating scales, and treatment records.

Quinn, P. and Stern, J. (1992) *Putting on the Brakes.* New York: Magination Press. Subtitled "a young people's guide to understanding Attention Deficit Hyperactivity Disorder (ADHD)," the authors combine simple text with illustrations to address the most frequent concerns of ADHD kids between the ages of 8 and 13.

Videotapes
ADHD in the Classroom (1994) 36 minutes. New York: Guilford Publications. (800) 365-7006. Ideal for teacher training, this excellent video addresses the double challenge teachers confront when ADHD students are in the classroom.
Provides hands-on demonstration and includes manual.

ADHD: What Can We Do? (1992) 36 minutes. New York: Guilford Publications. (800) 365-7006. Dr. Russell A. Barkley provides an overview of the most effective approaches to treating the problems associated with ADHD. Includes manual.

ADHD: What Do We Know? (1992) 37 minutes. New York: Guilford Publications. (800) 365-7006. Dr. Russell A. Barkley discusses the nature of ADHD, its frequently attendant problems, its developmental course and its likely causes. Includes manual.

Educating Inattentive Children. 120 minutes. Salt Lake City, UT: Neurology Learning Center. (801) 532-1486. ADD experts Sam and Michael Goldstein familiarize teachers with ADD-like behaviors and the problems they cause in school. Provides an easy-to-follow explanation concerning evaluation, medical and non-medical treatment and tells teachers what to do to successfully manage the problems these behaviors cause.

It's Just Attention Disorder: A Video for Kids. 30 minutes. Plantation, FL: ADD Warehouse. (800) 233-9273. This video is designed to explain ADD to children in a MTV-format using claymation and a comedian. Interviews with children and adolescents and advice from a former NBA coach on becoming a "winner" encourage children and adolescents in their efforts to cope with ADD.

Why Won't My Child Pay Attention? 76 minutes. Salt Lake City, UT: Neurology Learning Center. (801) 532-1486. Dr. Sam Goldstein helps parents with easy-to-follow explanations concerning the effects that hyperactivity and inattentive behaviors have on children at different ages.

Games

Look Before You Leap! King of Prussia, PA: The Center for Applied Psychology, Inc. (800) 962-1141. This fun-filled board game addresses the problems of impulsivity on many levels. Players must think before they move ahead, use real-life problem-solving and critical-thinking skills, and control their responses while using forethought to guide their behavior. Features a turning wheel under the game board.

The Self-Control Game. Dayton, OH: Cognitive Therapeutics. (513) 293-8901. This game addresses 24 specific behaviors associated with hyperactivity, including failure to finish things, difficulty in following rules, distractibility, daydreaming, disturbing others, and more.

Stop, Relax & Think. King of Prussia, PA: The Center for Applied Psychology, Inc. (800) 962-1141. This popular game recognizes that children with impulse control problems have complex learning styles and need an entertaining game which will keep their attention. Manual includes information on using the game as a diagnostic and therapeutic tool.

The **Educational Resources Information Center (ERIC) Clearinghouse on Disabilities and Gifted Education,** operated by the Council for Exceptional Children is a federally funded, nationwide information network designed to provide access to education literature. Call (800) 328-0272 or (703) 264-9474 for a catalog. Also, the **United States Department of Education Office of Special Education and Rehabilitation Services** sponsors and disseminates research on interventions for children and adolescents in the schools. Call (202) 708-5366 for more information.

Two computer networks which disseminate information on ADD are **SpecialNet** [(800) 927-3000], which carries research studies and ADD information on the PROGRAM.EVAL bulletin board and **CompuServe** [(800) 524-3388; Representative 464], which carries research studies and ADD information on the ADD Forum.

Periodicals Addressing ADD

Journals
Attention!
Children and Adults with Attention Deficit Disorders (CH.A.D.D.), 499 NW 70th Ave., Suite 109, Plantation, FL 33317; (305) 587-3700. Published quarterly as membership benefit. Features articles and departments devoted exclusively to ADD.

Exceptional Children
Council for Exceptional Children, 1920 Association Drive, Reston, VA 22091; (702) 620-3660. Published bimonthly; $45.00/yr. Contains current articles on critical and controversial issues in special education as well as credible articles on research and developments in the field.

Journal of Developmental and Behavioral Pediatrics
Society for Behavioral Pediatrics, Williams and Wilkins, Inc., 428 E. Preston St., Baltimore, MD 21202; (410) 528-4000. Published bi-monthly. Individual: $98/yr.; Institution: $138/yr. Covers learning disabilities, behavioral reactions of children, and family dynamics. For pediatricians, child psychologists and psychiatrists, and special educators.

Journal of Learning Disabilities
Pro-Ed, Inc., 8700 Shoal Creek Blvd., Austin, TX 78757-6897; (512) 451-3246. Published 10/yr. Individual: $45/yr.; Institution: $90/yr. Covers practice, theory and research articles about learning disabilities and related disabilities such as ADD.

School Psychology International
Sage Publications, Ltd., 6 Bonhill St., London, England EC2A4PU; (71) 374-0654. Published quarterly. Individual: $82/yr.; Institution: $190/yr. Highlights the concerns of those who provide quality mental health, educational, therapeutic, and support service to schools and communities throughout the world.

School Psychology Quarterly
Guilford Publications, 72 Spring St., 4th Fl. New York, NY 10012;
(212) 431-9800. Published quarterly. Individual: $32/yr.; Institution: $65/yr. This American Psychological Association journal promotes a scientific understanding of school psychology. It covers new concepts in enhancing the life experiences of children, families, and schools.

School Psychology Review
National Association of School Psychologists; 8455 Colesville Rd., Suite 1000, Silver Spring, MD. 20910; (301) 608-0500. Published quarterly. Individual: $40/yr.; Institution: $60/yr. The official journal of the National Association for School Psychology, it contains articles on theory, research and opinion related to the practice of school psychology. Three of four issues in each volume cover specific themes; the first covers general topics.

Newsletters   (other than those published by ADD organizations)

ADHD Report

Guilford Publications, 72 Spring St., 4th Fl. New York, NY 10012;
(212) 431-9800. Attn: Journals Dept. P. Published bi-monthly. Individual (first time):
$49.95/yr. Institution (first time): $59.95/yr. Special rate for parents of children with
ADD by calling Journals Dept. Created by Russell Barkley, Ph.D., this newsletter
presents information about the nature, course, outcomes, assessment, management,
and education of children and adults with ADD.

Challenge

Challenge, Inc., P.O. Box 488, West Newbury, MA 01985; (508) 462-0495. Published
bimonthly. Individual: $20.00/yr. Support group rate available for orders of 10 sub-
scriptions or more. Formerly the newsletter of the Attention Deficit Disorder
Association, *Challenge* is now published separately. It provides articles by professionals on the treatment, assessment, and related concerns for individuals of all ages
with ADD.

BRAKES is a bimonthly newsletter for ADHD children ages 7-14. Each issue features fun facts, feature stories, interviews, and games written expressly to help
ADHD kids cope with attention disorders. Edited by *Putting on the Brakes* authors
Patricia O. Quinn, M.D. and Judith M. Stern, M.A., this interactive newsletter is
packed with mazes, cartoons and puzzles, poems, drawings and jokes, and much
more. Each issue contains a special parent/teacher supplement with information on
ADHD developments. Annual subscription: $24. Call (800) 825-3089 for more infor-
mation.

- Video Reviews -

"ADHD in the Classroom: Strategies for Teachers" "Educating Inattentive Children"

Russell Barkley's "ADHD in the Classroom: Strategies for Teachers," and Goldstein and Goldstein's "Educating Inattentive Children" both provide an inside view into the difficulties that children with ADD and their teachers face in the classroom. While ADD exists in the child, the degree to which the child will experience difficulty with its symptoms depends to some significant degree on the nature of the environment with which the child is interacting. The school classroom presents a particularly challenging environment for the child with ADD because its rewards are inconsistent and not immediate; its punishments are inconsistent, delayed, and at times fail to take into account the nature of the child's intentions and difficulties; it places a high premium on sustained attention; and it requires a significant degree of physical stillness.

Barkley's video presents basic information about ADD and demonstrates a variety of behavioral interventions that are being used in his special kindergarten program for children with ADD. The teachers who run the program discuss their interventions, and examples are shown as they occur in the classroom setting. The interventions used include regular positive reinforcement and a positive reinforcement token system that encourages children to monitor their progress.

The class as a whole is also reinforced as it earns points that lead to a special event. Reinforcers that are used on a daily basis are a choice of activities for free play. The use of a time-out procedure and response cost are also demonstrated. Rules are simple and brief and are rehearsed throughout the day either by the class or individually. It is helpful to see these procedures as they are carried out and the teachers' positive and realistic perspectives serve to highlight the practical aspects of the interventions. The video also makes the point that many of these behavioral techniques translate well into the regular classroom and benefit not just the child with ADD, but the entire class, as they create more consistency and structure.

The tape is designed to be integrated into a presentation on ADD and the classroom, and is broken into different segments which allow for natural breaks in a presentation. Basic ideas are listed at various intervals, and Barkley speaks clearly and slowly, making it possible to take notes easily while viewing. The manual provides a comprehensive and concise discussion of ADD.

Goldstein and Goldstein's video is somewhat more didactic in its design, and presents solid discussions on identification of ADD, assessment, medication, and interventions. The majority of the video is of a lecture that Goldstein and Goldstein gave to a group of teachers. They are effective speakers and interweave their own experiences with children, schools, and families into a well-organized and delivered talk. Stress is placed on an interdisciplinary model, which actively includes the parents and physician in the teacher's efforts to work with the child. Comments from regular classroom teachers who have worked with ADD children in their classrooms provide good insight into the experience of the teacher and how the child with ADD looks from their perspective. The comments are well-thought-out and convey the concern and warmth these teachers have for their students.

At the end of the tape a question and answer session is presented. The bottom line message is that teachers have the ability and power to have a positive impact on children with ADD, an impact that will endure beyond the academic year in which the teacher and child interact.

"ADHD in the Classroom: Strategies for Teachers." (1993) New York: Guilford Publications. Featuring Russell Barkley, Ph.D. 40 minutes. Manual.

"Educating Inattentive Children." Neurology, Learning and Behavior Center, 230 South 500 East, Suite 100, Salt Lake City, UT 84102; (801) 532-1484. Featuring Sam Goldstein, Ph.D. and Michael Goldstein, M.D. 120 minutes.

- Book Review -
ADHD in the Schools:
Assessment and Intervention Strategies

By George J. DuPaul, Ph.D. and Gary Stoner, Ph.D.

Experts in the study of ADD, DuPaul and Stoner have written a state-of-the-art text, and perhaps the first book to focus directly on school-based assessment and treatment of children and adolescents with ADD. Each chapter is carefully researched, and discusses practical interventions as well as the theoretical basis and empirical evidence for various interventions. The topics covered are: assessment, ADD and learning disabilities, classroom-based intervention strategies, medication therapy, adjunct therapies, and treatment team/systems communications. Case studies are used to demonstrate the application of the information and appendices with examples of assessment instruments, medications, determination of eligibility for special education, handouts, and other practical information are included at the end of every chapter.

The foreword by Russell Barkley, Ph.D. creates the setting for DuPaul and Stoner's work. Barkley states that ADD is best conceptualized not as a disorder of attention but as a problem in response inhibition which leads to neuropsychological irregularities in the realm of executive functions. Executive functions are essentially the operations involved in assessing present and past, and planning and executing activities either in the immediate, short- or long-term future. Barkley writes, "Thus, at its core, ADHD represents a profound disturbance in self-regulation and organization of behavior across time..."

Because of its nature, it is difficult to identify ADHD by psychometric tasks, and yet the child's difficulty in delaying responses across time leads to problems which are easily observed on a daily basis by teacher and parents. The implications of this for school-based interventions include that ADD must be viewed as a disorder of "dysregulation not of deficit," and that whereas with learning disabilities there is a gap between the child's IQ and academic achievement, with ADD the gap exists between the child's IQ and his/her level of functional adaptation.

The best way to assess a child for ADD is through observing the child's behavior in the child's environment. While a child or adolescent with ADD may be able to focus in the novel and time-limited setting of a standard psychological evaluation, s/he will not be able to maintain this level of control in his/her daily activities. Likewise, treatments must be focused on the behaviors and situations that are problematic for the child or adolescent. While adjunct therapies may assist the child in several ways, they will not address the core issues of ADHD.

Thus given the current understanding of ADHD, the most appropriate sites of treatment are in the home and in the school. While much work on home management of children with ADHD has been done, school management is a newer frontier. A recurrent theme in this book is the importance of data collection in all phases of treatment and for all treatments provided, including medication therapy. Research has shown that children's reactions to all of the available interventions are highly individual and that successful programs while sharing the same psychological principles, must be designed to meet the child's unique style and personality. In addition, as the child improves changes in the treatment regime need to be made with the goal of having the child manage his/her behavior independently of interventions.

The importance of and difficulties involved in the team treatment of children with

ADD is thoughtfully and practically discussed in a chapter devoted to issues of professional communication. The authors write:

The wide range of issues and concerns requiring professional involvement with children diagnosed with ADHD clearly warrants interdisciplinary collaboration. Also warranted are frank discussions about appropriate roles and responsibilities for the professions involved. School psychologists and special educators, in particular, may be faced with challenging demands for service delivery in light of recent decisions regarding eligibility for special education services of children identified with ADHD under the 'Other Health Impaired' category of IDEA (Individuals with Disabilities Education Act).

The authors emphasize the ethical standards set by the National Association of School Psychologists for communicating fully to the parents and child or adolescent about all aspects of treatment. They also discuss the need to clearly identify the values of the various team members and devote a section to issues related to medicating children with ADHD.

The treatment of ADD is viewed as occurring at several different levels and this is an important dimension the authors bring to the ongoing discussion of ADD. While providing detailed information on the individual assessment and treatment of the child, they never let the reader forget the larger coordination of systems required for effective treatment delivery. For example, in terms of medication they recommend the creation of "district- or school-wide policy and communication systems for collaboration with community physicians" and the establishment of a "system-wide outcome evaluation system for use with children being treated with stimulant medication" (p. 208). (See Interview with George DuPaul in this chapter for a description of a regional ADD consultation program for school systems.)

DuPaul and Stoner have written a brilliant book that will most likely become required reading for psychologists, educators and others who are involved in the treatment of children with ADD. Its balance between scholarly and practical discussion, and between individual and systemic applications, give it a depth and thoroughness rarely seen in clinical texts.

ADHD in the Schools: Assessment and Intervention Strategies. George J. DuPaul, Ph.D. and Gary Stoner, Ph.D. New York: Guilford School Practitioner Series, Guilford Publications. 1994. 269 pp.

ADD Organizations and Programs

Organizations
Attention Deficit Disorder Association

P. O. Box 488, West Newbury, MA 01985; Support Group Referral and General Information Line: (800) 487-2282. The mission of ADDA is to provide a resource network, provide support to people with ADD, to advocate for the development of community resources to meet the educational, health and social needs of those with ADD, to provide support for parents, and to provide media outreach and public education. *ADDA,* the group's official publication, is included in its membership fee.

Children and Adults with Attention Deficit Disorder (CH.A.D.D.)

499 Northwest 70th Ave., Suite 109, Plantation, FL 33317; (305) 587-3700. CH.A.D.D.'s mission is to help children and adults with ADD to succeed and to provide support for parents of ADD children. It is a large organization with over 20,000 members and 500 chapters working at the national, state and local levels. CH.A.D.D. provides family support and advocacy, public and professional education, and support for scientific and educational research. Individual membership benefits include a monthly newsletter; *ATTENTION!,* a quarterly magazine; and a set of ADD fact sheets. Organizational benefits include the aforementioned as well as 20 copies each of the organization's publications.

Programs
Barkley-Worcester, Massachusetts Program

University of Massachusetts Medical Center, 55 Lake Avenue North, Worcester, MA 01655; (508) 856-3260. Developed and directed by Russell Barkley, Ph.D., this is a kindergarten program for children with ADD provided in collaboration with the Worcester, MA public school system.

Hyperspace Support Group

The Family Resource Center, 3603 8th Avenue South, Birmingham, AL 35222; (205) 328-1717. Contact: Kirsten Boorhees. This program provides an education and social skills training support group for ADD children ages 5 through 10, as well as a support group for their parents.

Lehigh University Regional Consulting Center for Adolescents with Attention Deficit Disorder

Lehigh University, Bethlehem, PA 18015; (610) 758-6384. Directors: Edward Shapiro, Ph.D. and George DuPaul, Ph.D. Funded by the U.S. Department of Education, this program provides training to school-based personnel in addressing the needs of ADD students between 5th and 9th grades (see Focus on Programs in this chapter).

The Chesapeake Institute

2030 M Street NW, Suite 800, Washington, DC 20036; (202) 785-9360. A research organization that produces information on ADD for parents and teachers.

The University of California, Irvine and Orange County Department of Education Program (UCI-OCDE Program)

The Child Development Center, 4621 Teller, Suite 108, Newport Beach, CA 92660; (714) 833-8588. This program provides an ongoing special school for ADD children, intervention in public schools, and participation in a national research program funded by NIMH to study the treatment of children with ADD (see Focus on Programs in this chapter).

Research Triangle Institute

P.O. Box 12191, Research Triangle Park, NC 27709; (919) 541-6000. This group is involved in research concerning education, learning and ADD.